D1355975

The Genealogist's Encyclopedia

BOOKS BY THE SAME AUTHOR

The Stuarts of Traquair
The House of Wavell
The Middle Sea
The Story of Heraldry
Trace Your Ancestors
The Golden Book of the Coronation
They Came with the Conqueror
The Story of the Peerage
Tales of the British Aristocracy
The House of Constantine
Teach Yourself Heraldry
The Twilight of Monarchy
A Guide to Titles
Princes of Wales
American Origins
Your Family Tree
Ramshackledom
Heirs of the Conqueror
Heraldry, Ancestry and Titles: Questions and Answers
The Story of Surnames
After Their Blood
Tradition and Custom in Modern Britain

The Genealogist's Encyclopedia

by L. G. Pine

DAVID & CHARLES · NEWTON ABBOT

7153 4473 0

For

RICHARD LESLIE PINE

ἡ γνῶσις φυσιόι
ἡ δὲ ἀγάπη οἰκοδομέι

Published simultaneously in the USA by
Weybright and Talley Inc New York

Printed in Great Britain by
Clarke Doble & Brendon Ltd Plymouth for
David & Charles (Publishers) Limited South Devon House
Newton Abbot Devon

Contents

PART 3   THE CLAN SYSTEM

List of Illustrations

Author's Preface

Usually left unread—but please read this one, as it is a key to the book.

WHEN I first began to study family history, I found many of the guide books extremely hard to understand. I had the task of teaching myself, and then of elucidating for others the dark matters which had perplexed me. First, I wrote of English genealogy, which as I had forbears who had lived in England for many centuries was but reasonable. It is impossible to consider English genealogy without studying, even superficially, the Scottish, Welsh, Irish and European continental genealogies with which it is connected. One's knowledge gradually widens out, until genealogical interest begins to embrace the whole of humanity.

As one studies genealogy, it is inevitable that references will be found to heraldry, to the coat of arms of an individual, or of a family. Just as naturally, titles occur as soon as one's study of family history passes beyond a narrow limit. There are references to succession to titles, to peerages dormant or abeyant. Many times, orders of chivalry are mentioned and curiosity aroused. Finally, if we carry our study of family history outside the national structure of the modern world, we shall come upon the concept of clans in more primitive societies.

Sketched out as I have shown it above, the plan of this book is strictly logical. As the glossaries have been placed at the end, it is perfectly possible for the reader to start at page 1, and read on to the last page of the narrative. Reference to the heraldic glossary will become necessary when the section on Heraldry is used as an introduction to wider heraldic study. The terms in the general glossary are explained in the text, but are also put together so that the reader has them to hand for quick reference.

Therefore my advice to a neophyte would be, start by reading Chapter 1 and go on until you come to a section which is not immediately germane to your purpose. You may not want to read about Peerage Law, but it is there for your reference if and when you want it. There is the apocryphal story about the Indian student who set out to learn the *Encyclopedia Britannica* by heart, or at least to read it through. Apart from the lesser bulk of my book, it would be possible for a student without suffering mental indigestion to read the *Genealogist's Encyclopedia* from beginning to end.

However, many people do not come to the studies which are the matter of this book in a strictly connected manner. My own primary interest was in heraldry, then in titles and orders, and it was a considerable time before I became interested in genealogy as such. Then I found myself conversant with its problems every day. It follows that some readers will want to use a particular section first. This they can do, since each part is independent of the others, although all succeed one another in an orderly fashion. It is a fact, as far as my own experience goes, that while the devotees of heraldry do often become genealogically minded, the student of genealogy who begins as such rarely, if ever, becomes a heraldist.

I welcome letters of inquiry as they have frequently assisted me in the elucidation of many matters, and here I wish to acknowledge the enormous amount of help, encouragement, interest, friendship—yes, and amusement—which my correspondents throughout the world have given to me. With many whom I have never met I have formed by way of letters a friendship which is very dear.

For critics, I fear that I cannot always speak as well. Honest criticism is very valuable, even essential, but such objective outlook is rare among genealogists. The *odium genealogicum* is scarcely less virulent than the *odium theologicum* of days past. It is no longer possible for Calvin to have Servetus burnt to ashes, but it is well within the capacity of the offended genealogist or heraldic Sanhedrin to try to ruin the reputation of anyone who dares to impugn some cherished belief. This trait is unfortunately not confined to the genealogical world. We have it on the highest authority that 'the imagination of man's heart is evil from his youth.' From an authority of more vicarious nature comes what must surely be, in this age, the greatest of understatements. 'Man is very far gone from original righteousness.' Indeed he is, and historians, some of whom, though a fast dwindling minority, affect to underestimate genealogical study, are apt to regard the PhD as a trade union ticket, and those who do not possess it as outside the pale. One of the greatest universities in the world informed me, in writing, that research apart from a university could not be regarded as research. Well, that is unfortunate because genealogical studies have been brought to their present carefully worked-out principles and their vast wealth of knowledge by persons who, though often enjoying the benefits of university education, have never-theless—at least in the British Isles—not held university research posts. Yet today the greatest modern writers of history in the English language employ the resources and techniques of genealogy. The endowment of a chair of genealogy at an English university is still awaited.

I mention these details concerning historians lest it be thought that genealogists are more given to vituperative criticism for personal reasons than those who work in other disciplines. From the beginning of my work in a position of authority, in 1946, I have striven to substitute facts in place of fiction, myth or legend, to dispel an entirely unnecessary and false air of mystery in the exposition of the subjects treated in this volume, and to work without personal bias, either towards critics or friends. I have been rewarded. Some works exist now which could not have been published in their present form, and might not have been published at all but for my labours. I have advocated in and out of season, for many years, reforms in the British peerage which are now being carried out by government policy. I have urged reforms in heraldic procedure which, stymied in England, are being vigorously practised in America. I have, again in writing, been able to predict the outcome of many matters affecting the British royal family and the British aris-tocracy, and this not by any method of divination, like Joseph seeking outlines of the future in his great cup, but by plainly employing the rational faculty. On the whole, I have been well served by my publishers; other writers have shown their appreciation by using my works as a genealogical quarry. To the latter, I say, I don't mind being quoted, but please do not simply lift or transplant the material or you will be sure to get into a terrible muddle.

To the tiny minority who find my handling of their officialdom some-what irreverent, or who are hurt to the quick because I deny them the doubtful distinction of Normannity, I say, as Richard Coeur de Lion did to Prince John, 'Go, brother, forget my forgiveness as quickly as I shall forget your injuries.'

LESLIE G. PINE

Bodiam, High Street, Petworth, Sussex, England

PART 1

Genealogy

CHAPTER 1

Introduction

FROM the time of the earliest civilizations the keeping of genealogical records or family histories has been regarded as of the greatest importance. Two early examples of the extreme gravity with which the matter has been viewed are to be found in the books of Ezra and Nehemiah, the two leaders in the return of the Jewish exiles from their captivity in Babylon, circa 536-433 BC.

'And of the children of the priests: the children of Habaiah, the children of Koz, the children of Barzillai; which took a wife of the daughters of Barzillai, the Gileadite, and was called after their name.

'These sought their register among those that were reckoned by genealogy but they were not found; therefore were they as polluted, put from the priesthood.' (Ezra, ch 2, v 61-62).

'And my God put into mine heart to gather together the nobles, and the rulers, and the people, that they might be reckoned by genealogy of them which came up at the first, and found written therein,

'These are the children of the province that went up out of the captivity; of those that had been carried away, whom Nebuchadnezzar the king of Babylon had carried away, and came again to Jerusalem and to Judah, every one to his own city.' (Nehemiah, ch 7, v 5-6).

These two passages underline very heavily the importance attached in certain times and places to a correct genealogy, lack of which could entail loss of office and privileges. Also to be noted is the bearing of the surname derived from the mother, a phenomenon which occurs again and again in some sections of genealogical study. To the Jews returned from exile to Israel and surrounded by enemies, the proper keeping of their family descents was of the greatest moment.

A far distant time and place, removed from modern outlook? By one of the cruellest ironies of history, the possession of a Jewish genealogy could, some 2,500 years later in Hitler's Germany, mean exclusion from that country, loss of property and even of life. Under the Hitler regime,

the study of genealogy greatly increased when thousands of Germans found it imperative to prove pure Aryan descent. There is a persistent story that Hitler himself had a Jewish grandmother—a possibility since there were Jewish Hitlers—but the latest biographers do not accept this view. (See Note 1). It remains true, however, that the bitterest of human hatreds often spring from a fact of ancestry fully known but deeply resented. Incidentally, the collocation of Hitler's real name of Schicklgruber, with the well known 'Heil' would clearly have been impossible.

Surnames are of great importance in the study of genealogy but at the outset it is well to realise that they have frequently been very fluid. In English-speaking countries the use of an alias is generally thought to denote something questionable in the user's character. Not so in the past, for some of the greatest men were content to write 'alias' after their surnames—Oliver Cromwell alias Williams (his name in the male line); Richard Hooker alias Vowel, for the founder of Anglican theology and the writer of great English prose. Surnames varied almost as much as the spelling of other words, and as far as the latter is concerned, it began to be consolidated only with the publication of Dr Samuel Johnson's *Dictionary*.

The sudden interest in genealogy in Hitler's Third Reich was only one of the more recent examples of the way in which the science has been used in a highly practical manner. Gone are the times when family history was regarded as the preserve of the spinster or the proper study for an eccentric uncle. In the first half of the nineteenth century one of the greatest of English historians, Lord Macaulay, swallowed whole the legendary origins of the chief families in the British aristocracy. His critical acumen readily detected the fabulous portions of Livy's history of early Rome, yet he was able simply to accept the origin of the great house of Hastings from a Norse sea rover of the ninth century. Again, he elevated the De Veres, admittedly famous as Earls of Oxford, to the rank of the greatest barons merely on the strength of legend. Today no such treatment of family history will be found among responsible historical writers. Sir Frank Stenton and his wife, Lady Stenton, both use the rich resources of English genealogy to illustrate English medieval history; so, too, did Sir Lewis Namier employ valuable family records to unravel the intricacies of eighteenth-century British politics.

Indeed, without a proper evaluation of genealogical sources, English or any other history frequently becomes incomprehensible. The tedious struggle of Lancaster and York, in the Wars of the Roses, is at once lightened by the realization that it was an affair of cousins. Edward III (reigned 1327-77) had six legitimate sons, several of whom survived the horrors of medieval nursing to reach manhood and propagate their kind. As no caste system then existed in England, the royal scions married daughters of the nobles and their offspring allied themselves in turn with the gentry, and these with the mercantile classes. From this widely flowing royal blood come the very large number of English and, of course, American pedigrees which ascend to Edward III and through him to many royal lines of western Europe. It was not that Edward was a man of phenomenal physical prowess, but simply that his children lived to manhood. There are six large volumes of the Marquis de Ruvigny's *Blood Royal of the Plantagenets* containing some 40,000 names of persons having legitimate descent from Edward III, a fact which gives fresh reality to the old saying that a king is the father of his people. Moreover, the 40,000 represent only those whose ancestry had been traced at the date of publication (1907 or thereabouts), whereas Ruvigny estimated that there were a known 100,000 descendants of Edward III.

With the cousinship of Edward's sons extended among the nobility, a contest for the crown became a struggle among relatives, with nearly all the nobles personally involved. The formal term 'cousin', used in old-style addresses from the sovereign to the greatest nobles, reflects a time when the greatest of the dukes and marquesses were indeed closely related to the reigning king. (See Note 2).

Genealogy also explains the extraordinary emergence of the Tudor dynasty. How came a Welsh squire of mixed blood to inherit the English throne? Without a genealogical table this cannot easily be understood. Nor can the strife of Stuart and Hanover be other than meaningless unless it is understood as a quarrel between kinsfolk, one branch of whom remained Catholic and so forfeited Britain's throne, while the other and German line became Protestant, and thus acceptable to the English requirements of regal succession.

Outside England a knowledge of pedigree is essential to understand many great institutions and events. How else to evaluate that great medieval international conception, the Holy Roman Empire? At first elective, the empire came eventually into the House of Habsburg. The House had two branches, of Austria and of Spain, and at times the rivalry of these relatives bedevilled European politics. It even extended to a dual claim to the Order of the Golden Fleece, so that a chancellery existed in both Madrid and in Austria. The order originated in the Netherlands from Philip the Good, father of Charles the Bold of Burgundy, to add another complication to the study.

Again, how to understand the coalescence into one realm, just in time

B

for the discovery and development of America, of the half-dozen or so small Spanish kingdoms? Or how the Bourbons came to reign on both sides of the Pyrenees? Or why Austria should ever have controlled part of the Netherlands? And how came it that a Prince of Orange, a small principality in the south of France, ruled in Holland and was crowned King of England? The only explanation of these strange national juxtapositions lies in dynastic history, and that *ipso facto* is inexplicable save by pedigree.

It may of course be said that all such happenings of earlier days are of concern only to Europe, and that the New World has long since left them behind. Certainly there is no monarchy in the Americas, except in Canada, and no titular aristocracy or even an order of knighthood in the USA. But this is not to say that the leading citizens of the United States are indifferent to their genealogies and, in fact, what the Norman Conquest is to England, the sailing of the *Mayflower* and the settlement of New England are to the USA. The settlers seem often to have wished to forget their place of origin, a wish heartily regretted by their tenth, eleventh, or twelfth generation descendants who are thus handicapped in their researches by the brief statement that the immigrant ancestor sailed from London or Plymouth, which was merely the port of embarkation. The crucial question of where he lived before coming to the port is one which only genealogical aids can answer.

In the course of my thirty years' study of American genealogy I must have seen several thousand American pedigrees and, in consequence, was not surprised, though extremely interested, to read in an American genealogical magazine an account of the Presidential dynasty of the USA. The word 'dynasty' is here used, not in the sense of hereditary rulers imposed upon a people, but of elected magistrates who, nonetheless, belong to what the author of the account calls 'a still tighter ring of some twenty-four families (who) have contributed four or more members to elective Federal Office. This list includes some twenty-three (of the thirty-six) Presidents, three Vice-Presidents, three Chief Justices, and two Speakers of the House of Representatives. . . . It is of this innermost two dozen that some twelve, all interrelated among each other, can be singled out to form the interlocking "Presidential dynasty". These twelve, the families of Adams, Bayard, Breckbridge, Harrison, Kennedy, Lee, Livingston, Lodge, Randolph, Roosevelt, Taft and Tucker are the core of our dynasty.' (*The Augustan*, vol 10, no 4, April 1967, article by Robert W. Formhals). In another issue of this same publication (Vol 10, no 6, August-September 1967) an account is given by Walter Angst of 'An Armorial Banner for President Kennedy'.

In 1939 I prepared an article on the Kennedy family for the *Burke's Landed Gentry* of that year, which contained a Supplement of American Families. Joseph Kennedy was then the American Ambassador at the Court of St James's. The ancestry went back only a few generations and was certainly not distinguished by the possession of a coat of arms. This lack has now been remedied. The Irish government decided to make the late President Kennedy a grant of arms as a St Patrick's Day gift. The description of the arms is: sable three helmets in profile or, within a bordure per saltire gules and ermine. Crest—Between two olive branches a cubit sinister arm in armour erect, the hand holding a sheaf of arrows, points upwards, all proper. The author states: 'These arms were presented to President Kennedy at a White House ceremony on St Patrick's Day of 1961. It certainly seems unique that the government of a free republic grants a coat of arms to the head of state of another sovereign republic.'

Incidentally, there are two republics carved out of the former British Empire which have renounced any British claim to sovereignty over them yet have set up heralds of their own. These two are South Africa and Ireland, and there is nothing inherently wrong in a republic possessing heralds or orders of chivalry, or even granting titles to its subjects.

There is a rapidly growing interest in family in Canada, Australia, and New Zealand, mostly with emphasis on descent from persons in the British Isles. In South Africa, the genealogical interest is partly concerned with Dutch descent, since the ruling race in the republic is the Afrikaaner. No doubt, as in pre-war Germany, interest in genealogical research is being stimulated by the apartheid policy, since it is often of vital importance for a man to be able to prove his all-white descent.

In Latin America, from the Rio Grande to Cape Horn, there is keen interest in genealogy and heraldry. Many ancient Spanish and Portuguese families are represented in Latin America, and there are flourishing societies devoted to these interests.

Only one area of the world is silent on the study of ancestry and, evidently, the science is viewed as dangerous to the peace of mind of citizens of a people's republic. In Czechoslovakia, to give one instance, the genealogical society was one of the first casualties of the Communist regime, though there would now seem to be some lifting of the veil as some useful publications for the genealogist are now coming from Czechoslovakia through the state publishing house. In Russia, the population is officially regarded as beginning in 1918, from which date a record of births, marriages and deaths has been maintained in the state archives. It has not proved possible to obtain information about the genealogical sources of the former regime.

Genealogy would therefore appear to be a study which is a prerogative of the free world, and within that world it flourishes as never before. As in Western Europe, so in the USA are there many societies, from Texas to New England, which publish magazines of genealogical interest, and it may well be that in future decades the USA will become the genealogical centre of the world. Already in Salt Lake City the Mormons are building up a magnificent collection of microfilm records, and though these are not primarily intended for genealogical purposes, they will nonetheless be of priceless value to the researcher.

CHAPTER 2

Ancient Genealogies: Oral Tradition

THE word 'genealogy' comes from the Greek γενέα, birth and λόγος study, and means the science of studying family history. 'Pedigree' is the word used to denote the setting out of a genealogy in chart or other written form and derives from two Latin words, *pes*, a foot, and *grus*, a crane, the reference being to a sign somewhat resembling a crane's foot which was used to indicate lines of descent in early western European genealogies. Variations of this have appeared since, such as an arrow shape, or double lines ||. The usual modern form is ⌐──¹──¬, familiar to most people from the charts of kings' pedigrees in school history books. The sign = denotes marriage, and a line thus ∿∿∿, implies illegitimacy. It has been written that the use of the term 'genealogy' originated in England during the fifteenth and sixteenth centuries but this can hardly be correct as St Paul, in his epistles to his spiritual sons, uses the word in the original Greek; eg, 1 Timothy ch 1, v 4. 'Neither give heed to fables and endless genealogies' (1611 version, with Greek original, μηδὲ προσ ἔχειν μυθοις καὶ γενεαλογίαις ἀπεράντοις which passed into the Latin Vulgate, as *neque intenderent fabulis et genealogis interminatis*) and again, Titus, ch 3, v 9 'But avoid foolish questions, and genealogies, and contentions, and strivings about the law; for they are unprofitable and vain' (μωρὰς δὲ ξητησεις καὶ γενεαλογιας K.T.L., *stultus autem quaestiones et genealogias*). Judging by his reference to the law, meaning the Mosaic system, the apostle must almost certainly have had in mind the numerous Jewish genealogies when he wrote of genealogy, and he would of course have been familiar with these from boyhood. They were an integral part of the Bible but, like many other matters in the Hebrew Dispensation, had become rather formalized by the first century AD. (For further details of Hebrew genealogies, see Note 3).

With genealogy, then, as with most other sciences, we begin with a Greek term, even though it existed long before the Greeks gave it a name. In the earliest civilizations of Sumer and Akkad in the Middle

East—formerly called Mesopotamia, the land between the rivers Tigris and Euphrates—there are lists of kings before and after the Great Flood, evidence of which was discovered by Sir Leonard Woolley and identified with the Noachian Deluge. In a sense, these are rudimentary genealogies since a king would normally be succeeded by a kinsman if not by a son. In Egypt more elaborate descents are recorded. The royal house of the Pharaohs was regarded as divine, and as such was unable to marry outside its own table of affinity. Even the last independent dynasty of Egypt, that of the originally Greek Ptolemies, adopted this incestuous habit and Cleopatra would have been married to her small brother, a boy of nine or ten. The great importance of kinship in Pharaonic Egypt stimulated the keeping of pedigrees and a similar *motif* of divinity and semi-divine descent later played a very important part in European genealogies as well as becoming a recurring theme throughout the world.

There are three stages in genealogical development. The first is the period of oral tradition, then that of committing pedigrees to writing, and finally, from the sixteenth century onward, the attempt to record all members of a people and not merely the higher classes. Learned men have written a great deal of pretentious nonsense about tradition over the last 200 years, but a far more sensible attitude is now being taken by modern scholars. Tradition is seen often to be more reliable than written records, and, especially when illiteracy prevails, may embody the knowledge of a whole people. Memory is always stronger when men are unable to make notes, and even when a people has been generally literate it was often a point of honour to memorise a text, particularly of a religious rite. Among the ancient Jews there was the saying 'a good disciple is like a well, he loses nothing.' Macaulay, we know, could recite Milton's *Paradise Lost* by heart and, even in these present days of reliance upon writing and recording machines many people are able to memorize long and difficult texts. Many members of the Church of England know the Communion Service, and Evensong or Matins by heart, owing to simple repetition. In Masonry, the book is used for learning but discarded in the actual ceremonies, reliance then being placed on memory to recall long and involved texts.

This being so with our possibly degenerate memories, it was much more the case in times and places when writing was unknown. Instances can easily be provided from the Celtic portions of the British Isles. Irish pedigrees were once a subject for merriment and ribald scorn, and as they originally appeared in print from the sixteenth century onwards the ancestry of the Irish kings and princes was traced to Milesius, King of Spain about 1,000 BC, and from him to Noah and Adam. In some pedigrees the prophet Jeremiah, having disappeared from Palestine and the Old Testament, turns up in Ireland with a Pharaoh's daughter for wife and becomes progenitor of a royal line. All of this has now been given up. 'History begins with writing, and Irish history begins with the introduction of Latin learning and letters in the fifth century AD; so far as we know, the primitive pre-Christian alphabet called Ogam was used only for inscriptions over graves.' Thus the greatest authority on the Irish genealogies, Professor David Greene of Trinity College, Dublin, writing in *Burke's Landed Gentry of Ireland*, 1958.

The corpus of Irish pedigrees is reliable as far back as AD 600, while some pedigrees may be genuine as far back as the fifth century, that is about 1,500 years ago, a length of family history not easily to be matched elsewhere in Europe. The reason for this is that after the coming of St Patrick in 432 (the traditional date), monastic institutions with a literate practice rapidly developed. What more natural than for the monks to write down a string of names, those of the traditional ancestors of the local king? And why should anyone invent such a string? Invention usually gives us some events and persons of grandeur, but there is nothing particularly exciting about a line with the following names: Niall of the Nine Hostages, Connall Cremthainne, Fergus Cerrbeoil, and Diarmid. Niall, High King of Ireland, was killed about AD 405 on the Garonne, and Diarmid was definitely an historical personage who gave the first recorded decision in copyright dispute between his cousin St Columba and St Finnian of Moville. Diarmid lived at a time when historical records could lighten his story, so why doubt his great-grandfather's existence? We are dealing here, of course, only with the pedigrees of the greatest men—kings and princes. Ancient Ireland was composed of four provinces, Leinster, Munster, Connaught and Ulster. Each province had its king, one of whom was the Ard-Ri or High King. The O'Neills, descendants of Niall, held the position for centuries, and when Brian Boru, or Boroimhe, ancestor of the famous O'Brien family, became High King, he defeated the invading Danes at the battle of Clontarf in 1014. Later, the supremacy passed to the ancestors of the O'Conor Don until, in the Anglo-Norman invasions of 1167-72, the High Kingship ended and the Kings of England became Lords of Ireland.

The compilation of vast pedigrees going back to Biblical personages was the work of monastic chroniclers. They wrote down accurately enough the oral traditions of their kings, but embroidered the earlier part of the pedigree. The divine beings who very often figure at the beginning of a West European pedigree were explained by the monks as heroes who had been deified. In this they were probably correct and were unknowingly applying the criterion of Euhemerus who, in the fourth century BC, had similarly explained the gods of ancient Greece as being deified heroes.

Welsh pedigrees go through the same cycle as the ancient Irish genealogies, and many of the present day have a proven family descent of a millenium or more. These are based on documents, but behind these is the oral tradition which affixes the line to one of the more celebrated Romano-Britons in the break-up of the Roman province of Britain in the fifth century. In an instance to hand, Magnus Maximus, Governor of Roman Wales was proclaimed Emperor of Rome by his soldiers in AD 383; despite his subsequent defeat, he was claimed as an ancestor by several Welsh princes and in our time actually figured, in some accounts, as ancestor of the Philipps family, that of Lord St Davids.

Oral tradition also plays a part in the pedigrees of the Scottish Highland chiefs, but not so successfully as with the Welsh and Irish. Few Highland family trees go back to the year 1,000.

In a highly literate society, tradition is often suspect and may, in fact, be merely a reflection of some written suggestion. The writings of Sir Walter Scott (1771-1832) rekindled an interest in the middle ages and encouraged many romantic ideas about the Crusades and other medieval events. Scott was a man of vast knowledge, but sometimes *Homerus etiam nutat* and in one of his novels, *Ivanhoe*, he refers to descendants of St Edward the Confessor, King of England 1042-66. In fact Edward, although married, lived as a celibate and preserved his chastity. Scott's readers, however, were not expected to be straitened by historical fact and began to think of themselves as descended from noble knights and barons, even though their grandfathers had made their fortunes by sweat shops in the industrial revolution. Then arrived the most potent of all genealogical writers, Sir Bernard Burke, son of the founder of the world famous Burke publications. Despite his great knowledge and never failing memory he could not resist the call of romance. He committed himself to the statement that most of the landowning class in England were descended from the Norman Conquerors, in the male line; he put Guy of Warwick, our delightful and gallant childhood hero, into the undoubtedly ancient Arden pedigree; in his famous first edition of the *Landed Gentry*, then under the name of *Burke's Commoners*, he found a place for the Dragon of Wantley and allowed a tenth-century Viking to appear as the ancestor of the genuine sixteenth-century family of Blacker. All this obscured much otherwise excellent work and underlines the small reliance to be placed on English traditions.

A powerful factor in the transmission of oral traditions was the work of the bards. These men were not simply singers or entertainers, though that side of their work existed. They often had a duty to recite the pedigrees of their kings. This was so with the sennachie of the Scots kings from whose office developed the position of the Lord Lyon, head of the heraldic system of Scotland, who was a great officer of state when Scotland was a separate kingdom. Each sennachie had the duty of teaching others; the information was passed on orally, and should there be a mistake in recitation the pupil received a blow from a rowan rod.

Oral sources, then, have given the supremacy in age to the Irish and Welsh pedigrees, not only in the British Isles but in the rest of Europe. No families, not even the royal houses, can make a sound claim to bridge the chasm of the dark ages and establish a proven connection with the period of the later Roman Empire. Efforts made to give Charlemagne a late Roman ancestor are not substantiated and, this being so for the great imperial line, we may accept Edward Gibbon's dictum that the most important European royal families struggle through from the darkness of the early middle ages.

Claims to Roman descent have sometimes been advanced, as with the Italian Prince Massimo who has been described as descended from the Roman dictator, Fabius Maximus, who foiled the great Hannibal in the third century BC. The Prince Massimo of Napoleon's time, when asked by Bonaparte what was the evidence for his claim, replied nonchalantly, 'People have been saying it for 2,000 years, so I suppose it is true,' a *bon mot* but not evidence, nor can there be evidence in such matters. Rome fell; her governors and her emperors were replaced in western Europe by barbarian kings, and it is from these that the erstwhile proud monarchies of Europe descend. The British sovereign is sixty-second monarch in descent from King Egbert of Wessex (in southern England) who achieved supremacy over the other kings in Britain about 825, and thus bore the title of Bretwalda, or Ruler of the Britons, roughly corresponding to the Ard-Ri in Ireland. Egbert descended from Cerdic, the founder of the kingdom of Wessex, about AD 500. The latter was Woden born, that is, descended from the deity of the Saxons, Woden or Odin. A bare string of names, some ten generations, lies between Cerdic and Woden. Woden must have been a towering personality, who perhaps saved his people in some forgotten cataclysm and was rewarded by an apotheosis, like that of Romulus, the founder of Rome, who became the god Quirinus.

If Europe cannot penetrate even in her most august lines beyond the third or fourth century, and that only by a line of demi-gods, what of other continents? Probably the most astonishing of all royal pedigrees is that of the Emperor of Ethiopia. The *Kebra Nagast*, or 'Glory of Kings', translated by Sir Wallis Budge, is held to represent a written tradition dating from the fourth century AD. Behind this may lie other versions but, even so, the events narrated in this ancient book pertain to a fantastically earlier period, that of the reign of Solomon, King of Israel, about 1,000 BC. Everyone knows the Old Testament account of the visit of the Queen of Sheba to King Solomon. The Ethiopian history takes up the story from that point. Makeda, Queen of Ethiopia, visits Solomon and after some protracted love play, they marry. The queen returns home but promises to send a son of the marriage to Solomon. In due time young Menelik arrives in Jerusalem and is made much of by his father. By a trick, the prince gains possession of the Ark of the Covenant, which he takes home with him and places in Axum, the holy city of Ethiopia. He reigns as David II and from him the subsequent emperors of Ethiopia descend. In the *Kebra Nagast* there is no claim that the story is true; it is simply stated as a fact. The most that can be said is that it may be true, and certainly the Ethiopians have always shown remarkable tenacity in maintaining their national traditions. When converted to Christianity, they held to it despite being surrounded for 1,000 years by fierce Moslem races. In modern times they have preserved their native Catholicism against Roman Catholic proselytism, and in this century, with British help, they succeeded in throwing off the Italian yoke. There is a strange turn to the story of Solomon and Menelik. Solomon was an ancestor of Christ; both Christ and Menelik could be called a son of Solomon and by Ethiopian ideas they were akin to each other. 'But Christ was the son of God, and therefore being the kinsman of Christ, Menelik was divine. And Isaac the Ethiopian, holding this view, maintains in the *Kebra Nagast* that the Kings of Ethiopia who were descended from Menelik were of divine origin, and that their words and deeds were those of God.' (Sir Wallis Budge). Here, once again and with added emphasis, is the divine origin of kings.

Leaving Africa and coming to Asia, we might expect long centuries of descent when we think of the immemorial traditions and ancient history of China. Here is the only nation in the world which has been the contemporary of the Pharaohs and of the empires of the Fertile Crescent in the Middle East. Before Greece and Rome were, China existed as a great civilized state. The most widely spread and tenaciously held belief in China is ancestor worship, and to worship properly one must be aware of one's ancestors. The greatest sage of China, Confucius, taught respect for ancestors and due performance of all customary rites. He received great honours after his death, and respect was always paid to his descendants, whose genealogies would thus span 2,500 years, or more than eighty generations. The imperial system in China rested upon a fiction, that the first emperor of a new dynasty was, in fact, the lineal successor of the last ruler of the old dynasty, whom he had quite often deposed. This being so, imperial pedigrees would not as a rule be much longer than the history of the particular dynasty. How far the pedigrees of the nobles could be traced it is impossible now to state, but, some noble titles were allowed to exist for twenty to twenty-five generations, which would argue a descent of some 500 years.

In India, long pedigrees exist, going back to periods well before the beginnings of the Christian era, if full reliance can be placed upon them. How much reliance there can be is shown by the ascription of divine origin to the royal races of various Hindu kings, and by the inclusion of mythical happenings. Still, even when all due allowance has been made for these impossible items, the pedigrees of many of the Hindu royal houses are unquestionably very ancient. Among the Rajputs, pedigrees extending to over 1,000 years are by no means unknown. The classic work on the subject, by Lt Col James Tod, once British political agent to the western Rajput states, is entitled: *Annals and Antiquities of Rajasthan, or the Central and Western Rajput States of India.* First published in 1829-32, it is an immense tome and the 1950 edition runs to close upon 1,300 closely-printed pages. Making the reservations required whenever one considers studies by Europeans of Asian or African nations—that is, discounting the enthusiasm of a convert—it is nonetheless clear that many Rajput pedigrees antedate the European genealogies. The same would not apply to other Indian princely lines, many of which arose out of the chaos caused by the decline of the Mogul empire in the eighteenth century. Provincial governors elevated themselves to independent princes, though many of them were of lower rank in their origins than the Rajput princes. As there were over 500 Indian princes when the British handed over their sovereignty to India and Pakistan, there was ample margin for the existence of over 200 royal lines with an antiquity exceeding a millenium.

In other parts of Asia, war, conquest and the rise and fall of empires have all hampered systematic record keeping. In the large area of country formerly known as Indo-China between the eleventh and twelfth centuries AD, the Khmers possessed a very great empire, and an ability to arrange and carry through public works equal to that of any other ancient civilization. Yet the Khmer empire declined to such an extent that, by the sixteenth century, mighty cities like Angkhor Vat had become buried in the jungle, where they were discovered by the first Europeans to penetrate the country in that age. When these enormous ruins were later cleared and investigated by French archaeological expeditions, the natives disclaimed all knowledge of them, even saying that they had made themselves. In such a state of knowledge, or rather of ignorance, pedigree-keeping could have little place. Again, in the neighbouring country of Thailand, or Siam, we have it on the authority of a member of the royal family, HRH Prince Chula, that few even of the greatest Thai families can trace ancestry further than 200 years—a poor length of pedigree for anyone in England or America.

Japan is sometimes mentioned as possessing a very ancient imperial line, but the pedigree of the Mikados, like the history of their country, is so involved in myth that length of genealogy has to be cut down to get away from the exploits of the sun goddess. The Mikado—a term little used by the Japanese themselves—is supposed to derive from the rape performed by the god of lust, Susanoo, upon his sister, Amaterasu, the sun goddess. The descendant in the fifth generation from this incestuous though heavenly bastardy was the first Emperor Jimmu, who ascended the throne in 660 BC. The earliest Japanese historical writings, the *Kojiki* and the *Nihongi*, date from about AD 722. The pedigree of the imperial line may, therefore, be traced to a period some centuries later than that of the British royal house. How far the pedigrees of the Japanese nobles can be taken back is not known, but it is a fact that heraldic emblems originated in Japan many centuries ago, completely independent of European influence. The Japanese use a symbol called the *mon*, which corresponds very much to the badge or crest in western heraldry, and as all their noble families possess a *mon*, usually of ancient date, the Japanese nobility presumably have pedigrees at least comparable to those of their European counterparts. (See Note 4.)

In western Asia, many genuine pedigrees are traced from the seventh century when Mohammed founded the religion of Islam. Interest in pedigree among the Arabs was by no means confined to their famous steeds. Mecca before the time of Mohammed was a religious centre, though not of monotheism. The Black Stone, the Kaaba, was an object of pilgrimage and the affairs of Mecca were managed by a number of aristocratic families, the Koreish, of whom Mohammed was a member. He conceived his mission, not as the founding of a new religion, but as recalling his contemporaries to the worship of the one God, which had been corrupted from the pure teaching of Mohammed's predecessors, Moses, Christ and others. After Mohammed's death, his work was carried on by his successors, the caliphs, and the main controversies in

Islam have arisen through dissensions as to the lawful holders of the caliphate. Unquestionably, however, Moslems do pay a certain reverence to descendants of the Prophet, and after 1,300 years these are quite numerous, tracing their descent from Fatima—the only daughter of Mohammed to survive and have children—who married Ali, one of Mohammed's favourite disciples. HH the Aga Khan descends from this marriage but many other descendants of the Prophet are far from wealthy or famous. Other Arab or Moslem pedigrees exist of much the same length.

The writing of what is now called scientific history is a western product and full elucidation of eastern history has been prevented by difficulties in research and of language. Eastern genealogy has suffered to an even greater extent and far too little research has been devoted to the genealogies of Asians, either of the Near or the Far East. Consequently, the present work has been confined, save for one or two excursions, to the study of European genealogy. After all, from Europe has come the civilization of both the Americas, of South Africa, Australia and New Zealand, and it is to Europe and its records that families in these countries must look if they wish to go beyond the records of their own lands.

Meanwhile, other instances can be given relevant to the present consideration of ancient, and traditional genealogies. In the Pacific, it has been proved that many ancient traditions exist. Thor Heyerdahl, for example, has shown in *Kon-Tiki* that some Pacific islanders have traditions of origin from a land to the east a very long time ago. Whether that mother country was Peru has not yet been proved. Again, the Maoris had no knowledge of writing before the coming of the white man, but their legends and a system of record keeping with beads enabled us to establish that they arrived in New Zealand in the fourteenth century, although their pioneers had discovered it in the tenth century. The fact that such distant voyages in primitive craft were possible over the wide Pacific should give pause to the rejection of many native traditions in various parts of the world. Clearly, in times before the writing of history, tribes did migrate over vast areas and even such a fiction as the Milesian pedigrees in Ireland should not blind us to the fact that migrations thither by tribes from Spain, or even from Greece, are not impossible in view of the wanderings in the Pacific of races like the Maoris.

In contrast to the lengthy traditions of the Maoris are the scantier oral records of the Zulus, of which a recent writer has this to say: 'Each of the Nguni clans in the Mtetwa paramountcy had its own history but very few of them could trace their story back more than a generation or two. In the absence of written records or of any oral epic tradition, there was little enough to go on. Clans could recite the direct genealogy of their chieftains for perhaps a dozen generations, but the names that came so readily to their lips were those of people whose lives and deeds had already dropped into limbo.' So wrote Donald R. Morris in *The Washing of the Spears: The Rise and Fall of the Zulu Nation*, p 42, published in 1966.

In ancient Peru, before the Spanish Conquest, the pedigrees of the Incas and their kinsfolk, the nobles, were carefully preserved, not only by oral tradition but no doubt by means of the *quipus* (*quipu* = knot), an arrangement used mainly for arithmetical calculation but capable of assisting the memory in other tasks. As Prescott points out in his *Conquest of Peru*, (Ch. 1) no account of the Inca dynasty allows of more than thirteen princes before the Conquest. The keeping of such a pedigree would not entail much difficulty but it was otherwise with the Inca nobles. They were all related to the sovereign, who was polygamous and might easily sire a hundred or more children. Retention of the different genealogical connections after two or three generations must have been a rare feat of memory.

The earliest Americans in the northern part of the western hemisphere are the famous but strangely named Red Indians. Unfortunately, very little of their traditions has been collected as they had the misfortune to be colonized before the advent of properly trained observers with an interest in their history. They stood in the way of American expansion and must inevitably have been overcome, yet their history could have been of great value. In Canada, the system of the totem pole comes very close to the use of an heraldic device; in fact, it is of the same order, especially when it is remembered that the greatest civilized nations follow the practice of the Indian tribes in having animals as national symbols. In Canada, too, among the Indians, there was the political federation of the Six Nations which tribal traditions suggest as originating from about AD 1400. Perhaps it was this phenomenon which caused the great historian of Rome, 200 years ago, to sigh for an Iroquois book, a treasure even then scarcely possible and now altogether out of reach.

The Indians of North America put up a strong resistance to invaders. Viking settlements on the mainland appear to have been abandoned as the result of Indian hostility, and both British and American regular forces perished in battle with the Indians. As late as 1875 the destruction of General Custer and his force was due to a combination of tribes, and it was not until 1890 that the frontier was officially closed. Nominal rolls exist of some tribes from 1840 onwards, with an increase after the close of the war between North and South. These records, which originated from treaties the Indians made with the American government, are now kept in the national archives in Washington.

Over the several centuries of white colonization of North America some mingling of blood was inevitable and one of the earliest cases had considerable genealogical consequence. Powhatan, a chief in Virginia, had a daughter, Pocahontas, who saved the life of Captain John Smith, one of the leaders in the colony of Jamestown, in the reign of the English and Scottish king, James I (James VI of Scotland). In 1614, when she was about nineteen years old, Pocahontas married an Englishman, Captain John Rolfe, and went with him to England. Being presented at court, she was treated by King James as a sister in regality and regularly styled Princess. She died in 1616-17 and was buried at Gravesend, in Kent, one of the first American victims of the English climate. Short as was her life, she was yet able to leave descendants, and several eminent families in both Old and New England descend from her. Nor was James I alone in giving royal recognition to Indian chiefs and kings. In the records of the reign of Charles II there is an account of four small crowns or coronets in thin silver plate gilt and adorned with false stones of various colours which were designed as 'presents to Indian kings and queens now tributary to His Majesty within the colony of Virginia.' An Indian sachem, whom the English called the King of the Pamunkeys, had done the settlers good service and when he died his queen appealed to the Virginian House of Burgesses for an award in recognition. As a result, Charles II sent her a cap of red velvet surmounted by a silver plate to which were attached some chains. These and other similar instances are given in Lord Twining's magnificent account of European regalia. The Indian chiefs were regularly accorded the regal title, as witness the well-known affair of King Philipp's war, where the treatment was very different from the attitude reflected in a later saying, 'The only good Indian is a dead Indian.'

CHAPTER 3

Ancient Genealogies: The Period to AD 1100 of Committal to Writing

HISTORY begins with writing and genealogy is a part of history. Just as genealogical considerations explain much in national history so, conversely, national history will determine the nature of the family histories which are possible in a particular country. The most familiar example is that of England, which has a written history of just over 2,000 years counting from the first invasion by Julius Caesar in 55 BC and taking the history of the Roman province of Britain as part of the history of England.

Two events of great importance decide what can and what cannot be proved in the study of English or, if we prefer the term, British genealogy. The Roman government of what is now England lasted 400 years, until AD 410-11. Then the Roman official connection ceased and so, with the exception of a sermon or moral exhortation by St Gildas, did written record until St Augustine, sent by the Pope, St Gregory the Great, landed in Kent in 597 to convert the English. This is the only gap in the otherwise well-documented history of England. At the beginning of this well nigh 200-year period, the Roman province is in being, shaken by barbarian onslaughts north, west and east, but still recognisably part of the great Latin empire of civilization. At the other side of the gap, the Roman province has disappeared and in its place are a number of petty kingdoms peopled and ruled by folk who speak an ancient form of English and whose ancestors have crossed to Britain from the North Sea coasts of Germany. In short, Britain has turned into England. From the genealogical standpoint one thing is clear. No English person can claim descent from anyone living in the old Roman Britain. As we have seen, some of the princely Welsh families try to assert a claim to a Roman or Romano-British descent, but this can never be proved or even taken as more than a possibility. It most certainly cannot be predicated of anyone of English descent.

The second event of crucial importance in English history is the Norman Conquest. From 597 to 1066 the English kingdoms gradually evolved into one realm, partly owing to the necessity of resisting the Danish Viking onslaught. Four Danish kings ruled in England, but the English line was restored, and in any case the country remains England and the language English, not Daneland or Danish. Then, upon this realm which, except in the arts of warfare, had a higher culture by far than its conquerors came the tremendous cataclysm of the Norman Conquest. In 1066 the land was held by English and Danish landowners. In 1086, when William the Conqueror's Domesday survey was completed, only a small proportion of the landowners bore English or Danish names. Supplanting them were persons of continental origin, having mostly French names. The former native ruling class had largely disappeared, either slain in battle or removed by the simple process of dispossession in favour of William's companions. The genealogical moral, and one which many writers of family legends have found it impossible to draw, is that, with a very few exceptions, no one can genuinely claim a pre-Conquest pedigree.

The exceptions are Arden, Berkeley and Swinton, and anyone who has perused the very short pedigrees which have been recovered and recorded by W. G. Searle will realize this. The title of his work is *Anglo-Saxon Bishops, Kings and Nobles: The Successions of the Bishops and the Pedigrees of the Kings and Nobles,* 1899 and half the pedigrees in the second part of this book are those of the royal lines of Kent, Sussex, the Isle of Wight, Essex, East Anglia, Mercia, Bernicia and Northumberland, Deira, Lindsey, Wessex (ie the royal house of England), showing descent, with the possible exception of Essex, from Woden, the god of the pagan ancestors of the English. Of the second portion of the second half of the book—the genealogies of the Anglo-Saxon nobles—the author says that they 'are mostly very short and fragmentary. That they are not more complete is due to the circumstance that no history of any of these families exists. All that was possible was to put together such information as could be derived from the scattered notices of the members of these families found in the histories and charters, from the wills which contain references to them, and from their signatures appended to the charters.' (*op cit*, p xi).

This means that even the very greatest nobles of pre-Conquest England possess only scanty pedigrees of not more than five or six generations. How impossible then to trace a pedigree from one of these magnates. The great hero, Hereward the Wake, the last man in England to resist the Conqueror, has been claimed at different times as ancestor of the

c

Wakes, baronets; of the Howards (the Dukes of Norfolk); and of the Harwards. The problem cannot be solved, yet every now and then someone comes along with a claim based, not always accurately, on the possession of a Saxon surname and asserts his descent from the pre-Conquest English. King Harold II, who fell at Hastings in 1066, had seven children. We know what happened to one daughter, Gytha, who married Wladimir of Novogorod, son of Uselovod, Tzar of Russia, and who figures in many of the Russian pedigrees. But of the remaining six —Hakon, Godwin, Edmund, Magnus, Gunhild and Ulf (whose name may have been Harold)—we know nothing beyond the fact that two of Harold's sons made a Viking-like descent on the Somersetshire coast near Bristol in 1068-9. This noble line which had produced a king of England then vanishes from history. What happened to the Godwinsons? We simply do not know. And if a family of this magnitude is lost to view, how can someone assume, merely on the strength of possessing an Old English name as surname, that his family is traceable to ancient Saxon times?

The suffixes -ham and -ing occur very often in Old English place-names, and the majority of English place-names are pre-Conquest and Saxon in origin. The suffix -ham meant a home or place, -ing often denoted a tribe. Bodiam in Sussex, the site of a famous medieval castle, was the ham or settlement of one Bod, whose name has survived, rather as Lucan says of Pompey, *stat magni nominis umbra*, save that Bod is only the shadow of a shade. He has bequeathed his name to after ages; nothing more. Beddington is the ton or town of the tribe of the Beddings. Now, if someone's surname happens to be Beddington or Bodiam, it means, not that he is of ancient Saxon ancestry, but only that a forbear of his who may have been a Frenchman lived at this place at some time from the twelfth to the sixteenth century when English surnames were being formed. Another interesting example is the name of the smallest English county, Rutland, which derives from Ruta's land. Who Ruta was we have not the faintest idea, nor why by the time of the Conquest this county had become the dowry of England's queens.

If this particular point should seem to have been laboured it is because experience has shown that only the most stringent precautions can hold in check the undisciplined pedigree maker. It is not that they deliberately and fraudulently make up pedigrees, but rather that they ignore the hard facts of genealogy. When we come to consider the claims to Norman ancestry we shall find that it is only a little less difficult to prove descent from a first generation Norman in England than from a pre-Conquest Englishman. Had Harold won the battle of Hastings there would have been many more pedigrees of English folk dating from before 1066. Clearly, the pride of the great English families would have consisted in tracing descent from the heroes who had beaten the Norsemen under Harold Hardrada, and the Normans under Duke William. Instead, the pride of the English nobility has been to assert a Norman origin. A strange national trait, to be proud of one's conquerors! In England in 1966 there were celebrations for the ninth centenary of the Norman Conquest. Can anyone imagine the French celebrating Sedan or Waterloo, or the Germans joyfully commemorating their surrender in 1945?

Much the same stringent considerations apply to the study of western European pedigrees. As already mentioned, claims to descent from Roman notables can be forgotten. The only likely exception to this rule is in some of the pedigrees of the grandees of Spain. Even then, this will not amount to a link with Rome, for Spain was conquered by the Visigoths, who were among the barbarians that overran the Roman Empire. I have been told that Spanish genealogists now exercise much the same caution towards such claims as we in English-speaking countries do towards claims to Norman ancestry. In most west European lands the invaders were few in comparison with the natives and soon after the barbarian conquests there began a mingling of conquerors with the old Roman provincial population. This certainly took place in France, Spain and Italy, countries which, not unreasonably, are called Latin lands, because their language and much else besides derives from Rome. Britain was an exception to the rule; although we do not know the exact fate of the population in the English Conquest, it is fairly safe to say that a large number must have perished or fled. The cities were usually deserted, at least at first, the English tribesmen often preferring to settle in a new place of their own, or near the Roman settlement. Language is by no means always a guide to race, but the Latin and Celtic languages were completely replaced by English dialects though, strange as it may seem, a number of Celtic place-names survived, as in Avon and even London. In North Africa, too, the Roman population disappeared after the Moslem Conquest in the seventh century, the wealthier classes withdrawing to Italy and Sicily and the poorer being absorbed into Islam.

No family history can better illustrate the impossibility of tracing descent from Roman notables than that of Mountbatten. This, since 1917, has been the surname of the family of the Marquess of Milford Haven, of which Earl Mountbatten of Burma, and his nephew, Prince Philip, Duke of Edinburgh and husband of Queen Elizabeth II, are cadets, or junior members. Of this line, a modern historian who wrote the revised account of the family states: 'As the mist of the Dark Ages clears away, their ancestors in the direct male line are already found as soldier statesmen maintaining order in parts of what is now Belgium and Luxembourg' (*Burke's Peerage*). The documented history of the Mountbattens begins with one Gislebert, Count of a portion of land round the river Meuse and of Masau, or Maasgau in modern Belgium. He can be dated between 841 and 863. In 846, in the fashion of those times, he abducted Irmgard, daughter of the Emperor Lothair, but got back into the emperor's good relations through the intercession of his uncle, Charles the Bald, King of the Franks. Count Gislebert was unlikely to be a new man, if he had this degree of kinship, and in fact eight generations of the family are given in the type of traditional genealogy which has been mentioned in connection with the classic Irish pedigrees. The oral pedigree begins with Duke Ydulf in the sixth century and goes through seven generations—Brunulf, Aubri, Walter, another Walter, Albo, Mainier and Gainfroi—to Count Gislebert. The Mountbattens are described as one of the oldest traceable families in Christendom. Certainly their story is a useful illustration of the manner in which barbarian chiefs took over provinces of the old Roman Empire and gradually evolved, through the influence of Christianity, into something resembling gentlemen. Rough, turbulent, bloody and commandment-breaking were their careers, but it remains true that the most polished royal and aristocratic dynasties of Europe have such gangster-like types for their revered ancestors.

Before going on to describe the second great period in European genealogy, when from the ninth century onwards the oral traditions were being written down in conjunction with documentary evidence, it is as well to look at the genealogical information current in the Roman Empire. Like other races which possessed heroes and heroic literature, the Greeks, with the Iliad and the Odyssey of Homer, had genealogies of their greatest men, though those given in Homer are often short. There is no great corpus of Hellenic genealogy, mainly because much of the material from which it might have been composed has perished. Much the same is true of the Romans, and few pedigrees can be constructed for more than a few generations. The Greeks were absorbed by Rome, and though Greece became the Roman province of Achaia she was still able to exert a great influence on her Roman masters and not least in genealogy. As everyone knows, the great Latin poet, Virgil, wrote his poem 'The Aenead' in an attempt to emulate in Latin the work of Homer. Among other things, he took over the legend that the Romans derived from Troy, and that a band of Trojans under Aeneas, fleeing from the doomed city, reached Italy and founded the Roman state. This legend may have contained some element of truth but was mainly a reaction against the Greek predominance in so many spheres. Greek influence also showed itself in the false pedigrees which now began to appear. Roman notables, like their counterparts in Elizabethan England, could not bear to think of themselves as merely rich and successful; they had to be noble as well. In both periods persons, some learned, some not, came forward to gratify their patrons' wishes. Sometimes they had a disconcerting reception. The Emperor Vespasian, who became ruler in AD 70, knew himself to have come from honest farming stock and used to laugh at the huge family histories of illustrious descent made up for his delectation by his courtiers.

The House of the Caesars affords probably the most interesting example of a Roman pedigree. It begins with Caius Julius Caesar, the great Dictator, who bestowed upon the world's dynasties his name of Caesar as a title—Caesar, Tzar, Czar, Kaiser, and even for the British sovereign from 1877-1947, Kaiser-i-Hind. Caesar's family was supposed to descend from the goddess Venus, another instance of the ascription of a semi-divine origin to a great family. He did come from one of the noblest houses of Rome, but his ancestry, like that of the other Roman notables under the Republic, cannot be traced in exact detail. The matter-of-fact Romans used a very concrete way of denoting their predecessors; in the hall of a great house a Roman noble would show a wax image for every ancestor who had held office in the state. This method at one glance discriminated between the member of an old family and a *novus homo*, a new man, the expressive Roman phrase very much used and corresponding to our self-made man. Such a manner of pedigree delineation was very inexact and liable to destruction. While a new arrival like Marcus Tullius Cicero would have a hall bare but for his own bust, Caesar's hall would be filled. *Vides omnes has imagines, quae implevere Caesareum atrium?*, asks the philosopher Seneca. 'You see all these images which fill up Caesar's hall?' and then adds the caustic comment, 'there is not one not marked by something unpleasant.'

Turning to the pedigree derived from Julius Caesar, we have the name of his father, Caius Julius Caesar, who married a lady named Aurelia, and had by her the Dictator, bearing the same names as his father, and a daughter, Julia, living in 52 BC, who married Atius Balbus. Her daughter, Atia, married as her first husband, Caius Octavius, who died 59 BC, having been the father of Caius Octavius, born in 63 BC. The Dictator had no son, and by his will adopted Octavius as his heir and as a member of the Julian family. Octavius was to become the Emperor

Augustus, first emperor of Rome. He was by adoption the son of Julius Caesar. Augustus, in turn, had no son, and after many losses in his sister's family he adopted his stepson, later the Emperor Tiberius. The latter was succeeded by his great nephew, Caius Caesar, known as Caligula, or 'Little Boots'. In his turn he was succeeded by Claudius (in whose reign Britain was successfully invaded by the Romans), the nephew of Tiberius and uncle of Caligula. Claudius, who died in AD 54, married as his second wife his niece, Agrippina, who had a son by a previous marriage. This son, Nero, who has attained an almost unparalleled notoriety, is the original of the famous Number 666 in the Revelation of St John—the signification of Neron Kaisar in Hebrew letters. He succeeded his great uncle after the latter's murder in AD 54. Nero was Claudius' adopted son, in accordance with the Roman practice when no real son was available. On Nero's death in AD 68, he was 'the last of the family of the Caesars, the last of the divine Julian-Claudian dynasty. The last drops of the united blood of Octavius, of Agrippa and of Livia (wife of Augustus and mother of Tiberius by a previous marriage—L.G.P.). . . . Intermarriages had led to the natural consequences. The germs of disease that might have been dissipated by the admixture of fresh and vigorous blood were accumulated in the Caesarean stock by consanguineous marriages, till all the members to the last perished, either as madmen, or as victims to the mad fears of their blood relatives and natural protectors.' (S. Baring Gould, *The Tragedy of the Caesars*, 1923, pp 637-8).

The above is about the best pedigree of a Roman imperial dynasty until the fifth or later centuries, and up to that time there is no instance of an imperial succession going into a third generation. The empire was the prize of the most ambitious and powerful general, who was succeeded by his son until the latter was murdered. It is true that in the second century AD the Antonines preserved the Roman state and gave to Roman humanity what Edward Gibbon regarded as a golden age. The Antonines, however, used very freely the method of adoption which secured the wellbeing of the empire, but is obviously unconnected with genealogy.

Nor can we expect the pedigrees of the nobles in ancient Rome to supply us with very much information. Under the Republic there were two orders—patricians and plebeians—but these gradually lost their exclusive distinction as the political offices in Rome provided the plebeians with a growing supply of wax images for their atria, or halls. The older patrician families had stories of ancient descent like that of the Caesars from Venus. The evidential value of these may be gauged from the fact that Brutus, one of the conspirators who murdered Julius Caesar, was popularly supposed to be descended from the Brutus who 500 years earlier had driven the Tarquins from Rome; an ascription based on identity of name as no evidence other than that of a vague tradition has come down to us. Another factor militating against the preservation of the nobles' pedigrees was the wastage among the nobility caused by war, tyranny and consequent executions. In several periods of the empire, a new nobility came into existence, so that length of pedigree was never a distinguishing feature.

The practical Romans did, however, devise a system of surnames which was very useful and may have served as a model for Europeans in later times. As a general rule, a Roman had three names. The first was the *praenomen*, which corresponded to our Christian or forename; this was followed by the clan or race name, and last of all came the *cognomen*, or surname. As illustrations we have Caius Julius Caesar, or Marcus Tullius Cicero; in these cases Caius is the *praenomen*, Julius is the name of the *gens* or clan, and Caesar the *cognomen*, or surname, and so on with Cicero's names. Such a precise Roman system was a great advance on the Greek practice of using the expression, 'son of' with only a few rare clan names similar to our surnames. The Romans had the custom of bestowing upon a victorious general a title which was added to his surname and then often became the surname of his descendants. Scipio Africanus gained the latter name or title from his victory over Hannibal at Zama in 202 BC. Later he was given the title of Asiaticus, because he had led the Romans to victory in their first Asian campaign. His descendants were known by these titles, which had become part of their surnames. Similarly, the last name of Quintus Fabius Maximus Cunctator (delayer) derived from the delaying tactics by which he had frustrated Hannibal. Plutarch mentions cases in which the title of Maximus (the greatest) had been bestowed in peace as well as in war, and that this title, like that of Africanus, was carried on as a surname in the families of descendants. An interesting modern parallel is the British habit of commemorating the victories of a great commander by adding the name of one of his most famous battles to his title: thus Viscount Montgomery of Alamein, Earl Mountbatten of Burma, titles which will descend in the families of these peers.

Genealogies in the sense in which they were built up during the middle ages did not, of course, exist in the Roman Empire, and this fact, coupled with the breakdown of Roman administration and its replacement by barbarian kingdoms, renders claims to descent from persons of the old classical world out of the question except in one or two royal families. If one may use a lighter touch, the pedigree of some sixty or seventy generations devised by the famous romancer, Sir Rider Haggard, in his novel, *She*, is a good example of a fictitious pedigree. The family of Vincent or Vindex is traced from Greek, Roman and medieval English sources, with the wise precaution that none of the family is accorded any eminence. Pedigree fakers always claim too much. Content with a long pedigree of nobodies, a genealogist might escape censure; except for the fact that a pedigree of small people stretching back a thousand years is impossible, since records of the small fry were not kept, at least not in a connected form. To give one example, in the time of Charlemagne, on an estate near Paris called Villaris, belonging to the abbey of St Germain, there was a man named Bodo, who owned a little farm with a few vines. His wife's name was Ermentrude and his children were Wido, Gerbert and Hildegarde. He owed days of labour to the monastery, like all other serfs. History has paused sufficiently to lift the veil of obscurity which hangs over the lives of such ordinary folk, but we cannot find any pedigrees for their descendants. We catch a glimpse of them and they are gone. (Eileen Power, *Medieval People*, 1937). As Charles Kingsley says of his unforgettable character, Martin Lightfoot, in *Hereward the Wake*, 'But when Martin Lightfoot died, no one can say, for none kept trace of such footpad churls in those days.' The story of genealogy, as of history generally, in these last 400 years has been one of ever widening interest until in this twentieth century anyone, however poor or lowly, is better documented than a king 1,000 years ago.

In the committal to writing of the oral pedigrees and their extension by the scribes, only the greatest persons are thus provided with family histories. Plenty of names of obscure individuals are mentioned in old chronicles, because they are essential to the narrative, but only the eminent have anything like a genealogy. Fortunately, a first-class specimen is available to show how a royal pedigree was constructed in the 9th-10th centuries. Here is the genealogy of the kings of Wessex, who became kings of England, and thus the forbears of Queen Elizabeth II. It comes from the *Anglo-Saxon Chronicle* (Everyman's Library, 1953, p 66).

'(The year) 855. In this year the heathen for the first time wintered in Sheppey. And the same year King Ethelwulf granted the tenth part of his land over all his kingdom by charter for the glory of God and his own eternal salvation. And the same year he proceeded to Rome in great state, and remained there twelve months, and then made his way towards home. And Charles, King of the Franks, gave him his daughter as Queen, after that he came to his people, and they were glad thereof. And two years after he came from the Franks, he died, and his body lies at Winchester, and he reigned eighteen years and a half. And that Ethelwulf was the son of Egbert, the son of Ealhmund, the son of Eafa, the son of Eoppa, the son of Ingeld; Ingeld was the brother of Ine, King of Wessex, who afterwards went to St Peter's (Rome) and there gave up his life afterwards; and they were the sons of Cenred and Cenred was the son of Ceolwald, the son of Cutha, the son of Cuthwine, the son of Cealwin, the son of Cynric, the son of Cerdic, the son of Elesa, the son of Esla, the son of Gewis, the son of Wig, the son of Freawine, the son of Frithugar, the son of Brand, the son of Baeldaeg, the son of Woden, the son of Frithuwald, the son of Freawine, Frealaf (this part of the pedigree is not clear. It seems that an additional name slipped into the ancient manuscript—L.G.P.), the son of Frithuwulf, the son of Finn, the son of Godwulf, the son of Geat, the son of Taetwa, the son of Beaw, the son of Sceldwea, the son of Heremod, the son of Itermon, the son of Hrathea, who was born in the Ark (in another version the name of this unique personage is given as Sceaf—L.G.P.): Noah, Lamech, Methu-salen, Enoch, Jared, Mahalaleel, Cainan, Enos, Seth, Adam, the first man, and our father who is Christ. Amen.'

There are in this pedigree several very illuminating features. First, it has forty-six generations to cover 4,859 years (Usher's chronology). The last ten generations cover 2,349 years. This gives thirty-six generations to span 2,210 years, which leaves a gap of 800 years (even allowing forty years to a generation), but perhaps Hrathra and some of his immediate descendants were long lived as befitted the Noachian strain. One genera-tion is possibly omitted, unless Hrathra or Sceaf is regarded as Noah's own son, instead of being the offspring of one of Noah's sons. Secondly, the pedigree is composed of three elements. The first part is the descent from Cerdic, an historical person, the first king of Wessex. There is no reason to doubt at least some of the generations from Cerdic to Hrathra, and, indeed, all of them may be accurate for what reason would anyone have for inventing them? The third part of the pedigree comes, of course, from Genesis.

The other illuminating feature of this pedigree is to be found in the central portion in which the name of Woden appears, showing in common with many other pedigrees of kings in the dark ages, a semi-divine descent. Because descent from the gods is to be dismissed as fabulous there is a real danger that the generations represented by these names may be discarded as equally improbable. The key to the pedigree lies in a realization of what the ancients believed about their gods. It is not hard to imagine some pagan king coming round to accept the White Christ, yet still retaining belief in the old gods, not as objects of worship, but as his ancestors. The early missionaries to these pagan lands were usually very sensible, almost broadminded men. They insisted on the destruction of the idols, but they did not ridicule their converts' genealogies. Then came the next, more settled Christian generation. Monasteries are founded, learned men arise; the native Christians absorb all that their teachers can impart and then go on to produce works of their own.

So it was with the generations which followed St Patrick in Ireland, which became known as the island of saints and scholars. The monks begin the national history with their chronicles. They write down the pedigrees of their great men, and they do not balk at the mythical divinity of some of the ancestors. 'Why, in thirty or forty years, were there no books, any great man would grow mythic, the contemporaries who had seen him, being once all dead. And in three hundred years, and in three thousand years! . . . Enough for us to discern, far in the uttermost distance, some gleam as of a small real light shining in the centre of that enormous camera obscura image.' (*Heroes and Hero-Worship*, Thomas Carlyle, The Hero as Divinity, writing of Odin or Woden).

Similarly, connection of heroic ancestors with the Biblical genealogies is the most natural thing once one has assumed that the Bible is literally and entirely true. The human race has descended from Adam and Eve, and here is an old genealogy stretching back beyond recorded history, so obviously it must be joined on to the patriarchal lines given in Genesis. Hence the suture effected by the Irish monks between the Noachian line of descent and the Milesian pedigrees of the Irish kings. In old Ireland the divine may not have formed an element in the finished genealogies; the Irish heroes and monarchs were content to be heroic. In countries where the Norse or Germanic mythology prevailed the ancestors are gods, Woden in the old English royal lines, and Odin, the same god but known by this form of the name in the north. Thus the writers of the *Anglo-Saxon Chronicle*, and Bede in his *Ecclesiastical History*.

So, too, later, in Norway, Denmark and Iceland. We have the sagas of the Norse kings by Snorre Sturlason, who was born in Iceland in 1179. He begins his work, known as *Heimskringla* (Everyman's Library, 1951), with the semi-mythical Ynglinga Saga. This is the story of the Yngling family from Odin to Halfdan the Black. It begins with Odin, who is regarded as a very great man, the inventor of various arts, a wise leader who brings his people from Asia into northern Europe. He has twelve companions, or assistants, called Diar or Drotner. Odin's death is recorded: he tells his friends that he is going to Godheim, 'and would give a welcome there to all his friends, and all brave warriors should be dedicated to him; and the Swedes believed that he was gone to the ancient Asgaard, and would live there eternally. Then began the belief in Odin, and the calling upon him. The Swedes believed that he often showed himself to them before any great battle.' (*op cit*, pp 13-14). Here then, in the most matter-of-fact manner, is Odin's death and the burning of his body; the deaths also of the other gods, as the Diar are called. Clearly, then, Odin and his fellows were accepted as having been real people of flesh and blood, who in some way lived on as superior spiritual beings after their bodily death. Remembering that Sturlason was a Christian, we can see how easily the monks accepted the old gods simply as generations in the pedigrees, as it were baptizing them posthumously. Not only were the tribal genealogies linked to those in the Old Testament; they were modelled on them. In the pedigree of the old English kings previously quoted, two incidents are mentioned which break the monotony of the string of bare names. It is a feature reminiscent of the genealogies in St Matthew's first chapter where women are mentioned only four times, one of them anonymously, 'David the king begat Solomon of her that had been the wife of Urias.'; and only two incidents are glanced at, 'the time they were carried away to Babylon', and 'after they were brought to Babylon.'

A large amount of genealogical material is found in early written records like the *Heimskringla*, but it is always given in general terms without exact details such as dates. The latter can come only with a more settled and more complex way of life, with more of what is termed civilized living. Much of the *Heimskringla* is taken up with the exploits of Harold Haarfager, Harald the Fair Haired, who in one respect might have been accepted by youth today. He had sworn not to cut his hair until he reigned as sole king of all Norway. In the plain fashion of the times, the matter is thus recounted in Sturlason's chapter 23. 'King Harald has his hair clipped—After King Harald had subdued the whole land, he was one day at a feast in Möre given by Earl Rognvald. Then King Harald went into a bath and had his hair dressed. Earl Rognvald now cut his hair, which had been uncut and uncombed for ten years; and therefore the king had been called Harald Luva (ie, The Lousy!). But then Earl Rognvald gave him the distinguishing name—Harald Haarfager—and all who saw him agreed that there was the greatest truth in that surname, for he had the most beautiful and abundant head of hair.'

This Earl Rognvald (or Reginald as it has sometimes been rendered) was the father by a woman called Hild, a daughter of Rolf Nefja, of the great Viking warrior, Rolf Ganger. He was so called because he was too big for a horse to carry him and had to walk wherever he went. He did not escape King Harald's wrath although his father was the King's dearest friend. Rolf was banished and, after some plundering expeditions, settled in Normandy or Northmandy, which he obtained by force from the French king. He was the ancestor of William the Conqueror, he being the first Duke of Normandy, and William the seventh.

The Norman duke's pedigree went back into the ninth century but there are few dates in it and, not knowing when he was born, we are not sure how old William the Conqueror was when he died. Nor can we be sure if Gundreda, who married Earl Warenne, Earl of Surrey, after the Conquest, before 1078, was the Conqueror's daughter, expert opinion being inclined in the opposite direction. With such gaps in our knowledge we can see how imperfect is the information about the centuries from 500-1100, when pedigrees were being written down. There are a few cases in which the history of a distinguished family can be traced into the eleventh century in the male line and, as we have been considering Viking stories, it is pleasant to be able to refer to one of their pedigrees which is still alive. The Clouston family of Clouston and Smoogro in the Orkneys can show a male line descent from approximately 1050. This is how the account begins in *Burke's Landed Gentry*. 'Havard Gunnason, Chief, Counsellor to Haakon, Earl of Orkney, *circa* 1090, married Bergliot, who had the odal lands of Clouston for dowry. She was the daughter of Ragnhild, the 4th daughter of Paul Thorfinnson, Jarl of Orkney, by his wife, daughter of Haakon Ivarson, Jarl of the Uplands in Norway, 1054-64, by his wife, Ragnhild, only daughter of Magnus I, "the Good", King of Norway, 1036-47.' In this involved paragraph seven generations are given. The family has remained for 900 years in possession of its lands and the records of this holding have naturally assisted in the preparation of the pedigree. It is to be noted that the history is ultimately that of a royal line. Without a kingly connection and the consistent ownership of land, a pedigree cannot be traced before 1100.

Apart from such male-line descents, there are numerous persons who can show a female-line descent from Charlemagne, coming very often through Edward III of England. Charlemagne's male-line descent is from St Arnulf, Bishop of Metz, who died about 635. There are five generations between Arnulf and Charlemagne, whose father was Pepin the Short, last Mayor of the Palace to the Merovingian kings and himself King of the Franks in 751. Pepin's father was Charles Martel, famous as the man who stopped the Moslems from overrunning Europe when he defeated them at Tours in 732. Martel himself was the illegitimate son of Pepin II of Heristal (Mayor of the Palace 680-714) who was the grandson of St Arnulf. It is said that the pedigree can be taken back even further into the fifth century. It is not so surprising that the great emperor for whom the Holy Roman Empire was founded should have come of distinguished forbears.

From 1100 onwards we are in the feudal period, when this system has replaced completely the broken-down Roman civilization. Life becomes more regular and the evidences of genealogy more frequent. From this period many more male-line descents are found, though always connected with lands, until in the thirteenth century we actually encounter pedigrees of villeins, a term applied to those who lived at a vill or villa, a country estate from which they could not go without permission of the feudal lord. In short, they were serfs, tied to the land, but not slaves since they were not the property of another person. The basis of genealogy is widening and we are moving towards the condition of the sixteenth century when there is the possibility of providing everyone with a pedigree.

Medieval Genealogies: from AD 1100-1500

THIS is the period of the later middle ages or the middle ages proper. The earlier period from 500 to 1100 is often known as the dark ages, which means that in a comparatively small area of the world, western Europe, there was a recession in civilization after the collapse of the western Roman Empire. The eastern or Byzantine Empire certainly did not undergo a dark age. It was a splendidly civilized state at a much higher level than the barbarian kingdoms which had arisen on the ruins of its western counterpart. The Moslem world also was far from darkness, in fact the time when western Europe was struggling forward was one of exceptional brilliance for the Arabs and the rest of the Moslem civilization.

The greatest achievements in western Europe during these 600 years were those of the Church, which by the year 1000 had succeeded in converting most of the European peoples to Christianity. As always happens, whether in medieval Europe or in modern Africa, some learning came with religious instruction. Very soon after the conversion of the people in Ireland, England and Scotland, schools and writing begin. Literature comes, as with the committal to writing in England of poems like 'Beowulf', which had been handed down orally. Historical writing in England commences with Bede's *Ecclesiastical History of the English People* which though written in Latin provided the example for later works, annals like the famous *Anglo-Saxon Chronicle* of the ninth century, in the vernacular.

The light of Irish civilization shone brightly and steadily for several centuries after the conversion of the country by St Patrick in the fifth century. Most people have heard of the Book of Kells, now in Trinity College, Dublin; which is a copy in Latin of the Four Gospels written on vellum, most probably in the seventh century. It has been described, and with good reason, as a work with which no other book in the world can compare for beauty of execution. Many other early works written in the Irish language still exist: the 'Book of the Dun Cow' written before 1106 and containing material from 592; the 'Book of Leinster', written about 1160; and the famous 'Annals of the Four Masters', finished in 1636 but based on and containing ancient records. Many persons from England and other countries came to study in Ireland; many Irish missionaries went to Europe to preach the Gospel and in many towns in France, Germany and Italy, the patron saint is an Irishman. The great Emperor Charlemagne, who died in 814, gathered around him many scholars from different lands, such as Alcuin from England, and John Scot Erigena from Ireland—John the Scot—a considerable philosopher and a Greek scholar at a time when knowledge of that language was a rarity in western Europe.

This fair and flourishing state of learning was destined to be obliterated by those pests of the ninth to eleventh centuries, the Vikings or creek dwellers (from vik—a fiord or inlet), commonly called the Danes or Norsemen. They came in fact from Norway and Denmark, whereas the Swedish Vikings found their way mostly to Russia, where the ancient royal dynasty was founded by Rurik. It is thought that the barrenness of their native soils impelled the overflow of population, so that the Vikings sought other lands for settlement. In due course the Danes did colonize other countries but their raids towards the end of the eighth century were at first purely destructive. They colonized Iceland, which they found uninhabited; they wrecked the Irish civilization and succeeded in holding ports like Dublin and Waterford. They were defeated in a great battle at Clontarf in 1014 by Brian Boru, at that time High King of Ireland, and ancestor of the O'Briens, which prevented them from over-running the whole of Ireland. In France they gained control of one of the fairest provinces which was called after them, Northmansland or Normandy. In Scotland, the Vikings made incursions, though the poverty of the country did not attract them; the latest invasion was that which was decisively defeated at Largs in 1263 by the Scots king, Alexander III. Even after that they retained their hold on the Orkneys and Shetland until the fifteenth century, when a peaceful transference to Scottish control was made. Of pedigrees, apart from the Clouston example already mentioned, little trace has been left; and this applies also to Ireland, which is the more remarkable in that every other wave of invaders has left its mark on the genealogy of that country.

In England the Danish invasions caused widespread disruption in the sphere of learning and of civilization. Like the Irish, the English after their own conversion applied themselves to the conversion of their continental kinsfolk. St Boniface became the Apostle of Germany; as far as Finland the English missionaries preached the Faith. Norway and Denmark enriched themselves with English spoils, many of which remain in the art collections of those countries. Later, in the early tenth century, the debt owed to England was more honourable, for those who evangelized Norway and Denmark were either Englishmen or men like St Olaf, the patron saint of Norway, who had been converted in England. The Danes won control of the north-east of England which, like Ireland, was divided into a number of kingdoms. Each of the four Irish provinces had its own king, one of whom, often the O'Neill, would assert overlordship above the rest. In theory, he was obeyed by the other rulers but in practice each fought for his own hand. In England, the kingdoms of the Heptarchy—Kent, Essex, Wessex, Mercia (the midlands of England), Sussex, Northumbria and Deira—were independent one of another. The strongest of them for the time being had a supremacy which enabled its ruler to be called the Bretwalda, or Ruler of the Britons.

When St Augustine came to Canterbury in 597 the king of Kent was the Bretwalda. Afterwards supremacy passed to Northumbria and to Mercia. The greatest king of Mercia was Offa (757-796), a contemporary of Charlemagne, with whom he had diplomatic relations. Thereafter Mercia went into decline, and by 825 the Bretwalda was King Egbert of Wessex, who has been mentioned as the ancestor of Queen Elizabeth II. About the same time the Vikings began to invade England, and it was the severe defeat that Egbert inflicted upon them which, for a short time, checked their ravages. They succeeded later in conquering much of England, and in the time of Egbert's sons and grandsons they nearly conquered the whole country. Alfred the Great emerged from hiding in the marshes of Athelney, in Somerset, to beat the Danes and to recover the kingdom of Wessex, which came to mean the area of southern England from Devon to Kent, ie, south of the Thames. Under his son, and the succeeding kings, much of the Midlands were recovered, London, became the *de facto* capital of England as opposed to Winchester, and the whole of England came under the one crown. The House of Wessex thus became the Royal House of England.

Such was the position by the year 1000, a century after Alfred's death. Then fresh Danish onslaughts disrupted the country and drove the English monarchy into exile in Normandy, where the wife of the English king, Ethelred II (Ethelred the Unready, or Evil Counselled), was sister of the reigning duke. In consequence of these happenings four

Danish kings—Sweyn, Canute, Hardicanute, and Harold Harefoot—ruled as Kings of England. Canute, a wise and Christian ruler, who has been called the Great, was also King of Norway and of Denmark. Meanwhile, in Normandy, the two sons of Ethelred, Alfred and Edward, grew up with a Norman education. They were recalled to England after Canute's two sons had ended their lives in sottishness and violence; the elder, Alfred, was murdered, the younger, Edward, became King of England in 1042. He is known to us as St Edward the Confessor, so great was his reputation for sanctity, and so revered was he by both English and Normans that his body still remains in his ancient shrine in Westminster Abbey, the only English saint to survive the ferocious zeal of Henry VIII and the Protestant reformers.

Thus, both in Ireland and England, the Danish invasions wrought havoc, though in England they actually had the effect of consolidating the country into one realm. An interesting instance of this process occurs in the pedigree of the Scottish family of Swinton, who are known to Scots as 'of that ilk', meaning that the surname is the same as the name of the ancestral property and is derived from it. For more than 850 years the Swintons of Swinton have held the family estate of that name in Berwickshire. They were descended from the Edulfings, a royal house which had ruled the area known as Bernicia, the region between the rivers Tyne and Forth. Their seat then was Bamburgh Castle on the Northumberland coast, five miles off the main road from Scotland to England, and now a place of attraction to tourists. The Danes cut across this district and left it isolated from the rest of Christian England. The ruler in 886 was Edulf, who submitted to King Alfred the Great and ruled henceforth in Bernicia as a sub-king. With the Norman Conquest the heads of the family withdrew into Scotland where they became powerful landowners, some of them as the Earls of Dunbar, others like the Swintons among the lesser nobility. A similar acceptance of Alfred's overlordship occurred in Mercia where the sub-king accepted the Old English style of nobility—Alderman—on his marriage with Alfred's daughter, Ethelfled, the Lady of the Mercians.

Thus England had become a kingdom well before the Norman Conquest. After 1066, it remained for the Normans to finish off the outlines of the realm by taking in Cornwall and Cumberland, and by preparing the way for the conquest of Wales. The Normans cemented the kingdom and were careful to maintain all claims and rights of their predecessors. The English kings had possessed a vague overlordship vis-a-vis the Welsh princes and the kings of Scots, but William the Conqueror made this claim much more precise by exacting homage from King Malcolm of

D

Scotland and from the Welsh princes. The last Viking invasion was in 1066, when Harold Hardrada, King of Norway, came to claim the English throne but found instead a grave in English earth. Never again did the Vikings invade the country. Their fleet threatened a descent in William the Conqueror's time, but he bought them off. Later, Norwegian kings claimed sovereignty over all the western British islands including Man, whose bishopric is still called Sodor—Norse for south—and Man, to remind us of the Norse connection.

Consideration of the Norman Conquest should finally destroy two unfortunate myths which still exist in the minds of many people. One is the idea that the Normans made England. They certainly organised and stabilized it, but it remained England, not Norman land. Nothing is more indicative of a nation's culture than the possession of a literature, and the history of English literature begins in 700, not 1100. By the time of the Norman Conquest, the English already possessed an extensive literature of poetry, history, fiction, sermons, translations and philosophy. By contrast, the Normans had nothing written but were more proficient in the arts of war.

The second myth is that the English people are a very mixed or mongrel race. This idea is frequently put forward in some verses of Daniel Defoe—who should have known better—about the true-bred Englishman. The ingredients which he quotes as making up the Englishman of the seventeenth century—Briton, Roman, Saxon, Dane and Norman—do not add up to anything like the multi-racial mix-up which characterises modern England. It is very doubtful, as already mentioned, if there is a Romano-British strain in the English people, and Saxon, Dane and Norman were all cousins, the first having come from Denmark and western Germany, the second and third from Norway and Denmark. Since Defoe's time only one large influx has been assimilated, that of the Huguenots. The Jewish community has remained, as in most countries, distinct, though there have been marriages into the British peerage. In the period since the start of Hitler's persecutions in the late 1930s, many Jews of foreign extraction have come to England; as have also numerous Poles, Czechs, Hungarians, Pakistanis, Sikhs, West Indians and Kenyan Indians.

Returning to the eleventh century, there was then made in England the first survey or census in any European nation. Known as the Domesday Book, because no one was allowed to question its authority, its record like that of the Last Judgment being irreversible, this was a survey of all the land of England, undertaken by commissioners sent out by William the Conqueror in 1085. The results were set forth in two massive volumes, in Latin, which are still preserved in the Public Record Office at Chancery Lane in London. Northumberland, Durham and London are not described in the survey; most of Lancashire, the south of Westmorland and part of Cumberland, are reckoned in with the West Riding of Yorkshire. Otherwise all England is covered. Though much genealogical information is derived from Domesday, this was not, of course, the Conqueror's object and every place named in Domesday is accompanied by the following information; the name of the person who held it on the day King Edward the Confessor died, who held it in 1086, and what was the nature of the land, its value and the number and condition of persons who lived on it.

From a study of the Domesday survey it has been possible to deduce, as a rough estimate, that the number of people living in England in 1086 was a million to a million and a half. The number of knights has been put at 5,500; and that of great tenants directly holding their lands from the Crown at less than 200. The theory of feudalism was that the King owned the land and let it out to tenants-in-chief who, in their turn, let out parts of their land to under-tenants, in subinfeudation as it was termed. The unit of land was referred to as a knight's fee and consisted of two carucates of land, about 100 acres, though it is thought that in some cases a fee might amount to much more. The word 'carucate' derives from the Low Latin *carucca*, a plough, and was originally as much land as a team of oxen could plough in one season. The term 'fee' meant simply the amount of land sufficient to maintain an armed horseman with a small following of retainers, and derived from the Latin *feodum* or *feudum*, rendered into Old French as 'fief', and into English as 'fee'. It meant an estate in land held of a superior by a vassal, and was of the essence of the feudal system. The owner or holder of a fee did not always go to war himself but he was responsible for supplying the necessary armed men for the feudal army. Many references may also be found to the possession of more than one's knight's fee, or to half a fee. The same feudal system of landowning prevailed throughout western Europe, adapted to the needs of war as well as for the supply of food. The great men who possessed many manors, or lordships, were wont to journey from place to place, staying long enough to exhaust the resources of a manor and then moving on to another.

The conception of feudalism is that of a society in which classes exist subordinate to others and in which land tenure is the most important factor. Feudalism comes, then, from the Latin *feudum* or *feodum* and also from the Frankish *fehu-od*, much the same as the German *vieh*, cattle. In Old English it was rendered as *feoh*, cattle or property, and especially property in land. In England after the Norman Conquest, the system came to a considerable development. It had existed in pre-Conquest England but in a much looser form than in France. There had been in Saxon England many freeholders without any lord to whom they owed homage; after William's conquest everyone had his lord, whose man he was. Soon, in English usage, the fee came to mean a free inheritable tenement, and the term used was *tenementum per servitium militare*, a tenement or property held on condition of knight's service, the knight's fee mentioned above. In present-day English law a freehold estate is still said to be in fee simple.

The whole system came from the barbaric kingdoms which replaced the western Roman empire. By an act of *commendatio*, or commendation, a man placed himself under the protection of a lord, to whom he owed obedience and from whom in turn he received assistance and protection. The lord then rendered to the vassal as he was termed (from a Low Latin word *vassus*, from the Celtic *gwas*, or boy) the aid known as *beneficium*, or land bestowed in consideration of the homage. The last term came from the Latin *homo*, a man, because the vassal in the ceremony of homage put his hands between those of his lord and said, 'I am your man' or words to that effect. This was the *hominium*, or act of homage, followed by an oath of fealty (faith). The relationship between the lord —often called the suzerain—and the vassal was binding. If the vassal broke his part of the bargain he could be dispossessed of his fief. On the other hand, the overlord could not push his powers beyond certain well-defined limits. In England, where the vassals of the Crown were bound to serve for forty days on military service, many quarrels between king and barons were due to the barons' refusal to extend their military obligations. As a result, the English kings came to accept financial aid in lieu of knight service, and with the money thus obtained paid for the services of professional soldiers. This explains the numerous victories gained by small English armies in the fourteenth and fifteenth centuries, particularly against the French. The latter relied upon the old feudal levée en masse, but when they came up against a well-trained professional army as at Crecy, Poitiers, Agincourt and many other battles, their much greater numbers were of little avail.

There were lengthy disputes between Church and monarchs in the eleventh and twelfth centuries as to the investiture of the bishops. These were not only spiritual persons but also temporal lords, and as such had to do homage for the temporalities of their sees, ie, the lands which they held from the Crown. The ecclesiastics were not required to give personal military service but, as holders of fiefs, they had to find soldiers to discharge the duty in their place. (See Note 5).

The Pipe Rolls

After the Domesday Book there is a gap in English records of some two generations until the time of the *Pipe Rolls* or *Great Rolls of the Exchequer*, so called because the parchment or vellum documents were rolled round a rod or pipe. The records were written on a roll or rotulet: 'The roll of each year consists of a set of rotulets between 13½ and 14 in wide and between 3 and 4 ft 8 in long. Each rotulet was made up of two skins or membranes sewn together to form a single length.' (*Chambers' Encyclopedia, sub* Pipe Rolls). A series of these Pipe Rolls extends from the reign of Henry II (1154-89) to that of Queen Victoria, but earlier specimens exist from the end of Henry I's reign (1100-35). In the pedigree of a family now extinct in the male line, the Okeovers of Okeover in Staffordshire, the line of descent was traced from Ormus Helsweyn or Halesgen, otherwise called Orme de Okeover, who in 1113 obtained from the abbot of Burton-on-Trent, a holding of land (Okeover). This Orme may have been the son of Eddulph, who was mentioned in the Domesday as tenant of Okeover, though the gap in records from 1086 to 1113 makes this impossible to prove. And if the affiliation to the Domesday tenant cannot be proved in this type of case, where a family remained in its own property from 1113 to 1952, what chances are there of joining up the various claimants to Norman or Domesday descent whose proven ancestry starts in the 1600s or 1700s? In nearly all the test cases I have encountered, claims to entries in the Domesday Book could be forgotten, and if anyone thinks it a little hard that his ancestors were not given a name and place in the survey, he can take refuge in the thought (genealogically almost irrefutable!) that his forbears were there anonymously.

William spared no one in the census. The old monk who describes the Bastard's doings almost allows us to see his lip curl with scorn when he relates how William ordered the details of the survey. It was shameful to say what he did, records the monk, who was an Englishman, but he (William) thought it no shame to do. Every wood, meadow and cornfield, together with the domestic animals was recorded, as was every labourer or serf. Sir Henry Ellis laboriously worked out that 283,342 people are mentioned in Domesday, though only a small minority by name; the great bulk of the anonymous humans might as well have been cattle or swine. Still, one can always console oneself with having descended from the best people, for none but the fittest could have survived the wars, famines, plagues and other horrors which make the middle ages sometimes so reminiscent of our own century.

The records in the Pipe Rolls were much taken up with the problem of subinfeudation, by means of which the magnates could have avoided paying their dues to the King. When a great feudal lord had been assessed for a certain amount in the Pipe Roll, and had afterwards created a larger number of knights' fees than had formerly existed on his estate, on the next occasion of assessment the Crown would require a return of the number of fees on his property and the amount due would be reassessed. The value of these financial records was summed up by the Rev Joseph Hunter in 1844 (*The Great Rolls of the Pipe for 1155-1158*): 'The Pipe Rolls which have now been printed all belong to the period before the reign of King Henry the Third. For much of that period they are almost the only records we possess, and thus contain innumerable notices of persons, places, and transactions of which there is no other memorial whatever. The earlier of them place us amidst the persons who lived before the time of legal memory. If we desire to know what names were great in England in the reign of Henry the Second, we must peruse with attention the Pipe Rolls of that reign.'

(The limit of legal memory mentioned above is 1189, the year of Richard I's accession, and the date before which English law takes no cognisance of events.)

The series of the Pipe Rolls runs from 1130—with a break until 1155—to 1833. Receipts were given in the form of tallies and a few relics of these have survived the fire which destroyed the old Palace of Westminster—the Parliament House—now superseded by the present structure.

In 1166 a Great Survey of England was undertaken in order to bring the feudal returns up to date. This survey is known as *Liber Niger Scaccarii, The Black Book of the Exchequer* and the following is a good example of its use as a guide to family history and to the fate of old English families after the Norman Conquest. In the Domesday (the Warwickshire portion translated by J. H. Round in the *Victoria County History of Warwick*, 1904), Turchill of Warwick, an Englishman, is shown possessed of considerable properties. In the Black Book, his grandsons, Henry and Hugo de Arden, are sub-tenants of the Earl of Warwick, the family no longer being independent landowners. We also see how, in the twelfth century, families of English origin had adopted French Christian names, a practice which makes it impossible to determine the racial origin of most of the old families. Only in a few cases is there an English Christian name at the foot of a long family tree; where this is not so, we simply cannot tell whether a family like the Traffords or Tichbornes is French or English.

Demonstrably the starting point for the majority of folk of English descent must be in the twelfth century, about 1150. If this applies to English pedigrees, it applies also, *mutatis mutandis*, to other European countries. The general rule is that, with the exception of royal pedigrees with which we have already dealt, the European nobility cannot be traced earlier than the twelfth century. The Crusades had then begun, signalizing the recovery of Europe from the pagan onslaughts of the earlier centuries. The feudal system had been fully established and a much more peaceful and organised existence prevailed. The Vikings had become Christians and some of them, the Normans, were the Church's most devoted sons. The Moslems were being rolled back in Spain and Sicily, and the success of the First Crusade (1095-99), bolstered up the Eastern Byzantine Empire and enlarged the boundaries of Latin Christendom by taking in, for nearly a century, Syria and Palestine. A healthy life had arisen in western Christendom which, in the twelfth and thirteenth centuries saw a great blossoming of human creativeness. The Gothic cathedrals; the origination and development of trade guilds, of civil liberty and of Parliament; the growth of law; the rise of European literature, in particular, Dante's epic portrayal of the human tragicomedy; and finally, the majestic synthesis of divine revelation and human knowledge in the works of St Thomas Aquinas—all these features of the period from approximately 1150-1270 give it fair claim to be the greatest for all-round achievement in human history.

It is with this period that our concern now is. The English records may not unreasonably be described as fairly akin to those in other western lands, since the same system of land-holding—the basis of pedigree record—also existed there.

Monastic Records

Turning from Domesday and the Pipe Rolls, we come to Monastic Records. At the Reformation in England (and this applies to other countries which became Protestant), one of the most powerful motives assisting the Protestant reformers was the desire on the part of many laymen to obtain the lands of the monasteries. When these monasteries were dissolved—in 1535-40 in England—no care was taken to preserve their libraries or art treasures. Splendid collections of manuscripts and other works were destroyed, and in many instances documents which would now be considered priceless were dispersed as waste, the parchments being used by cooks and for other domestic needs. In this way the epic poem of Beowulf was nearly lost, surviving only through a single manuscript.

There was, however, one type of document found in the monasteries which the spoilers were most careful to preserve and this related to the chartularies of the monasteries. These chartularies (from *chartularium* = register), were, as their name implies, parchment or vellum books which contained copies of all the charters relating to the lands and properties of the religious houses. As might be expected, these valuable records are now scattered throughout libraries in England, many in public, but some in private, collections. In the old work by Richard Sims of the British Museum (produced in 1888, originally in 1878) entitled *A Manual for the Genealogist, Topographer, Antiquary and Legal Professor*, there is a list of the English chartularies, arranged alphabetically under the monasteries and running to twelve closely-printed pages. There are also three pages showing the whereabouts of Welsh, Irish and Scottish chartularies, as well as a list of family chartularies. The Okeover family, previously mentioned, had its own chartulary which is now in the Bodleian Library at Oxford, and there was a monastic house at Burton, the Lazar (ie, sick or leper foundation), Hospital, whose chartulary is in the British Museum, in the Cottonian Mss—a collection formed by a great antiquary, Sir Robert Cotton, in the reign of James I, 1603-25. An American inquirer need not conclude that a great English family extinct in England did not leave descendants in the American colonies, and one who is fortunate enough to belong to an English county family—fortunate because the records of such families go back to the twelfth century—should also consult the book by G. R. Davis, *Medieval Cartularies of Great Britain, A Short Catalogue*, 1958. In this will be found the names of works which list chartularies, including Sir William Dugdale's *Monasticom* and the works of R. Sims.

Another monastic record which has gained a notoriety far beyond any other, and for obvious reasons, is the Battle Abbey Roll, which was supposed to contain the names of William the Conqueror's companions at Hastings. No original of this exists but copies—all discrepant—are to be found. As far back as the days of William Camden (1551-1623) the view of trained investigators was that no reliance could be placed on the Roll. The monks of Battle Abbey added to the Roll the names of benefactors of the abbey, as though conferring a posthumous Norman ancestry, and certainly no modern genealogist would give any credit to a reference in the Battle Abbey Roll.

A muniment room or muniment chest (from the Latin *munire*, to fortify, ie, to strengthen or make good a claim) is possessed by all old landed families, and its contents may go back for centuries, as with that ancient Norman family, the Curzons, whose head is Viscount Scarsdale. This family has owned the estate of Kedleston in Derbyshire for 850 years and, not surprisingly, has a very large collection of ancient documents relating mostly to land transactions, leases to tenants, conveyances etc. The surname is derived from Courson in Normandy, whence an ancestor came to England, and the family may have offshoots in America spelling their name as Curson.

Sometimes the monks, if specially pleased with a benefactor, placed his portrait in a document, and the records of St Alban's Abbey, Hertfordshire, now in the British Museum, contain a drawing of Sir Nigel Loring, who was a pious benefactor of the abbey. He was the name original of the hero of Conan Doyle's romances, *Sir Nigel* and *The White Company* and was also, in truth, one of the founder knights of the Order of the Garter.

The use of charters was not confined to the monks, and large numbers survive from the period before the Norman Conquest. There are six large volumes of the *Codex Diplomaticus aevi Saxonici*, prepared by J. M. Kemble, an immense compilation embracing the charters—usually granting land, or privileges and rights—of the old English kings. Volume I contains the charters of the kings of the Heptarchy from Ethelbert of Kent (604) down to Egbert of Wessex (838). Charters of ecclesiastics and noblemen are also included. Most are in Latin but some are in Old English. Volume II embraces the period from 839 to 996, and deals mainly with the House of Wessex. Volume III covers the period from 966 to 1016, the time of Ethelred the Unready and the Danish wars. Many wills, leases and settlements written in English are in this volume. Volume IV brings the history down to the reign of Harold II (1066). Out of 254 charters 137 are in English. Volume V contains charters omitted from earlier volumes, as also does Volume VI, which includes about 150 documents, nearly one-third of them in English.

Charters continued during the whole medieval period for both public and private transactions, among the best known being the Magna Carta, or Great Charter of 1215, in which King John made important concessions to his principal subjects, and which was confirmed again and again by later kings. There was also the Charter of the Forests, guaranteeing rights to the use of the forests to various eminent subjects. Again there are the Charter Rolls from the time of King John (1199) to the reign of Edward IV (1483), recording grants to various bodies, of privilege to hold markets, or fairs, or of titles, honours and the like. There was a medieval baronial family of Bermingham (the old spelling of Birmingham, the city), the heirs to which may still exist, whose representative in the reign of Henry II, Peter de Bermingham, had a charter from the Crown under which he was allowed to hold a weekly market on Thursdays at Birmingham. The grant also gave him the power of punishing offenders within his own bounds, and obliged all who lived in the area to plead in his manorial courts.

With the dissolution of the monasteries (1535-40), the name 'charter' gave place to the term now used, 'title deed', by means of which conveyance of property is customarily made.

Other records of great service to the genealogist who delves into medieval times are the 'Red Book' and the *Testa de Nevill*. The former, or *Liber Rubeus* of the Exchequer, was the work of Alexander de Swereford, Archdeacon of Shrewsbury, who died in 1246. R. Sims in a *Manual for the Genealogist*, p 40, wrote: 'It contains among many miscellaneous entries respecting the court and kingdom at large, serjeanties, knights' fees and *prima scutagia* of the reigns of Henry II, Richard I, John and Henry III. In substance, it is much the same with the Black Book and with the *Testa de Nevill*.' Scutage was a tax imposed on those feudal tenants who, perhaps because they could not, had not fulfilled their military obligations; in other words, a payment in lieu of military service. Swereford wrote in 1230 a pedigree for the then King of England, Henry III, which he traces through the mother of the Empress Matilda (daughter of Henry I who had married the English heiress of the old royal line), and so on through the House of Wessex, via Woden to Adam, just as in the *Anglo-Saxon Chronicle*, but ignoring the Norman line before Henry I.

The *Testa de Nevill sive Liber Feodorum in Curia Scaccarii* (Book of Fees in the Exchequer Court) contained an account of the feudal dues and services in the reigns of Henry III and Edward I. It was named either from Ralph de Nevill, a clerk in the Exchequer under Henry III and mentioned in the copy printed in 1807 (p 39), or from Jolland de Nevill, an itinerant judge or justice of that time. It is about 600 pages in length, with about 75 pages of index. Many of the names it contains are known now—Bagot, Bastard, Boteller, Burnell, Wake, Gorges, Tremlett, Giffard, Frere, Corbet, Kyme, Luttrell, Malet, Marris, Neville, Percy, Pomeroy, Pine, Piggott, Sandford, and Segrave.

The Placita, or Pleas

These are extremely valuable records, being those of law cases which came before the royal courts of justice. In former centuries there were two important differences compared with English law as it is now: the first was that there were other courts, those of the great barons and lords of manors, besides the King's courts, though in course of time, the royal courts and royal justice superseded the others. The second difference was that until 1876 there were two legal systems existing side by side in England, that of the Common Law and that of Equity. Persons who applied to the courts where the Common Law of England was administered and who failed to obtain satisfaction—probably because no remedy existed at Common Law—very often petitioned the King through his Lord Chancellor, or Secretary (an official who is found functioning as early as the reign of Edward the Confessor). The Chancellor then considered the case and gave an equitable decision, or as Roman lawyers would have said, a decision in accordance with natural justice, a term not liked by English lawyers. It was not until 1876 that these two systems were fused; it was then decided that in the event of a conflict between the principles of Common Law and Equity, the latter should prevail. Previous to 1876 there had been two Lord Chief Justices, one of King's Bench, the other of Common Pleas. After 1876, only one Lord Chief Justice was left, with the Lord Chancellor above him as head of the whole legal profession. The different courts then became divisions of the one High Court; Chancery Division, Probate, Divorce and Admiralty Division etc. Above them is the Court of Appeal and, highest of all, the House of Lords in its judicial capacity. A Court of Criminal Appeal was established in 1907. The nineteenth century in England was a period of great law reforms and this explanation is necessary for the researcher who may be puzzled by the names of courts now defunct or otherwise named.

The *Placita* relate to eleven different courts:

(i) of the *Curia Regis*, or King's Court, dealing with pleas touching the Crown, and common pleas of both civil and criminal nature. From the time of Henry II (1154-89), the King's judges were itinerant, and the expression 'Justices or Proceedings in Eyre' is often found in old documents. Eyre is from Latin *errare* to wander or rove, through French *errer*, the judges having as it were a roving commission.

(ii) Of the Forest, to deal with pleas concerning the demesne of the Crown.

(iii) Of the Crown, *Placita Coronae.*

(iv) Of Parliament.

(v) *De Quo Warranto*, literally, 'concerning the warrant which'. This form of plea was instituted by Edward I (1272-1307), on his accession, to inquire into various abuses, especially as regards the revenues of the Crown. It was in connection with this procedure that there occurred the famous incident of Earl Warrenne, Earl of Surrey. On being asked by the King's commissioners for the title deeds to his estates, he produced a rusty sword and said that his property had been won by the sword and that he would keep it by the sword. His ancestor, William de Warrenne, had been a close kinsman of the Conqueror, who had made him Earl of Surrey. He had been married to a lady named Gundreda, who was formerly described as a daughter of the Conqueror, (see above). The Pleas of Quo Warranto are said to be the original of the Hundred Rolls, (see below).

(vi) Pleas of the Court of Chancery, beginning in the reign of Richard II (1377-99).

(vii) Common Pleas: this court, as distinct from that of *Curia Regis,* began in the time of King John.

(viii) The Ecclesiastical Courts for many centuries dealt with matrimonial offences and with wills, until in 1858 wills came under the Probate Division of the High Court. Today they handle only ecclesiastical affairs.

(ix) Court of Exchequer dealt with matters touching the public revenues.

(x) Court of King's Bench, of whose proceedings it has been said that 'these records abound in curious matter illustrative of the general history of the country, of the descent of landed property, and of the manners and state of society in the twelfth and thirteenth centuries'. (Sims, *op cit,* p 71).

(xi) Court of Star Chamber, instituted under the Tudors and abolished by the Commonwealth. It dealt principally with offences by great persons, and had a considerable influence on the law's treatment of libel.

The records of all these courts, if printed, are likely to be in the British Museum, otherwise they can be consulted in the Public Record Office.

The Rotuli or Rolls

Mention has already been made of the Pipe Rolls and others of importance for the genealogist are:

(i) The Close Rolls: these were records of private transactions which were sent out closed or sealed and addressed to one or two persons only. They range over a vast number of subjects from the time of King John to the beginning of the present century.

(ii) Also from the time of John date the Patent Rolls, so called because they were open or patent for all to read, and were sealed with the Great Seal of England. They refer to grants of office, honours, privileges, to both individuals or to bodies corporate.

(iii) The Fine or *Oblata* Rolls: these record fines which were levied by the King for permission to perform certain acts, eg, to stay at home instead of accompanying him abroad, or to have the wardship or right of marriage of an heiress which normally belonged to the Crown.

(iv) *Liberate* (ie, set free) Rolls were orders to the royal treasurers to pay various sums of money.

(v) Hundred Rolls: so named because the areas in question were supposed to be able to maintain 100 families. The purpose of these rolls has been explained above.

(vi) Escheat Rolls: 'escheat' was the term applied to the process by which property went to the Crown, not always for treasonable actions.

(vii) Coronation Rolls: these contain accounts of claims put forward at the coronations of English sovereigns by various individuals or families to perform certain services. The latter are a feudal relic, for under that system lands were held under service of grand serjeanty (there is also a petty serjeanty). See Note 6 for further explanation and illustrations.

(viii) Copyhold Court Rolls. The economic unit of medieval Europe was the manor, and lords of the manors held their lands from the Crown; the manor was termed a barony, and each manor had a court of jurisdiction called the Court Baron. Slavery had gradually changed in Christian times to serfdom, so that although the lord of the manor did not own the people who lived on the soil, they were nonetheless bound, together with their children and effects, to his property, just like the cattle or stock of the manor. A man who was a villein (the original spelling of our 'villain' from the Low Latin *villanus*, Latin *villa*, the equivalent in economic terms of the manor in Roman times), could not leave an estate without the lord's permission, and had to work for him so many days in the year without pay. In return, he had protection by the lord against outside interference. 'Villeins and their children having been permitted to enjoy their possessions without interruption in a regular course of descent, the Common Law gave them title to prescribe against their lords, and on performance of the same service, to hold their lands in spite of any determination of the lord's will. For though, in general, they are still said to hold their estates at the will of the lord, yet it is such a will as is agreeable to the custom of the manor, which customs are preserved and evidenced by the Rolls of the several Courts Baron in which they are entered, or kept on foot by the constant immemorial usage of the several manors in which the lands lie. As such tenants had nothing to show for their estates but these customs, and admissions in pursuance of them, entered on these rolls, or the copies of such entries witnessed by the steward, they now began to be called tenants by copy of court roll, and their tenure itself a copyhold.' (Sims, *op cit*, p 86). See Note 7 for further details and family illustrations.

(ix) Coroners' Rolls. The modern coroner has the duty of investigating a death when a medical certificate is not forthcoming, and also in cases of treasure trove, which technically belongs to the Crown. These duties are relics of much more considerable medieval functions, for the coroner in former days had to conduct inquiries as regards not only sudden death, but also wounding and rape. The records were returned to the Crown Office, and can be inspected at the Public Record Office.

(x) Memoranda Rolls: these cover a vast amount of material both secular and religious, but are mainly concerned with various claims of the Crown.

The Public Record Office

This office in London, to which frequent reference has been made, was set up as a result of an Act of Parliament in 1838. Previously, many of the invaluable records mentioned above were kept at the Tower of London and in a highly unsatisfactory condition; also in the Rolls Chapel on the site of the present Record Office, in the Chapter House of Westminster Abbey and in other places. Damp, dirt and rodents, in the

Tower at least, were allowed freedom with the public records. In 1800 a Records Commission was appointed which began the printing and publication of the old documents. At last the Record Office was established, on the site of a *domus conversorum*, a medieval home for converted Jews, later turned into the Rolls Chapel. The head of the Office, called the Master of the Rolls, is a distinguished judge, who is also a member of the House of Lords. Anyone wishing to search and study in the PRO must apply for a ticket to the Secretary, Public Record Office, Chancery Lane, London, WC2 and printed guides to the contents of the Office are available. The references to places where records are stored, as given in Sims' work, or in M. S. Giuseppi's *Guide to the PRO*, no longer apply and the modern guide must be used. The useful leaflet supplied to all inquirers states: 'The PRO contains many millions of documents relating to the actions of the central government and the courts of law of England and Wales from the eleventh century, of Great Britain from 1707, and of the United Kingdom from 1801 to the present day. There is no comprehensive index, but paragraphs 6 and 7 (ie, of the leaflet) indicate how to set about finding the records required. Readers will save themselves a good deal of time and trouble if, before coming to the Office, they have familiarised themselves with the printed sources for the subject of their research and have a clear picture of the material they can reasonably expect to find.'

Inquisitiones Post Mortem

Meaning literally, 'inquiries after the death', these were the medieval equivalent of the estate or death duty, as it is called in modern Britain. In some ways the medieval form was more rigorous, for an heir could not enter upon his inheritance until he had paid certain dues to the Crown, the feudal theory being that all land belonged to the King and an estate reverted to the Crown on the tenant's death. A tax, called a 'relief', then became due to the King and the heir had to pay this before he could take possession of the property; he had also to pay homage and only after both had been done could he receive delivery (or livery) of his inheritance. Should the heir be a minor, the property reverted to the Crown until he came of age and was able to render homage. These wardships, as of heiresses already mentioned, were of great value to the Crown and an unscrupulous monarch often managed to retain control of lands, and of course their financial yields, after the time of due delivery. Heiresses were married off to persons who could afford to pay for the privilege. Ecclesiastical benefices, too, were often kept vacant so that the Crown might enjoy the revenues from the land. On the death of a tenant-in-chief, the royal officer in the county, known as the escheator, received a writ from the King, *De Diem clausit extremum*, 'Concerning the death etc', which ordered him to empanel a jury to ascertain:

(i) the lands held by the late tenant.
(ii) the rents or services by which they were held.
(iii) the name and age of the heir.

The returns were made upon oath and a record of them exists from Henry III (1216-72) to Charles I (1625-49). They are of great value to the genealogist because, clearly, all the information provided can be relied upon. In many pedigrees of great families, the abbreviation, *Inq post mortem*, occurs with a statement that, eg, in 1360 the heir was of full age. We cannot get the exact date of birth but the general estimate is extremely useful.

Inquisitiones ad quod Damnum

Meaning literally, 'to the damage which', these are similar to the previous inquiries but relate, not to the inheritance of an estate, but to some act such as the alienation of land by a tenant, the granting of a fair or market, and especially to the granting of land in mortmain. The Crown would possibly suffer loss by these transactions. Mortmain was particularly disliked by the kings. It meant 'the dead hand' and referred generally to what we should call a charitable or religious foundation which would be unable to discharge the warlike duties of feudalism. Statutes against mortmain were passed in medieval England; the writs referred to were collected from the reign of Edward II.

Fines and Recoveries

These have already been mentioned under the Fine Rolls, and relate to proceedings which were taken in order to convey estates and to free them from various charges such as the dowry of wives and the entailment of the estate upon an heir. Breaking an entail is a process which still goes on under English law. In most cases a payment of money was made to the Crown. The records of these transactions have been preserved from the reign of Richard I. As with many other old documents, some of the Fines and Recoveries have been calendared, ie, arranged in chronological order with a summary of contents, and these calendars are in the British Museum.

To illustrate the kind of happening in a fine and recovery there is the story of Roger Stafford, who was the last of the Lords Stafford, of the creation of 1299. This was an old barony by writ whose holders had fallen into great troubles in the Wars of the Roses in fifteenth-century England. At length the last holder but one of the barony died in 1637, unmarried, and the barony was claimed by a poor old man, Roger Stafford, who had been brought up in obscurity by a servant and had apparently been known as Roger Floyd, the servant's name. When he petitioned the King, Charles I, for the barony, the King decided that as the said Roger Stafford had neither land nor money, he should resign all claims to the barony for His Majesty to dispose of as he should see fit. Roger Stafford was therefore induced to surrender the barony, and in 1639 a fine was levied in the Common Pleas, in which the King was the plaintiff and Stafford the defendant. By this action Roger Stafford quit claimed (ie, gave up) for himself and his heirs for ever any rights to the barony. Behind the jargon in which this manifest injustice was clothed, was the fact that Charles I wanted the title of Baron Stafford for Sir William Howard, who was married to Mary Stafford, heir general of the Stafford family, and these two were accordingly created Baron and Baroness Stafford in 1640, with a viscounty two months later. Viscount Stafford was executed on a false charge of treason in 1680.

Parliamentary Records

These begin with statutes as far back as the reign of Henry III. Parliament as known in England consists of the Sovereign, the Lords and the Commons. The House of Commons did not begin to exist until 1265, when Simon de Montfort, Earl of Leicester, who was in rebellion against Henry III, began to call the Knights of the Shire, (whom we would now call the MPs for rural areas), and the burgesses of the towns, to the councils of the nation along with the great lords. The device was adopted by Simon's conqueror, who became Edward I, but laws were being made by King and Lords long before the Commons were summoned, so that the earlier statutes of the realm were made without the presence of the Commons. The Statutes are printed and can be consulted at the British Museum. So can many private Acts of Parliament which are very valuable for genealogists. As no divorce court existed in England before 1858, a marriage could be dissolved only by private Act of Parliament. Then many private Acts deal with settlement of family estates, the

F

naturalisation of foreigners (denization as it was then called), attainders and their reversals, legitimation of issue, all of which are of service in the study of family history.

Hearth Tax

This tax was introduced into England from France after 1660. Like many of the taxes mentioned earlier, it has valuable incidental aids to genealogy, for the number of hearths which a man possessed will indicate his social status. In the returns for Oxfordshire for 1665 the Lord Chancellor, the Earl of Clarendon, had forty-three hearths in his house at Cornbury, and Lord Anglesey had thirty. This tax lasted only a few years, being abolished in 1689, but the records are obviously very useful. In mentioning this tax we have over-passed the date of 1500 given earlier for the medieval genealogies and this overlapping should be explained.

The most important feature of the feudal system as regards royalty was that the King had very large demesnes in different parts of the country. How these originated it is impossible in most cases to discover, and many Crown lands are described in Domesday Book as being of ancient demesne. The income from the lands made the King the richest man in the country, and many of the squabbles between King and nobles were due to the barons' insistence that the King should 'live of his own'. They meant that he should run the country on his private revenues, but as this proved impossible, there were repeated attempts at raising taxation. During the Tudor period (1485-1603), many taxes were endured simply because it was felt that the country was facing unprecedented difficulties and needed the strong government provided by the monarchy. With the accession of the Stuarts, the money difficulties increased and Charles I (1625-49) set himself to recover many old financial rights of the Crown which had fallen into desuetude. Hence the cause of trouble with the Parliament and the ensuing civil war. When the monarchy was restored in 1660, there was a great outburst of loyalty. Acts were passed by the Restoration Parliament for the Attainder of Regicides (1660), on Treason (1661), and for a Free and Voluntary Present to His Majesty (1661) of money to relieve his distresses. At the same time there was also passed the Tenures Abolition Act (1660), by which the old feudal services and dues were done away with. The amusing feature of this Act was that the Courts of Wards and Liveries had been effectually abolished by the rebel Parliamentary government in 1645. This was now confirmed by the ultra loyal 1660

Parliament, so that the very matter over which the civil war had been fought was now conceded on all sides to have been right. 'It hath been found by former experience that the Courts of Wards and Liveries and tenures by knights' service either of the King or others or by knights' service *in capite* or soccage *in capite* of the King and the consequents upon the same have been much more burdensome, grievous and pre-judicial to the kingdom than they have been beneficial to the King' says the opening section, 'The reasons for passing this Act.'

To make good the money thus lost to the Crown, a grant of £1,200,000 a year was made to Charles II. The duties on beer and ale were also granted to the King, but these did not raise enough money, and one of the new taxes imposed was the Hearth Tax. By an Act of 1662 it was ordered that two shillings a year were to be paid, in two half-yearly instalments, on every fire, hearth and stone in each and every house. When the tax was abolished, it was speedily replaced by a window tax which lasted right into the nineteenth century and was the cause of the many bricked-in windows still to be seen in old houses in England.

With the reign of Charles II, then, we have passed completely into the modern era. As we shall see in the next section, the modern and medieval periods inevitably overlap. Before 1500 we are concerned with the great families. After 1500 it becomes increasingly possible and even fairly easy to trace ordinary families.

Muster Rolls

Muster Rolls extend almost from the Conquest period, for Domesday Book is a record of the knights on whom the Conqueror could depend. Later on, in the thirteenth century, commissioners were appointed in each county whose task it was to return lists of all men between the ages of sixteen and sixty. These lists have sometimes been preserved in public sources, in libraries and in the archives of families. The family of Hooke of Crookes Park, which has held land in Gloucestershire for over 550 years, has in its records descriptions of family servants of the seventeenth century who were deemed fit to bear arms. In the Muster Rolls will be found the Christian names, surname and rank of each man, his weapons and, at times, his age, value of property etc. Modern military records are very considerable and are kept in the Public Record Office for the earlier portions, and in the offices of the three Services for the more recent sections. These records give not only names of officers but of enlisted ranks also. On several occasions I have traced private soldiers who served in the British Army in the wars against Napoleon; for an even earlier period, the time of the American War of Independence, I obtained particulars of the career of a British officer who was a member of the Birch family in America.

Revenues of the British Crown

The personal position as regards the revenues of the British Crown is that, ever since the accession of George III in 1760, it has been the practice for each sovereign to surrender to Parliament the hereditary revenues of the Crown which, as previously explained, are derived from very ancient lands of the Crown in England. In return, Parliament has granted in each reign a fixed annual income known as the Civil List. This practice could, in theory, be revoked by a new sovereign, but the enormous strength of tradition in Britain makes this most unlikely. It is an unfortunate practice because it has given rise to the constantly repeated complaint that the British monarchy, or royal family, is too great an expense to the country. The Civil List amounts to not more than £700,000, of which £475,000 goes to the Queen. The produce of the royal estates amounts to £2½ millions per year, so that, in fact, the national treasury is the gainer by over £1½ millions. This does not, of course, include private property of the sovereign, such as the estate at Sandringham which was purchased by Edward VII. It follows that so far from the British nation having to find money for the upkeep of the monarchy, it is actually making a good profit out of the 200 year-old handover.

Another important feature of the British scene which ought to be understood is that the terms 'aristocracy' and 'nobility' are not confined to persons of title. In the examples of family history which have been quoted, some have been of peers, others, of untitled families. Sir Bernard Burke, son of John Burke, the founder of the many Burke publications, summed up the matter well when he referred to the 'untitled aristocracy'. This is a feature peculiar to Britain. In all other countries where nobility has existed, it has included all the members of a family, whereas in Britain only the reigning peer and his wife are regarded as technically noble. Thus, even the grandson of a duke will be plain Mister, as was the case with Sir Winston Churchill who, for the greater part of his life, had no title of any sort until he accepted the knighthood of the Garter from the Queen. Yet he was the grandson of a Duke of Marlborough. Consequently those families who possess no hereditary title are of the same social class and status as the titled. The former are usually given a place in *Burke's Landed Gentry*; the titled families—the peers and baronets—are in *Burke's Peerage*, though among the 50,000 or so persons in the latter volume there are probably 40,000 without a title who are known as the cadets, or junior members of a family. The position is quite different in Continental volumes such as the *Almanach de Gotha*, or Ruvigny's *Titled Nobility of Europe*, where no one is entered who does not possess a title. The real determining factor in separating noble from non-noble was, and is, the possession of a coat of arms. This is known as nobiliary status and the best account of it, with examples drawn from many European countries, is to be found in *The Nature of Arms* 1961, the work of a Scottish heraldic authority, Robert Gayre of Gayre and Nigg.

NOTE: page 51. The number of knights has been variously estimated between 4,200 and 5,500. Thus F. W. Maitland reckons 5,000, while Enoch Powell thinks the total was 4,200. (*The House of Lords in the Middle Ages*, p 44.) Probably the discrepancy arises owing to our ignorance of the numbers of knights who received their lands from the great lords under the King in cases where the number of fees had not been specified.

CHAPTER 5

Genealogies from AD 1500

THE beginning of the sixteenth century is marked by a great increase in record keeping. A very considerable source of information on family history derives from the work of the heralds. Heraldry originated in the twelfth century as a means of identifying men clad in complete armour. From warfare it spread into civil life and by the sixteenth century had come to be used by all manner of persons who could claim gentility. With the spread of the use of arms, the kings in various countries came to exercise control over arms, and to do this they used their heralds. In England, the method employed was that known as the Visitations, by which the heralds were given commissions by the sovereign to visit a particular area and there inspect the arms used by the different families or institutions. The records of these Visitations were entered in the archives of the College of Arms (another less correct name is Heralds' College) which still exists in London. Not only coats of arms were entered but also pedigrees, and as these Visitations extended over a period of some 160 years they constitute a body of genealogical information of great value. The first Visitation took place in the reign of Henry VIII in 1529-30 and the last in the reign of James II (1685-88). One of the most important facts about the Visitations is that if the researcher can show his male-line descent from a person in the Visitation pedigree who had the right to bear arms, then the searcher has the right to those same arms. This is the rule in English heraldry.

Where are these records to be found? In their original form, only in the College of Arms, which is not open to public inspection. Anyone can make inquiries at the College, but they will be conducted by the heralds, who charge fees. The College is the only large repository of records in England which is not available to the public for personal inspection. All others, such as the British Museum Library, the Public Record Office, and Somerset House (with the exception of census records after 1861), are available on application either free or for very small charges. This privacy of the College of Arms records does not mean that it is impossible to study the Visitations as, fortunately, many copies of them were made and have now been printed, notably in the volumes of the Harleian Society. These are to be found in most large libraries in England, including the open shelves in the Reading Room of the British Museum, and also in the Library of the Society of Genealogists at 37 Harrington Gardens, near Gloucester Road, London. This society has many thousands of volumes in its collections, all devoted to genealogical subjects, and the rooms are open to searchers for a small sum each day. In the manuscript collections in the Colleges of Oxford and Cambridge there are also many copies of Visitations, nearly all of which are believed to have now been printed either in volumes dealing with the particular county or in the volumes of the Harleian Society.

A list of Visitations is given in Sims (*op cit*, p 161) and in a modern work by the present Garter King of Arms, Sir Anthony Wagner, entitled *The Records and Collections of the College of Arms* (1952). On copies of the Visitations he remarks: (p 63) 'Copies were made for various purposes. . . . In these and similar circumstances many copies or purported copies of Visitation books were in fact made in the 16th and 17th centuries and are now to be found in many public and private collections. The trouble with them is that, until they have been collated with the originals, their character and authenticity are quite uncertain. And it is from such copies that the editions printed by the Harleian Society and others are for the most part taken.' There could be a good deal of exaggeration here, for if Sir Anthony agrees that the copies were probably made for the convenience of the heralds or their deputies in the different counties it seems unlikely that such copies would be flagrantly wrong. Again, since these copies were made, further information has in some cases been added to the originals, but this need not be anything but an advantage unless it appears (as one can almost always detect) that a false pedigree has been concocted. The inventors of the spurious rarely content themselves with an ordinary John Smith, son of John Smith! In any event, it is always open to the College of Arms to settle the possiblity of error by permitting a collation of its records against the copies, just as it could also bring order to most of the heraldic chaos in England by producing a list of those to whom arms have been granted.

The inquirer can, then, use these printed versions of the Visitations, though with the same reservations that must generally be given to a document copied from an original and which has then passed through other hands, with editings on the way. Probably the best up-to-date critical account of the Visitations is in the booklet by G. D. Squibb, *Visitation Pedigrees and the Genealogist*, 1964. Here he says: 'No genealogist whose interests lie in 16th- and 17th-century England can afford to neglect Visitation pedigrees. They must be used critically, but so used, they are invaluable.' (p 25). These remarks are made, be it carefully noted, of the original Visitation pedigrees preserved in the College. Mr Squibb, who is Norfolk Herald Extraordinary and has worked on the records of the Court of Chivalry in the College, then goes on to speak of the printed copies of the Visitations. 'Printed Visitations need to be used with special care. Some of them are very bad, some so bad as to be worthless. On the other hand some are very good. It is therefore a mistake to dismiss printed Visitations as a class as being unworthy of serious consideration. Used with discretion they are an indispensable section of the genealogist's library.' Elsewhere (p 11) he remarks 'there are even a few Visitations printed from texts which are better than any in the College of Arms.' (See Note 8).

Some information may at this stage be useful concerning printed sources of pedigrees. Two volumes exist which give the names of nearly all families in Great Britain and Ireland whose pedigrees appear anywhere in print. The second volume is a continuation of the earlier work after a gap of fifty years. The earlier work is the *The Genealogist's Guide to Printed Pedigrees*, by George W. Marshall, published in more than one edition, the latest being that of 1912. The sub-title gives an idea of the nature of the book: 'Being a General Search through genealogical, topographical and biographical works, relating to the United Kingdom, together with references to family histories, peerage claims etc.' About 50,000 references to sources are given. The second book is entitled: *A Genealogical Guide. An Index to British Pedigrees in continuation of Marshall's Genealogist's Guide*, by J. B. Whitmore, (1953). This extends to 658 pages and must contain at least as many references as Marshall's book. Since it was finished there has been the publication of *Burke's Landed Gentry* (1952) containing 3,000 pages and listing about 4,500 families, some of which had no pedigree in print before their record in the *Landed Gentry*. A new edition of this work is now being produced in four volumes, the first two of which have appeared. Also published in 1958 was the fourth edition of *Burke's Landed Gentry of Ireland*, 800 pages, with about 800 pedigrees, many of which had not appeared before.

These sources enable an inquirer to dispense with all other lists of pedigrees, such as those found in Sims, and also to be sure that in the overwhelming majority of cases he can refer to a printed pedigree of the family which interests him. The Marshall book has to be obtained second-hand; that by Whitmore is still in print and can be bought through most good booksellers. The investigator can also make good use of *Burke's General Armory* (last edition 1884, but available in a modern photolithoed copy), which contains descriptions of some 100,000 coats of arms and also has some genealogical details. With these three books, the inquirer can be confident that he will find most family names which have any heraldic or genealogical information concerning them in print in the British Isles. He must, of course, bear in mind that the inclusion of arms in the *General Armory* does not mean that they are registered with any heraldic office, but only that they were used by the persons whose names are given in the book. Also, the mere fact that a family has a printed pedigree somewhere does not mean that anyone with the same surname is necessarily of the same family. Still, these three books are tools of the genealogist and, as such, are a useful aid to research but not a substitute for it.

Other records of an heraldic nature are found in the series of the Rolls of Arms. These were made mostly before the Visitations of the heralds and were records of great occasions, such as a warlike expedition or a tournament. The Rolls are of great beauty and value. They show the arms of the persons mentioned and sometimes give a few details about them. They start in the middle of the thirteenth century and go on into Tudor times. In Scotland they date only from about 1540, though there is a Scottish section of the French *Armorial de Berry* which dates from about 1445. In England, there are such specimens as the Falkirk Roll, which gives the arms of those who served with Edward I at the battle of Falkirk against the Scots in 1298, recording 111 persons, among them being Percy, Wake, FitzWilliam, Hastings, Moulton, Despenser, Clifford, Basset, De Vere and Martin. Another Roll was that of York, about the same time as that of Falkirk, and containing 268 coats of arms. Perhaps the most interesting is the Roll of Caerlaverock, written not long after 1300. It is a poem written in Norman French and describes the siege and capture of a small castle in Dumfrieshire, Scotland, by Edward I. In it the author, who may have been a herald in Edward's train, describes 87 banners and over 100 coats of arms, giving pen pictures of their owners and not always flattering descriptions.

Besides these sources the searcher who visits Britain should be on the look-out for monumental inscriptions in churches and on tombstones, which often contain quite a lot of genealogical information. Seals give a clue to coats of arms, and were used in round form when belonging to kings and other great persons, whereas clergy used the oval shape. Later in the twelfth and thirteenth centuries triangular seals were used, and in the thirteenth century the seal became generally oval, more or less acute, though there are many of circular and heater shape to be found. In the fifteenth and sixteenth centuries seals were often of non-heraldic type.

Some of the greatest of the heralds set out the results of their research in accessible form in books. An example of this is the work of the great Sir William Dugdale (1605-85), who at the time of his death was Garter King of Arms. He wrote the *Monasticon* already mentioned, the *Antiquities of Warwickshire* (1656) and the *Baronage of England* (1675-76). These works are available in most large libraries and with the researches of William Camden (1551-1623), Clarenceux King of Arms and author of *Britannia, Remaines Concerning Britain* and other studies, go some way to compensate for the other heraldic personages of Tudor times who were none too scrupulous in dealing with pedigrees and arms.

The counties of Britain received much valuable attention from many learned men from the eighteenth century onwards. Many most useful county histories exist, packed with genealogical knowledge and references to family and coats of arms. Also of great help to the searcher is the Victoria series of County Histories dealing with English counties, a series begun many years ago and not yet complete. Often in this series, that part of Domesday which is relevant to the county is translated.

The Parish Registers

A few years after the beginning of the Visitations another great step was taken towards documenting all the people in England. The order for this was given in 1538 by Thomas Cromwell, who held the office of Vicar General to Henry VIII. In earlier life he had been familiar with conditions in Italy and is supposed to have brought back with him ideas of regimentation until then unknown in England. This may, however, be a calumny prompted by the intense hatred in which he was held in England as Henry's instrument and favourite in dealing with the suppression of the monasteries. As long as he continued to fill Henry's coffers and to manage his affairs successfully, he had Henry's support and was unassailable. When he was so foolish as to recommend to the King a marriage with a plain, boorish woman, Anne of Cleves, his fall was certain. He had a patent from the King to become Earl of Essex but never lived to enjoy it, for he was duly beheaded at the King's order.

From the genealogical point of view Thomas Cromwell rendered invaluable service, for his order of 1538 made it the duty of every parish clergyman to keep registers of baptisms, marriages and burials. At first, the order was honoured in the breach rather than the observance, as though most registers date from at least the seventeenth century, very few are dated 1538. At St Giles in the Fields, London, magnificently kept registers are to be seen which go back 400 years. This church was very fashionable right up to the early nineteenth century and very many members of aristocratic families have their names in the registers, including an illegitimate daughter of the poet Byron. It is said that the registers of most of the old London churches have been kept from 1558; this may have been due to the nearness of the seat of government. In small country parishes and in remote places the local clergyman went very much his own way. Again and again the authorities of Church and State made orders for the better keeping of the parish registers, and for the rendering of transcripts or copies to the bishop of the diocese. Many of these transcripts survive and have often supplied information which was wanting from the registers. No amount of direction could ensure that the registers, even when kept regularly, would be safe from dirt, fire, carelessness or the destruction caused by rodents. During the troubles of the Civil War, many registers were not kept up, Parliament, the victorious party, being generally Puritan and hostile to the Church. When the King had been executed, the Puritans abolished episcopacy and banned the Book of Common Prayer. Thus it is understandable why during the war, from 1642 to 1649, the registers were not properly kept, even though in 1644, and again in 1653, Parliament did order them to be kept.

When the monarchy was restored in 1660 the Church came back, too, and from then on the registers were fairly well kept. They are the main source of pedigree information for the inquirer and by their help he can often get back 300 years. Many cases exist in the peerage today where the ancestors were simple folk living for generation after generation in one place. This is so with the famous Harmsworth family of newspaper proprietors whose head is Lord Rothermere. They lived in a parish in Hampshire for nine generations, recalling the famous lines in Gray's *Elegy written in a Country Churchyard* about the rude forefathers of the hamlet. Even more remarkable was the family history of the late Viscount Nuffield, William Morris of car manufacturing fame. His proven genealogy went back from Elizabeth II to Elizabeth I, and all were simple people who did not move from their native Oxfordshire. In this instance there is a distinct probability that the family was there in the time of King John, so that for some 700 years the Morrises had been small tenant farmers in the same county.

To find that his family have been living in one area for a long time is the hope of most research workers, for he may thus have a clear run through the registers for as many as ten generations. In the days before the industrial revolution and before the advent of railways, it was not so easy to move from one county to another. The industrial revolution occurred in England in the second half of the eighteenth century, with inventions like the spinning frame invented by Sir Richard Arkwright. The demand for workers in the new factories led to mass movements of people, especially in the developing north and midlands. The invention of the steam engine and the railways next affected the whole country and made movement a possibility for all. Before these great changes, only some classes of the population would be likely to travel about much: clergymen, schoolmasters, doctors and paupers.

A. M. Burke's useful *Guide to the Parish Registers of England and Wales* lists them as they were about forty years ago and can be consulted in libraries or bought second-hand. Apart from the breakdown during the Commonwealth period, other national events have, of course, affected the keeping of the registers. Thus, the Great Fire of London in 1666 destroyed thirty-five churches, which were never rebuilt. The same kind of result followed the bombing of London in 1940-41. Many of the destroyed churches have not been replaced, but where their archives still exist, these are now lodged in a nearby church. The only way to discover the whereabouts of the registers is to write to the secretary of the bishop of the diocese for guidance in the case of registers of destroyed or otherwise non-existent churches, or, if you know the parish still exists, to look up the clergyman in charge (rector or vicar, usually rector in the country), whose address can be found in *Crockford's Clerical Directory of the Church of England*. Since the last war some new arrangements have been made as regards parish registers in London. The greatest number of registers of parishes within the diocese of London, which have been deposited, are held at the Greater London Record Office, The County Hall, London, SE1. Application should be made to the Head Archivist. Where, however, registers of parishes in the ancient city of Westminster are concerned, they, if deposited, are at the Archives Department of the City of Westminster at Buckingham Palace Road Library, London, SW1. Similarly, registers of parishes in the City of London are either with the incumbent or in the care of the Corporation of London at the Guildhall Library, Basinghall Street, London, EC2. A Survey of the Parish Registers of the Diocese of London,

Inner London area, edited by Miss Joan Coburn, Assistant Archivist, Greater London Record Office is to be obtained from the Information Centre, Greater London Council, County Hall, London, SE1.

Some general notes may be useful. All parish registers have more entries of burials than of baptisms. Many registers contain more information than just the details of baptisms, marriages, and burials; eg, that someone was the base (ie, bastard) son. In the case of marriages, the parentage of one party is sometimes omitted. Old registers occasionally record marriages which did not take place in the parish. Some people have their decease registered in two places. A peculiarity in times gone by was to give the same Christian name to two children in a family, particularly when one child died and it was desired to keep a Christian name going in the family. Until the early eighteenth century, the style of every unmarried woman was Mistress. The bishop's transcripts, referred to above, are now usually preserved in the Diocesan Registry and application to consult them should be made to the bishop's secretary. Many parish registers have been copied, and a large number are in the keeping of the Society of Genealogists, who have a printed catalogue of them. Of very great value in this connection is *Boyd's Marriage Index*, which covers a great many but not all English counties, and which is also kept at the society's rooms.

Nonconformist Records

It must be remembered that from the separation in 1533 of the English Church from the Church of Rome until 1662 it was the settled view of the majority of Englishmen—government and individuals alike—that all Englishmen should belong to one and the same church. From the time of Elizabeth I, a number of persons refused to attend their parish churches, and were known as Recusants or Papists, or as we should say now, Roman Catholics. They were the first Dissenters or Nonconformists from the Established Church, which itself was heavily involved in a contest to decide whether the Puritans should prevail. After 1662 those with Puritan views were expelled from the Church, some 2,000 clergymen resigned their livings and the history of the Nonconformist bodies began. This had an important bearing on the keeping of records, as these new Dissenting congregations no longer came to the parish church for baptism, marriage or burial. They had their own records. In 1836 a commission was appointed to inquire into the existence of such records and it required that they should be surrendered to the custody of the commissioners. As a result, about 7,000 registers were handed over under an Act of 1840, and the most part are now deposited in the Public Record Office.

These registers covered seven main classifications:

(i) The Protestant churches whose members came from abroad, particularly from Holland and France as a result of persecution. These immigrants began to arrive as far back as 1567, increased after 1572 when there was the massacre of St Bartholomew's Day, and swelled to even greater numbers after the revocation of the Edict of Nantes in 1685. Gradually these immigrants were absorbed into the English population and their congregations and churches declined to such an extent that their separate registers were no longer kept. Some prominent English families have preserved the memory of their French origin—often the surname is clearly recognisable as French or even as Norman but instead of coming over with the Conqueror in 1066, their ancestors came under William III (1688-1702). The actor, Sir Laurence Olivier, has his family history beginning with Laurent Olivier of Nay, France, who was born about 1520. One of his descendants was a French Protestant (Huguenot) clergyman, the Rev Jourdain Olivier, whose grandson, Daniel Josias Olivier, was a merchant in the City of London. There is a Huguenot Society which maintains records of the immigrant families and inquiries should be addressed to The Hon Secretary, The Huguenot Society, c/o Barclay's Bank, Pall Mall East, London, SW1. There are records of this group in several places in London, but it would be advisable in the first instance to consult the society, as sometimes there is a vague tradition in a family of Huguenot ancestry which is incorrect, and if this false idea is dispelled it will aid other researches.

(ii) The Presbyterians, Independents and Baptists. These are the oldest Nonconformist bodies in England, apart from the Roman Catholics. Their registers have a few early entries from the time of Charles I, and no doubt the troubles over religion at that period were already leading to separation from the Established Church. After 1662, these separate bodies came into being, and over 2,000 registers were deposited following the Act of 1840. In the case of the Baptists, there is no baptismal record since this denomination gives baptism only to adults, though a child is said to be dedicated and this fact is recorded.

(iii) Besides the above, there are some 1,400 registers covering a number of the later Christian bodies. Their titles, together with the date of the commencement of their registers, are as follows: Bible Christians (1817), Calvinists (1762), the Countess of Huntingdon's Connection (1752), Inghamites (1753), Moravians (1742), New Connection Methodists (1779), Primitive Methodists (1813), Swedenborgians (1787), Wesleyans (1772). Some records of these Dissenting bodies are best consulted in the archives of the society concerned. This is so with the Quakers (the Friends), although their early registers, like those of the others listed, are in the Public Record Office. Anyone whose ancestors belonged to the Society of Friends should consult the secretary of the society at Friends' House, Euston Road, London.

Jewish and Roman Catholic records were not deposited under the 1840 Act, being dispensed from this requirement. Jewish details will be found under the Jewish section further on. For Roman Catholics, application should be made to the Secretary, The Catholic Record Society, St Edward's, Sutton Park, Guildford, Surrey. The legal penalties against the practice of what was called Popery were very harsh, and so effective were the efforts made to stamp out the Catholic religion that when Catholic Emancipation came in 1829 only about 70,000 Catholics were left in England. For over 300 years almost any reference in English literature to Catholicism was couched in most offensive language. An instance of the prevailing prejudice occurs in Bunyan's *Pilgrim's Progress*, where he refers to two giants in a cave, one being Pagan, now dead, and the other Pope, practically helpless and only able to mouth and gibber at passers-by. At the other end of the scale a learned, cultured poet like Milton could describe the Paradise of Fools as full of cowls, monks, rosaries etc. Even as late as the nineteenth century Sir Walter Scott, though constrained by the very nature of his writing to describe Catholic persons, dogmas and rites, never does so without a half-apology. For an excellent account of the Disabilities of Nonconformists, including Roman Catholics, see an article with that heading by an English lawyer, F. H. Cowper, in *Who's Who in the Free Churches*, (1951). It is as well that the above facts should be understood, as they go far to explain the difficulties in tracing Catholic families.

Other records of a similar nature to those just listed are: Records of Dr Williams Library: these are registers formerly kept at this library, a very fine collection of theological and other books, in Gordon Square, London. They dealt with the Protestant Dissenters (Presbyterians, Independents and Baptists) from 1742-1837, plus a few entries from 1716 and 1742, and seventeen registers dated 1698-1833. Records from the

Chapels Royal and Somerset House Chapel: the former run from 1647-1709 and from 1687-1807; the latter from 1733-75 (baptisms), 1714-76 (marriages) and 1720-70.

The Fleet Registers

These are registers of marriages solemnised by clergymen who, though regularly ordained, were men of low character residing within the Fleet Prison, to which they had generally been confined for debt. This was in the eighteenth century and many distinguished families are said to have been damaged and sometimes ruined through these marriages. The irregularity was not stopped until 1754 when Lord Hardwicke's Marriage Act put an end to the abuse. The Fleet records of baptisms and marriages cover the period 1674-1756. Of a similar nature were the baptisms and marriages celebrated in the King's Bench Prison, and in the Mint in Southwark. The Mayfair Chapel also shared in the obloquy of the prisons. Its records of marriage are from 1728-54, and three additional volumes of its registers, now in the Church of St George's, Hanover Square, relate to baptisms 1740-53 and to marriages from February 1735 to March 1754.

Events in Hospitals

These are for Greenwich and Chelsea Hospitals, the Foundling Hospital, and The British Lying-in-Hospital in the eighteenth and nineteenth centuries.

Cemetery Records

These relate to Protestant Dissenting burial grounds, of which Bunhill Fields, the burial place of John Bunyan, is the most famous. It was first used in 1665 with records from 1713-1854. The other cemeteries are Eccelsall Bierlow, Sheffield, Yorkshire, records 1836-38; Leeds, Yorkshire, 1835-37; Liverpool (Everton), Necropolis or Low Hill General Cemetery, 1825-37; Walworth East Street, South London Burial Ground, 1819-37; and Victoria Park Cemetery, London, 1853-76. Besides the above, there are records of graves or tombstones removed under licence or in accordance with private Acts of Parliament.

The Allegations

These are useful in seeking records of marriages, as they are copies of applications to the bishop of the diocese asking him to grant a licence for a marriage. In older days, marriages did not take place so much by the calling of the bans in church on three successive Sundays, as by the granting of licences, at least in the case of the better educated classes. When a licence was required, application had to be to the bishop, or in some cases to the archbishop, or to a dean of what was known as a Peculiar, the term applied to a particular type of ecclesiastical administrative unit. The licence, when granted, went to the person who sought it, but the original application, or allegation as it was called, was preserved. One very interesting case of this kind concerned the marriage of William Shakespeare and Ann Hathaway. The entry for this could not be found in the registers, but in the last century, in the archives of the diocese of Worcester, the allegation for the marriage was discovered. Even now we only know that the ceremony was performed in an unidentified church of the Worcester diocese, the register of which is lost. 'Within six months of the marriage bond, in May 1583, a daughter was born to the poet, and was baptized in the name of Susanna at Stratford parish church on the 26th.' says Sir Sidney Lee (*A Life of William Shakespeare,* 1915, p 29) and goes on to point out that it was not usual for persons in the middling classes of society to obtain these allegations. In Shakespeare's case the explanation is that this was what is known in popular parlance as a 'shot-gun wedding', and the sureties to the bond were substantial farmers, friends of the bride's late father.

Registration of Births, Marriages and Deaths

The first half of the nineteenth century was a time of great awakening of public interest in national records. Just as the public records were removed from uncertain and dangerous places of storage to the Public Record Office, and just as the non-parochial records were brought into safe custody of a public nature, so the keeping of the vital statistics of the nation were no longer to be left to the parish. The Births and Deaths Registration Acts of 1836 made the registration of births, marriages and deaths compulsory with effect from 1 July 1837, and the General Register Office was set up, with the Registrar General at its head. The registration is organised by districts and full returns are rendered to the Registrar General of Births, Marriages and Deaths at Somerset House in London. Only a very small number of births were not registered and that only in the early days of the system. The failure to register a death has been a matter of the greatest rarity. Marriage registration has been complete, and penalties are incurred for failure to register. The registers from 1 July 1837 are available for inspection by callers at Somerset

House; for those who have to work at a distance, an application by post is strictly attended to. Copies of certificates can be obtained on payment of a small fee.

The Census

This has been held in England since 1801; in the USA since 1791; in Scotland since 1755. In ancient Rome the office of censor combined that of enumerator of the Roman citizens with the duties of censuring certain kinds of conduct. In Israel, in the time of King David, his attempts to number the people brought down the divine wrath, although in many other parts of the Old Testament there are references to the numberings of the people of Israel and of Judah.

There having been no census before 1801, historians have had to guess the size of the English population. In 1948 the Registrar General wrote: 'For many centuries after the Norman Conquest the population of this country remained small. It was a period of small growth interspersed with heavy losses, by far the greatest of which was due to the Black Death (plague) which ravaged the country in 1348 and 1349 and reduced the population by anything from one-third to a half. It is held by historians that in spite of these repeated losses from war and disease, the population of England increased in some six centuries from the estimated one and a half millions of Domesday Book to five and a half millions in 1700. There was still no systematic recording of the basic facts about the number and condition of the people.' (*Matters of Life and Death*, HMSO, 1951).

An attempt was made in 1753 to arrange for a census but the Bill did not pass Parliament. In 1800, the Census Act was passed, and at the first census in 1801 it was found that the population of England and Wales was just under nine millions. The contemporary population in Scotland was one and a half millions, in Ireland between five and six millions, and in France twenty-seven millions. The greater interest in the lives of its citizens taken by the modern state very often involves much tedious interference and restriction, but from the genealogical standpoint it is invaluable. The use of the registration of births, marriages and deaths is obvious; the census records are almost of greater value, though, unfortunately, the actual records have not been preserved from any census before 1841. The 1841 census records were content to ask the person filling in the form if he or she were born in the place of residence in that year. In the 1851 census this was replaced by the much more sensible question, 'Where were you born?', so that by means of this record it is often possible for the inquirer to trace the parish where his ancestor was born. By looking for the earliest possible certificate in Somerset House records, the searcher can discover where the ancestor lived in 1841 and 1851, and thus trace the ancestral parish. Often this is a small country place, because English people did not move about very much before the nineteenth century. The census records of 1841 and 1851 are preserved in the Public Record Office, where they can be consulted personally by an inquirer, and to these have now been added the returns for 1861, in the belief that all who were alive in 1861 are now either dead or uninterested in the investigations of researchers.

Wills

Nothing can exceed the value of wills in tracing family history, as they contain so many family references. Somerset House has a rich collection of wills, some of them dating even from Saxon times. The Church had much to do with the making of wills, as she urged a man who was approaching death to make a will if he had anything to leave. This being so, it is not surprising that the custody of wills came under the jurisdiction of the Church. In 1858, however, a law was made which set up the Probate Court and wills then had to be proved therein. Thus from that year onwards an inquirer has been able to trace a will through the records of this court, now kept at Somerset House in the department of the Principal Probate Registry. Photostat copies of wills can be obtained and seldom cost more than a few shillings.

Wills which date in the many centuries before 1858 present a much more complicated problem for researchers. Where the property of the deceased was in more than one county or district, it could, and usually does, mean that the ecclesiastical court in the area was not able to deal with the will because it had no jurisdiction over the area adjacent to its own territory. In such an eventuality, the will had to be proved, not in the Archdeacon's Court—let us suppose at Wells in Somersetshire—but in the Prerogative Court of the Archbishop of Canterbury or York. The Canterbury Court is referred to in documents as the PCC, and wills proved in PCC have been deposited in Somerset House. So far the procedure is straightforward, but when the property left under the will was in one ecclesiastical jurisdiction only it is a much more difficult matter. 'Before the establishment of the Principal Probate Registry in January 1858, the probate of any will could have taken place in one of at least 300 courts, depending on the disposition of the lands of the deceased.' Thus A. J. Camp in the preface to his valuable work, *Wills and Their*

Whereabouts (1963). In this book of 137 pages there is a detailed account of the repositories of wills in the different counties of England, in the Channel Islands, Ireland, the Isle of Man, Scotland and Wales. It is impossible in the space here available to do more than refer the inquirer at this stage to Mr Camp's work, which he describes in his sub-title as 'a thorough revision and extension of the previous work of the same name by B. G. Bouwens'.

Most popular expositions of the distribution of repositories of wills leave out some details, but at least one piece of negative information should be given. The records of wills for the diocese of Bath and Wells, which had been deposited in the Probate Registry at Exeter, were destroyed by the bombing of Exeter in 1942. As a result, genealogical research in the counties of Somerset and Devon has been severely curtailed, and such records as still exist in the form of copies of wills etc, should be sought from the Somerset Record Office, Obridge Road, Taunton, Somerset.

Printed Books

Some of these have already been mentioned. They are of two kinds in so far as they assist the genealogist.

I. Those which contain specific information, eg, of a profession or a class. *Crockford's Clerical Directory*, previously mentioned, gives records of the clergy of the Established Church of England. These records go back about a century starting with the *Clergy List*, an earlier publication than Crockford's. The *Medical Directory* deals with the doctors and gives full professional information, although it gives nothing in the way of family details. Neither, for that matter, does *Crockford*. The *Law List* gives particulars of the two branches of the legal profession in Britain, (i) barristers-at-law, and (ii) solicitors. The information is very formal with far less detail than in the two works just mentioned. Much further information is available at the various Inns of Court, and three of them, Gray's, Lincoln's and the Middle Temple, have published lists of their entrants. These give the parentage of the student, and are very valuable in this respect.

The Army, Navy and Air Force each have their official lists which give information about officers and their ranks. Lists in book form exist for other and more modern professions, such as chartered accountants, dentists etc, but these give only professional qualifications. It is almost always possible to check the facts about a professional man. There is no general reference work on the clergy of the Dissenting bodies (except the one edition, mentioned above, for the Free Churches), but very exact information can be obtained from the headquarters of the bodies concerned. Catholics are served by the *Catholic Year Book,* and there have been editions of the *Catholic Who's Who,* now well out of print but still useful for past entries.

There is in Britain a wealth of information in the form of university registers and the registers of public schools. Obviously, any university or any school with a continuing life is going to be able to supply information as to the identity of its members. There is, however, often an easier way of obtaining details than by writing to a particular university or school as many large libraries have volumes of their registers. The Society of Genealogists has probably almost all. The names and details of alumni of Oxford and Cambridge are given in several large volumes, which are usually found in any good reference library. An account of the career is given for each person who attended the school or university. In some biographies the details are very scanty owing to the defective original records on which the compiler had to draw, but generally the name of the father of the pupil or undergraduate is given. Models of this kind are—for a school—the *Record of Old Westminsters* which, in three volumes, gives the careers of all boys who attended that famous school. For a university, Venn's *Alumni Cantabrigienses* is a work of wonderfully exact knowledge from which a small pedigree can sometimes be constructed, if for two or three generations the men of a family went to the university. For Oxford, Joseph Foster's *Alumni Oxonienses* (1891), is very useful.

II. The books just mentioned can be of nothing but assistance to the searcher, whereas those in this second category must be used with great caution, including the County Histories previously mentioned. If the pedigree of a family whose name is the same as the searcher's appears in any work, the searcher must never assume the identity of that family with his own unless he can prove it. No more fruitful source of error exists than the assumption that identity of name spells sameness of family tree. There are thousands of pedigrees in *Burke's Peerage* (over 100 editions) and in *Burke's Landed Gentry* (in its eighteenth edition) beside *Burke's Landed Gentry of Ireland,* (fourth edition) and *Burke's Family Records.* They may be very useful in supplying hints as to where to look, but they must not be used as a substitute for effective research. There appears to be a mesmerism about the printed page which has persuaded many an inquirer to seek no further, once he has seen his own name at the head of a family. He feels dimly what was so well expressed by the Major General in the Gilbert and Sullivan opera, 'The Pirates of

Penzance', when he boldly claimed the persons buried in the chapel on his estate as his ancestors. He had bought the place, so the dead must belong to him, too.

Chancery Proceedings

For those who are able to trace their ancestry beyond the limitations which may be imposed by the social position of their forebears, the Chancery Proceedings may well provide much additional information. In their original manuscripts, they are in the Public Record Office in London, but indices can be seen in some libraries. They are records of legal proceedings, often between members of the same family. The references given may yield only the fact that the two members, plaintiff and defendant, were alive at the time of the suit, a useful piece of information certainly. In other cases some rudimentary pedigree details may be gleaned, the more important because they occur in documents completely remote from pedigrees and therefore the more reliable genealogically. The term 'terrier' may occcur often in such documents. It is derived from Latin *terrarium* (*terra* = land), sometimes spelt 'terrar', and meaning a roll or survey of lands which shows the amount of the land holding with the tenants' names. The Exchequer records have a terrier of all glebe land in England, made in 1338.

The Calendar

Researchers are sometimes puzzled by references in pedigrees to a date, eg, 31 Jan 1633/34. The explanation lies in the reform of the English Calendar in 1752. The first reform of the calendar in Europe, which gave it the main outlines it still possesses, was made by Julius Caesar who, when he became Pontifex Maximus, found that the seasons had shifted about two months from their true positions. As a result of his reformation in 45 BC, the lunar month disappeared from the reckoning and the calendar year became purely solar. Some further reforms were made in 8 BC by Augustus, the first emperor and successor of Julius Caesar. Julius had changed the name of the month Quintilis to Julius (July) after himself, so Sextilis then became Augustus (August), and was given an extra day taken from February. The numbering of the months was originally from March, as is evident from the terms September (7th), October (8th), November (9th) and December (10th). Quintilis was the fifth month and Sextilis the sixth, the Julian Calendar being based on the old Roman calendar which had ten months. January and February are thus intercalated to make twelve months. By the Julian reform, an extra day was added every fourth year, thus making the average length of the year 365¼ days. Augustus fixed the number of days in the four months after August. After some 1,500 years an error began to be noticed in the Julian Calendar. By making the average length of the year 365¼ days, there was an excess of eleven minutes, which would add up to about eight days in 1,000 years. Thus the dates of the seasons were slowly moving backward.

In 1577, Pope Gregory XIII undertook a further reform of the calendar, completed five years later. The vernal equinox fell on 11 March, which was too early by ten days. The Pope, by means of a Bull dated 1 March 1582, abolished the ten days, so that the vernal equinox came on 21 March, and 5 October 1582 became 15 October. By a further reform in connection with leap year, the calendar length of the year differed from the solar year by some twenty-six seconds, which would cause a discrepancy of twenty-nine hours in 4,000 years. Unfortunately, religious differences prevented the adoption of the papal reform by all Europe, and in England it did not occur until 1752. Then, by Act of Parliament, it was ruled that eleven days were to be omitted after 2 September 1752, with 14 September as the next day. The year 1751 was shortened by three months. Previously, the year had begun on 25 March, but from 1752 it began on 1 January. There was rioting that year in England over the eleven lost days, as though life had been shortened by the change. It was not until the twentieth century that Russia and Turkey adopted this reckoning, and in the United Kingdom the financial year still begins on 5 April.

Overseas Records (other than American)

Right up to the year 1947, a quarter of the Earth's surface was under the British flag, forming the British Empire and Commonwealth. This has now dissolved and hardly any colony will remain to Britain by 1970. But the records of these many countries are still linked with those of Britain and some notes may be of assistance to inquirers. Each country of the Commonwealth keeps its own records as to births, marriages and deaths. In many countries these records date back for over 100 years, but in others only from the time of independence after the Second World War (1945).

Any citizen of a Commonwealth country seeking to trace his ancestors in the country from whence they came must first do so in whatever Commonwealth or former Commonwealth country he lives. Before he can start searching any records in the British Isles, it is essential that he be quite sure of the immigrant ancestor who left these islands. With this name, and any further information he may have as to place of origin, age at death etc. the inquirer will then have something concrete to go on. A very useful work is published by Her Majesty's Stationery Office as a guide to this type of record. It is entitled: *Abstract of Arrangements respecting Registrations of Births, Marriages and Deaths in the United Kingdom and the other countries of the British Commonwealth of Nations, and in the Irish Republic.* Editions have been published from 1904 to 1952 and cost a few shillings. Two cautions are necessary. The political changes in the Commonwealth may cause certain alterations in the whereabouts of records. Secondly, anyone using the *Abstract* should carefully consult both the appendix and index before writing to an address because there are in the main body of the work statements which require to be supplemented by those in the appendix. Particulars are given in this *Abstract* for the territories from Aden to Zanzibar. Of particular importance are the non-Anglican non-parochial registers listed above.

Turning now to registers likely to be of particular interest because of their overseas connection, there are the following which are kept at the General Register Office, Somerset House, London, WC2. (i) Records of events occurring at sea in merchant shipping or in the Royal Navy. (ii) Reports by the Irish Free State for 1924 to the General Register Office of events at sea. (iii) Army and Royal Air Force Returns, record of events occurring abroad. (iv) Events in India and Pakistan. (v) Returns from (former) Protectorates in Africa and Asia. (vi) Air Register Books maintained in accordance with the Civil Aviation Act, 1949, and containing record of births, deaths and missing persons from 1949. (vii) Records kept by British consuls abroad and other foreign records, including the many English Church chaplaincies overseas.

There is also a number of records which are not kept at Somerset House. These include (i) Details of baptisms, marriages, and burials, in foreign places; these are deposited at the London Diocesan Registry, 1 Dean's Court, Doctor's Commons, London, EC, and are mostly nineteenth-century records. (ii) The records of the Diocese of Gibraltar and the Lisbon Registers are with the Vicar General, 1 The Sanctuary, Westminster, London, SW1. (iii) Other ecclesiastical records of events outside the United Kingdom are kept at the Commonwealth Relations Office, King Charles Street, London, SW1.

Indian Records

Besides the records mentioned in the above *Abstract*, mostly dating from the last century, reference should be made to the records of the Honourable East India Company. This was a trading company granted a charter in 1601 by Elizabeth I to trade in India. Gradually it acquired wealth and influence and in the century from 1757 to 1857 it became the paramount power in India. After the Indian Mutiny of 1857, India was brought under the direct rule of the British Crown. In India there was a large Anglo-Indian community whose records come under those mentioned in (iv) (page 88). The records of the Honourable East India Company are invaluable for tracing any connections with India, and there are many books in the British Museum and in the Society of Genealogists which will also be of great assistance to any whose ancestors served in the Company. The records of the East India Company will be found in the India Office Library, Commonwealth Library, at 197 Blackfriars Road, London, SE11. Reference should also be made to India House, and to Pakistan House, in London.

Naval Records

Many of those employed by 'John Company', as the East India Company was called, served in the Company's army, so it is not inappropriate here to mention the records of the regular British Navy and Army, to which some reference has already been made. As regards the Navy, there are very large sources of MS information at the PRO, and in addition to these, which may be somewhat bewildering, there are printed works of reference on naval officers and their biographies, such as W. R. O'Byrne's *Naval Biographical Dictionary*, which goes back as far as 1845. There are also, of course, the *Navy Lists* of each year, for more modern careers.

Army Records

These are also at the PRO, but if they are not easily accessible—due to pressure of space or of time—there are useful collections of Army material at the Society of Genealogists. It may be added that the great help which the society renders to the researcher is to have assembled under one roof books which are available elsewhere but which, as at the British Museum, are not on the open shelves.

One final caution: fortunes in Chancery are often the objective of researchers' investigations. Many inquirers, both in America and in England, have set their hopes on fortunes held in Chancery for them by the kind thoughts of benevolent ancestors and only awaiting their claims. So much is this the case that the Supreme Court Pay Office, at the Royal Courts of Justice, Strand, London, WC2, have deemed it wise to issue a leaflet on the subject of 'Dormant Funds in Court'. If anyone thinks he has a claim to such a fund, application should be made to The Chief Accountant at the Supreme Court Pay Office. The leaflet stresses that any sums held are likely to be small, and an express warning is given against belief in the existence of unclaimed millions which simply are not there.

CHAPTER 6

Scottish Records

 ${\rm T}$ HE genealogy of every country is determined by the course of its history; conversely, the history of a country is elucidated by its genealogy. It was a great English genealogist, Sir Harris Nicolas, who said, 'It is asserted after much reflection, that there is scarcely an important fact in the annals of this country, but either had its origin or became intimately involved in a point of genealogy.' If true of England, it is also applicable to Scotland. The outsider thinks that 'Mac' is the distinctive sign of the Scotsman, whereas it indicated the Highland Scot who is of a quite different race from the Lowlander. Until a little over 200 years ago Highlanders were regarded by those Scots who lived in the Lowlands, in and below the waist of Scotland, rather as Americans in the eastern states would have viewed the Red Indians of the middle west. The Lowlander had little if any good to say of the Highlander. Some Lowlanders understood the economic hardships which often drove the Highlander to plunder his Lowland neighbour, but generally the men of the Highlands were to their southern compatriots, thieves, 'rievers', 'caterans', or plainly, scum. In fact, they were not always looked on as countrymen, and as late as the 1470s one of the greatest clan leaders, the Lord of the Isles, the MacDonald, head of the clan Donald, behaved as if he were independent of the King of Scots, and signed a treaty of alliance with the English king.

In addition to troubles with England and a 300-years war with that country, Scotland has also been vexed with Norse invasions. The perils and insecurity engendered by these difficulties, and the unsettled internal condition of much of Scotland, especially of the Highlands, has led to many Scottish records being destroyed, or removed to England. In consequence, many Scottish records begin later than their counterparts in England, though on the other hand they are in some respects better than those of England.

Registration of Births, Marriages and Deaths

This dates from 1855 in Scotland, and is on the same lines as the English system but with more detail in some respects. Why the system began eighteen years later than in England is not clear, but it should be remembered that Scotland, after the Act of Union with England in 1707, preserved her own legal system and a law passed at Westminster did not and still does not necessarily apply in Scotland. Thus there are numerous differences between both the legal systems and the laws of the two countries and these can have important consequences. For instance, a barrister in Scotland is usually termed an advocate, and a solicitor, a Writer to the Signet (WS). One of the most important genealogical results of the differing systems is that the Scots equivalent of the English Earl Marshal, the Lord Lyon, is a judge of the Court of Session, the Scots High Court of Justice. As such he can make his judgments prevail like any other High Court judge, and as he is in charge not only of heraldry but also of matters relating to claims to peerages and the chieftainship of clans, an enormous amount of genealogical information and genealogical decision is lodged in his office. The address is: The Rt Hon the Lord Lyon Kings of Arms, At His Court, HM Register House, Edinburgh, Scotland. Inquiries regarding matters of birth, marriage and death from 1855 should be made to: HM Registrar General, HM Register House, Edinburgh.

Parish Registers

These, as a general rule, do not go back as far as those in England, and in most cases are not earlier than 1700. They have one advantage over their English counterparts, that they are all kept in one place, HM Register House. If a bomb had fallen on this building in the last war, the history of Scotland would have been deprived of most of its original sources. The records can be searched and extracts made from them, as with the state records from 1855. The parishes mentioned in the registers are, of course, those of the Kirk of Scotland, the Established Presbyterian Church. There are over 900 such parishes.

Census Records

These are available from 1841, 1851, 1861 and 1871; forms of application and details of the rules for searching are obtainable from the Registrar General, The New Register House, Edinburgh.

Wills

Before 1836, wills were proved before the Commissary Courts, the old ecclesiastical courts similar to those in England which operated up to 1858. In 1830 the jurisdiction in matters relating to marriage, separation, divorce, and legitimacy was transferred to the Court of Sessions, and for alimony to the Sheriff Court. The records of the Commissary Courts are of great importance. They are listed below with dates for their earliest records:

1715 Aberdeen (though much was destroyed by fire in 1721)
1674 Argyll
1576 Brechin
1661 Caithness
1637 Dumfries
1539 Dunblane and Perth
1667 Dunkeld
1514 Edinburgh (where the records extend to 154 volumes)
1547 Glasgow
1564 Hamilton and Campsie

1630 Inverness
1661 The Isles
1663 Kirkcudbright
1595 Lanark
1561 Lauder
1684 Moray
1644 Orkney and Zetland
1681 Peebles
1802 Ross
1549 St Andrews
1607 Stirling
1700 Wigtown

Inquiries about wills should be addressed in the first instance to the Register House.

University Registers

These exist in printed form for the four ancient Scottish universities, Edinburgh, Glasgow, Aberdeen and St Andrews. In most cases the name of the undergraduate's father is given. Inquiry should be made of the chancellor of the university if the printed books are not accessible.

Kirk Session Records

These give information as to the date and the reason for a person leaving a parish. The records are in the keeping of the minister. Generally, letters of permission (or demission as they were called), had to be obtained before anyone could leave a parish.

Land Registers

In England, registration of title to possession of land is now being steadily extended all over the country, whereas in Scotland it has been the rule from at least the early seventeenth century. In consequence, there exists for Scotland a very large series of records of land sales, transfers etc, among which are those known as the Return of Heirs, or to give it its full name, 'Rettours of Services and of Heirs'. This is in three volumes and gives the inheritance of most of the landed property in Scotland from about 1500 to 1700. In these documents the relationship of the heir to the person from whom he inherits must be shown. Then there is the Register of Deeds, a collection of 621 volumes from 1554 to 1667, not all of which have been indexed. It contains all deeds which have a clause of consent to registration.

Scottish Societies

Very important here is The Scots Ancestry Research Society, 4a North St David Street, Edinburgh, 2. It was started in 1945 by the then Secretary of State for Scotland with the object of assisting persons of Scottish blood in tracing facts about their ancestors. Forms of application can be obtained from the Secretary.

The Scottish Genealogy Society is also of value to inquirers. The society meets monthly in the St Andrews Society Rooms, 24 Hill Street, (Castle Street end), Edinburgh. Inquiries should be made to The Secretary, at that address.

In addition, there are very many Scottish clubs which deal with archaeology and research, and publish records of their transactions which often contain details of a genealogical nature. Most of them could probably be contacted through the Society of Antiquaries of Scotland— itself a very worthwhile association, which publishes volumes of transactions of great interest—at the National Museum, Queen Street, Edinburgh.

Printed Books

It will be evident from what has been said that it is not as easy in Scotland as it is in England to trace beyond the sixteenth century. Nevertheless, owing to the clan system and the closer links in Scotland between members of a family, much useful information may be gleaned from printed books. It would be advisable for the beginner to know the main outlines of the history of Scotland and on this the best book is the four-volume work by Andrew Lang, now out of print but obtainable at second-hand or in libraries. Also useful is Brown's *History of Scotland*, a one-volume book and still likely to be in print. Scottish law terms necessarily occur in many pedigrees. They are far too numerous to be listed here, and the reader is recommended to *Principles of the Law of Scotland*, by John Erskine of Carnock, Advocate, whose book went through many editions and can usually be obtained second-hand. There is also a very good account of the Scots legal system in *Chambers' Encyclopedia*, while *Bartholomew's Gazetteer to the British Isles* is as useful for Scotland as for England or Ireland.

As to guides to family records, an excellent work with a preface by a former Lord Lyon, Sir James Balfour Paul, is *Scottish Family History*, (1930) in libraries or at second-hand. Written by Margaret Stuart, it is described as a 'Guide to Works of Reference on the History and Genealogy of Scottish Families'. A *Guide to the Public Records of Scotland Deposited in HM Register House, Edinburgh*, written by M. Livingstone, is, obviously, of great service, though not all of it will be of interest for genealogical purposes. The work is divided into four parts: (i) Crown, Parliament, Revenue, and Administration; (ii) Judicial Records, eg, like those of the Commissary Courts (see above); (iii) Crown Grants and Titles to Lands, Dignities and Offices. This section includes the Register of Sasines which denotes the same thing as the medieval English, seisin, the taking possession, of land. It is the ancient register of land transfers, which is mentioned above; (iv) Ecclesiastical and Miscellaneous Records and Documents; these include proceedings to relieve destitution in the Highlands, and these transactions of the aid given to emigrants to the British Colonies in and after 1857 may contain the names of those whose descendants have become wealthy in the USA.

Sir James Balfour Paul edited the *Scots Peerage*, which is in eight volumes with an index. The immense value of this work is that it gives not only the title holders but their family history as well, together with the names and such details as are available of the younger sons from whom so many people claim their descent. A book of great use, though to be employed with caution, is William Anderson's three-volume *Antiquity of the Scottish Nation*, which has the family history of every Scotsman of note up to 1840. Hew Scott's *Fasti Ecclesiae Scoticanae*, in seven volumes and produced between 1915 and 1928, gives the records of the Presbyterian clergy.

Many Scottish records were taken to England, but a list of those which remain is given in a *Calendar of Scottish Documents deposited in HM Public Record Office in London,* by Joseph Bain. Even without these, there are still at the Register House in Edinburgh about 60,000 manuscript volumes and the equivalent in bulk of unbound warrant and other papers.

Contrasted with those of England, Scottish surnames are few in number and it is possible to deal with them in one volume. This is well done in a book by Dr George F. Black, *The Surnames of Scotland, Their Origin, Meaning and History,* published in 1962 by the New York Public Library. This is a monumental work and it is to be doubted whether any Scots surname has escaped the author's research and erudition.

Scots heraldry and the Highland clan system are extremely important to the student of Scottish genealogy, and these are dealt with later in the sections allotted to these subjects.

CHAPTER 7

Records of Wales, the Isle of Man and the Channel Islands

FROM 1542 Wales has been united in an administrative union with England, and the genealogical sources from that period are much the same. In 1284 King Edward I of England had conquered Wales and annexed it to his dominions; he divided Wales into the county system but the old Welsh law continued to prevail. By this, the property in a family was divided under the arrangement known as gavelkind, ie, equal division among the sons in a family. Because of this, the Welsh placed great emphasis on pedigree and a Welshman could run off half-a-dozen names of his forbears thus: Ievan ap Caradoc ap Griffith ap Meurig ap Gwillim ap Morgan. Ap meant 'son of' and thus provided an easy way of recounting a pedigree while at the same time dispensing with a surname. When union with England came in 1542, English law prevailed and consequently the Welsh imitated the English usage in adopting surnames. This explains why so many Welsh folk have the same surname. Jones (son of John), Williams (son of Gwillim), Griffiths (son of Griffith), Price (ap Rhys), Powell (ap Howell) and so on. Thus the greatest families of Wales share with the lesser known families the most common surnames. As with many other medieval pedigrees, those of the Welsh princes and lords were linked by monastic chroniclers with the Biblical genealogies and with the great names of the old Roman province of Britain. In the case of the most famous Welsh families, the pedigrees are genuine from 900-1200 and are known as those of the *bon heddig*, or free men. To make a complete study of them and their development through medieval times to the present day, a knowledge of the Welsh language is essential, as well as acquaintance with the facts of Welsh economic and social history. As time passed, various schematic arrangements were worked out whereby great Welsh families were held to descend from the Five Royal Tribes of Wales, or the Fifteen

Noble Tribes of Wales, somewhat on the same lines as in the stories of the Scottish clans.

For the majority of Welsh inquirers, the year 1542 will be their terminus, and probably much later than that. Especially is this so in the industrialised south where the inhabitants, pressed by their economic necessities, have long lost interest in their genealogy and in their original language, whereas in the north of Wales interest in both has been maintained.

For those who can see the opportunity of tracing before 1542, there is the aid of the very large and growing collections in the National Library of Wales at Aberystwyth, founded 1907-09. The library is one of the six in the British Isles which has the privilege under the Copyright Acts of receiving a copy of every book published in Britain. In 1955 there were 1,500,000 books in the library, with 30,000 volumes of manuscript and about 3,500,000 deeds. Much no doubt has since been added to these.

This library also has the finest collection of Welsh manuscripts ever brought under one roof, much of the material having been transferred from the Public Record Office in London to Wales. Some works of reference are essential to enable the inquirer to find a way through the riches of this great collection. There is a general guide to the library in pamphlet form by the National Library, under the title, *The National Library of Wales, A Brief Summary of its History and its activities*. Of particular interest to Americans will be *A Bibliography of Welsh Americana*, by Henry Blackwell of New York, edited and with an introduction by William Williams, 1942. *The Department of Manuscripts and Records in the National Library of Wales*, by E. D. Jones, 1947, is also of great assistance.

A large number of valuable genealogical collections have been bestowed upon the National Library by various individuals, and among its benefactors is the Honourable Society of Cymmrodorion. This society was founded in 1751 for the 'Encouragement of Literature, Science and Art as connected with Wales'. In 1951 it received a royal charter and is under the patronage of the Queen. The transactions of the society contain much information about Welsh genealogy, and the proceedings are published annually, most of the papers being in English but some in Welsh. A history covering the first 200 years of the society was published some years ago. The address of the secretary and of the society is: Ben G. Jones, LLB, Hon Sec, The Hon Society of Cymmrodorion, 118 Newgate Street, St Paul's, London, EC1.

Other Welsh Manuscripts

There are Welsh manuscripts stored in Bangor University College Library and the Cardiff Public Library. The Bodleian Library, Oxford, and the British Museum Library in London both have some early Welsh genealogical records. The Harleian Mss, which contain some Welsh papers, are in the British Museum Library, which has much other Welsh material. A catalogue of Welsh Mss was compiled by Edward Owen, and there are also the collections of Randle Holme, with pedigrees of many Welsh families. The Society of Genealogists has a large Welsh section, and most of the printed calendars which give an index to Welsh Mss are in the society's archives. Other useful material for the Welsh researcher are a *Report on Mss in the Welsh Language*, a volume issued by the Historical Manuscripts Commission; a list of Welsh wills proved 1601-78 at the Carmarthen Probate Registry; an index to the wills of the Peculiar of Hawarden; sixty-five volumes of pedigrees made by the Rev Thomas Williams; Sir Joseph Bradney's *History of Monmouthshire* and the *List of Parish Registers of the Diocese of Llandaff*.

Welsh Wills

These were proved in the Probate Courts of the four, ancient Welsh bishoprics and their dispositions are as follows: Bangor, in the Probate Registry; Llandaff, which includes wills of the diocese of Hereford at Llandaff; St Asaph at Bangor; St David's at Carmarthen. In each case, inquiry should be made of The Secretary, The Diocesan Registry, Bangor, or whichever is the diocese.

Welsh Records in the PRO London

Owing to the interrelation of Welsh and English affairs, many matters of interest to Welsh searchers occur in the medieval English records already mentioned. A useful source of information is the work by M. S. Giuseppi, *A Guide to the Mss Preserved in the Public Record Office* (1923). On pages 317-24 account is given of the records of Wales. From the latter part of the reign of Edward I, assizes were held in Wales and some of the assize rolls are in the records of the King's Bench and others in those of the Court of the Exchequer. After the union in 1542, Courts of Great Sessions were established, and four counties—Brecknock, Radnor, Denbigh and Montgomery—were added to the eight counties anciently set up by Edward I. Under the statutes of 1543 and 1544, sessions were held in each of the counties twice yearly, and the ensuing legal records are useful for genealogical details.

(i) Equity records, from the Chester, North Wales, Brecon and Carmarthen circuits, consisting of decrees, exhibits and pleadings. (ii) Common Law records, including Calendar Rolls from Henry VIII to Charles II, with abstracts of coroners' inquests for Radnor, Glamorgan, Cardigan and Pembroke; Fines and Recoveries from Henry VIII to William IV (1830-37); Jail Files; Henry VIII to William IV; and Plea Rolls which are not earlier than 1485, though the section on Ruthin records is from 1343. (iii) There is a mass of miscellanea, with 249 bundles and volumes from 1327 to 1830.

In the PRO, is the Golden Grove Book, consisting of three volumes and an index with a wealth of genealogical information. A transcript is in the National Library.

The Isle of Man

The Isle of Man is not bound by Acts of the United Kingdom Parliament unless specifically stated, as it has its own parliament, the Tynwald. The authority to consult is the Registrar General, Government Office, Douglas, Isle of Man. Wills are kept with the Probate Registry (of Deeds), Finch Road, Douglas. At the Registry of Deeds, (same address) will be found title deeds to real estate etc. At this centre will be found also some entries of baptism, marriage and burial before 1849, the date of compulsory registration in the island.

The Channel Islands

These comprise Jersey, Guernsey, Alderney, Sark, Herm, Jethou and Brechou. Jersey has the States of Jersey, likewise Guernsey has its States; on the latter the remaining five islands are dependent.

Jersey: Records of births, marriages and deaths are kept by the Superintendent Registrar, States' Building, St Helier, Jersey. Details of baptisms, funerals and marriages can be obtained from the Dean, St Saviour, Jersey, or on application to the incumbent of the parish concerned (see *Crockford's Clerical Directory*). Wills of real estate are registered in the Royal Court of the island, but wills of personalty in the Probate Division. Wills in the Public Registry of Contracts may be inspected on application to the States' Building, St Helier.

Guernsey, Alderney and Sark: The Registrar General's Office, Greffe,

Guernsey, has the record of births and deaths since 1840, of marriages from 1919 and of non-Church of England marriages since 1840. In the case of baptisms, marriages, and burials before 1840, application must be made to the parish or minister concerned. For the records of Alderney, application should be made to the Registrar General of Guernsey, as also for wills of realty; copies of wills of personalty are kept by the Registrar to the Ecclesiastical Court, 9, Lefebvre Street, St Peter Port, Guernsey. With regard to Sark, an interesting work, *The Story of Sark*, published in 1956 by A. R. de Carteret, gives the names of the original settlers. The De Carterets were settlers in the reign of Elizabeth I (1558-1603), and the island remains a feudal economy under the rule of the Dame of Sark, Mrs S. M. Hathaway, OBE.

Celtic Languages

Since it is impossible for the researcher into Welsh, Irish or Scottish Highland pedigrees not to encounter documents in languages other than English, Norman French or Latin, he should know what is meant by the term 'Celtic languages'. Professor Emrys Jones, in the Session 1967, Part I of the transactions of the Honourable Society of Cymmrodorion, has a very interesting paper, 'The Changing Distribution of the Celtic Languages in the British Isles' in which he writes: 'There are the six languages, in two groups: Scottish Gaelic, Irish Gaelic and Manx, Welsh, Cornish and Breton. Confining this paper to the British Isles, I shall say nothing about the distribution of Breton.' Neither need the researcher working on material in the British Isles. Cornish has ceased to be spoken since the early part of last century, though there is an effort to revive it. Manx has now hardly any native speakers, though in 1901 there were 4,500. Today there are only 75,508 Gaelic speakers. In 1961 there were 659,000 Welsh speakers. In Ireland, there has been a determined effort by the government since 1921, when Ireland became independent of England, to encourage Irish speaking. Everywhere in Ireland one sees notices in Irish, and a knowledge of the language is obligatory for those holding posts in the government service. Yet, as Professor Jones points out: 'It is almost impossible to estimate accurately the number of people to whom Irish is a mother tongue, but it is probably between 25,000 and 35,000 and they are found in the extreme west. Looking again at those areas where a majority speak Irish, we can see how they have progressively diminished during the last hundred years.'

The important factor is that there are persons who still speak Gaelic,

Welsh and Irish, not only the native speakers but others, too, who have learned them as a second language. Thus there are people who can help in the interpretation of documents in these Celtic tongues.

Latin Documents

After the fall of Rome, Latin still existed as the official language, largely because the Catholic Church used Latin in the services and in all her documents. Latin continued as the language of the only educated class, the clergy and the monks. Probably it was only in England that a literature in the vernacular had grown up by the eleventh century; the foundation upon which modern English literature has been built. The Norman Conquest interrupted this and led to a period of depression for English writers, from which they eventually emerged to resume the natural development of English.

Before the Conquest, many official documents were written in English but after 1066 they were written in Latin or a curious mixture, Norman French. This persisted until 1731 in the English law courts and has contributed many terms to English law, including words of such universal employment as 'culprit' (short for 'he is taken, ie, and we are ready to prove his guilt'). There was more reason for the use of Latin, since it was the language of all educated western Europeans. Thus, even Sir Isaac Newton's great work, the *Principia* (1687), was in Latin, and right up to the first half of the nineteenth century a scholar who produced an edition of a Greek or Latin author was expected to write all his comments and notes in Latin. In fact, it is not an advantage that Latin has ceased to be the medium for general communication among the learned. As regards documents in England, it had ceased to be used for all official purposes before the end of the medieval period but the researcher must be prepared to encounter it during several centuries.

For those who have no Latin, work is likely to be confined to the seventeenth century and after, unless they employ professional searchers. Even the good classical scholar has to realize that medieval Latin is a development from the older classical sources. It contains many words not used by the Romans, the spelling of classical words is often varied, and the grammar is at times a little away from the rules. Reading medieval Latin is rather like an encounter with Winston Churchill's French, very fluent, equipped with a large vocabulary, but with a curious pronunciation and quite probably an occasional divorce from the rules of grammar. Anyone reading medieval Latin will agree with Milton as to the use of words which would have made Quintillian stare and gasp. The best course for anyone who is coming to read Latin charters, writs etc, is to study an excellent book by Eileen A. Gooder, *Latin for Local History* (1961), which goes right through the grammar, showing the differences between classical and medieval Latin, with examples from Domesday Book to the sixteenth century, and includes a very useful word list which goes far to explain many terms likely to puzzle the inquirer. Generally speaking, however, no one who has a fair ground-work of Latin from his schooldays is likely to be seriously put out by the type of Latin met in records.

Styles of Handwriting

In former days these varied a great deal and many are liable to hold up the inquirer. The quickest way to solve this difficulty is to ask one of the professional searchers to translate the document into modern writing. Such searchers are listed in places like the PRO and have a regular tariff of fees. Alternatively, the searcher can, if he has extensive work to do, learn to read the old handwriting. *Court Hand Restored*, a good book on the subject by a man named Wright, was in its ninth edition in 1879, and presumably a second-hand copy could be obtained or may be seen in libraries. For Scotland, a useful work is *Facsimiles of the National Manuscripts of Scotland* in three volumes, also to be consulted in libraries. In the *Genealogist's Handbook*, published by the Society of Genealogists, examples are given of letters of the seventeenth century which are found in parish registers. As regards documents of an earlier period, the handwriting, once learnt, will be found to conform to established patterns and be fairly easy to make out. In this connection a useful small work, *How to Read Local Archives, 1550-1700*, by F. G. Emmison, County Archivist of Essex, is published by the Historical Association. Costing only a few shillings, it is not only good as an intro-duction but enables the reader to go on to more detailed studies.

CHAPTER 8

Irish Records

IRISH records have been very much governed by the history of the country. Until 6 December 1921 the whole of Ireland was under British rule, but after that date it became two countries. The six northern counties—Antrim, Armagh, Down, Fermanagh, Londonderry, and Tyrone—are known as Ulster, and the Government of Northern Ireland, or Ulster, is under the British Crown and sends MPs to Westminster. The rest of the counties of Ireland, twenty-six in all, then formed Eire, which some years later declared itself as the Republic of Ireland, and is completely independent of Great Britain. Belfast is the capital of Northern Ireland, Dublin of the Republic.

The English had been connected with Ireland from the time of Henry II (1166-72), when the Anglo-Norman barons, followed by the King himself, invaded Ireland and set up English rule. Effective control over the whole country eluded the English government until almost the end of the Tudor period. After that, there were a number of rebellions against the British Crown until, following the outbreak of terrorism by the Irish Sinn Feiners in 1918-21, the British government granted independence to the twenty-six counties.

The Irish remained Catholic at the Reformation, while England and Scotland became Protestant, and when, later, the northern province of Ulster was cleared of its native inhabitants, these were replaced by English and Scots settlers whose descendants remain to this day. The other provinces of Ireland are Leinster, Munster, and Connaught. The greatest of the Irish families were kings of these provinces, with the strongest of them as High King. Under the centuries of alien rule, and the difference in religion, many Irish families changed their surname to an English equivalent. Thus O'Cahane became Keane; O'Gowan became Smith, Maelseachlainn was Anglicised as McLoughlin. In other cases the Irish O' or Mac was dropped, resulting eg, in Kelly or Lysaght instead of O'Kelly or MacLysaght. Many of the Norman families which had settled in Ireland became very Irish, and the common Irish name of Burke is derived from the Norman de Burgo. Many English names are borne by Irishmen now in the Republic, and while there have been changes of name, the majority of the English-style names are probably derived from English settlers, like those soldiers of Cromwell or William of Orange who received land grants in Ireland. In the former ruling class of Ireland —'the old ascendancy', the peers and landed gentry—where the knowledge of pedigree has been maintained, the links with England and Scotland are not broken and most of them adhere to the Protestant faith, or at least are not Catholics. One sometimes sees references to the Duke of Wellington as an Irishman, a curious failure to understand psychology since that famous duke was essentially the stiff upper lip, no nonsense type of Englishman. As well make out a European born in Japan to be a Japanese.

From this brief notice of Ireland's turbulent history it will be clear that there are many gaps in the Irish records. By a wretched irony of fate, after the connection with Britain had been severed, quarrels broke out between the Republicans themselves. On 13 April 1922, the Public Record Office in Dublin, housed in a building called the Four Courts, was occupied by armed men and the history of Ireland, in the form of irreplacable manuscripts, was used to barricade the windows. In the subsequent fire, the records went up in flames. It has been observed that a parallel to the catastrophe in England would have involved the loss of the contents of the PRO and of Somerset House, plus the parish registers and the bishops' transcripts. The Irish parish registers, like those of Scotland, were collected together in one place and thus in one disaster no less than 817 were destroyed. All researches into Irish genealogy have to contend with this major difficulty and, although the loss cannot be made good, it has stimulated the efforts of Irish genealogists to find other sources of information.

Northern Ireland

It will be as well first to deal with the records of Northern Ireland. Before 1921, the Registrar General in Dublin kept the record of births, marriages and deaths for all Ireland. After 1921, a separate department was created for Northern Ireland. The address: The Registrar General, General Register Office, Fermanagh House, Ormean Avenue, Belfast. This office has records of births, marriages and deaths since 1921, also census returns for 1931 and 1951 (there was no census in 1941). A Public Record Office was created in 1923, and the Minister of Finance is *ex-*

officio Keeper of the Records. The permanent official is called Deputy Keeper, and to him all inquiries should be sent, addressed to the Public Record Office of Northern Ireland, May Street, Belfast. The records preserved go back in some cases before 1921 and include copies of wills for Northern Ireland district probate registries from 1838, and original wills from 1910. Many families, with pedigrees back to 1600, have given their private papers to the Office, and copies of some of the parish registers destroyed in Dublin are in Belfast. Presbyterian families should seek information from the Secretary, Church House, Belfast. There is also the Ulster Scot Historical Society, Law Courts Building, Chichester Street, Belfast. The inquirer whose ancestry is from Northern Ireland should certainly search the Record Office in Belfast but much of the desired information may be in Dublin.

The Republic of Ireland

Despite the great loss of records, the descendant of Irish emigrant stock can usually rely on tracing his ancestry for three generations. As a start to research, it is advisable to visit the locality where the family is known to have originated, a procedure followed by the late President Kennedy, in the course of which he discovered numerous cousins. Should anyone in the district remember the family, an affidavit can be obtained and will be accepted in a law court as proving the existence of, eg, the grandfather of the emigrant.

Births, Marriages and Deaths

These had to be registered from 1 January 1864, and the information is in the Registrar General's Office, Custom House, Dublin, where there are also records of all Protestant marriages from 1845.

Public Record Office

This was established in 1867 and the address is: The Deputy Keeper, Public Record Office of Ireland, The Four Courts, Dublin. Census returns were of great importance in Ireland, as in England, in bridging the gap between registration from 1864 and the period before this date. The census was first taken in Ireland in 1813, though after that it followed the same dates as the English system; and it was from the returns kept in the PRO before 1922 that old people were able to prove their age when the Old Age Pension Act was passed in 1908. Only remnants of the returns now remain. There are twenty-three volumes for county Antrim for 1851; fourteen volumes of the 1821 census for county Cavan; and six volumes for county Derry for the 1831 reckoning.

Parish Registers

Due to the depressed state of the Catholics, few of their priests were able to keep registers and reference to a parish register generally means to one kept by the Protestant Episcopal Church of Ireland. Owing to the English control of Ireland, the Protestant Reformation was made to apply to it. The buildings and endowments of the Church in Ireland therefore remained, and still remain, in the hands of the Protestants. The Irish Protestant Episcopal Church was disestablished in 1869, and its parochial records were constituted public records, under Acts of Parliament passed in 1875-77. The parish registers ought, therefore, to have been placed in the PRO, where they might well have been destroyed. Fortunately, there was a clause in the Act which enabled a parish clergyman to keep his parish records provided he could prove that he had a proper place of storage for them. This meant that more than 600 parishes still had their registers when the destruction of the Four Courts took place. These are mostly with the Protestant clergy, for whose addresses consult *Crockford's Clerical Directory*, or *Thom's Directory of Ireland* (Crow Street, Dublin).

The keeping of parochial registers in Ireland was ordered in 1634, but few registers are of that age. For various reasons, the names of Catholics can be found in the Protestant registers. With Catholic registers, very **few go back before the nineteenth century**, though some are 200 years old. Some registers exist for other religious bodies. The Baptist Church in Cork, for example, has a lot of information about the Riggs family, including the fact that Edward Riggs was married three times, though only one marriage is known from other sources. As usual, Quaker records are well kept and considerable family information is available in the registers of the Society of Friends. Also in Cork, the Unitarian Church has registers dating back to 1717, as well as minutes of church meetings with genealogical information beginning in 1600.

Wills

For many centuries these were proved in the church courts; in the diocesan courts when a man's property was in only one diocese but, when the property was in more than one diocese, the will was proved in the Prerogative Court of the Archbishop of Armagh. From 1858, as in England, the wills were proved in a special Probate Court. Even now, the PRO possesses over 300,000 Irish wills, the biggest collection in Ireland. From 1904 the collection is complete, and almost complete from 1858 for the district registries. Of the wills proved in the old church courts, only eleven of the Prerogative Court wills were saved in 1922, and only one of the diocesan wills. Some will books saved contain copies of wills, in a few cases from the seventeenth century. About 10,000 wills which had not been given to the PRO before 1922 have now been deposited there and card-indexed. Quite a large number of abstracts of wills are at the PRO. In the Genealogical Office in Dublin Castle there are abstracts of all the Prerogative Court wills before 1800, together with abstracts of the diocesan court wills of Dublin, Cork and Water-ford. These abstracts were made for genealogical purposes and contain the essential information in the will, stripped of all unnecessary wording.

The Registry of Deeds

Owing to the frequent changes in the ownership of land, it was necessary for records to be preserved. From 1708, abstracts exist of all transactions over landed property and these are kept by The Secretary, The Registry of Deeds, The Four Courts, Dublin.

Court Records

These provide much useful information, as most notable families have been involved in law suits. The following were in a fireproof room in 1922: the bill books of the Chancery Division; the judgment books of the Common Law Courts; and the bankruptcy petition registers.

Convert Rolls

These cover the period from 1703 to 1772 and give the names of Catholics who were converted to Protestantism, mainly in order to save their property. These Rolls are in manuscript volumes, the work of John Lodge and, along with many other valuable manuscripts of his, are in the PRO.

The Genealogical Office

For 400 years the Office of Ulster King of Arms was in Dublin Castle. The Ulster King was in charge of heraldic matters in Ireland from 1552 to 1940, when the last Ulster King of Arms to work in Dublin Castle died. In 1943, the then Premier of Ireland, Mr Eamon de Valera, wished to terminate the tenure of the Dublin Castle Office by the Ulster King, and the office of Ulster was then united by the British Crown with that of Norroy King of Arms, in England. The Norroy and Ulster King of Arms has jurisdiction over the six northern counties. In the Republic, De Valera set up the office of Chief Herald of Ireland, and he occupies the Ulster Office in the Castle and carries out the same duties as the former tenant. After over 400 years of record keeping, the Office contains rich genealogical material and it would be impossible to overestimate its value to an Irish searcher. To mention a few of the records in this Office: (i) *Linea Antiqua*, compiled by Roger O'Ferrall in 1709, which gives information about the pedigrees of the ancient Celtic Irish families. (ii) The Mss collection of Sir William Beetham, Ulster King (1820-53), twenty-four volumes recording pedigrees and over thirty volumes of chart pedigrees based on wills; (iii) abstracts made by Beetham of all the Irish Prerogative intestate administrations before 1800. (iv) Funeral Entries; in former days the heralds had to arrange for the funerals of distinguished persons, and the ensuing records contain much genealogical data. (v) Grants of arms which fill many volumes. (vi) Registered pedigrees likewise occupy numerous volumes. (vii) Visitations, of which only three were held in Ireland, those of Dublin in 1568 and 1607, and of county Wexford in 1618.

Other Sources of Information

Printed sources are of varied quality. A work which is very often mentioned in connection with Irish pedigrees is O'Hart's *Irish Pedigrees, The Origin and Stem of the Irish Nation*, published in 1875 by John O'Hart. It gives unbridled rein to the Milesian pedigrees, with descents from Adam. Statements in it must always be checked against other sources, but it is useful in the more modern portions. *Burke's Landed Gentry of Ireland* first existed as a publication separate from the *Landed Gentry of Great Britain* in 1899. The other editions are of 1904, 1912, and 1958. A great deal of critical effort was put into the last two editions, and the result is a very good collection of pedigrees. An example of the use of this type of publication to the overseas inquirer is seen in the genealogy of the O'Tooles (meaning 'son of Tuathal'), who descend from the King of Leinster in AD 950. The name is now usually Toole and the present head of the family is living in Canada, although he owns the ancestral property. Another useful source of information is *Lodge's*

Peerage of Ireland, by John Lodge, published in 1754 and republished with additions by the Rev Mervyn Archdall in 1798. The *Peerage* gives details of many lines of families only of distant connection with the Irish peers, and herein lies the great value of the work because, more often than not, it is precisely these obscure individuals who are passed over by the majority of works on such subjects.

That the 1958 edition of *Burke's Landed Gentry of Ireland* should ever be published would have seemed wildly improbable to those who lived in the 1921-39 period. The previous edition of 1912 was published when the British Empire was still in full strength, and when the present Irish Republic was a relatively minor part of the United Kingdom. The 1914-18 war, the subsequent economic difficulties in Britain, and the terrible troubles in Ireland in 1916-21, all militated against the continuance of the Irish landed gentry. In the 1937 edition of *Burke's Landed Gentry*, an Irish supplement of some 200 pages was included, with the underlying assumption that nothing could be done to produce a whole volume of Irish pedigrees. The second world war would seem to have given the last blow to any such project. However, with the reappearance of *Burke's Peerage* and of *Burke's Landed Gentry* (of Great Britain), there seemed some possibility of another Irish work. If ever a book answered to popular demand it was this. Clearly the Irish landed gentry refused to die. Many of them still possessed ancestral properties, and many more possessed family pride. Besides this, the effort made by Irish genealogists had borne fruit, and much material was available to assist in overcoming the gaps caused by the fires of 1922. The 1958 edition accordingly includes about 800 families; many of the very old Celtic families (now often landless) are included, together with a large number of the old ascendancy and some who, in recent years, have come from the Continent to make their home in Ireland. The result is a valuable addition to genealogical and heraldic knowledge. The book is prefaced by a series of useful articles on various matters of interest to Irish searchers: 'The Irish Genealogies', by Professor David Greene, gives an account of the ancient Milesian pedigrees; 'Irish Surnames' are handled by Dr Edward MacLysaght, and there are articles on the royal peers of Ireland; Irishmen in the British military service, the Bench and Bar in Ireland, and on the Irish Genealogical Society.

Alumni Dublinenses gives the record of all persons entered as students of Trinity College, Dublin and is of enormous value to the genealogist, since it records, wherever possible, the particulars of the undergraduate's father. It was compiled by two first-class genealogists; G. D. Burtchael, at one time Deputy Ulster and the careful analyst of the pedigrees in the

1912 edition of the *Landed Gentry of Ireland*; and T. U. Sadleir, who was Deputy Ulster after Burtchael and, from 1940-43, Acting Ulster. Very many sons of the old Protestant ascendancy went to Trinity College (abbreviated TCD).

D'Altons *King James's Irish Army List*, 1689, gives particulars of Irish officers and their families who settled in France and Spain after the battle of the Boyne (1690). A very large number of Irishmen became soldiers in the Continental armies, many of them rising to distinction. Descendants have in some cases returned to Ireland, as with the O'Kellys, and this list helps to check many details in earlier pedigrees.

Newspapers are of especial importance and fortunately there was one which began in 1763 and continued until 1924. This was the *Public Monitor, or Freeman's Journal*. It contains a vast number of entries about people, very often of well-known families. The files are kept at the National Library of Ireland, and the indexing of the newspaper's contents is being done by convicts, long-term prisoners of good education at Portlaoghise Prison. The work began in 1954 and it is estimated that it will take twenty years to complete, with some three million cards as the final result. Walker's *Hibernian Magazine* was also published from 1771-1812, and an index to Irish marriages recorded in its pages was compiled by Henry Farrar and printed in England in 1897.

Among libraries, the greatest in Ireland is that of Trinity College, Dublin. Under the Copyright Acts of the United Kingdom six libraries are entitled to receive one copy of every book published in the United Kingdom and TCD still remains one of these libraries, although it is no longer in the United Kingdom. The National Library of Ireland is in Kildare Street, Dublin, and has some 14,000 manuscript volumes, many of which are of genealogical interest. The indexing of this material was begun some years ago. Of special interest, too, are a document, *Forfeited Estates of 1688*, and, *The Book of Postings and Sales of Forfeited and Other Estates and Interests in Ireland*. The latter gives the names of persons who had owned the estates before the war of 1689-90 and who were deprived or forced to sell; the names of the new owners are also given. The library has large collections of Irish newspapers of 200-300 years ago.

In the Royal Irish Academy there is a manuscript, *The Books of Survey and Distribution*, compiled in 1677, which gives an account of all land in Ireland. The rebellion of 1640 was ultimately suppressed by Cromwell, and this document gives the names of the old owners of land in 1640, very many of whom were dispossessed. The address of the Royal Irish Academy is 19 Dawson Street, Dublin.

As Ireland is predominantly a Catholic country, not many Irishmen are masons, but there is a good masonic organisation with headquarters in Dublin; the address is: Grand Secretary's Office, Freemasons' Hall, 17 Molesworth Street, Dublin. Many persons belonging to the old landed families were masons and some genealogies are heavily indebted to masonic records.

The Irish State Papers Office in Record Tower, Dublin Castle, contains records of affairs of state, but there is also much genealogical information as many Irish families were in trouble with the authorities.

The affairs of Ireland, like those of Scotland, being so much inter-twined with those of England, many sources of information on Irish matters are to be found in the British Museum Library, and in the Lambeth Palace Library, London, the town house of the Archbishops of Canterbury.

Irish Families, Their Names, Arms, and Origins, by Dr Edward Mac-Lysaght should be seen by all persons of Irish descent. The author was the first holder of the post of Chief Herald of Ireland. His work has been produced in three volumes, separately by different publishers, and con-tains a wealth of information. Again, the user should always remember that the identity of his name with that of a great or historic family does not necessarily mean that he has a common ancestry with that family. Dr MacLysaght has also published a book on Irish Surnames.

The Irish Genealogical Research Society was founded in 1936 and has the following aims: (a) to promote and encourage the study of Irish genealogy; (b) to collect manuscripts and books of genealogical value and, above all, existing copies of records of particular interest to the family historian, which were destroyed at the PRO, Dublin, 1922; (c) to card-index the contents of all manuscripts acquired by the society. Meetings of the society are held at the Irish Club, 82 Eaton Square, London, SW1, to which inquiries should be addressed. A magazine, *The Irish Genealogist,* is issued.

To encourage those who may feel depressed by the references to the loss of Irish records, two Irish achievements can be recorded. The best family history I have ever read was of one of the Anglo-Norman families long resident in Ireland, and which may therefore be assumed to have run the gauntlet of the destruction of Irish records from various causes and in various places. It is the history of the Segraves, a family which began with Thomas de Segrave, described in the Domesday Book as part owner of Segrave in Leicestershire, England, whence the family took its name. Before 1400, the Segraves were large landowners in

Ireland, and Cabragh Castle, built by them, remained in their possession until 1912, over 500 years' ownership. The family history is a model of its kind because it assumes nothing, takes nothing for granted, states no legend or hearsay as fact, but proves every step of the pedigree. There is not the slightest attempt to extend the antiquity of the family beyond the limits of ascertained fact. The family has an article in the 1937 supplement to *Burke's Landed Gentry*. The author of the book, Charles William Segrave, was father of the famous racing motorist, Sir Henry Segrave, who was killed in 1930 in an attempt to beat the world's speed record on water. Luck played some part in bringing about this extremely well authenticated pedigree, as Mr Segrave had seen boxes of his family records lying about in out of the way places on the family property. Similar good fortune could be the lot of other inquirers.

In the second instance, that of Viscount Valentia, a much more difficult task was successfully essayed—the achievement of an old Irish peerage with an old Irish baronetcy as well. In the present century succession had passed to cousins on two occasions. Thus in 1949 the 12th Viscount died unmarried and his titles were assumed by his kinsman, the Rev William Monckton Annesley, who descended from the 1st Viscount but was distant from the line of the 12th Viscount. This 13th Viscount died without issue in 1951, and without having proved his claim to the viscounty and baronetcy. The task then fell to the new 14th Viscount who had to prove his own and his predecessors' claims. In 1959 he established his succession, having had the difficult duty of proving negatives as regards the descent and extinction of kinsfolk back in the preceding centuries, for unless they could be shown to have died without leaving male issue, the 14th Viscount could not have made good his claim. That he did so is a tribute to his own abilities and to the rewards which pertinacious effort can win from the depleted Irish records.

H

CHAPTER 9

Continental Records

IN dealing with Continental records we need to bear in mind three factors: (1) Europe can be divided into two sections, (a) that of the old Latin Christendom and (b) the area of Greek Christianity—covering Greece itself, Russia, and the Balkan countries. The only Slav people within the Latin or Roman Catholic fold are the Poles. (2) In the Latin or western portion of Europe the conditions mentioned in connection with England apply—in broad outlines—so that we have the breakdown of the Roman Empire, followed by the growth of barbarian kingdoms upon its ruins, the rise of feudalism, and the consequent development therefrom of the modern and democratic civilisation. This is, of course a generalisation, subject like all generalisations to many modifications. The Scandinavian states and most of Germany were never within the Roman Empire, so that the records of these lands are free from direct Latin influence until a late period. Then, too, England was unlike the Latin countries—France, Spain, Portugal, Italy etc—in that a complete breakdown of the old civilisation occurred, whereas in the Latin countries the Latin languages and many customs continued. Even so, it has not been possible to connect the western European princely lines with Roman predecessors, with the possible exception of Charlemagne's descent from St Arnulf. (3) The history of most European states has been much more disturbed than that of England, and many of them have suffered from centuries of disunion.

Factors (1) and (2) are clearly of great importance for the keeping of records. England was at last united by the Norman Conquest of 1066, and France was also a united country in the twelfth century. Spain was not one country for another 400 years, Germany and Italy not until 1870; the Netherlands (Holland) became free from Spain by a convulsive effort in the sixteenth and seventeenth centuries. The country now called Belgium remained Catholic and under Spanish rule until in 1713, by the Peace of Utrecht which closed the war of the Spanish succession, it became the Austrian Netherlands under the control of the Austrian branch of the Habsburg dynasty. After the Napoleonic wars Belgium was united for a short time with Holland until it became an independent state in 1830. Luxembourg, the third of the present Benelux countries (ie, Belgium, Netherlands and Luxembourg), was part of the Duchy of Burgundy, then passed to the Spanish Habsburgs in 1555, and in 1713 to the Austrian branch. Eventually, after a period following the Napoleonic wars when it passed between Holland and Belgium, it became in 1890 a dukedom ruled by a branch of the House of Nassau. Austria itself is now a small state with a capital city quite disproportionate to the area of the country; Vienna until 1918 was the capital of the Austria-Hungarian Empire, ruled by the Austrian Habsburgs, and included not only the present separate countries of Austria and Hungary, but also the new country of Czechoslovakia, the state which now includes the old Bohemia, Moravia and parts of Silesia and Slovakia.

The Austrian Empire was the successor state to the Holy Roman Empire which, though elective, became hereditary in the Habsburgs. Switzerland as a political unit originated as far back as 1291, when some of the cantons formed a league against the Austrians. The Swiss League grew in strength from the defeats it inflicted on the Austrians and, later on, the Duke of Burgundy. By 1499 practical independence had been gained from the Empire. Germany was a collection of kingdoms until one of them, Prussia, had, by 1870, become strong enough to weld Germany together as an empire. In the same year Italy was at last united under the rule of the House of Savoy. The Dukes of Savoy had become Kings of Sardinia and of Piedmont. The Papal States, which dated back 1,000 years, stretched across Italy from sea to sea, but in 1870 they were taken over by the Italian state. Behind this unification is a mosaic of small Italian states, and some not so small, such as Venice, whose influence reached far into the Levant, as anyone can see by reading the Travels of Marco Polo who, in the thirteenth century journeyed across Asia from the Venetian trading posts on the Black Sea to the court of the Great Khan at Peking.

The Slavonic countries—Albania, Bulgaria, Rumania, Yugoslavia—together with Greece, were all under Turkish rule until they freed themselves in the last century. Yugoslavia as such emerged after the 1918 war; it is a union of six republics—Serbia, Croatia, Slovenia, Boznia and Herzegovina, Macedonia and Montenegro. Other small states whose independence has been late, precarious and short-lived are the Baltic countries—Lithuania, Latvia and Estonia—now under the domination of Soviet Russia. As may be imagined records in the Balkan countries are not *prima facie* likely to be extensive, they have very little in the form of independent archives, and what records exist are under the control of the assortment of rulers they have known—Germans, Poles, Swedes and Russians. Then again, Russian records prior to the revolution of 1918 are not accessible, though there is good reason to suppose that they are well preserved. Politics tend to impede genealogical studies in any Communist-controlled state.

It need not, however, be assumed that all documents of the medieval past in Europe are defective or lost, though the searcher must bear in mind the history of these countries and the possibility of the records having been destroyed. In certain European countries, some of the records are older than their counterparts in England. This is so in Spain, where in quite a large number of cases parochial records antedate the orders made for the keeping of such records by the Council of Trent (1545-63). In Luxembourg, many records exist in registries back to the seventeenth century.

THE SCANDINAVIAN COUNTRIES

Beginning with northern Europe, there are five Scandinavian countries whose records are on the whole well preserved. These lands are Norway, Denmark, Iceland, Sweden and Finland. I have linked Iceland with Denmark and Finland with Sweden, because these countries were formerly united. Norway, Denmark and Sweden have much in common both linguistically and in their history. The descents of the Norsemen on other lands were principally from Norway and Denmark, while the Swedes tended to seek an outlet in Russia. After the cohesion of England under the Norman kings, the Norsemen turned their attention to the Baltic area. At length, in 1397, the Union of Kalmar was made, with one crown for all three kingdoms. It lasted until 1523 in Sweden, when Gustavus Vasa became king of that country. The union of Norway and Denmark endured until 1814 when Norway and Sweden were united under one crown. This latter union was dissolved in 1905. Iceland was united with Denmark until 1944, when it became independent. Finland was united with Sweden as a grand duchy from 1528-1809, when it came under Russian rule. It has been an independent state since 1917-19.

Norway

A great deal of information which would now be kept by the state in England or in the USA, is still recorded by the clergy of the Norwegian church. Civil registration of births, previously entered in the church registers, was established as from 1915, but even now marriages and deaths are registered by the clergy, as also are baptisms. These ecclesiastical records contain many other interesting particulars, as of the confirmation of the persons mentioned and the movements of people in and out of the parish. The records were ordered to be kept from 1687, but often do not begin until after 1700. The registers are under the supervision of the Central Bureau of Statistics, which has copies of them in its files. The address of the office is: The Demographic Section, Statistisk Sentrablyra (Central Bureau of Statistics), Dronningens Gate 16, Oslo, Norway.

In Norway a census was held in 1769, 1801, and every tenth year during most of the nineteenth century, certainly from 1890. The national archives of the country, the Riksarkivet, which contain the census papers, are housed at Bankplass 3, Oslo. It is unlikely that the earlier returns would assist the genealogist, but after 1865 the place of birth of each individual is given. Apparently Norway has the premier rank in census taking, as there are population rolls of the years 1664-66, though these may be merely statistical and without details of families or names of individuals.

Wills, when proved, are kept in the records of the Probate Court, the oldest registers of which date from 1660 and are preserved, together with local government records, in the regional state archives, the Statsarkivet. The national archives mentioned above contain many documents, as one would assume, from government departments, but unfortunately there is no official register of the contents. It is known, however, that the records here include some estate books for the period 1665-1723. The addresses of the regional state archives given in an official pamphlet published in 1959 by the Royal Norwegian Ministry of Foreign Affairs, Office of Cultural Relations, are as follows:

Statsarkivet i Oslo, Kiregaten 14-18. These cover the counties of Ostfold, Akershus, Oslo, Buskerud, Vestfold, and Telemark.

Statsarkivet i Hamar, Standgaten, 71, for Hedmark and Oppland counties.

Statsarkivet i Bergen, Arstdveien 32, for Rogaland, Hordalan, Bergen, and Sogn og Fjordane counties. The chief records for Rogaland are in the Statsarkivkontoret i Stavanger, Peder Klows Gate, 27.

Statsarkivet i Trondheim, Högskoleveian 12, for counties of Möre, Romsdal, Sör-Tröndelag, Nord-Tröndelag, Nordland, Troms and Finnmark. The principal records for Troms and Finnmark are kept at the branch Statsarkivkontoret in Tromsö; Petersborg Gate 21-29.

Sweden

As Sweden is a highly efficient country it is not surprising that its genealogical resources should be well organised. The Royal Ministry for Foreign Affairs issues through its Press and Information Service a booklet, *Finding Your Forefathers*. A considerable immigration of Swedes into the United States took place in the last century, and provided that an American of Swedish descent knows the name of his immigrant ancestor and, most important, the place in Sweden where he lived before setting out for America, he or she should find Swedish records of considerable assistance in tracing the ancestral background. In addition to the guide mentioned, there is a booklet, *Archives in Sweden*, written by Ingvar Andersson of the Swedish Institute, which all inquirers are advised to obtain.

To begin with, the clergy of the Swedish church have, by direction of the law, been charged for the past 300 years with the duty of parish record-keeping. These records began fairly late in Sweden, by contrast with England, because they were not ordered to be kept until 1686, and in many cases those which are preserved date from a later time. Where they have been kept, they contain much more information than their English counterparts. Beside the records of birth, marriage and death, the church registers contain the communion records, and from a genealogical standpoint the most valuable of all, particulars of movements of people in and out of the parish. Thus from about 1750 the household examination rolls contain records of the households in the parish, with all their members. Since 1946 when some alterations were made in the system of parish records, a personal record of each individual is made out in the parish and when he moves it is sent on to the parish where he then lives; thus a complete record of an individual follows him through life. If he dies or emigrates this record goes to the Central Bureau of Statistics.

Although this system in its present form dates only from 1946 the procedure of parish registration is some 250 years older and should yield the information required for periods before 1946. The rule is that local records, eg, from parishes, are to be sent to the regional or district archives when they are one hundred years old, but in some cases Swedish parishes have obtained permission to retain all their records. As many Swedish-born immigrants to the USA have been there within the last hundred years, it is possible to obtain information from the pastor's office, if the parish is known. Some Swedish consulates have a catalogue entitled *Sveriges Statskalender*, which has under the heading 'Eccle-siastikstaten' some information on the clergy of the Church of Sweden with their addresses. When the parish registers or records do not contain the required information, recourse should be had to the regional district and city archives, but before mentioning these attention should be drawn to the national archives. These—the Riksarkivet—are in Stockholm, Arkivagate 3, Stockholm 2. They correspond to the PRO in London or the Archives Nationales in Paris, and are divided into five sections, of which a brief account can be given, with indications of the value of the contents to the genealogist.

The first section contains some of the records from the Royal Chancery, which was that of the Council of State; this began in the thirteenth century and was reorganized in 1634. Many of these documents emanating from or connected with the king and the government are, of course, of great value in the history of Sweden. As with all other national archives, there must be much information about private people, though not necessarily cast in genealogical form.

The second section contains many constitutional documents and collections about the former Swedish possessions in Europe, south or east of the Baltic Sea. There are documents from the Swedish governors in these areas addressed to the central government, and other documents from provinces of the Swedish empire. It is unlikely that the first and second sections would be of interest to the general inquirer about Swedish ancestry, but if he has reason to think he comes of one of the major Swedish families, then search in these archives would be essential. For example, a branch of the Norman family of Montgomery from England was settled in Sweden, and a family history has been produced by one of its members. Conversely, notable Swedish families planted themselves in many Baltic and Central European countries and these had numerous ramifications.

The third section of the Riksarkivet contains the archives of the Swedish royal family up to the time of Gustavus III, and the archives of the four estates of the old Swedish Riksdag (Parliament) which was reorganized in 1865; also many collections of private family papers of the nobility, of great genealogical interest.

The fourth section has some older records of the Central Administrative Boards (ämbetsverk) which were separate from the Royal Chancery; the archives of the High Court set up in 1614. Among the latter are the inventories of property of deceased members of the nobility from 1737-1916. Not all of the administrative boards have transferred their records to the national archives.

The fifth and last section includes what are known as the Cameral Archives, with copies of census rolls and real property books which may be useful in tracing the ownership of farms. Address: Kammararkivet, Burger Jarls Torg 13, Stockholm 2.

The regional archives are those most likely to interest the searcher, as to these are transferred not only church records over 100 years old, but also those of the country administrative boards and of the lower courts for the countryside and the towns. The details of these archives are:

Landsarkivet, Slottet, Uppsala, for the districts (län) of Stockholm, Uppsala, Södermanland, Örebro, Västmanland, and Kopparberg.

Landsarkivet, Slottet, Vadstena, for the districts of Östergötland, Jönköping, Kronoberg and Kalmar.

Landsarkivet, Dalbyvägen 4, Lund, for districts of Blekinge, Kristiansand, Malmöhus, and Halland.

Landsarkivet, Geijersgatan 1, Göteborg for districts of Göteborg, and Bohus, Älvsborg, Skarabirg and Värmland.

Landsarkivet, Nybrogatan, 17 Härnösand for Gävleborg, Västernorrland, Västerbotten and Norrbotten.

The district archives are Länsarkivet, Bisborgsgatan, 1, Visby for districts of Gotland; and Länsarkivet, Museiplan, Östersund.

The city archives (Stadsarkivet) are: of Stockholm, Radhuset, Stockholm 8; Malmö, Kyrkogatan 6; Boras, Stadhuset; Västeras, Radhuset.

Separate sources of information are: (i) for officers and other military personnel, the archives of the War Office—Kungliga Krigsarkivet, Banérgatan 64, Stockholm, Ö. (ii) For Swedes who reside outside Sweden, and for diplomats, the Foreign Office—Kungliga Utrikesdepartmentelsarkiv, Gustav Adolfs Torg, Stockholm 16. (iii) The Central Bureau of Statistics—Statistiska Centralbyrans Arkiv, Linnégatan 87, Stockholm Ö. Here there are extracts from the registers of births, marriages and deaths for each year from 1860, with extracts also from household rolls and parish registers for each ten-year period from 1860. There are summary reports on population, and these have lists containing the full names of persons who entered or left Sweden. (iv) The archives of the House of the Nobility, Riddarhusets Arkiv, Riddarhuset, Stockholm 2.

There is a large amount of genealogical and heraldic writing in Swedish and several genealogical and research societies, but these will mainly be of value to the more advanced searcher.

Denmark

Parish registers are, as usual, the staple of research. In 1645 the Danish clergy were directed by law to keep records of the vital statistics, although some registers date from about 1600. From 1814, the keeping of the records became more systematic and it was ordered that two copies should be kept, one by the clergyman of the parish and the other by the local teacher. Up to 1891, the parish registers are collected in four registers, namely (1) Copenhagen, which embraces the districts of Zealand, Lolland-Falster, Bornholm, and the former Danish colonies; (2) Aabenraa (South Jutland); (3) Viborg (North Jutland), and (4) Odense (Fünen). From 1831, the rule has been that one copy of the registers for the past thirty years is lodged in the archives after being completed.

The office in Copenhagen is the principal seat of the archives. The Danish State Archives Department was established in 1889. This department (Rigsarkivet or Public Record Office) keeps the records of the kingdom, together with large quantities of the old private collections; also the archives of Copenhagen University and those of the War Office before 1868. The older wills are preserved in the Rigsarkivet.

Iceland

This was originally an independent republic, but in 1264 came under the Norwegian Crown, and in 1380 under that of Denmark. It again became an independent republic in 1944. As with other Scandinavian states, the records of births etc have been kept officially by the clergy from the time of their establishment to the present day. From 1746, by royal decree sent to the two bishops in Iceland, the parochial clergy were instructed to keep registers of births, marriages, confirmations, and deaths. Some records of these happenings exist from an earlier period, but from 1746 the records are generally unbroken. The clergy send in annual returns to the Statistical Bureau of Iceland and all the parish records are deposited with the national archives in the capital, Rejkjavik. The national archives—Thjodskjalasfr Islands—were set up in 1899, and all inquiries should be addressed there. Copies of wills are kept there. A census was held in Iceland in 1703, and it was required to supply names, occupation, residence and age of every person in Iceland. In the 1816 census for the first time, places of birth were given.

A work which would prove particularly useful to any North American of Icelandic descent is called *Almanach Fyrir*, 1895. It is published by Utgefandic and the author is Olafur S. Thorgeisson of Winnipeg. It contains a great deal of historical and genealogical material about the first Icelandic settlers in Canada and the USA.

Finland

The Finnish language belongs to the Finno-Ugrian group which includes Lapp, Estonian and Hungarian, and is thus apart from the main European linguistic stock. In few countries are the historical facts more important in their bearing upon the genealogy. For some 800 years Finland was connected with Sweden, and even now Swedish influence is very considerable. In 1157, the group of tribes known as the Finns was conquered by Sweden, and religion and civilization came to Finland from the Swedes. Swedish is an official language with Finnish to this day. As the Finns received Christianity from Sweden (by means of an English apostle), so too in the sixteenth century Finland, like Sweden, turned to the Protestant faith. Today 95 per cent of Finns belong to the Evangelical Lutheran Church; the next largest religious group is that of the Greek Orthodox Church, but this numbers only 70,000 out of a population of 4½ millions. Finland remained Swedish until 1809 when it was ceded to Russia and became a grand duchy. In 1917-19 it secured its freedom.

Since 1918, civil registration has been allowed in Finland; it is not compulsory, and either civil or church registration, but not both, is allowed. With regard to ancestor tracing, most inquiries will go back before 1918, and church registration is therefore very important.

The contents of the registers are (i) chronological lists of births, marriages and deaths, also of moves in and out of the parish—the usual Scandinavian practice in record-keeping; and (ii) lists of the members of the registers by families. The member lists are kept up to date and include the information in the chronological list. The oldest of the latter date from the middle of the seventeenth century, and some of the oldest books have been placed in the district registers. The central archives in Helsinki contain copies of all chronological lists before 1850. The address of the central archives is (in Swedish): Riksarkivet, Fredsgatan 17, Helsingfors (ie, Helsinki).

In Finland, wills are not much used but their place is filled by estate inventories. These must be delivered to the town or circuit courts before the widow or widower can be remarried or the estate divided between the heirs. Much genealogical information is included. These documents are in some cases with the district archives, in others in the town records, and do not date before the seventeenth century.

To get in touch with the local records, the following works are useful: *Statistical Yearbook of Finland*, with text in English as well as in Swedish and Finnish; and *Finlands Statskalender*, which gives a list of all Lutheran congregations and other religious bodies. There is also a Finnish genealogical society: Genealogiska Samfundet i Finland, Snellmansgatan 9-11, Helsingfors.

There was in former times a Finnish House of Nobility, modelled on the Swedish Riddarhuset. The long connection of Sweden and Finland led to many Swedish families settling in Finland, and to Finnish families seeking to show descent from Swedish nobility, which would then automatically bring them into the Finnish House of Nobility. Under Russian rule, noble families were added by the creations of the Tzar. Since 1919, no creation of nobility can take place in Finland. Inquiries about noble families in Finland should be addressed to Riddarhusgenealogen, Riddarhuset, Helsingfors.

GERMANY AND AUSTRIA

Germany

Research in this country is not rendered easier by the fact that (a) Germany was for so long divided into different kingdoms, and (b) religious divisions into Protestant and Catholic have increased this fragmentation.

The keeping of parish records begins somewhat earlier in the sixteenth century in south Germany which remained generally Catholic, than in the north, and so was influenced by the Council of Trent which ordered the keeping of these records. About 1550 there were a large number of parish registers in the area along the river Saale. In Brandenburg, the first parish register, that of St Catherine in the town of Brandenburg, dates from 1566; in Hanover, the first preserved register is of 1562; in Mecklenburg, the oldest is of 1580. In each district there is a catalogue of the records in that area. It is of great importance to know whether the ancestor being sought was Protestant or Catholic. The Rhineland and Bavaria are Catholic; Brandenburg is Lutheran, and so on.

With a law of 1875, civil registration was established for the whole of Germany. Every place in Germany had, from 1 January, 1876, to have a Standesamt (registry office) of its own, or was assigned to a Standesamt in the area. Records of birth, marriage and death are kept in these local offices and duplicates are passed each year to the superior authorities. Despite the German love of administration and centralisation, there has unfortunately been little attempt at the centralisation of archives. Every city possesses its own archives and records useful to the genealogist, whereas he would normally expect to find them in the national archives. Every province has its Staatsarchiv, probably because the province represents the former kingdom. For instance, Niedersachsen has state archives at Hanover, Braunschweig, Oldenburg, Osnabrück, and Aurich.

The best advice for the inquirer into German ancestry is to get in touch with the main genealogical society in Germany. This is Der Herold Verein für Heraldik, Genealogie und verwandte Wissenschaften. The head of the society is Dr Otto Neubecker, whose address is 62 Wiesbadan, Dieselstrasse 24. There are also many German genealogical societies which are concerned with particular regions of Germany. For parts of western Germany, inquirers could seek assistance from Herr Karl Egbert Schultze, Genealoge, of Papenhuder Strasse 36, Hamburg 22. There is a society known as Deutsche Arbeitsgemeinschaft der Genealogiischen Verbander (Union of German Genealogical Workers), address Hanover, am markt 4. This has a very wide range covering persons of German descent in countries adjoining Germany.

In Germany, there has always been a very great interest in nobility and in heraldry. German insistence on nobility and on the doctrine of the sixteen quarters (*seizième quartiers*)—which means that all of one's great-great-grandparents have to be noble—has resulted in a very elaborate system of aristocracy. There is a large body of information about German nobility in the following sources: Deutsches Adelsarchiv, am Glaskopf 21, Marburg, an der Lahn 16, which has information on the genealogical collections of the German Union of Nobility; this institution produces the *Genealogisches Handbuch des Deutschen Adels* (Genealogical Handbook of the German Nobility). Very useful for the inquirer is the *Taschenbuch für Familien Geschichts Forschung* (Pocket book for Family History Research).

The following addresses of registries in Germany will be of service:

> Standesamt Berlin Mitte (Middle), Berlin C2, Elizabethstrasse 28-29.
> Standesamt I, Berlin (West), Berlin-Wilmersdorf, Fehrbelliner Platz I.
> Standesamt I, Berlin (East), Berlin C2, Stralauerstrasse 42-43.
> Hauptstandesamt Hamburg (Chief Registry Office), Hamburg I, Johanniswall 4.
> Berlin Hauparchiv, Berlin-Dahlem, Archivstrasse 12-14.
> And for the archives of religious bodies:

Archivamt der Evangelischen Kirche Deutschland, Hanover, Militar-strasse 9.

Kirchenbuchamt für den Osten, Hanover, Militarstrasse 9.

Bischöfliches (Episcopal) Generalvikariat, abt fur Ostertriebene, Lim-burg/Lahn.

The Almanach de Gotha. This work, so often mentioned in connection with Continental nobility, was begun in 1763 and took its name from the town of Gotha in Thuringia, East Germany, which was a residence of the former Dukes of Saxe Coburg Gotha. The publishing firm of Justus Perthes was established in the town, and the *Almanach de Gotha* was one of its publications. It was a small thick volume of over 1,200 pages, described on its titlepage as—*Annuaire Genealogique, Diplomatique et Statistique.* The genealogical part dealt with the families of the sovereign royal houses of Europe, then of the mediatised sovereigns of Germany (ie, those whose states had been considered princely under the old Holy Roman Empire which ended in 1806, and who were accorded the titles of Serene and Illustrious Highness), and finally of the princely but non-sovereign houses of Europe. By princely, the editors of the *Almanach* understood the ducal houses of Europe, and families of lesser rank than ducal are not likely to be found in the book. This valuable publication maintained its existence during the troubled times of the French Revolution, the Napoleonic wars, the First World War, and right up to the year 1944. Then, on the liberation of Gotha by the Russians, the work was ended, the publisher escaped to Paris, and his famous *Almanach* remained in Russian hands.

Since its demise, various works have appeared which strive to take its place, such as the *Genealogical Handbook of the German Nobility*, mentioned above, or the publication in France by Guy Coutant de Saisseval, *Altesse Imperiales et Royales, Maisons Souveraines de l'Europe.* Valuable as these books or any books can be on the remaining royal families or European nobility, the fact remains that nothing has replaced *Gotha.* Indeed not only now, but even in the palmy days of sixty years ago, it was very hard to obtain details about European nobility. The most useful guide was the single volume produced in 1914 by the Marquis de Ruvigny, *The Titled Nobility of Europe.* It would have been beyond human ability to have included within one volume all the noble families of Europe, and Ruvigny's book was intended as a first essay on the subject. It was never continued. The inquirer must remember that in Continental noble families all the members have *noblesse*, all are noble, which means that they all have titles. Hence a partial explanation of the great multitude of counts, barons etc whom one encounters and whose credentials it is difficult, or in many cases impossible, to check. In Britain, on the contrary, only the peer and his wife are regarded as noble, and although their children often bear what are called courtesy titles, they are not nobles themselves until they succeed their parents.

NOTE: The inquirer into German genealogy may profitably consult the section on Jewry (Chapter 10) which by analogy gives many details of record keeping in the German states.

Continuing with lands which are contiguous to Germany and have Germanic connections and associations, we now deal with Austria, the Netherlands and Switzerland.

Austria

From 1438 to 1806 the Holy Roman Empire was ruled by the Habsburgs, with the exception of two emperors. The Habsburgs assumed the title of Emperors of Austria after the dissolution of the Holy Roman Empire in 1806, and also came to rule over the Low Countries, owing to dynastic marriages. Up to 1477 the Dukes of Burgundy, those dangerous rivals to the French crown (as readers of Shakespeare's historical plays will recall) ruled a middle kingdom stretching from Switzerland to the North Sea and taking in the Low Countries. When the Duke Charles of Burgundy, known as the Bold, was killed in battle with the Swiss in 1477, Louis XI of France secured possession of his territories, except for the Low Countries. These passed to Mary, the daughter of Duke Charles, who married Maximilian of Austria; the latter in 1493 became Holy Roman Emperor. The son of this marriage, Philip the Handsome, married Joanna, the daughter of Ferdinand and Isabella, the King and Queen of Spain, which they had united. From this marriage of Philip and Joanna was born the future Emperor Charles V, also King of Spain. His dominions therefore included Germany, Spain, Northern Italy and the Low Countries. On his death he was succeeded in his Spanish dominions by one son, and as Holy Roman Emperor by another. Hence the Spanish and the Austrian Habsburgs. The Low Countries remained subject to the former, although Holland (the Netherlands) broke away. The southern provinces of the Low Countries (Belgium) remained the Spanish Netherlands until, in 1713, they became the Austrian Netherlands. The male line of the Spanish Habsburgs had died out and their Spanish and South American dominions passed to a grandson of Louis XIV of France; hence the Bourbon royal line of Spain which still exists, the last reigning sovereign having been Alphonso XIII, who went into exile in 1931 and died in 1941.

This explanation will, it is hoped, make clear what must at first sight seem very strange to the reader, namely references to the Austrian Netherlands.

In Austria, as in most west European countries, we begin with the impetus given to record keeping by the Council of Trent (1545-63), although the oldest parish register, that of baptisms, is dated as early as 1457. There are two peculiar features of the Austrian records. One is that, with only a very small exception, registration of births, marriages and deaths was ecclesiastical until 1938. Only since then has registration been civil. The marriage records date from 1 August 1938, those of births and deaths from 1 January 1939. The second feature is that the age of records appears to decrease as the inquirer goes from west to east, so that in Austria, the Tyrol and Vorarlberg areas are the best documented. Records in the neighbourhood of Vienna date from 1684, after the second siege of that city by the Turks. The above theory appears to be borne out as one studies the conditions of records in the Balkan countries. Then again, in Austria there was hardly any toleration for religious bodies other than the Catholic Church. Even when, in 1781, the emperor allowed private records to be kept, they had still (until 1849) to be included in the local Catholic parish. Some Protestant records from the sixteenth-seventeenth centuries do exist, and inquiry should be made to the High Church Council—the governing body of the Protestant denominations—at Vienna I, Schellinggasse 12.

To find the various parishes, the Austrian Official Calendar should be consulted, and most Austrian embassies and consulates can help on this. The centres where records can be found are:

Burgenland, at Sauerbrunn.
Carinthia, at Gurk-in-Klagenfurt, dating from 1840.
Lower Austria, at Vienna, dating from 1797 and at St Polten, from 1785.
Upper Austria, at Linz, from 1819.
Salzburg, from 1816.
Styria, at Seckau-in-Graz, from 1835.
Tyrol, at Innsbruck, from 1921, and at Salzburg, from 1816.
Vorarlberg, at Feldkirch, from 1839.
Vienna. Records of City districts I-IX, from 1812; City districts X-XXVI, from 1797; the registers of deaths from 1648 with some few gaps.

The preservation of wills has lain, since 1900, with the law courts; before that date they are to be found in the archives of the cities.

The public records are kept mainly in Vienna, where inquiries should

be addressed to the Direktor, Staatsarchiv, Vienna III, Landstrasse Haup-
strasse 140. These archives include: (i) The records of the Habsburg
family, for so long the rulers of Austria; (ii) The Austrian state records;
(iii) The documents of the Holy Roman Empire covering nearly 1,000
years, and (iv) The Kriegsarchiv, or military records from about 1500.

THE NETHERLANDS, BELGIUM AND SWITZERLAND

Holland

The Dutch churches, as elsewhere, kept registers and these records
have been deposited in the national archives, which are located in the
provincial capitals. The system of civil registration began with the conquest of the Netherlands by Napoleon in 1811, and this arrangement was
preserved when Holland regained its independence. The main centre of
archives is the Algemeen Riksarchief, at Bleijenburg, The Hague. At
this centre are preserved the archives of the central government and those
of the province of Zuid-Holland. There are eleven provinces in Holland
and anyone seeking information about the provincial archives should
first inquire through the Rijksarchief, who will indicate the provincial
or town archive required. In each municipality a register is maintained
which includes details about persons who have resided in the municipality. This system began in 1850 and as so much immigration took
place after that date, some information about immigrant ancestors may
be found there. As regards wills, those from the last half century are
in the Central Testamenten Register or Central Registry of Wills; earlier
wills must be sought in the provincial archives. The Dutch have several
genealogical societies. (i) Koninklijh Nederlandsch Genootschap voor
Gelacht en Wapenkunde (Royal Society for Genealogy and Heraldry), 5
Bleijenburg, The Hague. (ii) Nederlandse Genealogische Vereniging,
Post Box 976, Amsterdam. (iii) Central Bureau voor Genealogie. It
supervises the genealogical collections of the state. Address: 18 Nassau-
laan, The Hague.

Belgium

Even more than Holland, Belgium has been the scene of much fighting
and consequent destruction of records by the armies of the great powers.
Not only this but, in peculiarly high-handed fashion, Belgian records
were removed to other lands, in some cases to France and to Austria.
Lest this should deter those of Belgian descent from seeking their fore-

bears, it should be mentioned that many lines of Belgian ancestry are traceable into the middle ages, being descents from the romantic Dukes of Burgundy; also that the Delano family in the USA is derived from a man called John de Lannoy who was born at Turcoing in about 1570. From him descended Franklin Delano Roosevelt. Similarly the Baillieus, the ancestors of the British Lord Baillieu, came from Belgium where they are traced 400 years ago.

The parish registers were kept by Catholic priests before Napoleon invaded and occupied Belgium, along with Holland. These old parish registers are nearly all preserved in the state archives or in those of the town or commune halls. The addresses of the various state archives are as follows: the language being either Flemish or French, since Belgium has a dual language system.

> Antwerp: 5 Door Verstraeteplaats.
> Arlon: Place Léopold.
> Bruges: 14-18 Akademiestraat.
> Ghent: Geeraard Duivelsteen.
> Hasselt: Bampslaan.
> Liége: 8 Rue Pouplin.
> Mons: 23 Place du Parc.
> Namur: 45 Rue d'Arquet.

From 1795 the system of civil registration was introduced by the French, who regarded themselves as liberators and civilisers rather than as invaders. The records of birth, marriage and death are kept in the town and commune halls in Belgium.

Wills dated before the French Revolution, are usually kept in the provincial capitals. (see above).

The national or general archives are: Archives Générales du Royaume, 78 Galerie Ravenstein, Brussels. This dates from 1815 (the defeat of Napoleon at Waterloo and the end of the Napoleonic era). The contents of the archives are:

(1) Printed records, which are often those of the state or government. There are also matters such as the particulars of the Monts de Piété (an institution known in France and Italy, designed to provide poor girls with dowries to enable them to get married); articles regarding contested lands, moneys, redemptions, administrations and subsidies—all matters which may provide genealogical details.

(2) Records not printed, which include not only charters of the Belgian cities but also documents relating to former rulers of Belgium, like Mary of Hungary and Count Charles of Lorraine.

I

(3) Ancient collections, which include many family archives, documents relating to heraldic cases and parish registers, including those from the communes in the province of Brabant. As in most democratic countries, genealogical societies exist in Holland, and the Service de Centralisation des Études Genealogiques et Démographique de Belgique will be found useful. Address inquiries to the secretary of the service at 26 Rue aux Laines, Brussels.

Switzerland

As a political unit, Switzerland formally began in 1848, but of course had been recognised as independent centuries before when, in 1291, three cantons—Uri, Schwyz and Nidevalden—formed an Everlasting League against the Habsburgs. The cantonal structure in Swiss political life is reflected in the keeping of records, so that there does not exist a central organization, like the national archives, as in many countries. The Bundesarchiv in Berne contains the official documents of the federal administration. Four languages are in use in Switzerland: German, which is spoken by the majority; French, Italian and Romasch, the last being the tongue of a small minority. Owing to the pressure of population in a small country, many of the Swiss have emigrated to other lands. Before 1848, civil registration had been a matter for each canton, with the result that the date for the beginning of registration varies from canton to canton. Since 1876 registration of vital statistics has been made by the civil authorities; before 1876 it took place in the parish records of the churches. The records of birth, marriage and death for 1834-75 were passed to the registrar's office in each of the cantons.

The Swiss system of civil registration records for each person the date of birth, marriage, death, divorce or nullity of marriage, particulars of children, change of place etc; in short, a complete sketch of the person's life. Access to the records is reserved to the officials of the state, though permission can be given to private persons to consult the registers. Extracts can be made from the registers by the officials for the benefit of inquirers. The old church records have for the most part been handed over to the civil authorities.

As in all European countries, there exist pedigrees of families going back several centuries, with coats of arms. There is a Swiss heraldic society under the name of Schweizerische Heraldische Gesellschaft (Société Suisse d'Héraldique) Zwinglistrasse 28, St Gall. This society is sufficiently numerous and powerful to have organised in 1968 a Congress of Genealogy and Heraldry in Berne which was attended by delegates from some twenty countries. It is often written that there are state heralds in Switzerland; this is not true, though I understand that in each municipality it was possible and indeed necessary for a person using arms to register them in the town's archives. Certainly there is a great deal of heraldic illustration in Switzerland; on many houses coats of arms, often those of former owners, are to be seen, and churches, especially old churches such as the Dom in Berne, are richly dowered with heraldic glass.

THE LATIN COUNTRIES: FRANCE, SPAIN, ITALY, LUXEMBOURG, PORTUGAL AND MONACO

France

Civil registration in France began in 1792, when the French Revolution got into its stride and everything in the old regime had to be changed. From 1792 the documents of what is termed 'civil status' (*l'état civil*) have been preserved in each commune, two copies being made of each entry. One is kept in the commune, the other is sent to the Office of the Tribunal of First Instance. Before 1792 the registration of baptisms, marriages and burials was made by the parochial clergy, this having become obligatory from the sixteenth century as was usually the case in western Europe. Two copies were made, one remaining in the parish and the other being sent to the office of the judicial organisation in the locality. In 1792 the parish registers were turned over to the archives of each municipality. In tracing ancestry, the department of origin must be known and, on inquiry to the archivist of the department (*département*), he will indicate the commune or communes of origin. Since 1792 the clergy in each parish have continued to keep records of baptism, marriage and burial, and one copy of the record is held in the parish while another is sent to the bishop of the diocese.

With wills, the custom is that they are the property of the notary who drew up the will. It is therefore necessary to know the name of the notary and then through the archivist of the *département* it should be possible to trace the will.

The national archives (Archives Nationales) contain five main sections:

(1) Section ancienne (old section) has a vast amount of genealogical information in connection with titles, reports from notaries, legitimisations, naturalisations, the royal family and household; the Army, Navy, colonies, clergy, nobility and the orders of chivalry.

(2) Section moderne (modern section) is concerned mostly with political and governmental matters from 1792 onwards.

(3) Sous-section—a sub-section of private, economic and microfilm archives—contains much genealogical material with many family archives deposited there.

(4) Minutier central (central minute board). In the département de la Seine, there were 144 studies by notaries (in connection with wills) which have been deposited in this section. The earliest date in the series is 1452. For the years 1780-1830 there is a card index of more than 1,000,000 names.

(5) Sceaux-seals, a particularly valuable section for heraldic information.

Heraldry owes its language and much of its development to the medieval French. In the work of reference, the *Grand Armorial de France*, in seven volumes, there are about 40,000 coats of arms mentioned. Information can be obtained from La Société du Grand Armorial de France, 179 Boulevard Haussmann, Paris. There is a Société Francaise d'Heraldique et de Sigillographie, 113 rue de Courcelles, Paris XVII. The address of the Archives Nationales is: Ministère de L'Éducation Nationale: Direction des Archives de France, 60 rue des Francs-Bourgeois (III) Paris.

For the addresses of the archives offices, the following are the details:

Ain : Préfecture, Bourg-en-Bresse.
Aisne : Préfecture, Laon.
Allier : 'Bellevue' Izeure.
Alpes (Basses) : rue des Archives, Digne.
Alpes (Hautes) : Préfecture, Gap.
Alpes Maritimes : Avenue E. Cavell, Nice-Cimiez.
Ardèche : Préfecture, Privas.
Ardennes : Citadelle, Mézières.
Arigège : Avenue de Général de Gaulle, Foix.
Aube : 48 rue Bringer, Carcassonne.
Aveyron : rue L. Oustry, Rodez.
Belfort : Préfecture, Belfort.
Bouches-du-Rhône : Préfecture, Marseille VIme.
Calvados : 1 Parvis Notre Dame, Caen.
Cantal : rue du 139 me. R.I., Aurillac.
Charente : 5 rue de la Préfecture, La Rochelle.
Cher : 9 rue Fernault, Bourges.
Corrèze : rue Souham, Tulle.
Corse (Corsica) : Préfecture, Ajaccio.
Côte-d'or : 8 rue Jeannin, Dijon.
Côtes-du-Nord : 9 rue du Parc, Saint Brieuc.

Creuse : 4 rue des Pommes, Guéret.
Dordogne : 2 Place Hoche, Périgeux.
Doubs : Préfecture, Besançon.
Drôme : rue A. Lacroix, Valence.
Eure : 2 rue de la Préfecture, Evreux.
Eure et Loir : 9 rue Cardinal Pie, Chartres.
Finistère : Préfecture, Quimper.
Gard : 20 rue des Chassaintes, Nîmes.
Garonne (Haute) : 11 Boulevard Griffoul Dorval, Toulouse.
Gers : 6 rue Ed. Quinet (BP No 6) Auch.
Gironde : 13-25 rue d'Aviau, Bordeaux.
Hérault : 40 rue Proud'hon, Montpellier.
Ille-et-Vilaine : 2 Place St Mélaine, Rennes.
Indre : 32 rue Vieillie-Prison, Châteauroux.
Indre-et-Loire : rue des Ursulines, Tours.
Isère : Préfecture, Grenoble.
Jura : Préfecture, Lons-le-Saunier.
Landes : 26 rue Victor Hugo, Mont-de-Marsan.
Loir-et-cher : 21 rue d'Angleterre, Blois.
Loire : Préfecture, Saint-Etienne.
Loire (Haute) : Boulevard Jules Vallès, Le Puy.
Loire-Atlantique : 8 rue de Bouillié, Nantes.
Loiret : 15 rue Chappon, Orléans.
Lot : 14 rue des Cadourques, Cahors.
Lot-et-Garonne : Place de Verdun, Agen.
Lozère : Préfecture, Mende.
Maine-et-Loire : Préfecture, Angers.
Manche : Préfecture, Saint-Lô.
Marne : 1 rue des Buttes, Châlons-sur-Marne.
Marne (Haute) : 1 rue Dutailly, Chaumont.
Mayenne : rue Noémie-Hamard, Laval.
Meurthe-et-Moselle : 1 rue de la Monnaie, Nancy.
Meuse : 44 rue du Petit Bourg, Bar-le-Duc.
Morbihan : 2 rue Alain le Grand, Vannes.
Moselle : Préfecture, Metz.
Nièvre : 1 rue Charles Roy, Nevers.
Nord : 1 rue du Pont-Neuf, Lille.
Oise : Préfecture, Beauvais.
Orne : Préfecture, Alençon.
Pas-de-Calais : 14 Place de la Préfecture, Arras.
Puy-de-Dôme : Préfecture, Clermont-Ferrand.
Pyrènèes (Basses) : Palais du Parlement, Pau.
Pyrènèes (Hautes) : rue des Ursulines, Tarbes.
Pyrènèes-Orientales : 11 rue du Bastion Saint Dominique, Perpignan.

Rhin (Bas): 5-9 rue Fishchartt, Strasbourg.
Rhin (Haut): Cité administrative, 3 rue Fleischhauer, Colmar.
Rhône: 2 Chemin de Montauban, Lyon.
Sáône (Haute): Préfecture, Vesoul.
Sáône-et-Loire: Préfecture, Mâcon.
Sarthe: rue des Résistants Internées, Le Mans.
Savoie: Préfecture, Chambéry.
Savoie (Haute): 4 rue du 30 RI, Annency.
Seine: 30 Quai Henri IV, Paris IVme.
Seine Maritime: 21 rue de Crosne, Rouen.
Seine-et-Marne: Préfecture, Melun.
Seine-et-Oise: 12 rue Neuve Notre Dame, Versailles.
Sèvres (Deux): Préfecture, Niort.
Somme: 88 bis rue Gaulthier de Rumilly, Amiens.
Tarn: Cité Administrative, Avenue du Général Giraud, Albi.
Tarn-et-Garonne: 5 bis Cours Foucault, Montauban.
Var: 1 Boulevard Foch, Draguignan.
Vaucluse: Palais des Papes, Avignon.
Vendée: Préfecture, La Roche-sur-Ypn.
Vienne: rue Edouard Grimaux, Poitiers.
Vienne (Haute): 2 rue des Combes, Limoges.
Vosges: 4 rue de la Préfecture, Epinal.
Yonne: Préfecture, Auxerre.

Spain

A great amount of genealogical information exists in Spain, not only as regards the nobility but also for other classes of the community because, as already mentioned, the Spanish parish registers are the oldest in Europe. In all European countries, except England and Scotland, the nobility have formed a class apart from the rest of the population, being in fact a caste. In every other country the privileged position of the nobility has broken down, and this would have happened in Spain on the establishment of a republic in 1931 but for the re-establishment of the more conservative elements by General Franco. The Spanish nobility possess vast wealth and influence, and in Spain, unlike some other countries, the study of genealogy is not regarded as an eccentricity but it is backed by the state. Thus there is the Instituto Internacional de Genealogia y Heraldica, y Federacion de Corporaciones afines—the International Institute of Genealogy and Heraldry and Federation of similar corporations—which is helped by the state in various ways and is an extremely valuable institution. All correspondence should be addressed to the Secretary, Apartado de Correos 12,079, Madrid. The institute publishes a leaflet about every two or three weeks—the *Hoja Informativa*—which is usually in Spanish, with occasional translations into French. It was the initiative of this institute that launched the series of International Congresses on Genealogy and Heraldry which have since continued so successfully.

Parish registers were formally established by Cardinal Cisneros, in the first synod of Alcalá at the beginning of the sixteenth century, thus anticipating the directions of the Council of Trent. However, even before that time registers of baptisms, marriages and burials were kept in many parishes. There are 19,000 parishes in Spain, and of these no less than 1,636 have registers which date before 1570, the year from which most parochial registers begin. The oldest register in Spain is that of the parish of Verdu in the diocese of Solsona, which started in 1394. When seeking access to parish registers or information from the local priest, the form of address is to The Revdo Sr Cura Párocco.

There is a guidebook of the Spanish Church, published by the General Office of Information and Statistics of the Church in 1954, which lists all the parishes in Spain with their dioceses and the date of their most ancient register in each of the three categories. Also mentioned in this work are thirty-seven other parochial registers which go back before 1400. It is possible that this guidebook could be inspected at Spanish embassies abroad and it is probably similar to the *Guia Ecclesiastica y Civil de los Pueblos de Espana*, which used to give the names of parishes in various localities in Spain. In the two great upheavals which have afflicted Spain in modern times—the struggle with Napoleon's forces and the civil war (1936-39)—some parish registers were inevitably destroyed. Civil registration began in 1870 and the offices function under the justices of municipalities, of districts and of the peace. The records are kept in the municipalities.

Wills are either made in the presence of a notary and deposited with him, or if of other types, ie, made by the testator privately, they must satisfy the Justice of First Instance, after which they are entered in the registries of the notary in the district. Wills which have been proved during the last twenty-five years are kept by the notary in his office; after twenty-five years they are sent to the archives of the notaries in charge of probate. These are situated in the capitals of the various provinces, which are: Albacete, Palma de Mallorca, Barcelona, Burgos, Caceres, La Coruna, Granada, Madrid, Pamplona, Oviedo, Las Palmas de Gran Canaria, Seville, Valencia, Valladolid y Zaragoza. From 1945 an historical section has been created in each archive of the probate, or protocols as they are termed, and in these are preserved wills older than 100 years, which are open to study by researchers.

In considering the many treasures of Spanish record, the influence of Spain's former division into half a dozen separate kingdoms has to be remembered. Thus, while nothing comparable to the Archives Nationales of France exists, there are many splendid archives in different parts of Spain. This may often cause trouble to the student but has one great advantage: the records are unlikely ever to be completely destroyed as happened in Ireland in 1922.

The following archives are likely to be of help in inquiries, though it must be understood that the records in these places deal mainly with nobility:

(i) The Historical National Archives of Madrid, which contain documents of the four great orders of chivalry—Santiago, Alcántara, Calatrava and Montesa. These orders began in the middle ages in the crusading struggle against the Moors. Most of the noble Spanish families had members in one or other of the orders.

(ii) Archives of Simancas, at Valladolid.

(iii) Archives of the Indies, at Seville, which relate to the former Spanish possessions in Latin America.

(iv) Archives of the Crown of Aragon, at Barcelona.

(v) Archives of the Chancelleries of Valladolid and Granada.

(vi) Regional archives of Valencia, Galicia and Mallorca.

(vii) The National Library, Biblioteca Nacional, at Madrid. There is a catalogue of genealogical documents and manuscripts.

In addition, there should be mentioned the General Military archives of Segovia: a work about this has been produced which contains 850,000 entries and gives the surnames, Christian names, ranks, service etc of military personnel of Spain from the seventeenth to the nineteenth centuries.

There are many publications dealing with Spanish American, or Latin American, families, the most outstanding being the result of the enormous labour of Alberto and Arturo Garciá Caraffa. It is called *Enciclopedia Heraldica y Genealogica: Hispano-Americana*, and gives the arms and histories of a multitude of families in Spain and Latin America. The work runs into scores of volumes and is in every major library in Spain. Incidentally, it may be mentioned that Spanish encyclopedias on general knowledge run to many more volumes than their American or British counterparts, and may well contain much information of interest to the genealogist. An interesting example to hand, of a private family history, is that of Lucas de Palacio, entitled *La Casa de*

Palacio (1923, Mexico) which traces the history of this family from 1360 to the present and shows the care with which families in Latin America have kept their records.

Portugal

Here, as in Spain, there are riches for the genealogist, though the best way to obtain information would probably be to visit the country, as otherwise it is not always easy to obtain the required details. Many magnificent works on Portuguese orders of chivalry and on Portuguese colonial history have been produced. These can be procured through the Portuguese embassies and, provided the inquirer can read Portuguese, he will be bound to find information bearing upon his genealogical studies. In any case it is essential for the inquirer to know the meaning of the terms encountered in dealing with Portuguese families, eg, *rico hombre*, cannot be literally translated as 'rich man'. It has a quite different meaning as applied to the old Portuguese nobility, although quite probably the *rico hombre* was a man well-endowed with worldly goods. He was rather the equivalent of the feudal baron, and one of the symbols of his status was the cauldron to denote that he had the power to feed his followers.

Parish registers in Portugal go back in some cases, as in Spain, before the Council of Trent. Over the past 100 years the registers have all, in theory, been kept in the civil registries, partly in the central archives at Lisbon and partly in the district archives. In fact, not all the parish registers have been deposited, and the best course for the inquirer is to consult the central archives, the address of which is: The Director, Arquivo dos Registos Paroquinais, Rua dos Prazeres, Lisbon.

Civil registration began officially in 1878, and the registers are preserved with the local officials. A form of civil registration was apparently used from 1832, and then approved by legislation in 1878. In consequence, there are some records over 100 years old and these are sent to the Inspector Superior of Libraries and Archives, of whom there is one in every conselho, or county. The Director-General's address is: Direccâo-Geral do Registo e Notariado do Ministerio da Justiçia, Lisbon. Here will be found particulars of (i) birth; (ii) filial descent; (iii) marriage; (iv) pre-nuptial contracts; (v) deaths; (vi) emancipation; (vii) care or guardianship of minors or criminal persons and (viii) cases of mental trouble judicially verified. These details are given for Portuguese citizens and for foreigners in Portuguese territory. Wills, when they are called public, are made by the notary and are registered by him in his records after the testator's death. They are later preserved in the national archives and partly in those of the districts.

The national archives are in the Arquivo Nacional da Tôrre do Tombo, and inquiries should be sent to the Director, in Lisbon. In the archives, beside registers and wills and other items of a genealogical character, there is the registration of armorial bearings. The bulk of the old registers were lost in the terrible earthquake at Lisbon in 1755, but some survive or have been entered there since.

Two bodies of value to the inquirer are: (i) Conselho de Nobleza (the Council of Nobility) which, as in other formerly monarchical countries, looks after the interests, titles etc of the Portuguese nobility. The heir to the Portuguese throne is the Duke of Braganza, and anyone who seeks some honour or distinction from him is investigated by the Conselho, and on their report will depend the progress of the aspirant in the grades of nobility. Should the monarchy ever be restored to Portugal, the record of the Conselho would be the foundation for any noble privileges and classes. This Conselho has also a commission which deals with heraldic and genealogical matters. The address is: Praca Luis de Camoes, 46, 2°, Lisbon. (ii) Instituto Portugues de Heraldica: Largo do Carmo, Lisbon. This is the only body in Portugal devoted to the study of heraldry and is prepared to consider inquiries both on this subject and on the related study of genealogy.

Italy

Here the researcher faces considerable difficulty owing to the existence over many centuries of a large number of states, with consequent fragmentation of records. Italy has been united only since 1870, and though most people of Italian origin are likely to be concerned with tracing descent from an immigrant before that date, the position is better than it seems at first sight. Since 1870 the records have been well kept and preserved in good order. Civil registration dates from 1860-70. From 1860 the bulk of Italy is covered and after 1870 the whole, because from that date the estates of the Church were merged with the rest of Italy under the Italian crown. The vital statistics are kept by the local mayor or syndic. Particulars as to civil registration are best addressed to: Istituto Centrale di Statistica, via Cesare Balbo 16, Rome. For the period before civil registration, recourse must be had to the usual source, the parish registers which began in the seventeenth century. Some old registers are deposited in the episcopal archives of the diocese but many have been left in the hands of the local parish priest. Census returns appear to have been made in Italy about 1600, but many have disappeared and it is likely that they were primarily for the purpose of taxation. In the south of Italy they were called *libri dei fuochi*—books of the hearth—and in the north, *libri degli estimi*. The Istituto Centrale di Statistica may be able to supply information as to whereabouts, and some may be found in the national archives, or Archives of the State.

Wills in Italy, as in other Latin countries, are deposited with the notaries, but in Italy they may be passed on in the families of notaries, whose position is often hereditary. The danger, of course, is that these documents may be dispersed, though many are sent to the Arquivo di Stato. Information on wills can be obtained from Archivio Notarile, Ispettatore Generale, Via Flaminia 160, Rome.

The national archives have a centre in Archivio Centrale della Stato; Corso Rinnascimento 40, Rome. But at Italy has had many small independent states, it is not to be expected that all the national records should be in Rome. Great archives of state exist at Turin, Genoa, Milan, Venice, Parma, Mantua, Modena, Bologna, Florence, Naples, Palermo, Siena and Lucca.

Heraldry and nobility are important in Italy in tracing the past. The Istituto Araldico Romano at Rome was founded in 1853 and issues a review—*Rivista Araldica*—and also a book on the lines of the *Almanach de Gotha*, known as the Golden Book of the Italian Nobility (*Libro d' Oro della Nobiltà Italiana*).

Luxembourg

This small independent state between Belgium, France and Germany is a grand duchy ruled by its sovereign, the present Grand Duke Jean. Owing to its chequered history and the several powers which have ruled it, its archives may not always be most useful for the researcher. Those who would like to read an interesting account of the duchy should try to obtain a copy of T. H. Passmore's book, *In Further Ardennes*.

In common with other countries adjacent to France, Luxembourg was liberated by the armies of the French Revolution, and civil registration began in 1796. The registers are placed with the communal administrations and, incredible though it may seem, there are no fewer than 126 municipalities in Luxembourg, each possessing an office with documents relative to its citizens. One copy is retained there, the other is sent to the authorities in Luxembourg or Diekirch. There are Decennial Tables (Tables Décennales) made every ten years, and available from 1793 onwards in the Public Record Office of Luxembourg. These tables give names in alphabetical order, with dates for births, marriages and deaths. For parish records, the registers exist in some cases from 1601, and in others from later in the seventeenth century, or from the beginning of the eighteenth. Inquirers on these and other family matters may profitably address themselves to the Archiviste de la Ville de Luxembourg, Hôtel de Ville, Place Guillaume, Luxembourg. In addition, there are the government archives, inquiries about which should be sent to the Conservateur aux Archives du Gouvernment, 4 Boulevard Roosevelt, Luxembourg. These archives contain census returns, old documents with copies of such matters as letters patent, descriptions of coats of arms, and proceedings before notaries on transactions concerning property. All of these may well provide genealogical details. (See Note 9).

Monaco

This tiny, independent state, which contains the famous Casino of Monte Carlo, exists through the forbearance of its great neighbour, France. It has been ruled by the Grimaldi family since 1297, the present ruler being His Serene Highness Prince Rainier III, whose wife is the famous and lovely Grace Kelly, daughter of John Brendan Kelly. As there are only about 20,000 inhabitants in Monaco, of whom only a small fraction form the Monagesque nation, it is probable that few genealogical inquiries may be made there. However, for the sake of the record, it may be stated that the records of vital statistics from 1600 are held at the Mairie de Monaco. As with other Latin countries, wills are kept by the notaries concerned. Inquiries as to whereabouts of these and other documents may in the first instance be addressed to the Office National au Tourisme et á l'Information, 2a Boulevarde des Moulins, Monte Carlo, Monaco.

San Marino

No useful information has been elicited from this very small enclave despite assistance from the agent or representative in London.

Liechtenstein

To round off the small states of Europe before passing to the large Communist-dominated bloc, Liechtenstein is a small independent country on the north bank of the Rhine, between Switzerland and Austria, whose present sovereign is His Serene Highness Prince Francis

Joseph II. Church records are kept in the various parishes, from 1640. Civil registration began in 1878, but the keeping of the civil registers was left to the Catholic clergy. Wills are deposited in court. Inquiries on any matter in connection with documents should be made to the Chancellery of the Government of Liechtenstein at Vaduz, Liechtenstein (Kanzlei der Regierung des Fürstentums Liechtenstein).

COMMUNIST AND BALKAN COUNTRIES

These include Russia itself, Poland, Czechoslovakia, Hungary, Yugoslavia, the former Baltic states (Estonia, Latvia and Lithuania), Albania, Bulgaria, Rumania, and Greece. Only the last-named is outside the orbit of Communist philosophy.

Communist domination has a most important bearing on genealogical inquiries and as anyone who has tried to obtain information on any subject from a Communist state will know, there are immense difficulties in the way. In the last ten years it has been possible to get statistical, geographical, even political information from the USSR and it is to be hoped that this less restrictive attitude will continue and that it will soon be possible to obtain genealogical details from these lands. There is reason to think that the records in Communist countries which date before the setting up of the regime are preserved, and preserved carefully, though ideological considerations may prevent release of such information. (See Note 10). Nevertheless, a certain amount of information is held by emigrés in western Europe, and this has been particularly well organised in the case of the Russian emigrés. As regards the Balkan countries, it is important to remember that they were ruled by the Turks for 400 years. During the period from the sixteenth to the nineteenth centuries, when Turkey controlled the Balkans, the keeping of records would have been unlikely, so that records in these countries tend to be of later date than elsewhere.

Russia

Regulation by the State is nothing new in Russia, which has always been an autocracy, first under the personal rule of the Tzars and, since 1918, under the Soviet system. The only real difference in governmental direction of the citizens is that the Soviet system is far more efficient than that of the Tzars. The first code of laws regulating the maintenance of civil registration of births, marriages and deaths was issued in 1918, after the great October Socialist Revolution. At the same time the Church was separated from the State. It should be understood that from 1918 the records have been kept with care, as the local offices are under the direction of the USSR Ministry of Internal Affairs. The entries are exact and give the precise information required by genealogists. The birth entries include first names, patronymics, address, occupations and ages of the parents. A marriage entry is recorded on the identity cards of the husband and wife, as well as, of course, in the registers. The identity papers of each person also record particulars of a decree of divorce, together with details of any change of name and of adoption.

Before the Communist revolution the maintenance of records was in the hands of the ministers of religion. The system of registration of civic status, as it was called, began in 1722 as part of the many changes instituted by Tzar Peter the Great (1689-1725). The keeping of records of vital statistics for the great majority of Russians was the province of the clergy of the Orthodox Church, then the established religion of Tzarist Russia. The clergy or officials of the minority religions—Roman Catholic, Lutheran, Moslem, and Jewish—kept similar records of their own. Only those who had no religion or belonged to a faith forbidden in Russia, such as that of the Baptist Church, had their statistics kept by the police. From about 1820 copies of the register were sent every year to the regional consistory of the Church. This is in accord with the practice of other European countries, as with the bishops' transcripts in England.

Most people of Russian descent are more likely to be interested in records of the time before the revolution. As everyone knows, there are thousands of Russian upper-class men and women dispersed throughout the world. In the old Russia, their records were well kept but today there is practically no chance of obtaining anything from the Soviet authorities as regards the records of the old regime. However, as in other cases when a republic has replaced a monarchy in this century, the emigrés have endeavoured to preserve records of their families, and such inquiries for Russia should be addressed to the President of the Bureau Genealogique, Union de la Noblesse Russe, 8 rue Gabrielle d'Estrées, Vannes, (Seine), France. A considerable amount of Russian genealogical information has also been produced in multigraph books from this source.

An interesting feature of Russian nobility is that it derived from the holding of various governmental posts. There was an older nobility in Russia on the feudal lines which we encounter in other parts of Europe, but from the sixteenth century, when a register of nobles was made, the Tzars decided that the rank of nobility should be regulated by the position in either civil or military employment held by predecessors in the family. This register, known as the Velvet Book (*Barhatnaia Knega*), was last copied in 1682.

Among the many innovations of Peter the Great were the introduction of titles and the status of nobility, together with armorial bearings for all who had reached certain rank, civil or military. Many volumes of armorial bearings were compiled, which have probably been preserved along with the register of the nobility by the Soviet authorities—just as they have carefully kept the palaces, even the clothes of some of the Tzars—but these are almost certainly inaccessible to the western inquirer. Some printed books published in the last century may be of use in giving historical information as, for example: *La Noblesse Titrée de l'Empire de Russie*, by Dr R. J. Emerin (1892), and *Les Principales Familles de la Russie*, by Prince Peter Dolgorauby (1859). There are also editions from the last and into the present century of the *Annuaire de la Noblesse de Russie*. In addition, some information can be gleaned from editions of the *Almanach de Gotha*, albeit the Russian personages there recorded are likely to be of the most rarified nobility, princes, grand dukes etc. As, however, all persons in a Continental noble family are noble, it happens that the lesser ranks of count or suchlike may be found in the *Almanach*, if they were junior members of a great family.

Poland

This country had an ancient hereditary monarchy which, when it ended in 1572, was followed by a system of elective monarchy and a period of such excessive freedom that Poland became weak and was easily dismembered by her neighbours, Russia, Germany and Austria. Thus Poland disappeared from the map of Europe from 1795 until 1918. On the collapse of the three partitioning powers, Poland became once more a political entity, but the record keeping had obviously varied in the different portions according to the methods used by the occupying power. The position before 1918 can be summarised as follows: in Russian-ruled Poland, the clergy were authorised to keep the usual records of vital statistics; in the Austrian-ruled districts, the parish clergy were treated as state officials, in much the same way, presumably, as are the present Swedish clergy; in the German areas, the records were kept by secular officials. These differences, existing for a century and a quarter, have produced a rare tangle for the inquirer. The unwinding can be made, if one knows the voivodship concerned (voivodship = *wojewodzkie*, roughly equivalent to an English county in administrative content). The scheme can be set out in this way: (i) In the western and northern voivodships, and in the northern part of the Katowice voivodship—in German-ruled territory—the registration was civil. (ii) In the eastern part of Bialystok voivodship and in the former eastern voivodships, in Russian-ruled areas, registration was with the church authorities. (iii) In the central and Silesian voivodships and in Cieszyn Silesia, in Austrian-controlled land, there was a mixture of ecclesiastical and civil registration according to the religious allegiance or non-allegiance of the persons being registered. Parish records must exist in certain cases from before the period 1795-1918, but information about them is slight. Civil registration dates from 1946, that is for all Poland.

There are central archives in Warsaw: for old records—Archiwum Glowne Akt Dawnych, Warsaw, Dluga 7; new records—Archiwum Akt Nowych, Warsaw, Dluga 7. In the former may be found information on the older historical records of Poland, including Polish heraldry, and details of the great noble and princely families who necessarily figure so largely in Polish history.

Lithuania, Latvia and Estonia

These three former Baltic states have been for so long under the rule of neighbouring lands that their records are dominated by this fact. They are now under Russian rule, which is indeed a resumption of the state of affairs before 1918. Lithuania was once a grand duchy which was united with Poland in 1385, and it is significant of the bonds which once linked the two countries that the famous Polish poem, 'Pan Tadeuz' by Adam Mickiewicz, has for its full title: 'The Last Foray in Lithuania: A Story of Life among Polish Gentlefolk in the years 1811 and 1812'.

The republic of Lithuania lasted only from 1918 to 1940 when Russian occupation began, followed for a few years by German and then Russian domination again. The Soviet authorities, following much the same pattern as their Tzarist predecessors who took over Lithuania in 1796, have incorporated the three Baltic republics into the Russian state. There is, however, one considerable difference. Under the Tzars, the nobles of states such as Poland, Finland, Lithuania, Georgia etc were accorded recognition of their titles and armorial bearings. Thus, when Lithuania attained its brief independence in 1918 there still survived a considerable knowledge of nobility and heraldry, so that in 1928 an Association of Lithuanian Nobility was formed and properly registered by the state. When the Russians took over, this association was forcibly closed, just as the Czechoslovak genealogical society was also dissolved.

Latvia and Estonia attained independent existence after 1918. The Latvians had previously been ruled in turn by Germans, Poles, Swedes, and from 1721 by the Russians. The Estonians were ruled by German nobles, and from 1721 came under Russian control.

To sum up the position of these Baltic records: before 1918 any records kept would have accorded with the regulations of the Russian empire; except for the pedigrees of the nobles, which depended very much on family archives. The Germans produced a Baltic nobility from scions of noble families who had gone to carve fortunes for themselves in the wild lands of the eastern Baltic. There exists a body known as the Union of Members of the Baltic Knighthoods: Verband der Ange-horigen der Baltischen Ritterschaften, whose address is c/o Munchen 13, Elisabethstrasse 5/1, Germany.

Taking each country in turn: (1) Estonia, on its independence in 1918, passed a law under which registration of births, marriages, and deaths was later transferred from the parish clergy to the local admini-stration as from 1920. It is not known if this law was ever actually applied, and it was superseded by one of 1925 which made new regula-tions for the registration of births, marriages and deaths. There was no Central Record Office. (2) Latvia established civil registration in 1919-20 at local offices, and all these records have now been removed to Moscow. There were also state archives, which were the repository of wills that had received probate and of all documents of any public interest. (3) Lithuania after independence continued the keeping of registers by the clergy of the different denominations, who were given the position of state officials. Copies of these registers and many of the older registers were then sent to the central archives in Kaunas. Wills were kept in the records of the law courts which proved them. Public records were placed in the central archives.

Czechoslovakia

This is the national state of the Czechs and Slovaks, consisting of Bohemia, Moravia and part of Silesia and Slovakia. It lost its freedom in 1621 in the religious wars of that period and came under the rule of Austria, for the most part. There are both Catholic and Protestant parishes and some of the former are as old as 1620. Until the reign of the Emperor Joseph II (1741-90) who was a reformer, no Protestant registers were kept, except no doubt as private documents. The parish registers were taken over by the state in 1950, and are kept in the state archives. Civil registration began in a limited way after 1918, but was

K

compulsory only for those who were not members of a church. In their cases registration was with a district office; all others registered with the clergy of their parish. Wills are kept by the state notary, who has an office in each town with district administration. Inquiries regarding records may be made to Archivni Sprava, Prague 6, Trida Obrancumiru 133; or (for Slovakia) at Slovenaska Archivni Sprava, Bratislava, Vajanskeho, Nabrezi 8.

In recent years there has been some relaxation in the attitude of the Czechoslovak authorities towards heraldic and genealogical studies, at least as regards civic coats of arms. The latter, unlike the arms of individuals, can hardly be said to encourage class distinction and thus a study of them is not to be condemned. In 1966 an interesting work was published in England: *European Civic Coats of Arms*, by Jiri Louda, a Czech author whose work is published in his own country by the government publishing house.

Hungary

Hungary was formerly a kingdom, and part of the Austro-Hungarian Empire. The sovereign of this empire bore the style of Emperor of Austria, as well as that of Apostolic King of Hungary, because the latter country was regarded as a separate realm. As with many other Catholic countries, the registration of baptisms, marriages and burials in Hungary begins in the sixteenth century; as early as 1515 for baptisms, as ordered by the Diocesan Council of Veszprém. The ecclesiastical records were formerly kept in the parishes but the older ones have now been placed in the state archives in Budapest. Civil registration began from 1 October 1895, and these records are kept in the National Centre of Archives—Leveltarak Orszagos Kozpontja, Budapest I, Uri Utca 54-56. This centre also holds the national records of the different government departments. Besides this centre there are twenty-one provincial archives situated in the regional centres.

In Hungary, as in most other countries, there were noble families from the end of the ninth century, when the Magyars conquered the country. Heraldry developed fairly late, after 1400, in imitation of the custom in western countries, but from the sixteenth century onward a large body of heraldry was built up. A register was kept in Budapest for those Hungarians who had titles of nobility and armorial bearings, and registration was obligatory. A very interesting account of arms in Hungary appears in *The Nature of Arms* by Lt-Col Robert Gayre, 1961, p 86.

Yugoslavia

The records here follow much the same pattern as that already set out above. Church registers were kept as usual, and probably with varying dates. Civil registration began in the territory of Voivodina only from 1895; from 1946 it has been the rule in the whole of Yugoslavia. Each person is required to supply information concerning birth, marriage, divorce, annulment, death, adoption etc, and the system operates under the State Secretariat for Internal Affairs. Because of the late arrival of independence, the state of the records leaves much to be desired; added to which, Communist domination has prevented reasonable access to such records as do exist.

Consideration of Yugoslavia leads naturally to the rest of the Balkan countries. These consist of Albania, Bulgaria, Rumania and Greece. In 1453 the Turks took Constantinople and destroyed the last remnant of the Byzantine or Eastern empire. The Turkish armies pressed on into Europe as far as to Vienna, and the Balkans remained under their control for the next 400 years. Albania was freed of the Turks in 1912. Bulgaria reached a measure of freedom in 1878, and full independence in 1908. Rumania had become free by 1878. Greece secured her freedom in 1821.

Albania

In this country prior to independence the Church, both Roman Catholic and Orthodox, kept the parish records, and this continued until 1929 when civil registration came into force. The birth, marriage and death records are kept by local officers in each municipality. The Moslems are a sizeable minority in Albania, and their records were not kept as well as those of the Christian churches. Many even of the Christian records have been destroyed by the Communists and it is a melancholy fact that there is very little likelihood of obtaining genealogical information from Albania.

Bulgaria

This country also presents a blank field for the researcher. Parochial registers were begun in 1860, when the Bulgarian Church became independent of the Greek Church. Civil registration began in 1893 and the records are kept in the offices of the local District People's Councils. Wills are deposited with the notary public or, if made privately, with the notary of the People's Court. The older documents are with the Ministry of Justice.

Greece

Here the hazards of record keeping and genealogical inquiry are not so great as with Greece's northern neighbours. Church registers have been kept from before the times of civil registration, though it is uncertain how far back these records extend. Civil registration of a sort dates from 1856 but was incomplete until 1931, when the keeping of civil registers was extended throughout the whole of Greece. Since 1912 it has been obligatory for church registers to be kept in all parishes, with books of births and baptisms, marriages and deaths. Local archives are maintained with the names of all Greek citizens, a system begun in 1933 but practised with more efficiency since 1954. Wills are kept by the notary public in the case of public or secret wills. The notary, on hearing of the death of the testator, sends a copy of the will to the secretary of the Court of the First Instance. A third type of will, known as the written will as distinct from the public or secret will, must also be sent on the testator's death to the Court of the First Instance at Athens, where copies of wills are held.

Despite the comparative poverty of the records in Greece, as elsewhere in the Balkans, many long pedigrees exist for Greek families. Some of these have found their way into British publications. In particular may be cited the family trees of the Rallis, the Ionides, Scaramangas, Schilizzis and Argentis.

Romania, or Rumania

Registrations of civil status were introduced officially in the nineteenth century, and put into application on 1 May 1831 in Walachia, and in January 1832 in Moldavia. These registers, named *mitrici*, were held by the churches of the Orthodox Church. The other religious bodies have kept registers of births, marriages and deaths since the second half of the eighteenth century. Up to 1 December 1865 the registers of civil status were held by the churches when, in virtue of the Romanian civil code, they were passed over to the offices of civil status, which function in the sections of the mayoral departments. The priests were, however, obliged to keep registers in their parishes of baptisms, marriages and burials. Before these registers became legally compulsory the churches had kept their own registers with lists of births, marriages and deaths.

In Transylvania, registers of the civil status were introduced on 1 October 1895. Up to this date the acts of civil status had been inserted in the parochial registers. Contrary to the religious confessions recognised by the state—that is the Roman Catholics, the Reformed, Unitarian and Lutheran—the Romanian Orthodox, although they formed the majority of the population, had the right to keep registers of a similar nature only from the year 1791, the date at which the Orthodox Church was recognised officially.

The date of introduction of the parochial registers of the civil status for the various religious bodies cannot be precisely determined, since they were not introduced systematically by way of general dispositions, but rather by the personal initiative of the priests. The acts of the civil status are kept for seventy-five years in the archives of the institution which has created them. At the end of this term they are put into the state archives of the respective territorial area with a view to permanent maintenance.

Wills are found in the archives of the tribunals and are passed on, with a view to permanent conservation, to the archives of state of the territorial zone to which the respective tribunal pertains. A similar procedure is followed with other documents which have a permanent value, in conformity with the legislation governing the maintenance of archives.

In Romania there are state archives in which the most important documents of the whole country are concentrated with a view to preservation. The director-general, being the only administrator, is thus enabled to organise, direct and exercise control over the archive activity of the whole country, which has thus a unitary character.

[The above account of Romanian archives has been supplied by the director-general of the state archives of Romania, whose address is: Directia Generala A Archivelor Statului, B-Dul Gheorghe Gheorghui Dej nr 29, Bucuresti, Romania.]

From this study of European genealogy several common factors emerge. As a general rule there are three periods in the genealogical evolution of each European nation: (i) A feudal period in which the families of the nobles, the great houses, are almost the only ones whose history can be traced. This period, which could also be called medieval, has lasted longer in eastern than in western Europe. (ii) With the growth of mercantile and middle classes comes the demand for more information about ordinary people. This means the establishment of parish records kept by the church authorities. (iii) Finally, with the growth of state concern, there is the creation of civil registers, and from the beginning of the present century a vast and ever growing documentation of the citizens, in the interests of state control. Additionally, in several European lands there has been legislation against titles, and hostility has been shown to genealogical research.

CHAPTER 10

Jewry

IT is best to try to treat the subject of Jewish ancestry away from the main theme of European genealogy, since for so many centuries the Jews were a separate community in Europe. Apart from the Moslems, with whom the majority of Europeans did not mingle, the Jews were the only non-Christians known to the people of the middle ages. They were forced to live in ghettoes unless they became converted to Christianity, a rare occurrence even when, as in Spain towards the end of the medieval period, many Jews were forced to become Christians, but reverted to their former faith as soon as they could.

In England there has been toleration for the Jews for the last 300 years and, since the nineteenth century, removal of all restrictions upon them. Nevertheless, even in England, the Jewish community tends to be a little aloof from the rest of the nation, and Jewish records likewise. If this is so in tolerant England, it is not difficult to imagine how very much more restricted are Jewish records in continental Europe. To add to the restrictions, there was the fiendish persecution of the Jews in Germany and throughout German-controlled Europe, resulting not only in the torture and death of very large numbers of Jews, but also the destruction of their records. Then, too, owing to persecutions in earlier times, many Jewish families have changed their countries and their surnames. Thus it comes about that the people with the longest historical memory in western civilisation, whose existence goes back to the third and fourth millenium, nearly 2,000 years BC, have, as regards their individual members, very often genealogies to be reckoned by merely a few generations. Before the last war, the longest Jewish pedigrees were probably those of the Viennese Jews, where descent was sometimes reckoned over periods of 500-600 years.

In preparing this section I have been able to work in a thoroughly genealogical manner, because it has been necessary to trace the whereabouts of Jewish archives from person to person, and country to country.

Eventually I was able to contact the director of the Jewish Historical Archives in Jerusalem, and through his assistance received a very valuable paper entitled: 'Registration of Births, Deaths and Marriages in European Jewish Communities in Palestine and in Israel'. Of this the director stated: 'A collective research work on the registration of Jewish births, deaths and marriages in European countries has lately been carried out in our archives. The survey contains an introduction, which covers several European countries, and refers to the internal registration made by Jewish communities mostly before the time the Jews were included in the general instructions given by the authorities. In the survey itself exact data and details on registration are given on Germany.'

This survey was published in *Archivum* vol 9, 1959 (*Revue Internationale publiée sous les auspices du Conseil International des Archives, Paris*). With the permission of *Archivum*, this survey is here reproduced practically *verbatim*, except for the omission of all the notes save one concerning Jewish emancipation, which is reproduced in its place of reference under Internal Registration etc.

Preliminary to this most important survey, it should perhaps be stated that a full genealogical study of Jewry will at once remove the myth of a Jewish race peculiar from other races, a myth which did much to bring about the appalling persecution of the Jews by Hitler. It is unlikely that diseased minds of the Hitlerite type would be amenable to reason, but lest others of more civilised outlook should yet fall victims to such racial prejudice it is as well to stress that Jewry is a community, a religious community, but not a race. Genealogical study shows that from the second century BC the Jews, whose ancestors returned from captivity in Babylon, began to absorb other peoples into their community. In any event, the returned Jews did not represent the twelve tribes of Israel. As any reader of the Bible knows, the country of Palestine after the death of King Solomon was divided into two kingdoms, Israel and Judah. Between 750 BC and 722 BC the Israelites were carried into captivity in Assyria. They disappear from the Old Testament record except for a reference in the second Book of Esdras, ch 13 v 40-42. '. . . these are the ten tribes which were led away out of their land in the time of Osea the king, whom Shalmanasar the king of the Assyrians led away captive, and he carried them beyond the River, and they were carried into another land. But they took this counsel among themselves, that they would leave the multitude of the heathen, and go forth into a further country, where never mankind dwelt, that they might there keep their statutes, which they had not kept in their own land. And they entered by the narrow passages of the river Euphrates.'

The record goes on to describe the journey of a year and a half to another land. This is the only account we have of the ten lost tribes, enough to open speculation about them, taking them into all sorts of regions of the world. One noble British writer located the ten tribes among the Indians of the New World; and there has been mention of the Afghans as being identical with the Israelites of old. A possible, almost probable theory is that the lost tribes eventually found a place in the British Isles. We know so little of the migrations of peoples before the appearance of written history that dismissal of this theory would be somewhat foolish.

The remaining small country of Judah, comprising the two tribes of Judah and Benjamin, plus a number of Levites (Levi had no territorial inheritance in Palestine but was dispersed among the tribes) was carried into the Babylonian captivity in 588 BC. A letter from the Chief Rabbi, London, dated 18 November 1918 makes the position quite clear.

'1. The people known at present as Jews are descendants of the tribes of Judah and Benjamin, with a certain number of descendants of the tribe of Levi.

'2. As far as is known, there is not any further admixture of other tribes.

'3. The ten tribes have been absorbed among the nations of the world. (See II Kings ch 17, more especially v 22-23).

'4. We look forward to the gathering of all the tribes at some further day. (See Isaiah ch 27, v 11-12, and Ezechiel ch 37, v 15-28.)'

(Reproduced from the Quarterly (British Israel World Federation), 19 December 1967, by permission of the Editor, to whom I am also indebted for some notes on the Sephardic (South European) Jews given below. L.G.P.)

In the last century BC the Edomites, or Idumeans, were forcibly made Jews, hence that terrible figure, Herod the Great, King of the Jews at the time of Christ's birth. Later, various Caucasian tribes were brought within the Jewish community. It should, therefore, be obvious to any careful observer that the modern Jews include many racial admixtures.

As regards the Sephardic Jews, they are descended from the Spanish and Portuguese Jews, who have always been looked upon as the aristocracy of Jewry. They were very anciently seated in the Iberian peninsula, in fact it is said by some Jewish writers, notably the Dutch Jew, Isaak da Costa (1798-1860), that some of the Iberian Jewish families claimed descent from families of Judah and even from the royal house of David. It seems fairly clear that a Jewish community was established in

Spain well before the Christian era, and this could account for the proposed journey of St Paul to Spain, which he mentions in Romans ch xv, v 24-28. His practice, as can be seen from the narrative in the Acts of the Apostles, was always to begin his tours by visiting the Jewish synagogues in the town or city which he had reached. He speaks confidently of going to Spain, so it is likely that there must have been Jewish centres there. In the course of a long history, some of the Jewish families intermarried with those of the Spanish grandees, and many of them acquired arms from the twelfth century onwards, as can be seen from the histories of families which eventually reached England.

The rest of the European Jewish community is usually known as the Ashkenazim, who were on a definitely lower social level than their co-religionists from Spain and Portugal. The bulk of modern Jews come from the Ashkenazim.

Support for the idea that the Sephardic Jews are the aristocrats of Jewry is found in the attempt by Benjamin Disraeli, Prime Minister of England under Queen Victoria and later Earl of Beaconsfield, to prove his own family to have been among them. Mr Robert Blake in his *Disraeli* (ch 1) has shown that this is quite incorrect and that the ancestors of Disraeli were Italian Jews, probably from the Levant. The idea of noble Jewish connections is based on the belief that the Sephardic Jews were of Davidic origin, and also from the fact of their being armigerous in many cases and allied to great houses of the Iberian peninsula.

Since the destruction of Polish Jewry, the American Jewish community is the largest in the world, numbering, however, only about 3 per cent of the American population, For their benefit, the following addresses may be of service:

> The American Jewish Committee, 165 East Fifty Sixth Street, New York 22, New York.
> The American Jewish Historical Society: 3080 Broadway, New York 27.
> The Yivo Institute for Jewish Research, 1048 Fifth Avenue, New York 28.

Jewish immigration into the USA did not assume any large proportions until after 1880.

In England, there will be older records of Jewry, because of some 300 years' residence in England by the older Jewish English families. For English Jewry, reference should be made to the Anglo-Jewish Association, Woburn House, Upper Woburn Place, London, WC1.

A great deal of information about the history of Jews in England, and of the Jewish community generally, will be found in the writings of the great scholar, Dr Cecil Roth, one of whose small works, *The Rise of Provincial Jewry*, gives the early history of the Jewish communities in the English countryside from 1740 to 1840.

We come now to the study of the survey previously mentioned, provided by courtesy of the Jewish research authorities in Jerusalem. It is a truly astonishing event of history, strangely lacking mention or comment among modern historians, that after an interval of not less than 1,900 years the state of Israel should have been restored as a political entity. For this reason it is highly probable that most genealogical information about the Jews on the continent of Europe will come from the very highly organised Jewish Historical General Archives at Jerusalem. It will be noted that most of the following references to Jewish registration and records concern Germany. As a very large proportion of surviving Jews descend from German Jews, this is no disadvantage; in any case, to cover the whole of the European continent would need much more space than is here possible, even if the information were available. Also, the arrangements as regards the Jews must not be seen as applicable only to them; the details given are useful as regards Gentile, ie, German, registration in the formerly separate states of Germany.

'Registration of Births, Deaths and Marriages in European Jewish Communities, in Palestine and in Israel,' written by R. Blumenthal, Ch. Fraenkel, Dr J. Raba: The Jewish Historical General Archives, Jerusalem.

Introduction: The first part of this survey describes the internal, ie, non-official—registration of births, deaths and marriages as it was carried out by the Jewish communities, mostly for religious reasons. This registration existed for a considerable time before the introduction of official registers and has been continued to a great extent up to—and sometimes during—the twentieth century.

The second part covers the official registers of births, deaths and marriages in European Jewish communities, as they were requested by the various governments. The third part covers the registration in Palestine and Israel where, as will be seen, a sharp distinction has been made in the keeping of registers of births and deaths on the one hand and of marriages and divorces on the other. The registration of marriages has always been in the hands of the rabbinical courts set up by the local community councils. In the State of Israel, the religious community councils were incorporated into the Ministry of Religion, so that this registration, which formerly, as in Europe, had been kept by the communities, automatically became governmental. Thus, some kind of fusion between former community registration and the new governmental registration has taken place in Israel.*

The survey has been carried out by the two competent Israel institutions: the Israel State Archives and the Jewish Historical General Archives.

The State Archives, which were established in 1949, and which received legal status by the promulgation of the Israel Archives Law in 1955, are the official repository for the files and documents of the government departments and institutions of the State of Israel and also of the Mandatory Government of Palestine, and of the Turkish authorities, as far as they are preserved in the territory of Israel.

The Jewish Historical General Archives, which endeavour to establish a national archive for the Jewish people in Jerusalem, collect documents —original and photographic—connected with Jewish history in all countries and of all times, archives of communities as well as of organisations, private archives and single documents.

The archives which were founded in 1939 by the Historical Society recognised as one of their first aims the transfer to Israel of the archives of the destroyed Jewish communities of Germany and other countries. Numerous other projects have since been carried out, all of them serving the purpose to create, in Jerusalem, a centre of research for the history of the Jewish people.

As far as possible, the examples of registers given in Part I and II are taken from original material stored with the Jewish Historical Archives. Archival material extant in non-Jewish archives, or documents which for other reasons cannot be transferred to Jerusalem, have been microfilmed for the archives. These microfilms bear the signature 'HM'. Other photographic registers (G5) are those copied for the Jewish Historical General Archives by the firm Gebr. Batermann, Hamborn (Germany) from microfilm, made originally—in 1944—for the German 'Reichssippenamt' by the same firm. The greater part of these microfilms are now stored with the Personenstandsarchiv in Brühl. The small photostatic copies made for the Jewish Historical General Archives have been arranged in the original book form. The examples of internal—non-official—registers have been chosen from various European countries, as internal Jewish registration was more or less the same all over Europe.

Germany has been chosen as a first example for the keeping of official registers in European Jewish communities, the main reason for this

* NOTE. The third part to which reference is made above was not supplied to me, but no doubt inquirers who wish to obtain details of the forms of registration in the State of Israel will be able to do so. See end of the account.—L. G. Pine.

choice being the large amount of archival material of that country stored in Israel and easily available for research. Surveys on other countries are being made and will be completed in the not too distant future, although in several countries of eastern Europe, as well as in Italy and Alsace, the bulk of the Jewish registers was, unfortunately, destroyed during the Second World War.

The various German countries are defined according to the frontiers and the political situation prevailing during the time this particular kind of registration has been kept. For the choice of the German countries the existence of material relating to the subject was decisive.

I.   INTERNAL REGISTRATION OF BIRTHS, DEATHS AND MARRIAGES IN EUROPEAN JEWISH COMMUNITIES

It should be pointed out that the internal registration was often more accurate than the official one, for the following reasons: in some countries a certain marriage oath had to be taken which conflicted with the Jewish religion and was therefore avoided by marrying according to Jewish law only. A further reason for avoiding official registration was the fact that the authorities usually allowed only the eldest son of the family to marry, so that the number of Jews should not unduly increase. Until the emancipation of the Jews at the beginning of the nineteenth century, the number of the Jewish population in a town or village was usually restricted to a comparatively small number. Apart from the 'Schutzjude' (protected Jew) who owned certain privileges and had to pay 'Schutzsteuer' (eg, Halberstadt IV, I, 39—Verteilung von Schutzsteuern, 1755) there existed in several German towns (especially in Frankfurt/M and Worms) the term 'Stättigkeit' (right for domicile) from the beginning of the fourteenth century up to the emancipation. The 'Stättigkeitslisten' always listed the names and the tax which had to be paid (eg, Frankfurt/Main, Stättigkeitlisten 1503, 1808—HM. 1843). (NOTE: This paragraph is the transposed note mentioned on page 152.—L. G. Pine).

Often, therefore, there was no alternative left to the second and third sons but to marry only according to Jewish law.

There existed several kinds of lists and registers: circumcision books (Mohel-books) kept by the circumciser, and usually listing the place, the name of the boy and his father, the date of circumcision and, sometimes, the name of the godfather. Since the post of circumciser often descended from father to son, there exist circumcision books kept for many years by the same family and covering comparatively wide areas.

The prayers to be said at the circumcision were usually included as well as religious and medical instructions. This registration has, of course, been kept up during the time of official registration, the language sometimes changing from Hebrew to the official language at a later date.

Often registration of marriages, marriage contracts and testaments was carried out by the rabbi. There exist collections of marriage contracts (Ketuboth) often written on parchment and beautifully ornamented.

The desire to remind successive generations of the communities' existence and especially of outstanding personalities who had lived and died for their religion, found its expression in the so-called 'Memorbooks'. These books were always written in Hebrew and usually contained the names of these communities in Germany and other countries, the names of famous rabbis and scholars and—in more or less chronological order, but often without exact dates—the names of the deceased, with a short appreciation of their achievements. The 'Memorbooks', which continue even into the twentieth century, later developed into lists of people to be honoured after death by their respective families. The entries frequently took—even in later years—the form of a short appreciation.

Exact lists of the deceased, containing their names and, usually, date and place of the funeral, have been kept by the 'Chewra Kadischa' (burial societies) founded by venerable men, who made it their religious duty to bury the dead. There exist, too, cemetery lists which, in more or less accurate form, contain particulars of the graves and the deceased.

II.   OFFICIAL REGISTRATION OF BIRTHS, DEATHS AND MARRIAGES IN EUROPEAN JEWISH COMMUNITIES

Germany

The first laws and instructions regarding registers of births, deaths and marriages appeared in most countries after the French Revolution with the modest beginning of the emancipation of the Jews, which later found its expression in the various 'Judenedikte'. In Germany, this form of registration ended mostly in 1876 with the introduction of the 'Standesamter', civil registry—offices, where, irrespective of faith and religion, all births, deaths and marriages had to be recorded.

Certain particulars requested by governments regarding entries in birth, death and marriage registers were approximately the same in every country, and in the following, we shall refer to these as to 'the usual particulars'. They include these items: in registers of birth, the name of the child, of his father and mother, the day, and often the hour of birth, and usually a column, legitimate—illegitimate.

In registers of marriages: the name and legal status of the bride and bridegroom, the date and place of their birth, the names of their parents, the date of marriage, the bridegroom's profession and the name of the rabbi.

In registers of deaths: the name, and often the profession of the deceased, his legal status, his age, the date and cause of death.

If the register referred to more than one town or village, the place where the birth, death or marriage took place had to be given. Usually the instructions covered also the safe-keeping of the registers, the originals as well as the duplicates. The originals were, if no other orders were given, kept in the community-offices.

Apart from the registers of births, deaths and marriages, so-called 'family-books' were kept almost everywhere, listing every member of the household, often including servants living with the family.

Into several birth registers of Bavaria, Braunscweig and Holstein entries were made in 1938 regarding the additional Jewish private names (Israel—Sara) requested by the government. The entries were made by the 'Polizei—präsidium', and in the Braunscweig registers the annulment of these names in 1951 has also been entered.

(i) *Baden*. In the year 1809, with the enactment of the Code Napoleon, the rabbis in Baden were appointed to act as registrars for the Jewish population. It was, however, established by a new edict (20 May 1811) that the registers were to be kept by the magistrates if—owing to insufficient knowledge of the German language—a rabbi could not fulfil his duty. In villages, the oldest vicar acted as registrar.

The decree of 28 April 1817 transferred the duty of register-keeping also in towns to the clergy, excepting Karlsruhe, Mannheim, Bruchsal and Heidelberg, but there exist nevertheless—eg, from Heidelberg for the years 1820-27—registers drawn by the Lutheran parson. Twice yearly the parochial offices had to send the Jewish birth-registers to a higher state authority. By the ministerial resolutions of June 1841 and October 1851, registration again became (with certain exceptions) the rabbi's responsibility. The law of 21 December 1869, enacted civil registers and civil marriage in Baden.

All register books were kept in three different sections (births, marriages, deaths) some of them on special formularies. A few communities compiled retrospective lists reaching back to the second half of the eighteenth century.

The very bulky birth registers of Heidelberg show frequently, in addition to the usual particulars, the names of two witnesses, the date of the parents' marriage licence, the date of circumcision and, if the child died early, the date of death. From the year 1820 onwards the entries are signed by the registrar. At the end of each volume of birth and marriage registers here, as in some other towns, an alphabetical index was added, listing, in marriage registers, only the name of the husband. The birth register of Bruchsal contains an alphabetical index in Hebrew script, with the dates of birth according to the Hebrew calendar.

Most registers end with the year 1869. Some communities continued registration until the end of the century for their own needs, the registers finally being turned into lists of names only.

(ii) *Bavaria.* Up to the year 1807, no law existed in the Bavarian kingdom regarding the keeping of Jewish birth, marriage and death registers. The early German written registers in the Jewish Historical General Archives come from Swabia, from the then margraviate (Markgrafentum) Burgau, which in that period (1722-84) belonged to Austria. In Bayreuth, too, a 'Metzgermeister und kommissionär' (butcher and commission agent) kept as far back as 1799 regular registers which, although his private pastime and written in Yiddish (Hebrew script), reached far into the nineteenth century. These were later used as a basis for official retrospective registers.

In the years 1807-08 the Jewish community began—in obedience to a decree issued by the royal county courts (Kgl. Landgerichte)—to carry out registration of births, marriages and deaths. Registers had to be made according to prescribed formularies and, before being given over to the royal courts, had to be verified by the 'Judensvorsteher' (heads of the community). Later regulations provided that the rabbi—or in places without a rabbi, the schoolteacher or the clerk (Gemeindeschreiber), under supervision of the district rabbi or the head of the community—should keep the registers. Only in the Grand-dukedom (Grossherzogthum) of Würzburg, then under the reign of Ferdinand of Toscana, does it seem to have been the vicar's duty to supervise the Jewish registers.

The edict on the status of the Jews (Verhältnisse d. isr. Glaubensgenossen), of 1813 prescribed the adoption of German family names, which were later entered into the official matricula. Only the Jew who had a number in the matricula was, with his family, recognised as a protected Jew (Schutzjude), and only if one family had died out could another take its place; a law abolished only in 1861.

Duplicates of the registers had usually to be handed over to the police or to the head of the community every three—or in other places, twelve —months. In some towns where registration was carried out according to instructions, birth registers contain, besides the usual entries, the house number, the name of the midwife (about 1820 at the earliest) and additional notes, eg, later profession, the date of eventual emigration or, if the child died, the date of death. The name of the godfather appears only with boys, and sometimes the date of circumcision is added. In retrospective registers, girls' names usually appear from about the year 1809 only, those registers being for the most part copies of circumcision books.

Most registers, however, are at first very primitive, birth registers in 1836 still containing, in form of simple notes, only the children's names, the date of their birth and, sometimes, the names of the parents.

In death registers the cause of death has always been entered, the physician's name only—and even then not regularly—from about 1820. The required names of witnesses appear only in marriage registers and much later, from about 1850, also in death registers. Printed registers came into use rather late: only the very exact registers of the community of Fürth in this form in 1876.

Sometimes we find in the register books—which in most cases contain the three registers one after the other—additional entries of other kinds. Hammelburg: particulars of dowries, accounts, copies of legal texts etc. Altenstadt: lists of house numbers and budget notes; and in Mulhausen, medical prescriptions, certificates of poverty, copies of legal texts and so on. The column 'further notes' contains from time to time particulars on the official matricula, eg, in Hammelburg and Altenstadt '. . . has handed over his matricula' '. . . this family became "empty" ' etc.

There also exist family books and census lists from some places, among them Diespeck (containing details on immatriculation, working concession etc.), Hammelburg, Bayreuth, Forchheim and Altenstadt. Usually there is one page for each family, including sometimes the names of the servants.

The birth, marriage and death registers end at different times, and many of them reach far into the period of civil registration.

(iii) *Braunschweig.* The birth, marriage and death registers of the Jews, which begin in the year 1809 (Wolfenbüttel, Seesen), have reached us only in the form of copies or extracts made in the second half of the nineteenth century. Only one book—which also contained changes of domicile—had been used for the three registers. The next registers of Wolfenbüttel, which begin with the year 1855, contain, apart from the usual particulars, the following information: marriage-registers: particulars of the banns and the parents' names; birth registers: the name and domicile of the 'Mohel' (circumciser), the Hebrew date and often

L

the Hebrew name of the child; death registers: the burial place and the Hebrew date of death. The registers close with the year 1899.

The register book of Seesen and those of Gandersheim are both written on formularies, the former containing the three lists one after the other, and the latter having every page divided into three parts. Two special columns existed in the Gandersheim registers: one, in the birth registers, requiring the entry: alive or still born; the other, in the death registers, for children having died under the age of three. All registers were kept by the head of the community.

(iv) *Frankfurt/Main.* The decree of the town council (Ratsdekret) issued on 14 March 1805 ordered the keeping of Jewish birth, marriage and death registers. The registers begin in April 1805 and, apart from the dates, were written in Hebrew script. Every register ends with an alphabetical index.

The birth registers give, at that time, only the names of parents and child; the marriage registers the names of bride and groom and the legal status of the bride. Death registers which fail to give the age of the deceased sometimes contain particulars of surviving or dead relatives. Every register was kept apart and, at the end of every month, had to be sent to the town authorities. The registrar was appointed by the head of the community. New registers written in German begin with the year 1808. As before, there are three different registers, in the form of simple lists without formularies, for marriages, births and deaths, the first two showing only the usual particulars; the latter, from about the twenties of the nineteenth century, often containing dates of birth and marriage and the names of parent and wife. From the beginning there appears, with the entry of a woman's death, the name of the husband or the father. The alphabetical indices from 1808 onwards were continued only in the birth registers. The registers close with the year 1876.

(v) *Free Hanseatic City, Hamburg.* In 1815 the Hamburg government issued an edict ordering all church and Jewish congregations to keep birth, marriage and death registers. Duplicates had to be sent to the town archives at the end of every year. The registrar was a Jew, responsible not to the Jewish community but to the 'Wedde' (special registration authority in Hamburg). By an order of 24 October 1851, mixed marriages and the births of children of these marriages were to be entered into special registers at the 'Wedde'.

For members of the Portuguese community, special instructions were issued. All these regulations remained in force until the year 1865.

(vi) *Hanover.* Jewish registers were already being kept during the time when Hanover was part of the Westphalian kingdom, ie, from

1808-13. After the Napoleonic period, registration seems to have been discontinued, and it was not until 1831 that the royal 'Landdrostei' in Hanover issued new regulations regarding the country rabbinate and ordered the chief rabbi to keep two identical birth, marriage and death registers for each of the three districts. At the end of each year one of these two registers had to be sent to the 'Landdrostei'. In 1832 the 'Landdrostei' in Lüneburg authorised the rabbi to appoint a Jewish registrar for every district. One book, consisting of three kinds of printed formularies, contained the birth, marriage and death registers one after the other. Dates were to be given either according to the German or to the Hebrew calendar. Death registers contained special columns for the birthplace and profession of the deceased.

In 1843 special regulations, based upon the 'law on the legal status (Rechtsverhältnisse) of the Jews' of 30 September 1842, were issued. According to these instructions, registration was to be carried out by the head or another member of the community, under supervision of the district rabbi and the authorities. At the end of every year, certified duplicates and the original register had to be sent to the authorities for inspection. The three registers, from then on kept separately, had to be written in German. The dates, too, had to be according to the German calendar.

(vii) *Grand-dukedom of Hessen*. Official registration, in the Grand-dukedom of Hessen, has never been carried out by the Jews themselves. The parson, later the 'Landrat' and his officials, and, finally, the burgo-master, had to keep the birth, marriage and death registers. A degree of 1732 ordered the parsons to keep a *'matriculum nascentium Judaeorum'* for registration of boys only. As stated in this and a later decree of 1787, the aim was to prevent marriages of minors among the Jewish popula-tion. The decree of 1787-88 stated the conditions for marriage licences among Jews, and contained new instructions for the registration of marriages and deaths. The births of girls, too, which previously had only occasionally been entered, had now officially to be registered. In some parish registers we find only entries of Jews from now on. In most cases, the parson kept, at the end of his register book, some pages for the entry of Jews, but there exist also some books for Jews only. The three different sections (for births, deaths and marriages) appear usually one after the other, but in some books every page is subdivided into three parts.

On 10 April 1800, there appeared a proclamation by the 'Hessischen Oberamt' ordering the various mayors to remind the Jews of their obligation to follow the regulations of 1788.

By the law of 15 December 1808, which ordered the adoption of German family names, register-keeping became the duty of the ducal officials. The Jewish registers, or extracts of the parish registers, previously kept by the parsons had to be handed over to these officials, who had to draw up special lists with the new names chosen by the Jews and to send the lists to the government. Exact regulations were now issued: the three registers were to appear in one book with three sections. Every entry had to be signed by the registrar, and in marriage registers, by both husband and wife; in birth registers, by the father of the new born and in death registers by two neighbours. The midwife had to testify to the exact hour of the birth.

New regulations under a law of 26 February 1823 decreed that registration was in future to be carried out by the burgomaster, who was to keep three different books. Each entry had to be signed by him, and in addition to the signatures previously required, marriage registers were to be signed by two witnesses, and birth registers by two witnesses and the midwife. The latter signature appears regularly only from about the year 1827.

The registers, as again stated in 1827, had to be in form of short reports made by the burgomaster. Beginning with the same year, the births in each family had to be enumerated.

The last regulations, issued by the Grossherzogl Hess, Ministry of the Interior on 9 August 1837, ordered the use of printed formularies, again in the form of reports. Every entry had to be made twice, the original formulary remaining with the burgomaster, the duplicate being sent to the district court. Special formularies had to be used for illegitimate children. The completeness of the registers had to be certified by the burgomaster at the end of each year and an alphabetical index had to be compiled for each bound volume of formularies. Registration fees, amounting to 20 Kr., in accordance with the earlier decrees of 1787-88 and 1823, were now cancelled. The registers end between the years 1873 and 1876.

(viii) *Hohenzollern-Hechingen*. Birth, marriage and death registers of Hohenzollern-Hechingen now in the Jewish Historical General Archives mostly begin with the year 1820 or 1828. A note in the birth register of Hechingen informs us that the registers were drawn by the rabbi according to the instructions of the ducal commissioner for Jewish affairs. The birth register of Hechingen contains—apart from the usual particulars—occasional entries in the 'special notes' column: giving the date of death, while the register of Heigerloch occasionally gives the names of two witnesses and the corresponding number of the family register. There exist, too, retrospective birth registers, reaching back as far as 1800, based upon school and circumcision lists. Most registers reach up to the thirties of the present century, showing less particulars as from the year 1876.

(ix) *Holstein.* The Jewish Historical General Archives contain Jewish birth, marriage and death registers of the communities of Kiel, beginning in 1841, and of Elmshorn, beginning in 1847.

In the Elmshorn registers, births and deaths are entered on the same page, every page being vertically divided in two. Men and women were entered separately. The particulars were few: in birth registers, the name of the child, its parents and the date of birth; in death registers, the name of the deceased, his age and the date of death. The registers are written in German, but they also contain many Hebrew entries.

The registers of the community of Kiel contain the usual particulars. In the marriage registers, we find the names of two witnesses with every entry. There exists one restrospective register, apparently drawn about 1850, and containing births from the year 1771, marriages from the year 1801 and deaths from the year 1846 onwards. The entries are presumably copies from circumcision books and other internal lists of the community.

The Danish law on the conditions of the Jews in the dukedom of Holstein (14 VIII, 1863) contained some instructions regarding the keeping of Jewish registers. In places where a synagogue existed, two identical registers had to be kept by the warden; in other places a government-appointed official acted as registrar. More exact instructions were to have followed but, for political reasons, were never issued.

The edict on the keeping of Jewish registers issued on 22 December 1866 by the Prussian 'Ober-Präsidium' for Schleswig-Holstein brought no special changes. The registers show the usual particulars and had, from then onwards, to be certified by the town authorities once a year.

(x) *Free Hanseatic City of Lübeck.* The first Jewish registers of the Hanseatic city of Lübeck (the Jewish community of Moisling) date from the years 1811-13 and exist only in the form of copies made in later registers. In the first birth registers copied there we find, with every entry, the signature and names of the father and two witnesses, and, sometimes, their ages and professions. The same book contains a copy of the birth register of 1814-47 which, from the year 1830 onwards, often gives additionally, the dates according to the Jewish calendar in Hebrew script. The death registers (1812-28) are extracts from the death register of the town of Lübeck; they, too, show the names and signatures of two witnesses.

The regular register books begin with the year 1848. Three different forms of statements for births, marriages and deaths took the place of the previous registers, and were kept in three different books. No special particulars were required. The entries in the birth registers were, up to the year 1853, signed by the father and the registrar, sometimes only by the latter. From 1853 there appears, in all registers, only the signature of the rabbi. The birth and death registers end with the year 1876; the marriage register—with slight alterations as from 1876—in 1918.

(xi) *Mecklenburg-Schwerin.* As early as 1797, lists of births, deaths and marriages had to be sent by the Jewish congregations to the district rabbi. A ducal decree of the year 1813 ordered the keeping of 'Jewish churchbooks'. These books, beginning at about that time and written mostly on printed formularies, have been kept more or less uniformly in two parts, one book containing the birth and marriage register, the other only the death register. The registers of the town of Brüel contain, additionally, entries in Hebrew script. In some places, retrospective registers have been made reaching back to the eighties of the eighteenth century.

(xii) *Oldenburg.* The first Jewish registers, which have reached us only in the form of copies made in 1836, were apparently drawn at the time of the Westphalian kingdom. These registers end in 1814, and from that time until the year 1828 no official birth, marriage and death registers were kept. On 14 August 1827, an edict regarding the civil status of the Jews was issued, which contained, *inter alia*, instructions on the subject. From the beginning of the year 1828, registration was to be carried out by the local parson, who had to follow the instructions for the keeping of churchbooks and the regulations regarding the use of German family names for the Jews of 1827. There was one Jewish churchbook for every parish, containing the three registers one after the other, beginning usually about the year 1825 and ending about 1850-51. The required particulars were few, the birth registers, for example, recording only the names of parents and child, and the date of birth.

From time to time there were entries of other kinds: eg, a list of German family names of 1828, of country rabbis (1829) and of teachers of the congregation (1829-37) in the register book of the community of Vechte.

New instructions were apparently given in 1850-51, as from then on there exists only one churchbook for all Jewish births, marriages and deaths in the whole dukedom. It was kept during the years 1851-75. The particulars were more or less the same as in previous registers, though sometimes we find the name of the person who announced the birth.

All these regulations were not, apparently, in force in the north-western part of the dukedom. The first statistical survey of the Jewish population, which served as the basis for later registers, was made in 1840, when the heads of the Jewish families were summoned to appear before the magistrate for this purpose.

(xiii) *Prussia*. The edict regarding the civil status of Jews in the Prussian State (Edikt, betr, die bürgerlichen verhältnisse der Juden in Preussischen Staate), of 11 March 1812 does not itself contain any instructions as regards the keeping of registers, but there appeared on 25 June of the same year a special rescript by v. Hardenberg, giving exact orders as to how and by whom registers were to be kept. The police authorities had to draw up two identical lists containing births, deaths, marriages and divorces of the Jewish citizens of Prussia and to send the duplicate to the government at the end of every year.

There exist some retrospective lists, reaching back to the beginning of the nineteenth century, which apparently are based on circumcision books etc, or on individual inquiries.

According to a further order issued by the royal government on 2 February 1818, the illegitimate birth of the child of a Christian father was not to be entered in the Jewish register. In 1819, the government of the Oppeln district (Silesia) reminded the police authorities that birth data had to appear not only according to the Hebrew, but also the German calendar.

In most of the new Prussian districts, where other regulations had been in force, the new system was introduced by 1825. In Westphalia, for instance, registration was at first carried out by the synagogue wardens and partly by the church. In 1821-22, the registers had to be sent to the authorities (burgomaster or 'Landrat') who thereafter kept them under regulations identical with those of the rescript of 1812. Notice of every event had to be given within twenty-four hours, but apparently these instructions were not always followed. The burgo-master of Minden, for instance, received as late as 1836 a letter from the Landrat suggesting that the wardens read out the regulations in the synagogues regularly on certain days during the year.

In some districts, register-keeping seems to have been the duty of the Jewish congregation itself, as at Halberstadt. In the province of Posen, where the legal status of the Jews was entirely different from that prevailing in the rest of Prussia, registration until the year 1834 was apparently carried out by the Jewish community. Only then, by the regulations regarding the keeping of Jewish registers in the Posen district of 28 January 1834, were the mayors or 'woyts' and the administrative heads of the Jewish corporations appointed as registrars. The original register had to be kept by the mayors and later sent to the superior authorities; the duplicates, kept by the Jewish corporations, were sent to the mayor's office. Both registers had to be supervised and confirmed by the Landrat.

Every entry had to be signed by the registrar, the person announcing the case and two witnesses. Only after registration were the necessary religious rites (circumcision, funeral, etc) allowed to be performed.

In the Bromberg district under an order of 1823, register-keeping in towns became the duty of the burgomasters and chiefs of police, and in the country of the mayors. Here, as well as in all other Prussian provinces, the register had to contain details of births, deaths, marriages and divorces.

The law of 23 July 1847 introduced identical regulations for the whole of Prussia. Particulars remained more or less the same but, thenceforward, the birth, death and marriage registers had to be kept by a judge-in-ordinary.

Registration was usually carried out in German. Only in the formularies attached to the 1834 'Regulativ' of Posen were the column titles printed in Polish as well. Some registers, additionally, contain dates and names in Hebrew script. The three required registers were mostly kept in three different books consisting of printed formularies, and again we sometimes find, under the 'special notes' column, additional particulars about property (marriage register of Verden on Aller) the date of death (register of Steele, district Minden), and even the subsequent profession and residence of the new born child (Unna).

(xiv) *Sachsen, Weimer, Eisenach.* The first regulations regarding the keeping of Jewish registers seem to have appeared in the 'Judenordnung' of 20 June 1823. The decree of 14 August 1838, issued by the 'Grossherzogl Sächsische Landesdirektion, Weimar,' referred to the same 'Judenordnung' and gave more and detailed instructions, supplying formularies for the three registers to be kept. Registration was to be carried out both by the parsons and by the district rabbi. In small places, the teacher or the reader in the synagogue had to keep the registers and, after careful comparison with those kept by the parson, send them to the district rabbi, who then copied the data into his general registers. In 1873, a supplement to this law ordered that, in places where no Jewish community existed, the vicar should notify the district rabbi, at the end of the year, of every case which had occurred in his parish. An alphabetical index, compiled separately for men and women, had to be added to each register book.

Besides the usual entries, there had to be the following particulars: in birth registers, the dates of marriage and death of the new born and the subsequent numbers of births in one family; in death registers, the family status of the deceased (if and how many times married etc). Marriages performed abroad and mixed marriages had to be registered.

On 3 June 1876, a ministerial decree ordered the continuation of the registers 'in the interest of the Jewish "cultus" '. The registers from then on were to be kept by Jews, and new consequent numbers had to be given. The lists had to be carefully compared with the civil registers to ensure that the entries were identical.

(xv) *Schleswig*. The Jewish marriage registers of Friedrichstadt on the Eider for the years 1847-54, which have been kept on printed formularies, contain very detailed records, not only on bride and bridegroom and their legal status, but on their parents as well (if alive or dead, the maiden name and birthplace of the mother). The birth registers, besides the usual particulars, contain the date and place of the parents' marriage, and there are similar entries in the death registers. Dates according to the Hebrew calendar have been added.

By an order of 6 February 1854, two birth, marriage and death registers had to be kept simultaneously, one by the warden of the synagogue and another by the police authorities. Twice yearly the warden had to send his registers to the government authorities, who had to confirm the identical character of the two copies. Not even for one night were the two copies to remain under the same roof.

The new registers, which begin in 1854 and end in 1874, and for which handwritten formularies have been used, contain only the usual particulars.

(xvi) *The Westphalian Kingdom*. By a decree of 3 March 1809, it became, *inter alia*, the duty of the Jewish 'syndici' to keep special 'synagogue books'. Births and deaths, both with indication of the exact hour, also marriages and confirmations had to be entered into these books, in four different sections. A list of the synagogue members had also to be drawn up.

The Code Napoleon ordered the supervision of the books by the rabbi in co-operation with the civil authorities. The rabbi was also required to supervise the use of German family names.

(xvii) *Württemberg*. The keeping of Jewish birth, death and marriage registers was enacted by a rescript of 15 December 1807, under which registration had to be carried out by the synagogue warden or, where there were no synagogues, by the head of the municipality. However, parsons, who, until 1820 had to keep Christian registers only, have in many places also carried out registration of the Jews.

New regulations appeared on 10 July 1820, after which it became the parsons' official duty to keep the Jewish registers. The required particulars had to be supplied by the former registrars. Registration, usually carried out on printed registers which showed only slight differences of form and content, began in 1808. Apart from the usual particulars, we now find in birth registers the father's profession and, from time to time, the maiden name of the mother. In most cases the date of circumcision has been entered only from about 1820 or later. Marriage registers frequently show, from 1822-23 onwards, the names of two witnesses. Every entry—in birth, death and marriage registers alike—gives the corresponding page in the family register.

GENERAL NOTE: Access to the registers—as to all other archival units stored with the Jewish Historical General Archives—is open to the general public. Special formularies have to be completed, giving the reason (historical research, genealogical work, etc) for wishing to use the documents, which may not be taken out of the archives. On request, microfilms or certified copies can be made. The Jewish Historical General Archives regularly send inventories of the material stored with them to other institutions.

In Germany, the Society for Jewish Family Research published from 1925-38 the *Mitteilungen der Gesellschaft fur Jüdische Familienforschung* (1-50).

In Israel, there are no special genealogical societies, but traditional genealogical work is being carried out in many private genealogical archives.

CHAPTER 11

The Orient and Latin America

Japan

IT is not easy to obtain genealogical clues and data for some countries inside Europe, and more difficult still for those lands outside, but where information is obtainable, as with the following notes on Japanese sources, it would be wrong not to include it.

In Japan, registration of the vital statistics is regulated by the Family Registration Law. The reference to this is given as Law No 224, promulgated on 22 December 1947, as amended by Law No 260 of 1948, Law No 137 of 1949, Law No 148 of 1950, and Laws No 106 and 268 of 1952. These particulars were supplied by the Bureau of Statistics, Office of the Prime Minister, Shinjuku, Tokyo.

The provisions of the Family Registration Law are comprehensive, as the different chapters indicate.

(i) General Provisions. These are mainly concerned with stipulating that family registration shall be undertaken by the mayor of a city or the head of a town or village (Article 7). Supervision (Article 3) is exercised by the head of the Legal Affairs Bureau or District Legal Affairs Bureau having jurisdiction over the district in which the office of city, town or village is situated. (ii) Family Registration Books. (iii) Registration in Family Registers. The particulars entered are both comprehensive and specific, as may be seen by the next section. (iv) Notifications include, birth, recognition (usually of a child to be legitimated) adoption, dissolution of adoptive relations, marriage, divorce, parental power and guardianship, death and disappearance, resumption of surname by surviving spouse and dissolution of matrimonial relations, disinheritance of a presumptive successor, entry into or separation from a family, acquisition of name or surname, and transfer of registered locality of family and establishment of a family register. (v) Deals with the procedure for the rectification of family registers.

To obtain information on these matters, inquiry should be routed through the Civil Affairs Bureau, Ministry of Justice, Tokyo. From the latter is derived the following account of the workings of the Family Registration Law.

The Japanese system of family registers ensures that all matters relative to the status of a Japanese national from his birth to his death are collectively recorded and attested. A person's family register is kept by the particular city, ward, town or village in which he lives and is not only the record of all matters concerning his status, but also the collective record of all those who are related to that person as man and wife, parent and child.

Birth, marriage and death are all entered in the family register. Notification of birth and death must be made to the office of the city, ward, town or village in which the event took place. It must be made by the person prescribed by the Family Registration Law to make such notification and must also be in the form and within the period prescribed by that law. Notification of marriage must similarly be made in the registered locality of the individuals concerned, and a marriage is legally recognised only when such notification has been made.

All notifications are entered in the family register of the relevant person by the mayor of the city or head man of the ward, town or village in charge of family registration. Where a notification has been made to an office other than that of the registered locality it is transmitted to the office of the registered locality for entry in the family register. When entered, the notification is sent to the Legal Affairs Bureau or its branch and kept on file for twenty-seven years, being open to public inspection. Where an entry or record is struck off the family register because of the death of all the persons concerned, it is then transferred to another file (called 'the file of struck-off registers') and kept for fifty years. Thus the period for which a family register is preserved is from the time it is prepared to the time it is struck off, plus the fifty years for which it will continue to be preserved.

The register is kept in the appropriate office of the registered locality and there is no system in Japan for gathering together, recording and preserving notifications in one central place. Nor is there any centralised Public Record Office as in England.

Wills: on this subject the Ministry of Justice writes; 'The attestation of a will is a form of proving procedure before it is executed. This is carried out in the case of wills drawn up in any form, with the exception of a will made in a notarial deed and for which the family court has authority for attestation. From the seventh or eighth centuries (monarchic age) until the early days of the seventeenth century (medieval age of Samurai government) it was not necessary for wills to have been made in a fixed form, though as a rule inheritance was by wills. In the eighteenth century (Edo age) inheritance among the commonalty was usually by wills, and in such cases the will had either to be sealed by the local government official or must be a holographic deed. In those days a will was customarily opened in the presence of relatives and local officials on a specific day, eg, the 17th, 49th, or 100th day from the death of the person who had made the will. Since the latter half of the nineteenth century (Meiji Era), inheritance has generally been in accordance with the provisions of the Civil Code, and few wills have been made.

'A will is kept either by the person who made it, the person to whom it is entrusted (eg, a trust, banking company or friend), or a notary public. When a will is drawn up by a notary public in a notarial deed, the original is kept by him. When the family court attests a will it enters in the protocol of attestation the form, standard and particulars of the will, and may sometimes have a photostat made. Such protocol of attestation is preserved for fifty years.'

China

For very many centuries ancestor worship has been a dominant feature of Chinese life, though it is said that, under the existing Communist regime, attacks are now being made upon this immemorial tradition of the Chinese. Here it is possible only to give such information as would have been applicable under the Republic of China, now represented by the government of Chiang-Kai-shek on Taiwan (Formosa).

1. Registration of births, marriages and death came under the Census Section of the Civil Affairs Department of every precinct or borough. It was the rule that every event had to be registered within fifteen days of its occurrence and failure to comply with this order made the offender subject to a fine. The records were held by the precinct or borough. In the event of a family moving from one precinct to another, it was necessary to notify the Census Section so that its records could be passed on to the next precinct.

2. The registration described was the only one necessary for all citizens. A certificate of baptism, in the case of a Chinese Christian, could be used as evidence.

3. Census records were kept only in localities and nothing resembling the PRO in Britain existed—not surprisingly considering the vast size of China.

4. Wills were regarded as strictly personal and seldom published. More detailed information might be obtained from: The Government Information Service, 1709 Chung Cheng Road, Taipei, Taiwan, or The Free Chinese Centre and Newsletter, Albany House, 324 Regent Street, London, W1.

Latin America

It is far from easy to obtain genealogical information from this part of the world. In Mexico, for instance, it is stated that for information relating to civil and religious registration, on wills etc, reference should be made to Jefe de la Oficina del Registro Civil, Netzahualcoytl No 94, Mexico 1, D.F. On matters heraldic, application should be made to: Jefe del Departmento de Biblioteca, Palacio Nacional, Mexico 1, D.F.

In Peru, there is a Peruvian genealogical society which publishes a *Boletin Interno Del Instituto Peruano de Investigaciones Genealogicas.* The address is: Ocharón 444, Miraflores, Lima, Peru.

In Chile, there is the Instituto Chileno de Investigaciones Genealogicas, Casilla 1,386, Santiago de Chile.

Inquirers wishing to obtain information about the genealogical resources of Latin America are advised also to consult the Instituto Internacional de Genealogia y Heraldica, 12079 Apartado de Correos, Madrid, Spain.

PART 2

Heraldry, Titles, Peerage Law and Orders of Chivalry

CHAPTER 12

Heraldry

GENEALOGY goes back to the days of the most ancient civilizations and indeed forms one of the most useful and important parts of the history of each country. Heraldry, in Europe at least, originated in the twelfth century, but although so much younger than the science of genealogy, it is of great service to it. The purpose of heraldic devices was to assist identification of individuals; thus use of the same coat of arms should indicate relationship, and in this way heraldry can provide a sign-post to the direction a genealogical tree ought to take. In the first centuries of heraldry there is no doubt that identity of arms was considered to indicate kinship of blood; hence the numerous disputes between those who used the same arms but were not related. Incidentally, these disputes arose only because, in early times, a simple coat of arms was often worked out by two or more persons in complete ignorance of each other. When, on coming together, they discovered that they possessed the same arms the resulting quarrel often ended in a duel or a law suit, as we shall see later in the famous English case of Scrope v Grosvenor.

In the dictionary definition of heraldry we find: 'Science of a herald; armorial bearings; heraldic pomp.' (*Concise Oxford Dictionary*); 'The art or office of a herald; the science of recording genealogies and blazoning coats of arms.' (*Chambers' Twentieth Century Dictionary*). To the average person, however, heraldry means something very different from these definitions and no matter how unfamiliar he may be with heraldic terms or descriptions, he will usually have a rough idea of what an heraldic illustration looks like. He may even have ventured upon an inquiry into the language of heraldry and found it full of mystery with talk of gules, lions passant or rampant, bends, fesses and the like, all quite unintelligible to him.

Again, most people have heard or read of crests, without being quite clear as to what they are. Newspaper and popular writers like novelists, often offend very badly in this respect by using the word 'crest' incorrectly. Therefore at the very outset it is essential to understand the meaning of the main heraldic terms. Fortunately they are simple to grasp; anyone of normal intelligence can learn the rudiments of heraldry in a few days and then fill in the sketch as and when required. There is no need to burden one's memory with all the items of heraldic lore, when there are dictionaries and glossaries to which to refer. At the time of Queen Elizabeth II's coronation, models of the various royal badges were made, including an extremely rare one of the yale, a mythical monster seldom used in heraldry. A term of such rarity as this need not be learned until it arrives within one's ken.

To begin with the word 'heraldry'. Clearly the dictionary definition does not correspond to the popular and well-established usage of the word. The correct term is 'armory' and it is now used to denote heraldic objects and practice only by those who have written treatises intended for experts, and only occasionally even by the experts themselves. There is, however, one famous instance where the word will live as long as heraldry itself, and that is in the title of the well-known work, *Burke's General Armory*, containing descriptions of about 100,000 coats of arms which are known in the British Isles. The Continental work by Rietstap goes under the same title, *Armorial Général* and so, too, with other national works, such as the French *Armorial Universelle*.

Heralds as the primal form of ambassadors have existed from very early times. The most learned modern writer on heraldry, the Rev John Woodward, remarked: 'Etymologically, a treatise on heraldry should be an explanation of the duties of a herald. Though an analogy has been drawn between the Greek Κηρυξ or Latin *fecialis* (scilicet *fetialis*) and the herald of later times, the latter was essentially a medieval officer whose name seems to be derived from *Heer*, a host, and *Held*, a champion.' (*A Treatise on Heraldry, British and Foreign*, 1892, p 1). Woodward hastens to add: 'The "science" or rather art, which teaches us the language, and instructs us in the origin and development, of these symbols, should with greater propriety be termed Armory. This is the designation applied to it by the earliest writers on the subject, both in England and in France, but it is one which for more than two and a half centuries, has greatly fallen into disuse; and the better understood name of Heraldry consequently appears in the title of the present work.' (*op cit*, p 2). Hence, too, the usage here of the term 'heraldry' which one can further define as the science and art of symbols used in families, and by transference, to institutions; in other words as hereditary symbols used by individuals, families and corporate bodies, the latter being viewed as legal *personae*.

The terms used in heraldry point most clearly to the times when it originated, for they are all connected with arms and armour. Symbolism has existed in all human communities, and a very common usage has been to adopt the figure of an animal as a symbol. An instance well known in America is that of the totem pole of the Canadian Indians, which serves both genealogical and heraldic purposes. As to the precise origins of heraldry, we simply do not know and are forced to rely upon such evidence as we possess. The earliest known example of an heraldic shield is on an enamel which shows Geoffrey Plantaganet, Count of Anjou, the son-in-law of the English king, Henry I (1100-35). Count Geoffrey is shown holding a shield given to him by his father-in-law and this bears some golden lions in a definitely heraldic form. The enamel dates from 1136. Next to this we have the evidence of seals which, in the period 1135-55, show the use of heraldic designs. As with the use of symbols, so with that of seals, which have been employed from very early times as proof of origin and authenticity of documents.

Documentary evidence of heraldry does not begin until the thirteenth century, about 1250 in England, when Rolls of Arms were drawn up to show the designs used on some particular occasion such as a warlike expedition or a tournament. With seals, however, we can see the first authentic example of the use of arms by a king of England, in the lions which began to appear on the seals of Richard I, Coeur de Lion (1189-99). The three lions in the present royal arms of England are derived from those used by Richard towards the end of his life, and it has been suggested that they originated in the arms of the Counts of Anjou mentioned above, where the lions are heraldically described as lioncels or young lions.

With this positive evidence of the appearance of arms, we can couple some negative evidence which, as we shall see, is of great importance. We are able to study a great historical event, the Norman Conquest, in pictorial form in the famous Bayeux Tapestry, generally accepted by scholars as having been executed within living memory of the Conquest. In many scenes it depicts warriors in battle armour, including William the Conqueror and Harold. In a few cases there are some very rough designs on the shields but they are not particularly heraldic; they alter from picture to picture and the two main characters are without them. Admirable reproductions of the entire Tapestry are to be found in the small work by Sir Eric Maclagan, *The Bayeux Tapestry*, 1943, and in the large second volume of *English Historical Documents*, 1042-1189, published in 1953. Passing on to the next generation after the Norman Conquest, to the time of the First Crusade (1095-99), there is a description of the western knights as they appeared to a trained observer. This was the Princess Anna Comnena, who wrote *The Alexiad*, a history of the reign of her father the Byzantine Emperor, Alexius I. She gives a clear account of the Frankish knights and their shields: 'An additional weapon of defence is a shield which is not round, but a long shield, very broad at the top and running out to a point, hollowed out slightly inside, but externally smooth and gleaming with a brilliant boss of molten brass.' This description corresponds with the appearance of the swallow-tailed shields in the Bayeux Tapestry and such an observer as the princess would probably have noted the appearance of heraldic designs had they then been extensively in use (p 341, trans. E. A. S. Dawes, 1967).

What, then, caused the growth of heraldic devices, since they were evidently not in use at the end of the eleventh century, yet are found well into the twelfth century? We cannot be precise. Some writers assign the origin of heraldry to the Crusades, which have long been ascribed as the cause of anything medieval not otherwise explicable. (Rather as English detectives in the nineteenth century, faced with an insoluble murder, sometimes assigned it to Jack the Ripper!). The Crusades may have had some influence, because they did bring together large numbers of men from different races, which might have resulted in the appearance of national symbols. Others think that the use of armorial bearings spread on to armour from the seals. The more probable explanation may be that the development of body armour made the identification of individual fighters very difficult. At the time of the Norman Conquest, the western warriors wore suits of chain mail which left the face open, except for a nose-piece coming down from the conical helmet. The armour did not cover the leg below the knee and the hands were bare. The armour was a western invention and unknown in eastern Europe, for Princess Comnena remarks on it: '. . . the Franks were difficult to wound, or rather, practically invulnerable, thanks to their breastplates and coats of mail. Therefore he (the Emperor Alexius) considered shooting at them useless and quite senseless. For the Frankish weapon of defence is this coat of mail, ring plaited into ring, and the iron fabric is such excellent iron that it repels arrows and keeps the wearer's skin unhurt.' (Armour of a different type had, of course, been known from earlier times, and was used in the eastern armies). A different view of their invulnerability was taken by the western knights themselves. They felt that they needed all-enveloping armour.

Some unimaginative persons say that, in the 1066 period, recognition of the individual warrior was still possible, but this opinion can hardly be shared by anyone who has studied the Tapestry. At the crisis of the battle of Hastings, William the Conqueror had to pull off his helmet to show that he was alive and meant to conquer. His descendant a century later, Richard Coeur de Lion, would have found the throwing off of his helmet a task requiring the assistance of his squire. Still, even if we grant some recognition as possible to the lighter armed warriors of 1066, it is certainly true that in three generations the body armour had become all-enveloping and plate was beginning to be used with the ring mail. The evolution of armour over the next 300 or 400 years was all in the direction of greater complexity, plate entirely replacing chain mail, until by the time of the English Wars of the Roses in the mid-fifteenth century a fully armoured knight had only very limited mobility. Anyone who has seen a collection of armour, as in the Tower of London, or in the Royal Armoury in Madrid, will readily understand how difficult, or rather impossible, it would have been to distinguish one mail-clad man from another.

As one writer on armour remarks, speaking of the elaborate helmets (heaumes): 'These heaumes, by concealing the face, intensified a difficulty already felt at Hastings, when Duke William was obliged to raise his helmet to contradict a rumour of his death. Recognition, now become impossible, led to the use of heraldic badges, at first painted on the helm, as they already were on the shield; and of crests, first in the fan or peacock's feather shape, as on the second seal of Richard I, and afterwards to more distinctive crests and badges.' (*Armour in England*, by J. Starkie Gardner, 1897, New York, The Macmillan Co).

Whatever its origins, heraldry was from the first associated with the wearing of armour and still retains the old language of that association hundreds of years after armour has ceased to be worn. 'Arms', 'armorial bearings', a 'coat of arms' all bear evidence to this. The term 'coat of arms' is derived from the surcoat which was worn over the armour with the object of keeping off the heat of the sun and preventing the armour from rusting. The surcoat was made of linen for ordinary everyday wear; of silk for special occasions such as a tournament. It was useful to depict on these surcoats the armorial bearings of the wearer, and they were also shown on his shield. Consequently, when we want to refer to an heraldic device, we can use one of four terms: we can say simply, a coat of arms, or armorial bearings, or (heraldic) achievement, or in a more poetic vein, a shield or escutcheon.

No mention has yet been made of a crest, since a crest is only part of a coat of arms; arms can exist without a crest but not vice versa. It is a solecism to refer to the whole of the arms as a crest, though this is a very common error. There is only one case on record in England of the grant of a crest by itself, and the circumstances were such as to inhibit most people from any desire to imitate. The petitioner for arms was shown a sketch of the proposed coat; he did not like it and sent it back, but as he had approved the crest it was entered in the books of the heralds. Before the rest of the arms were approved, the petitioner died.

There are still a number of cases of coats of arms without crests, and an interesting instance occurs in a branch of the family of Sir Winston Churchill, that of the Churchills of Muston. It is often said that crests were at first the appendages of families wealthy enough to take part in tournaments; be that as it may, it is certainly true that by 1500 many families bore arms but had no crest. In the period 1530-1686, the English heralds were touring the country in the Visitations (see below) and in a very venal way were selling crests to arms-bearing families. Many were acquired during that time, and a result of this practice was that it became customary in England always to grant arms with a crest. Those families who are still crestless know that their arms are considerably older than 1600.

We can form a picture of our early bearer of arms, in the time of Richard I. He would be a mounted man, with his arms painted on his shield and embroidered on his surcoat; a pennon or a small swallow-tailed flag on his lance would also bear his arms. If he were a great man he might bear a roughly-made crest of leather on his helmet. Somewhat later his horse might bear trappings, also embroidered with arms. An example occurs in the illustration of a manuscript work known as the 'Luttrell Psalter', dating about 1340. Here the arms are shown on the knight's surcoat and shield, on his horse trappings and on his lance pennon; also on the gowns of his wife and daughter-in-law.

The helmet is another instance of the retention of warlike terms in what has become an entirely peaceful context. The crest was tied to the helmet by the wreath, and the helmet is said to be befitting the degree (ie, rank) of the bearer. In the course of heraldic development, various kinds of helmet have been devised to denote the rank of the arms bearer. Thus the helmet of a king is of gold, full-faced (*affrontée*) and open, but having grilles or bars over the opening. (By open is meant that the visor is raised.) The helmet of a peer is of silver, placed in profile (looking toward the dexter), open and guarded by bars of gold. A baronet or knight has a helmet of steel, *affrontée*, open, without grilles. The helmet of an esquire or gentleman is in steel, in profile, and with the visor closed. These rules may seem a little pedantic but they are useful when looking through illustrations of arms. Americans will all have

the helmets of esquires or gentlemen since, under their national constitution, they are barred from using other than honorary titles. Nevertheless, many notable American families are of royal and noble descent,
so that it is as well for them to able to recognise the type of helmet
used by their ancestors.

The early coats of arms were simple, for the fairly obvious reason
that there were fewer of them and because immediate recognition was
required. The life of a soldier might very well depend on his instantly
recognising an advancing body of men as friends or foes, and for this
he usually relied upon recognition of the armorial bearings of the
leaders. Apart from these vital circumstances, there were also many
occasions when it was highly important for an illiterate population to
recognise the presence of important people. It is the very fact of this
underlying simplicity of heraldry that makes the modern conception of
the subject as something mysterious and reserved for experts so absurd.
Granted that in the 800 years of its existence heraldry has enormously
increased its range, and that with more and more arms being made each
century they have become liable to complication, but that is no reason
for anyone to be ignorant of the essentials of heraldry. (See Note 11).

To this day a grant of arms or a description of arms is in the same
language as of 600-700 years ago, when the terms used did actually relate
to warfare, weapons and armour. Everybody who has arms today in a
grant has a helmet and a shield. The crest is described as being on a
wreath of the colours. This wreath, also called a torse, is usually shown
as if it were a straight rod, of alternate colours, whereas, in reality, it
was the means of tying the crest on to the helmet. In a drawing of arms
one sees, coming down from the helmet on either side, things which
look like cloths. These lambrequins, or mantlings, had severely practical
use in their original state for they were actually cloths hanging down
from the helmet, partly to keep off the sun's rays but also to divert sword
cuts. The description of the arms is known as the blazon, and to blazon
a coat is thus to describe it.

The motto in many coats of arms is shown under the illustration, and
sometimes there are two mottoes, one over the arms, the other below.
Scottish mottoes are usually put above the arms. Many inquirers imagine
that their family motto was a war cry or *cri de guerre* used by some
chivalric ancestor in days when knights were bold, whereas, in fact, it
probably only originated with their great-grandfather. Certainly, however, a few mottoes do come from remoter times and were war cries in
origin. Thus, the royal motto of the English sovereigns, *Dieu et mon
droit*, was first used by Richard I towards the end of his reign, when he

was fighting against the French king. It was dropped by his successors until revived in 1340 by Edward III who was then claiming the French crown and no doubt considered the Coeur de Lion motto very appropriate. But what had begun in about 1195 as a *cri de guerre*, in 1340 had become simply a motto.

Another motto derived from a war cry is that of the FitzGeralds, Dukes of Leinster—'crom a boo'. It is Old Irish, meaning *crom*, a castle in county Limerick, and 'for ever'. An undoubtedly ancient motto, 'Furth fortune and fill the fetters' is used by the Duke of Athol, the Earl of Dunmore, Lord Glenlyon, and some Murray and Stewart families. The explanation of this motto can only be said to be lost in antiquity but it is worth quoting an old account of it, though its accuracy cannot be vouched for. 'During the reign of one of the early Scottish kings a robber was in the habit of plundering the country. One of the Murrays, ancestor of the Duke of Athol, undertook to put a stop to the annoyance, and as he was setting out the king is reported to have said to him, "(Go) forth, (good) fortune (attend you), and (may you) fill the fetters (with your captive)".' This explanation is given by C. N. Elvin in *A Handbook of Mottoes*, p 73, 1963, reprint of 1860 edition, a useful work with translations of all the mottoes given.

Before going on with the subject matter of heraldry and its language, it will be as well to clear up the rest of the component parts of a coat of arms. As mentioned above, the shield is the essential part without which the other portions of the achievement have no existence. Above the shield is the helmet with the crest secured by the wreath, and from the helmet hangs down the lambrequin or mantling. This is the coat of arms as it exists for any man who is armigerous. Passing now to supporters, we come to additions to a coat of arms, which pertain only to certain classes of armigers. Supporters are the figures seen on either side of the shield; very often they are of animals, like the lion and the unicorn on either side of the royal arms of England. Supporters are the prerogative, in England, of peers, knights of the Garter, and of some other orders of knighthood. In Scotland, supporters are often borne by old untitled families, but they are generally of the old feudal nobility.

In the case of peers a coronet, which varies in appearance according to the owner's rank in the peerage, is placed above the shield and below the helmet. Sometimes the shield may be encircled by insignia of an order, as with Earl Mountbatten who is a knight of the Garter (KG). When there are supporters, they are usually shown standing on something, which in many Victorian drawings of arms looks somewhat like the old-fashioned bracket that used to hold a gas jet and light, but is really supposed to be a piece of scroll work. The more modern practice is to show the whole heraldic achievement on a piece of ground, often having grass or plants or flowers growing on it. The resting place of a coat of arms which has supporters is called a compartment.

In connection with crests and helmet, mention should be made of the chapeau, or cap of maintenance. This originally denoted that the bearer was a peer, because the chapeau was worn in Parliament by peers. Thence the usage passed to members of the peerage families who were not themselves peers. When the chapeau is shown below the crest the torse, or wreath, is omitted.

The crest coronet was used at first to denote rank, and is a crown, generally of gold, with strawberry leaves like those used in a ducal coronet. It is often described as such though it differs from the coronet of a duke. 'It was much employed in the Low Countries and in Germany, where, however, it is properly considered an adjunct to the helm rather than a portion of the crest. . . . The use of a coroneted helm is said by some writers to be peculiar to those who are of tourney nobility—whose ancestors had taken part in those conflicts.' (Woodward, *Heraldry*, pp 614-15). Some varieties of crowns, such as the naval, military and mural, are granted in England to persons of distinction in different spheres of action.

Standards were always used in ancient and medieval times, and instances are too numerous for examples to be needed. It still survives today, as with the royal standard of Queen Elizabeth II, which when flown over a building, such as Buckingham Palace, or from the royal yacht, denotes that the sovereign is in residence or on board. Other flags of a similar nature can still be seen occasionally in Britain, as when a nobleman flies his family standard above his house. In armies, too, there are many instances still remaining of the use of standards, at least on ceremonial occasions, though in the present century there can be few cases of flags being carried in actual battle, unless perhaps the Japanese did so in the last war. It is a common practice for British regiments to lay up their colours in churches.

The standard bore the arms of the owner, but as coats of arms became more complicated it proved more useful to have a single device shown on the flag. This was very often the origin of the badge. Badges were sometimes the originals of crests, and they have been used extensively in past times in connection with the clothes of retainers. Most readers of romantic historical fiction will be familiar with stories about badges, standards, the liveries of retainers and the like. With the advent of the Tudor dynasty, the practice of keeping large numbers of retainers was severely discountenanced, and the badge was then frequently transferred to be the crest in the Tudor heralds' Visitations. Many of the old badges survived, and even today one sometimes hears of the grant of a badge or a standard to a modern family. The wearing of liveries by servants survived, and in the seven editions of A. C. Fox-Davies' great work, *Armorial Families* (last issued in 1929-30), the livery colours are nearly always given for the family concerned. These colours are the same as those used for the mantling or lambrequin, ie, the outside being a colour derived from the coat of arms and the inside (lining) being of the metal. Of badges, Fox-Davies remarked, 'Another instance of a badge used at the present day in the ancient manner is the conjoined rose, thistle and shamrock which is embroidered front and back upon the tunics of the Beefeaters and the Yeomen of the Guard' (*Heraldic Badges*, 1907, p 21). Visitors to the Tower of London can see this example of the old use of a badge and will then understand how in feudal times badges were worn on the liveries of servants in great households.

Mantles and pavilions are items which apply only to the arms of kings and nobles and are, as it were, the backcloth behind the whole achievement. A mantle is often of crimson lined with ermine. When surmounted by a crown, it is a pavilion or crown canopy. For examples, see Burke's *Landed Gentry*, 1939 edition, also issued, as regards its American supplement, separately as *Burke's Distinguished Families of America*, 1947. In these volumes will be found, with a canopy for background, the arms of HH Princess Engalitcheff, formerly Bransford—or an eagle sable, the dexter wing extended, the head contourné, resting on a rock proper covered with grass, and holding in the beak a crown of laurel proper. The shield surmounted by a princely coronet. These arms are Russian.

Also in this work, under the Carpenter Marmon article, are the arms of HIH Prince Zourab Tchkotoua and of HIH Prince Nicolas Tchkotoua. These arms are of the Russian Empire but are enrolled at the College of Arms in London. Surmounted by a princely coronet, quarterly 1 azure, in pale, a Maltese cross and a crescent or. 2 gules a figure of St George on a horse argent, helmeted and reined or, piercing with a spear, a dragon proper. 3 gules on a mount vert, a stag statant contourné or. 4 azure a golden fleece. On an inescutcheon ensigned by a coronet or quarterly 1 and 4 vert a Maltese cross or; 2 and 3 azure a lymphad in full sail, oars in action or.

Women also have the right to armorial bearings with certain marked differences, though, with one exception, a woman never bears a shield or a crest. She is not supposed to take part in warfare and therefore her arms are shown on a lozenge (diamond shape) while she is unmarried. This applies to a single woman, whether she is a spinster, a widow or a divorcée. On marrying, a woman uses her arms in conjunction with those of her husband, provided of course that he is armigerous. He then takes his shield, divides it in equal parts from top to bottom, places his arms in the right or dexter side, and his wife's in the left or sinister side. This is known as impalement. Should his wife be an heraldic heiress, then a different arrangement prevails. The husband's coat of arms occupies the whole shield, and his wife's arms are shown on a small shield, known as an inescutcheon of pretence, set in the middle of the husband's shield. An heraldic heiress is, of course, the only or eldest daughter, without any brothers, and not a financial heiress. A recent example of the arrangement just mentioned occurred in 1933, when the 2nd Earl of Inchcape married 'Princess Gold' (Leonora Margaret Brooke), the eldest daughter of the British White Rajah of Sarawak. The Brooke arms appeared as an inescutcheon in the middle of the shield of Lord Inchcape's arms. In these cases, children of the marriage can quarter their paternal with their maternal arms; that is, the shield is divided into four portions with the father's arms in the first and fourth quarters and the maternal coat in the second and third. One other matter which may otherwise cause confusion should be explained here. As one looks at a shield, it must be remembered that it is supposed to be held by someone. Therefore the right or dexter side of the shield is that facing one's left, and the left or sinister side faces one's right.

The derivation of quartering is the cause of the somewhat squashed-up and very overloaded illustrations of coats of arms often seen in connection with old historic families. Not only can two coats of arms be shown together in this way but, if a succession of heiresses has been brought into a family, many quarterings are possible. Some great families have hundreds of quarterings, and one or two dukes in Britain are said to have as many as 1,000 quarterings in each case. Mercifully, no one has tried to illustrate them all. However, many families do have quarterly coats, and double crests are known.

Within the last 200 years there have been many marriage alliances in Britain which have entailed the groom taking the bride's surname in addition to his own, or in consequence of a will a double surname has resulted. The latter practice derives from what are known as name and arms clauses in a will. Their object is to perpetuate the name of a family which might otherwise die out owing to the failure of the male line, and also to ensure the continuance of the estate. This is the reason for many of the double, treble or even quadruple surnames found in Britain.

A fair number of court cases have arisen in this connection, from which the following conclusions can be deduced: (i) a name taken in accordance with a will must be taken in perpetuity and if not persisted in would have the effect of divesting the user of the property to which he has succeeded under the will; (ii) should there be uncertainty in the wording of a name and arms clause it can be void for uncertainty as happened some years back, in *Re Murray* (1955) in which an apparent conflict took place between two clauses of the will; and (iii) an objection can be taken to a name and arms clause on the grounds of public policy, eg, in which a testator has imposed upon a married woman an obligation to take a different name from that of her husband.

The exception mentioned earlier of a woman entitled to have the full coat of arms with crest, helmet and shield, is that of a queen regnant— one who reigns in her own right and not as consort of a king. The obvious example is Elizabeth II of England. As sovereign, the matter of her sex does not come into consideration. She is the Fountain of Honour from whom flow out honours and cannot therefore be without all honours herself.

The language of heraldry is old French, which was used throughout a large part of western Europe as a *lingua franca* among the ruling classes, just as Latin was the language of educated men. In England before the Norman Conquest, there was a very healthy and considerable growth in native literature and many even of the official documents were written in English, not in Latin. The Norman Conquest stopped the latter trend, and documents reverted to Latin, while the spoken language became French instead of English so far as the upper classes were concerned. English, of course, continued to be the speech of the bulk of the English people, and even English literature went on, but it was not until the fourteenth century, 300 years after the Conquest, that great writers again appeared in English, such as Chaucer, Langland and Gower. In the latter part of the fourteenth century, English began to be once more the speech of the ruling classes and this was definitely so in the fifteenth century. Latin remained the language of the Church until the Reformation. Under Henry VIII, the Bible was allowed in an English translation; under his son, Edward VI (1547-53) the services of the Church were rendered into English and, apart from the reaction under 'Bloody' Queen Mary II (1553-58) have remained so ever since. Latin continued as the language of many legal and court records until 1733, at which date the strange jargon used in court pleadings—Norman French—also disappeared.

The Normans were in male-line descent Northmen or Vikings, but by

1066 they had more or less forgotten their ancestry. The Norse speech had almost died out in Normandy, and the Normans spoke French. They were a conquering race and subdued all the lands they invaded, from England to Palestine. Their conquests were in northern France, England, south Wales, Ireland, southern Italy, Sicily, Malta, and the Holy Land, and they also penetrated into lands which they did not conquer, like Scotland. They helped to extend the speaking of French, much as the enormous extension of American power has widened the use of English in the modern world. As French was the language of the knightly ruling caste, it was only natural that it should also provide the language of the gentleman's insignia, in heraldry. About 1400 there was a movement in England to substitute English heraldic terms for French but this did not succeed and the language of heraldry remains French to this day.

In treating earlier of mottoes, reference was made to legends, or rather myths, about the symbols used in coats of arms. On this subject the late A. C. Fox-Davies remarked very truly, 'That an argent field meant purity, that a field gules meant royal or even martial ancestors, that a saltire meant the capture of a city, or a lion rampant noble and enviable qualities, I utterly deny. But that nearly every coat of arms for any one of the name of Fletcher bears upon it in some form or another an arrow or an arrow head, because the origin of the name comes from the occupation of the fletcher who was an arrow maker, is true enough.' (*A Complete Guide to Heraldry*, p 5, 1961).

It is true that in modern coats of arms there are symbolic uses, as of spears, swords etc, for soldiers, and so on with allusion to the occupation of the arms bearer, but all the alleged symbolisms so dear to family myth should be discarded. Much of this sort of thing is really akin to the curious natural history of the middle ages. Most people have seen representations of dragons, wyverns, griffins and other entirely mythical creatures; some must know the story of the pelican in her piety, ie, the pelican wounding herself to give her blood as nourishment to her young; or of the precious jewel set in the toad's head. This fabulous material is found in innumerable books of medieval times and right up to the seventeenth century. Shakespeare's plays contain many references to this (to us) absurd natural history. In ages when the human population was so much smaller than it is now, and when wild creatures abounded within reach of the cities, it seems strange that so many errors could flourish. Did no one ever dissect a toad to find the jewel? Or is the explanation that the observation of nature was left to the unlettered forester, while the learned refused to look beyond the pages of their text books? 'Great clerk, little sense' is a saying of the middle ages which may reflect this. Certain it is that anyone who reads the ancient works on heraldry will weary of the nonsense they contain as to the origin of symbolism in arms.

The truth is that only after heraldry had been in use for more than 200 years did anyone begin to write of it. The historian of the motor-car or of the aeroplane has the files of newspapers to help him from the very beginning. Something new will always be noticed by the journalist but newspapers, unfortunately, are creations only of the last 300 years. A newspaper file of the middle of the twelfth century, if such a miracle could happen, would do more to solve our historical problems in that era than all the careful researches of the medievalists. In the absence of it, we have had, as we have seen, to rely on conjecture based on evidence. The medieval writers were not hampered by our scruples, nor did they understand the meaning of an historical anachronism. Anyone can see this who looks at medieval paintings or sculptures. The figures of Biblical characters are shown in contemporary medieval dress. The understanding of historical change is not innate in man; he comes to it only by means of an elaborate educational system. As our minds are dominated by the idea of evolution, of change, so the human mind before the eighteenth (almost the nineteenth) century had the conception of a static universe. Consequently it was not all unnatural for a medieval writer on heraldry to assume that, as kings and nobles of his time, eg, 1400, bore coats of arms, they must always have done so. Thus he gave arms to Caesar, Alexander the Great, Alfred the Great and Edward the Confessor. The ascription of arms was extended in space, as well as in time; The Grand Soldan (the Moslem Sultan), of course, had a coat of arms; after all, even Saracens could be called gentlemen and as such must have had arms. In the *Book of St Albans* written towards the end of the fifteenth century, and usually ascribed to Dame Julyana Bernes or Berners, the author specifically refers to Saracen arms, and says that a Christian yeoman on killing a gentlemanly Saracen is entitled to assume his arms.*

The earliest writer on heraldry was Bartholus or Barto di Sassoferato (1314- *circa* 1356) who wrote a *Tractatus de Insigniis et Armis*. He was a professor of law at Bologna, Pisa and Perugia in turn and has been called the father of private international law (C C. Cheshire, *Private International Law*, p 30, 1949). The earliest writer in English is usually said to have been Johannes de Bado Aureo, who in 1394 produced a

---

* NOTE : I would like to make it clear that I do not believe in the reality of these Saracen or other non-European arms, but merely that early writers held them to exist.—L. G. P.

Tractatus de Armis, in which he refers to Bartholus as an heraldic authority. (The late H. Stanford London, in an article in the *Society of Antiquaries Journal*, London, vol 33, referred to other early English heraldic writers, in manuscript form but none earlier than 1440). Johannes is thought to have been indentical with a John of Guildford, and his treatise was printed in 1654, with a later work, *De Studio Militari*, of Nicholas Upton, written about 1440. These two treatises, with the *Aspilogia* (science of shields = coats of arms) of Sir Henry Spelmann (1564-1641) were all edited by Sir Edward Bysshe, Garter King of Arms in 1654.

Whatever views as to the origin of arms or their symbolism were entertained by these writers, they were soon equalled by those of the sixteenth century. Such English books were Gerard Leigh's *Accedens of Armory*, published in 1562, and Sir John Ferne's *Blazon of Gentrie* in 1586. The author of the *Book of St Albans* had already described heraldry as beginning in heaven with the different orders of angels. Christ was a gentleman on His mother's side, and bore coat armour; so also the twelve apostles were gentlemen of armorial bearing. And lest it be thought that these opinions were simply wild fancies, it is a fact that an escutcheon put up in the cathedral at Mayence bestowed arms upon Christ, the shield having twenty quarters in five vertical rows and the arms being the instruments of Our Lord's Passion and other devices. One cannot go higher than the court of heaven, or on earth than with Christ, but Gerard Leigh certainly did not fall overmuch behind. He thought that arms were used at the siege of Troy (approximately 1,000 BC) and in a list of the Nine Worthies so dear to medieval writers, he assigned coats to Duke Joshua, Hector, David, Alexander, Judas Maccabeus (the Jewish patriot of the 2nd century BC), Julius Caesar, King Arthur, Charlemagne, and Sir Guy, Earl of Warwick. Sir John Fearne even thought that the use of furs in heraldry came from the coats of skins of Adam and Eve after they were turned out of Paradise.

The publication of Guillim's *Display of Heraldrie* in 1611 marked the beginning of a more historical and rational approach to the subject. In his introduction, Guillim remarks that 'the antiquity of gentilicial arms in Britain will prove of far later date than many of our gentry would willingly be thought to have borne them.' Guillim did nonetheless hold the same views as his predecessors about the symbolism of heraldic devices, and it was not until the nineteenth century that this nonsense was given up. As regards the antiquity of arms, a French Jesuit, Pere Menestrier, wrote in 1680, the *Origine des Armoiries*. He could not find in western Europe a monument showing arms earlier than

1010 and his view was that, as arms could not have existed at such an early date, they had been added to the tomb in question (that of a Count von Wasserburg in St Emmeran's church in Ratisbon) when it was repaired. The addition of the arms to this tomb is typical of the ascription of arms to people in the past on the unconscious assumption that they must have had them.

Some of the most interesting of the post-mortem ascriptions of arms are to be seen in England to this day. At Westminster, in the abbey and in the famous school, one can see displayed the arms of Saint and King Edward the Confessor (1042-66). These were never borne by the Confessor, but they do appear in the reign of Richard II (1377-99), who had a great devotion to the Saint and wished to impale his arms with those of the Confessor. It would indeed be of enormous interest if we could discover how these arms of the Confessor were invented. Probably it occurred in much the same way as the arms of the Nine Worthies— such people simply must have had arms, being of the same class as our armigerous persons and, ergo, as we cannot find a coat for the Confessor the following is the sort of coat which he must have had. Accordingly he was given—by whom we know not—a coat, azure a cross patonce between five martlets or. These arms Richard II put in the dexter side of his shield, and the royal arms of England in the sinister, and to the present time the Confessor's arms appear over Westminster Abbey in its flag. Again, the arms of the University of Oxford—azure three open crowns, two and one, or—are supposed to be those of St Edmund the Martyr, the king of East Anglia. University College, Oxford, was supposed to have been founded by King Alfred the Great and thus has his arms. Needless to add, these ascriptions to St Edmund and King Alfred are unhistorical.

Did heraldry exist at all outside western Europe? The old writers on the subject had no doubt that it did, but on discarding their fancies can we find any proof of the employment of heraldic devices in non-European lands? The use of symbols has been constant in civilisations past and present; indeed symbolism has been widely used in communities which are not fully civilised or are even savage. Totemism is familiar to most people, and the use of an animal symbol is universal. This is not heraldic, but heraldry derives from it and is closely connected with it. Many of the charges, as they are called in heraldry, are of animals or natural objects, like trees, plants, flowers. It is generally in later heraldry that man-made objects appear, apart from the honourable ordinaries.

Heraldry being, then, a development of symbolism, it would be strange if nowhere else in the world had a system similar to that of the west arisen. In the first place, in the Bible, in the book of Numbers (ch 2, v 2), we have the following significant passage: 'Every man of the children of Israel shall pitch by his own standard with the ensign of their father's house.' These standards and ensigns are not given in the text of Numbers but were apparently based on the blessings bestowed by Jacob on his twelve sons in the 49th chapter of Genesis. The most familiar to us is the symbol of the Lion of Judah, now used by the Emperor of Ethiopia by virtue of his traditional descent from King Solomon and the Queen of Sheba. The symbols of the twelve tribes of Israel are still shown on standards in certain branches of masonry. Such being the case as regards 'the ensigns of their father's house' in Israel, one can understand old writers thinking that ancient Scriptural heroes like Judas Maccabeus had coats of arms. Some heraldic scholars are also inclined to think that the noble families of Athens in the fifth century BC had something in the nature of armorial bearings.* There are, too, descriptions of shields in the works of Homer, Aeschylus, Virgil and other writers, but these are matters of symbolism not heraldry.

The only proven instance apart from medieval Europe of the use of heraldry is in Japan, and in the Japanese Peerage, *The Japan Gazette*, published in Yokohama in 1912, each article on a noble family was headed with the *mon*, the hereditary symbol of Japanese nobility. Robert Standish, in his novel, *The Three Bamboos*, gives a device of three bamboos as the ancient *mon* of the Fureno family, who form his chief characters. The Japanese *mon* bears the closest resemblance to our crest, or more exactly our badges. It is used on armour, on breastplates, helmet or shield. As in Europe, it is also used in decoration, on objects in the house and on clothes, corresponding in this way to the use of the badge. In the illustrations of the *mon* given here, the reader will see the difference in representation of the objects from that in our heraldry. (See also Note 12).

CHRYSANTHEMUM OR ROYAL FAMILY MON

The Japanese had a chivalry as colourful and romantic as anything in western annals. That this system of Bushido did not preclude the most

* I cannot say definitely that this was so, but mention it as being the view of some authorities.—L. G. P.

N

horrible cruelty and ill treatment of the helpless was all too painfully made manifest to thousands of Allied servicemen and civilians in the 1941-45 war with Japan. The Japanese cult of Bushido was indeed an even grimmer chivalry than anything known in the west. The knights of Japan were the samurai, who were the retainers of the daimios, or great feudal nobles, under the old Japanese system which prevailed until the guns of Commodore Perry's squadron shattered the samurai swordsmen. Lovers of cold steel, delighting in combat and with a contempt for death, the Japanese knights were every whit as dauntless in their armour (considerably lighter) as were their western counterparts; their ladies were as lovely and enchanting; their giants and dragons as terrible; their castles and fortresses as hard to capture. Nor did they end their chivalric age with the sixteenth century and the mockery of a Cervantes. A nobleman of Japan expected to order his suit of armour for ceremonial occasions right up to the end of the nineteenth century, and examples of their suits can today be seen in the museums of Europe and America, with the *mon* upon the helmets and breastplates. The old feudal system was abolished in the Meiji era beginning in 1867, but the samurai spirit was somehow infused into the ordinary Japanese soldier, and in the 1941-45 war the Japanese was the only modern army in which the words 'no surrender' were taken literally.

We have, then, two heraldic systems, located in fairly small territories on either end of the Asiatic–European land mass. In Europe, heraldry was confined to the western portions of the continent, and to those western nations which were feudal or closely linked with the Catholic Church. Thus Poland alone among the Slav nations is Catholic, and has received the Latin culture and is the only Slav country to possess an indigenous heraldry. The Celtic fringe of the west—Ireland, Wales, and the Scottish Highlands, peopled by the Celtic race—was, of course, Catholic from early times, but the system in those lands was clannish rather than feudal. The great families of the Celtic countries received their heraldry through the influence of other western countries. In some cases even now great Irish families of regal descent do not possess arms in the sense in which they are generally understood.

In the pedigree of Maelseachlainn (McLoughlin) in the *Landed Gentry of Ireland*, 1958, the family descends from Niall of the Nine Hostages (see Chapter 8 on Irish Records), High King of Ireland, AD 400. The head of this line was for ages High King of Ireland but, like many other native regal lines, they were in trouble with the English governors of Ireland. Often the head of the family had to live in an obscure corner of Ireland, and one of the chiefs in the early sixteenth century, Morogh

Dubh O' Melaghlin, built a house of refuge on a small island in Lough Meelagh, Kilronan, in order to be safe from his enemies. It is clear that in such a case arms as anciently understood and used would not have been registered in recent centuries. A man wanted by the English for rebellion would hardly have gone to Dublin Castle to register his arms or he might have left his head on the battlements! These ancient Irish royal families possessed symbols of great interest such as the royal standard of Tara borne by the Maelseachlainn. The fabric of the standard was royal blue in colour and showed the Rising Sun centred in white, superimposed thereon a wheeled cross in gold. Within the wheel, centred, a Crown seven-pointed in gold positioned above a gold gorget of antique pattern. In each quartering at the outer corner, and suitably proportioned, a small crowned Harp in gold, the Crown, showing five points and the Harp twenty-one strings. Seven rays in white were shown in each quarter as proceeding from the Sun centred.

However small the area of medieval Christendom and correspondingly circumscribed the extent of heraldry, after the sixteenth century it expanded enormously as a result of the development of the world by the Europeans. In the Americas, heraldry became firmly established, and was also taken into southern Africa where its history has been traced from the Portuguese explorers through the Dutch, British, German and Afrikaans elements by Dr C. Pama. (*Lions and Virgins*, 1965). In the present Republic of South Africa, heraldry is so strongly entrenched that an Act of Parliament was passed in recent years which made provision for the establishment of a bureau of heraldry, with a state herald and a heraldry council, and for grants, registration, and protection of coats of arms, badges and other emblems connected therewith. Reference has already been made to the establishment of an heraldic office by another of the republics carved out of the former British Empire—that of the Republic of Ireland, which now has a Chief Herald in Dublin Castle. (See Chapter 8 on Irish Records).

In Australia and New Zealand there has always been, owing to their connection with England, a certain amount of heraldry. Since the Second World War this has grown considerably and there are now flourishing genealogical societies in these countries, so that heraldic knowledge is also increasing. Much the same is now true of Canada, for as a society becomes more sophisticated it will usually be more interested in assessing its past.

Of heraldry in the United States there is so much to say that a special section is devoted to it later in this chapter.

Heraldry in Latin America clearly has already become of great importance and there are many families of Spanish—and in Brazil, of Portuguese—descent who treasure both arms and pedigrees.

In India, influenced by British rule of the huge peninsula for about 200 years, the ruling princes gradually adopted coats of arms. These conformed to the main outlines of a coat, but had many additional features in the form of figures drawn from the Hindu faith.

In the east of Europe and in Russia, heraldry was adopted much later than in the west; in Hungary in the fifteenth to sixteenth centuries and in Russia in the eighteenth century on the initiative of Peter the Great. Thus the heraldry of western Europe has been exported on a world-wide basis.

Since we do not know the precise origin of heraldry, we cannot tell if it originated from a single mind. This in one way seems unlikely, because the phenomenon of heraldic devices is found in all western European countries at about the same time from the twelfth century onwards. On the other hand, as the basic rules are the same from Scandinavia to Spain, and from France to Poland, it would seem to have been a remarkably spontaneous development. Perhaps it did originate from one inventor, possibly a soldier of the First Crusade seeking to solve the problem of distinguishing between various bodies of men. A modern parallel can be found in the 1939-45 war when there were over 500 army devices or signs for British and Allied commands and formations, and such distinguishing marks as shoulder flashes and other signs.

Whatever the origins of heraldry, it developed spontaneously once it had started. Much unnecessary difficulty has been raised over this part of the subject, and the fact that, in England, three different and unrelated families in separate parts of the country bore the same arms is clear proof that arms were devised and developed by men to suit themselves and not in accordance with rules prepared by a central authority. When a gathering of knights took place, either for war or for some other occasion such as a tournament when arms were displayed, there was very often a dispute between two unrelated individuals as to the ownership of the identical coat of arms. Among the Rolls of Arms mentioned above, there is one written about 1350, the Roll of Caerlaverock, a small fortress in the south of Scotland in Dumfriesshire which was besieged and captured by Edward I's army. The Roll may have been written by a herald who was in the train of King Edward. Whoever he was, he described the arms of those who were present and said of Brian FitzAlan and Hugh Pointz that each bore the same arms, barry or and gules. Again, in the French wars of the later part of the same century, Sir William Scrope captured a French knight, the Sieur Philippe de la

Moustre, who bore the same coat as himself, azure a bend or. Later, in 1395, Lord Scrope, another member of the same family, was appointed as a commissioner to decide a dispute between Thomas Baude and Nicholas de Singleton as to their respective rights to bear the arms, gules three chevronels or. This same Lord Scrope had himself, when Sir Richard Scrope, been the main actor in a dispute as to the right to the arms, azure a bend or.

Fortunately for our knowledge of this part of heraldry we have two thick volumes, translated from Norman French and edited by Sir Harris Nicolas, called *The Controversy between Sir Richard Scrope and Sir Robert Grosvenor in the Court of Chivalry, 1385-1390.* The facts are very simple. Scrope was a great and powerful noble from Yorkshire, Grosvenor a knight of Cheshire. Both belonged to the same social class, but Scrope was far richer and more influential. Both used the same simple coat of arms and, as there was no apparent blood relationship, Scrope, been the main actor in a dispute as to the right to the arms, azure to do so. This occurred during an expedition against the Scots and as such quarrels were likely to cause serious trouble in the army, there was a tribunal—the Court of Chivalry—before which such disputes could be brought. Over it presided two high officers of state (when it sat in the most official cases, otherwise conducted by a constable and a marshal temporarily appointed) (see below); the High Constable and the Earl Marshal. The latter office still exists and has been for the past 300 years hereditary in the family of the Duke of Norfolk. Whoever succeeds to the dukedom, becomes also Earl Marshal, arranges the Coronation and other royal ceremonies and is permanent head of the English College of Arms. The office of High Constable was abolished as a permanent post in the reign of Henry VIII, but is now temporarily granted to a nobleman at the Coronation.

To return, however, to 1385 when the Court of Chivalry with these two officers was in full power. As it could not at the time of Scrope's original complaint settle the argument, further sittings were held and the main body of the report in Nicolas's edition is taken up with the evidence of witnesses on one side or the other. Many famous names appear—John of Gaunt, Owen Glendower, Geoffrey Chaucer. Both sides argued that their ancestors had borne the arms from the Norman Conquest, a contention which proves how much that event had sunk into the consciousness of the proud knighthood of England, and also how implicitly they assumed that coats of arms had always existed. The upshot of the case was that the Court decided in favour of Scrope and ordered the Grosvenor defendant to put a difference mark in his arms to show that he was not of the same family. Sir Robert Grosvenor was not pleased with the decision and appealed to the King as the final umpire. The sovereign then was Richard II, who was prone to sudden and hasty judgments, as readers of Shakespeare's play will know. He decided that a difference mark was insufficient to distinguish arms of two persons unconnected by blood and ordered Grosvenor to give up the Scrope arms. In the sequel, Grosvenor adopted a fresh coat, azure a garb or, which is now borne by his descendants, the Dukes of Westminster.

There is an interesting rider to this story which should really precede it, for it occurred in 1359. A Cornish squire named Carminow was found in the English army in France to have the same arms as Scrope, azure a bend or. He did not wait to be challenged by Sir Richard Scrope—who later became a peer as Lord Scrope—but challenged Scrope to prove his right to the arms borne by Carminow. When Scrope alleged that his family had borne the arms since Norman times, Carminow countered with the reply that his ancestor, having been a knight at King Arthur's Table, had derived his coat of arms from thence. This was a hard saying for the Court of Chivalry, whose members must have been placed in a quandary. They may have doubted the existence of Arthur; on the other hand Cornwall had for long been a foreign country from England, almost a separate kingdom, and the king of a country could grant what arms he pleased. The Court therefore contented itself with ordering Carminow to put a canton for difference in the top right of his shield. Sometimes the Carminows carried this out, more often they did not in the 300 years during which the family persisted in the male line. The important fact is that in these four cases—three in England and one in France—gentlemen used the same coat of arms. It was a simple coat, this azure a bend or, just a blue field with a gold bar across it from left to right. The moral surely is clear, it was the sort of coat which anyone who took arms might think of, which is precisely why four separate families did so. It follows that there was no one to regulate the assumption of arms. They were very practical, needed mainly for purposes of identification in time of war. There were no elaborate rules, just general, easily understood and remembered principles.

The heralds were at first simply persons who made a study of arms, perhaps in their own locality. They were very useful people, and gradually they were taken into the households of great nobles, and of the sovereign. To this day the heralds of the English College of Arms are members of the Queen's household. They are not civil servants or government nominees but are appointed by the Queen on the recommendation of the Earl Marshal. Two of the great families of medieval

England, the Percys and the Nevilles, had their own heralds, named Esperance and Vert Eagle from the motto or design of their masters. In Scotland, even now, three of the noble families can maintain their own private heralds, and sometimes do, as the Countess of Erroll appointed her own Slains Pursuivant (from *poursuivre*, to follow, the title given to a junior herald). Scotland is also very much a museum piece for heraldic illustration; a practice which has vanished elsewhere persists there. In England, private heralds gradually disappeared, and the only heralds who remained were those of the royal household. In 1484, the English king, Richard III (1483-85) formed his heralds into a corporation, the College of Arms. The French king had already done this in 1406, and it seems curious that his example was not followed for seventy-eight years. In the reign of Edward VI (1547-53), the English heralds moved into a building on the site of the present College of Arms in Queen Victoria Street, London. This was destroyed in the Great Fire of London in 1666, and the present edifice dates from the restoration of London after the Fire. The college possesses a magnificent collection of records, unfortunately not accessible to the public, and was lucky to escape damage or destruction in the Second World War. The great gates into the college courtyard were repaired and renovated some years ago, much of the cost being borne by American subscribers.

The Earl Marshal, as head of the college, has under him thirteen officers. They are three Kings of Arms: Garter, Clarenceux, and Norroy; six heralds: Richmond, York, Lancaster, Chester, Somerset and Windsor; and four Pursuivants: Rouge Croix, Blue Mantle, Rouge Dragon, and Portcullis. Such names have a delightfully romantic and medieval ring, and are mostly derived from territorial sources. The Garter King was created by Henry V (1413-22) for the service of the most noble Order of the Garter. He deals with peers and baronets and acts as right-hand adviser to the Earl Marshal. Clarenceux is named from the Duke of Clarence, the third son of Edward III (1327-77). His jurisdiction extends over that part of England lying in the south, west and east. Norroy is the King of Arms dealing with the north of England, north of the Trent (ie, Nord Roy). He also now unites with Norroy the office of Ulster King of Arms (from Ireland). Of the six heralds, Windsor is named from the royal castle there and was created by Edward III, who had been born at Windsor. The other five take their titles from counties and shires which have been the appendages of the younger sons of the sovereign. Lancaster is named from John of Gaunt, Duke of Lancaster; Chester recalls the earldom of Chester, a title of the Prince of Wales, York was from Edmund of Langley, Duke of York, another son of Edward

III. Henry VIII had a bastard son, Henry Fitzroy, Duke of Richmond and Somerset, and this accounts for Somerset Herald. The office of Richmond Herald occurs in the reign of Edward IV (1460-83). The Pursuivants take their names (i) Rouge Croix instituted by Henry V, from the Red Cross of St George, (ii) Blue Mantle from the blue with golden *fleur-de-lis* of the French royal arms; (iii) Rouge Dragon and Portcullis were created by Henry VII, the former being named from the dragon device of the Welsh princes and the latter from the badge used by this king.

It is clear from cases such as that of Scrope v Grosvenor that, while arms were assumed originally for practical reasons, they were subject to the authority of the Crown as the Fountain of Honour. With the incorporation of the heralds into a college, the Crown intended to extend its control of arms, and the two methods it used were the Visitations and the Court of Chivalry.

The Visitations have completely ended, although like many other English practices they have never been abolished. The customs of the age are against their revival. They were instituted by royal commission, first under Henry VII in 1529-30, directed to the College of Arms, instructing the heralds to visit a particular county in England and there to inquire into the use of arms within that area. If the arms were correctly borne according to the laws of arms, they were entered in the heralds' records. If they were not correctly borne their users were told to give them up. The records of the Visitations soon began to contain pedigrees, although the heralds' task was not at first to prepare genealogies. The Visitations lasted until the reign of James II (1685-88), after which they were discontinued. It is thought that the sovereigns who immediately followed James II—William and Mary, Anne, George I and George II—did not wish to disturb the ancient gentry of their realms. Besides, three of these monarchs were foreigners, one a Dutchman (William III) and two Germans (George I and II), who were not very interested in English customs.

With the cessation of the Visitations the heraldic authorities still had the weapon of the Court of Chivalry. Much that is inaccurate has been written about this court partly because of a misunderstanding about its name, and partly because the court records have not been, and are not now, available for general study. As regards the title, the court was quite often termed a Court Military or Court Martial, and from this it was assumed that the Court of Chivalry was the origin of the courts martial known to everyone connected with the armed forces. This is not correct and is based on a wrong translation of the Latin name of the court, *Curia*

Militaris. Miles = knight, and so the correct translation would be Court of Knighthood, ie, Court of Chivalry. The court was the Court of the Constable and the Marshal, and this court did exercise disciplinary powers over the army. These powers were exercised in virtue of what were termed the Statutes and Ordinances of War, which were set forth by the sovereign to govern the conduct of the army on a particular occasion. References to a Constable and Marshal, who were always present in a medieval army, by no means indicate that these persons were identical with the High Constable and the Earl Marshal, who were great officers of state, unlikely to be present on every military occasion and obviously unable to be present in both Scotland and France when simultaneous military measures were being taken against both countries.

From the Ordinances of War developed the Articles of War which were embodied in the Mutiny Act 1689, itself forerunner of the 1955 *et seq* Army Act which regulates courts martial in the British Army today. As in feudal times disputes over arms would have been likely to engender strife in an army, the Court of Chivalry, as one would expect, took special cognisance of these. The records of the court, such as they are, have now been studied and the results distilled in a work by G. D. Squibb, QC, *The High Court of Chivalry* (1959). Mr Squibb remarks (Preface, p ix). 'Unfortunately the surviving records of the court cover but a comparatively short part of the six centuries of its erratic and eccentric existence. . . . The manageable bulk of the records (mostly contained in two large boxes of files and loose documents and eight bound volumes) has made it possible to read every document.' The records thus analysed by Mr Squibb are of the seventeenth and early eighteenth centuries.

The type of case brought before the court varied considerably; some were of a kind which later came under the jurisdiction of the English Common Law courts; all were more or less concerned with questions of honour, personal in the case of duels, or of allegations of opprobrious words (denying that such or such a man was a gentleman) or they might be cases brought before the court by officers of the College of Arms, very often alleging that arms had been wrongfully used in the management of a funeral. There was in the period covered by the extant records very great opposition to the court. In 1640 the House of Commons took strong exception to it, and it did not sit again until after the Restoration (1660) of Charles II. Yet under the rule of the Parliamentarians matters relating to arms were not neglected, and they appointed commissioners drawn from the Lords and Commons to deal with heraldic abuses. The Court of Chivalry sat on 4 March 1737 and did not sit again until 1954.

In this long suspension of function, it was still deemed by the best legal minds, like William Blackstone, author of the famous *Commentaries on the Laws of England*, to exist and to possess jurisdiction. During these 217 years the misuse of arms in England and Wales went on unchecked, and I estimate that today there are probably not less than 50,000 cases of the use of incorrect arms in England and Wales.

At last, in 1954, an attempt was made to rectify the situation. The Court of Chivalry sat once more, under the presidency of the Earl Marshal, with the Lord Chief Justice (then Lord Goddard) acting as Surrogate or Deputy to the Earl Marshal. A test case was brought before the court. The City of Manchester had a coat of arms granted by Queen Victoria. For many years a place of popular entertainment, the Manchester Palace of Varieties had been using these arms on its drop curtain and on its company seal. The City now sued the Palace before the revived Court of Chivalry. It was not very difficult to settle the merits of the case, as the Palace had clearly no right to use the arms of the city. When the Surrogate gave his judgment early in 1955, he decided that the court existed and that it had jurisdiction; that the Palace must cease to use the city arms and pay the costs of the action (£300); he also advised the conveners of the court that, if they intended to make much future use of it, they ought to get an Act of Parliament to confirm and strengthen it and to give to the court the pains and penalties it ought to have. This has not been done, and the net public result of the reassertion of the court's existence was that the corporation of the City of London was persuaded to register the crest and supporters of its coat of arms with the College. The City's shield—the essential part of the arms —had been registered centuries before. Otherwise heraldic anarchy throughout England and Wales continues, and the threat of penalties from the Court of Chivalry is merely that of a birch above the door.

Far otherwise is the position in North Britain. Once one crosses the Tweed into Scotland, heraldic jurisdiction is a fact. This is because, under the Union of England and Scotland in 1707, the Scots kept their own legal system which differs considerably from that of England. In 1672 the Scots Parliament passed an Act under which arms had to be registered in Lyon's records or else would be deemed illegal. This is plain and simple, and as the head of the Scottish heraldic system, the Lord Lyon, is a judge of the Court of Sessions (the High Court of Scotland) it follows that refusal to obey his rulings amounts to contempt of court. Successive Lords Lyon have seen that the law is carried out and even the greatest Scottish nobles and the most important cities and institutions have been compelled to obtemper (ie, obey) the law. In 1867 the Lyon

Court Act (of the United Kingdom Parliament) confirmed the style and dignities of the Lyon which had been officially set forth in the Scottish Parliament Act of 1663.

The office of Lyon is ancient and was that of a great officer of state in the days of the separate Scottish realm. The title is derived from the lion symbol in the royal arms of Scotland. No Visitations were ever held in Scotland and the practical Scots, by making heraldry part of the law of Scotland, have ensured that it will be properly conducted. In Scotland, too, the system is simpler and yet more exact than in England. A grant of arms does not, as in the south, carry with it the right of every descendant of the grantee to bear the arms. In each generation there has to be matriculation, that is registration in Lyon's register. This means that the matriculator and his eldest son have the sole right to the arms; younger sons must matriculate in their turn. The costs are not high and this method means not only that the arms are properly differenced, but also that in Scotland only genuine arms are in use.

It should be of interest to Americans of Scots descent to know that they can apply to the Lord Lyon to record their arms and, if they wish, their pedigrees. He also adjudicates on the headship of clans, and on matters of title, in all Scottish families. Appeal from him lies only to the House of Lords, the highest court in the United Kingdom.

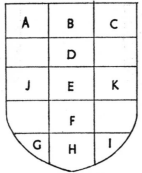

Points of division of a shield.

The points of division of a shield are shown above. A, B and C are the chief; A being the dexter chief point; B the middle chief point; and C the sinister chief point. D is the honour point; E is the middle or heart point, known as the fesse. F is the navel point; G, H and I are the base, G being the dexter base point; H is the middle base point; I the sinister base point. J and K are, respectively, the right and left flanks of the shield. The shield is said to have a ground on which the various charges are shown, and this ground can be one of different tinctures or colours. The colours are of three kinds; metals, colours as such, and furs. One of these must form the ground of the shield. Whatever is then placed upon the ground is said to be charged upon it. The shield is accordingly charged with whatever objects are placed on it.

The metals are or = gold, and argent = silver. The colours are: azure (blue), gules (red), vert (green), sable (black) and purpure (purple). There are references to two other colours, murrey or sanguine, which is between gules and purpure; and tenné or orange. The furs are ermine = a white field with black spots; the reverse, ermines = a black field with white spots. Erminois = a gold field with black spots. Pean = a black

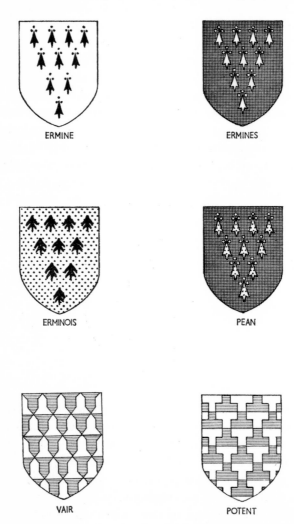

ERMINE   ERMINES

ERMINOIS   PEAN

VAIR   POTENT

Heraldic furs.

field with gold spots. Vair was derived from the fur of a species of squirrel used for the lining of cloaks. The colour of the squirrel was blue grey on top and white beneath, and as the whole fur was used, the resultant vair was of argent and azure, arranged in rows. Vaire is the term used when the tinctures differ from argent and azure. Counter vair is when the bell-shaped figures (see illustration) are differently arranged. Another variant of the figure is called potent, and sometimes potent counter potent.

Three points before going on from the tinctures:

(1) In English, the term 'proper' (abbreviated ppr) is used of every animal, tree or other natural object depicted in its natural colour.

(2) The term 'counter changed' is employed to denote that the field is of two tinctures, metal and colour, and that the charge upon it partakes of both, so that the part of the charge which is of metal lies upon the colour, while that which is of colour lies upon metal. It is important to remember that it is a rule of heraldry that metal and colour are not to be placed upon metal or colour. To break this rule is to produce what is termed false heraldry, but there are many examples of a breach of this rule. Perhaps the most famous instance is the arms of the City of Jerusalem: argent a cross potent between four cross crosslets or. Many other instances are found in the heraldry of Germany, Denmark, Italy and Spain.

(3) The best way to show arms is in colour, but this is not always practicable, especially in book illustrations, owing to the expense involved. In the seventeenth century some systems were designed using lines and dots, at first sight reminiscent of the Morse code. In the end, at least so far as England is concerned, the system of an Italian, Sylvester Petra Sancta (1638), prevailed. Examples are azure shown by horizontal lines; gules by perpendicular lines; vert by lines from the dexter chief to the sinister base; purpure, with the lines in the opposite direction and so on. Or is shown by dots or points; argent by the shield being entirely plain. Sable is depicted by cross lines. The furs are (1) ermine; (ii) ermines; (iii) erminois; (iv) pean; (v) vair; (vi) counter vair; this differs by having bells or cups arranged base against base. (vii) Potent counter potent of figures like the heads of crutches.

OR   ARGENT   GULES   AZURE   SABLE   VERT   PURPURE

Depiction of metals and colours by the Petra Sancta method.

Partition lines divide the field or charge. They are best learnt in

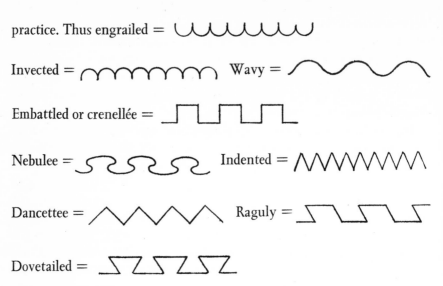

practice. Thus engrailed =

Invected =   Wavy =

Embattled or crenellée =

Nebulee =   Indented =

Dancettee =   Raguly =

Dovetailed =

When a shield is said to be party per pale or simply per pale, the field is divided into two equal parts. Quarterly means that the field is divided into four equal parts by two lines. Per fesse denotes a field divided into two equal parts by a horizontal line; per bend, that the field is divided into two equal parts by a diagonal line, from dexter chief to sinister base. Party per bend sinister has the division made in the opposite direction. Party per chevron is where the field is divided into two equal parts by two lines which meet like a pyramid in the fesse point, drawn from the dexter and the sinister point. Party per saltire is where two diagonal lines cross each other and the field is thus divided into four equal parts. In gyronny of eight, the field is divided into eight equal parts by four lines, two per saltire and two quarterly.

Once we have the field of the shield, we can go on to consider the charges upon it. Thus the arms of Burnell of Ireland and of Essex (England) are argent a lion rampant sable over all a baton gules. Here the field is silver, the charge is a black lion, while over the whole is a red baton as another charge covering the whole field. The Burnells of London had the following arms ascribed to them: sable on a bend argent three escallops of the first. This means that the field is black, the charge is a silver bend, which has on it three black escallops. Now in these two examples we have a charge—the bend—which is called an ordinary, the other—the lion rampant—is not classed as an ordinary, but is sometimes called a common charge. The reader is not likely to benefit much from the dry-as-dust minutiae of heraldry, the bulk of which evolved long after the beginnings of the subject in practical life, and the charges on a shield may most easily be divided into ordinaries and the others. Ordinaries can best be described as charges of very frequent occurrence, which are quasi-mathematical in form. Among the ordinaries, the most important are the chief, the pale, the bend, the fesse, cross, saltire, chevron and so on. It is important to know the meaning and form of these and they are best realized from illustrations.

The chief takes up a third of the area of the whole shield thus:

The pale also comprises a third of the shield, thus:

The bend we have already met in the description per bends, so that the bend is formed by two diagonal lines from dexter chief to sinister base, and also takes up a third of the shield. The bend sinister is merely the same form as the bend but with the lines from the reverse direction.

The fesse, thus,

is formed by two lines drawn across the middle of the shield, and like the other ordinaries noted above, takes up a third of the area of the shield.

The bar is a diminutive of the fesse and may be placed anywhere in the shield. With the exception of the word 'crest', probably no heraldic or semi-heraldic term has been so misused as the so-called bar sinister. In common and colloquially romantic language this means a mark of illegitimacy. 'He started life with the bar sinister on his shield' and the like expressions are found in many novels, and in more serious writings. On this subject, Woodward, (*op cit* p 550) remarks: 'The French name of the bend sinister is *une barre*, and from this circumstance originated the common, but utterly incorrect, expression, "a bar sinister", often used by persons who ought to know better. But the bar being a horizontal piece, a diminutive of the honourable ordinary the fesse, is not used like the French *barre* as a brisure for illegitimacy, a bar sinister is an absurdity and impossibility. The bend sinister, usually diminished to the size of a bendlet or baston, was then one of the earliest, and most generally used brisures adopted to denote illegitimacy.' Several methods were used in medieval times to signify bastardy, the canton, the placing of arms on a bend, the bordure and so on. In England, a baton sinister has been used, especially in the case of dukes who were bastards of King Charles II; in the last 150 years English heralds have inclined to the use of the bordure, which is a wavy border inside the shield and enclosing the arms shown on the shield.

The cross as an ordinary needs no explanation. It is very simple, but as one would expect in a Christian civilization, it was elaborated into many forms. There are said to be no less than 400 kinds of heraldic crosses, but of these not more than thirty are in fairly common use. The cross of St Andrew, well known as the national flag of Scotland and, since 1707, incorporated in the British Union Jack, is the Greek cross or saltire.

The chevron may be fairly likened to an inverted stripe as used in the stripes of a corporal or sergeant.

The border (or bordure mentioned above) occupies one-fifth of the field, and runs at equal distance around the field. It was originally used as a difference mark. The orle is an inner border and is about half the width of a bordure. It does not touch the edges of the shield, and the field is seen within it and round it. The tressure, so much used in Scots heraldry, is about half the size of the orle, and there is also a tressure flory, having fleurs-de-lis in it.

The inescutcheon has already been mentioned in connection with the arms of heiresses. The quarter occupies, or should occupy, one-fourth of the shield and is found formed by two straight lines in the top dexter chief.

The canton is smaller than the quarter and is very frequently used in arms. It occupies the same place as the quarter. The term comes from the French *cantonnée*, cornered.

Chequé is an arrangement of small squares on the field like a chess board. Billets are oblong figures, the numbers of which are specified unless they exceed ten, when the field is said to be billettée.

The paile, or pall, is made from the upper half of a saltire and half a pale. The pile is in the shape of an inverted pyramid. It issues from the chief and the tapering edge is towards but not touching the base. This ancient heraldic charge has been found very useful in modern heraldry, and has been used to denote a uranium pile in the arms of the British Atomic Energy Authority.

The flaunch, or flanque, is made by convex lines on each side of the shield, thus:

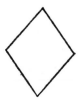

The lozenge is in the shape of the diamond, thus:

and has been already mentioned in describing the arms of a maiden lady. It is also used as a charge in coats of arms. The fusil is shaped like the lozenge but is longer. The mascle is a lozenge in which the middle has been voided (left out) so that the shield shows through the opening, thus:

A field is described as 'lozengy' when it is divided transversely by diagonal lines into equal parts in the form of lozenges.

The fret is an attractive ordinary. It is composed of six pieces, two long sets of parallel lines in saltire, over the whole of the shield from the extremities to the extremities; plus a square of four sets of parallel lines conjoining in the centre with the two pieces in saltire, thus:

o

FRET

The roundel is a round figure of metal. Various names are given to roundels according to their colour. When or, the roundel is a bezant; argent = a plate; gules = a torteaux; azure = a hurt; sable = an ogress or pellet; vert = a pomeis; purpure = a golpe; tenné = an orange; sanguine = a guze.

The annulet is similar to the roundel and is a plain ring of metal or colour. The label is used as a charge in ancient arms, and consists of a space enclosed by two straight lines and having three points. It is also very much used to denote cadency, particularly in the arms of the British royal family.

Charges other than the Ordinaries

Here the wealth of objects is practically boundless since heraldry, being a living and progressive science, is constantly being enriched by new charges. Prior to the nineteenth century, a telescope would have been unlikely to appear in a coat of arms, but in the arms of the British astronomer, Sir John Herschel, discoverer of the planet Uranus, there is the following really horrible description (horrible from the standpoint of true ancient heraldry): 'argent on a mount vert a representation of the forty-feet reflecting telescope with its apparatus proper, a chief azure, thereon the astronomical symbol of Uranus ♅ irradiated or.' In the present century the aeroplane has appeared in an English coat of arms, and when there is no existing heraldic symbol—such as the pile previously mentioned—which can express a modern discovery, then a new charge is taken into heraldry.

The following is a very brief sketch of the extremely varied charges found in heraldry; with the addition of a few items of interest here and there.

Animate Charges: (1) The human body. The whole figure is much more frequently found in Continental than in British instances. In continental Europe, many coats of arms contain whole figures on horseback or on foot, in armour or in civil attire. In Scotland, the naked man or savage is found in quite a number of coats, often as a supporter. Parts of the body appear in Scottish and Welsh, also in English and Continental heraldry. The heart in the arms of Douglas commemorates a genuine historical incident when Sir James Douglas tried to carry out the behest of the dying King Robert the Bruce and set out for the Holy Land to deposit Bruce's heart in the Holy Sepulchre at Jerusalem. He could not do so, as he was killed in battle with the Moors in Spain. The human head is a charge in the arms of some families belonging to nations which have fought long and bitterly against oppressors. Thus some ancient Welsh families bear Englishmens' heads in their shields, so commemorating a defeat of the hated Saxons. Several Hungarian families have Turkish heads as charges because of the long wars between their country and the Turks. This does not explain the presence of a Moor's head in England as a crest, and anyone who thinks that it derives from a long dead Crusading ancestor would be well advised to forget the idea. It could even be that an ancestor who made money had a great affection for an old inn.

(2) Animals, or rather Mammals. Here, again, we see the propensity, already mentioned in connection with the rise of heraldry, for mankind in all ages to take a symbolism from the beasts. The savage thinks that he will gain strength from the creature he kills and eats. In a sublimated form, the more civilised man likes to think that he possesses the qualities which he attributes to the animal. So, in heraldry, we find lions and tigers (the heraldic tiger—a cross between a lion and a wolf—would never be found in a zoo, or anywhere else in real life), the wild boar, the wolf, antelope, the Paschal Lamb etc.

(3) Birds. The favourite is the eagle, especially in Europe. Herons, storks, cranes, falcons also abound.

(4) Fish, reptiles and insects. There are many instances of fish, the most important being the dolphin, from which the seigneurs of Dauphiné, and eventually the heirs to the Crown of France, took their title. Serpents among reptiles, and bees among insects, are other examples in this category.

(5) Monsters or mythical creatures. These were part of the 'natural history' of the times, and include the griffin, dragon, wyvern, centaur etc.

Inanimate Charges: (1) Trees, flowers and fruits of many varieties, such as the English oak, palms, lilies (the fleur-de-lis of France), the Scotch thistle, and fruits like the pineapple and the pomegranate.

(2) Astronomical. The heavenly bodies have always attracted man's attention and this absorbing interest is reflected in heraldry. Sun, moon,

crescents, stars, rainbows, even storms, in addition to the Herschel monstrosity, attest the amount of astronomy in heraldic devices.

(3) Military, nautical and ecclesiastical. Clearly, swords, spears, castles and towers for military emblems; ships of all kinds, including the well-known lymphad or galley of the Campbells, the Dukes of Argyll; keys, croziers and bells.

Apart from these various classes, there are a large number of new charges. Animals unknown to the heralds of the middle ages, like the kangaroo and the springbok, the emu and the ostrich, have all made their way into coats of individuals as well as of cities, provinces and countries.

The language of heraldry in its basic elements can soon be learnt, a few weeks' careful study being sufficient to master the main facts of the subject. From then on the student should proceed to examine as many coats as he can find. The material is so vast that he is unlikely to lack examples. The best course is to study the examples and to blazon arms; when unfamiliar terms appear, he should look them up in glossaries like the one at the end of this book. This will be found a much easier way to remember them than by trying to learn long lists.

There are some simple rules in blazoning a coat. To begin with, the field must be described. Is it a colour, or a metal or a fur? The tincture must be given. It should be noted that an heraldic description needs no punctuation as it will, if correctly given, always make sense to the reader who knows heraldry. A simple blazon is azure a bend or, the arms of the Scropes. A blue field, and on it the charge, a gold bend. This is, of course, a very simple example. Here is one with an additional charge: sable a bend or between six fountains proper—the arms of Stourton. In heraldry, a fountain is not like any fountain in real life. It is described as barry wavy argent and azure, and looks like waves of the sea, in alternate colours. These arms do, in fact, symbolise the river Stour and six springs or fountains in Stourton Park in Wiltshire, which are the source of the river. To pass on: a coat may be divided per pale or per chevron. In this case, there are two tinctures to deal with, per chevron azure and gules, and the colour mentioned as the former will occupy the more important part of the shield. As a general rule, when a field is divided the description of the upper part comes first, and the dexter precedes the sinister portion.

The field having been given, we go on to the charge as in the Scrope and Stourton arms, but there may well be other charges beside the chief charge. Here is a coat chosen at random and ascribed to Dempsey: vert a lion rampant or between two swords wavy in fesse of the last. 'Of the

CROSS	PASSION CROSS	CROSS CALVARY	PATRIARCHAL CROSS
SALTIRE	CROSS CROSSLET	MALTESE CROSS	CROSS PATÉE OR FORMÉE
CROSS POTENT	CROSS PARTED AND FRETTY	CROSS TAU	CROSS PATÉE QUADRATE
CROSS MOLINE	CROSS BOTONNY	CROSS PATÉE FITCHÉE	CROSS COUPED

Sixteen varieties of the cross.

last' is used in order to avoid repetition of the word 'or', but anyone who has to blazon a complicated coat (that is, a coat with many quarterings) is advised to avoid this usage. Never mind about the repetition, it will be safer to give the colour in every case. When two objects are described followed by the term for one colour, this colour applies to both the charges. If a field is said to be semé (ie, strewed or powdered with) it must be so described before the charges are mentioned. When a principal charge appears between three others (all of the same kind) it is normally assumed that the three will appear as two in the upper part of the field, and one in the base. An animal, when described, must have its position stated, as rampant, dormant etc.

The best way to learn the art of blazon is to study the pictures in a book where the written descriptions also appear. Any volume of *Burke's Peerage*, or *Burke's Landed Gentry*, or *Debrett's Peerage* is useful in this way, and the student will have the advantage of studying the various styles of heraldry over a century or more. At present, most heraldic drawings are made as near as possible to the medieval style, and away from the eighteenth century or Victorian style of illustration. In the eighteenth century, heraldry was at a low level, and many bad pieces of heraldic design were made. Heraldic illustrations too can be studied to best advantage when they are in colour; this is not always possible, but examples can be found in the editions of Fox-Davies' *Armorial Families*. The 1939 edition of *Burke's Landed Gentry*, with a large American Supplement, contains very many illustrations in colour of arms borne by US citizens. Similarly, the 1939 *Burke's Peerage* and 1952 *Burke's Landed Gentry* (of Great Britain) contain a quantity of coloured pictures of arms. Reproduction in colour of heraldic achievements is always expensive and may quite often turn out poor results.

An account has been given earlier of the way in which a woman may use arms and how they are used in conjunction with her husband's and, in certain cases, borne by children of the marriage. Novelists and popular historians make great play with the term 'quarterings'. It is, in fact, quite haphazard for even an old recorded armigerous family to acquire quarterings, since this can come only from marriage with an heiress. However, it does happen and many of the more historic English families have, within ten generations, married six times with heiresses, thus acquiring a number of quarterings. Then in continental Europe there has been the doctrine and practice of the *Seize Quartiers*. This means simply that the sixteen great-great-grandparents of a man or woman must be entitled or have been entitled to bear arms, and the practice is known as the Proof of the *Seize Quartiers* or Sixteen Quarterings. The idea arose from the fact that in Europe, as opposed to England, the nobility formed a caste into which it was very hard to enter. Because of this, intermarriage among noble families was the rule, and consequently the families concerned were all armigerous. In England, on the contrary, there has never been a noble caste and as younger children of peers have married into non-armigerous families, the proof of sixteen quarterings is very rare in England.

Quarterings of coats can be applied apart from the inheritance of arms through ancestresses. A very well known example of quartered arms is that of the royal coat of Britain. In the form in which it has been used since 1837, the year of Queen Victoria's accession to the throne, the arms are: 1 and 4, England (the familiar three lions or leopards as they are often called in heraldry); 2, Scotland, and 3, Ireland. Throughout English history since the adoption of arms by Richard I, the royal arms of England have shown the growth of the English kingdom by the inclusion of Scotland, Ireland and, at earlier periods, of much of France and Hanover. A similar case is that of Spain, which has a quarterly coat of Castile and Leon to show the union of those two kingdoms, while Granada, the last Moorish kingdom to be conquered, is shown in the form known as pointe entée, the converse of the pile and issuing from the base of the shield.

Following on a number of marriages with heiresses and the consequent increase in quarterings, we get another arrangement known as marshalling—the ordering of several coats of arms in the same shield. This is described as 'quarterly of grand quarters', eg, in the arms of the Percys, the Dukes of Northumberland. The arrangement can be: quarterly: 1st and 4th grand quarters, 1st and 4th counter quartered etc for Lucy; and for Percy, 2nd and 3rd grand quarters, quarterly 1st and 4th, 2nd and 3rd for Drummond. This means that while the second and third quarters of the shield bear a single coat, the first and fourth quarters are themselves quartered. In the coat of arms of the Percy dukes, each quarter of the shield is itself quartered, with the inevitable result that in a small illustration it is almost impossible to make out any of the details.

A matter of some importance, but mostly outside English heraldry, is that of cadency, or differencing. This is a system designed to differentiate the younger lines of a family from the older and main stock. A cadet is a younger son or a junior member or branch of a family. The word is French and is supposed to be from a *capdet*, a diminutive of the Latin *caput*, head. A series of marks was worked out for nine sons: a label of three points for the eldest son; a crescent for the second; a mullet for the third; a martlet or bird without feet for the forth; an annulet the fifth; a fleur-de-lis the sixth; a rose the seventh; a cross moline the eighth, and a double quatrefoil the ninth. In England, the cadency marks have, in practice, disappeared; only members of the royal family bear cadency marks and these are shown on the labels which appear at the top of their coats of arms. In Scotland, the matriculation system ensures that a proper arrangement of cadency shall prevail.

Closely connected with the subject of cadency is that of bastardy, and it is worth careful study by anyone seeking more detailed knowledge of heraldry than can be given within the present sketch. There is a good account of cadency, marshalling, and the marks of illegitimacy in the second volume of Woodward's *Treatise on Heraldry*. An even more detailed and very interesting account is in *Heraldic Cadency* (1961) by Col Robert Gayre of Gayre and Nigg, this work having the advantage of being written by a learned Scottish herald who is conversant with an heraldic system in which cadency is very much employed.

Augmentations are, as the term implies, an addition made to an original coat. The augmentation is a rare honour, and refers to and commemorates a particular event in the life of an individual. It must be made by a sovereign and, when granted, applies to the individual whose deed is commemorated and to his family after him, unless otherwise stated. It can readily be imagined that many legendary, or more probably mythical, stories circulate among families as to some features in their arms having been specifically granted to an ancestor for warlike deeds. In some cases the legend may well be correct and the honourable augmentation have been granted even though no record of it remains save the family tradition. There are, however, plenty of accurate accounts of augmentation without resort to the fabulous; both Nelson and Marlborough received augmentations for their exploits, and the arms of British soldiers are not grudgingly marked with emblems of their valour against various nations throughout the world.

To American readers such augmentations may appear merely as hankerings after an imperial glory which has completely departed, and there are two of these which concern the United States. As a result of the fight between the *Shannon* and the *Chesapeake*, Captain Broke was granted an additional crest, an arm holding a trident and issuing from a naval crown, with the motto *saevumque tridentem servamus*. An even more obnoxious reference for Americans must be that of General Ross who won the battle of Bladenburg and captured the city of Washington. He died soon afterwards but his family were granted an augmentation of their arms to commemorate his exploits. This took the form of an arm holding the American flag with a broken flagstaff which is shown in the shield itself and as an extra crest. A good illustration of this coat is shown in A. C. Fox-Davies', *Complete Guide to Heraldry* (p 84).

Some of the most romantic of the genuine augmentations are connected with the escape of Charles II after the battle of Worcester (1651), when he was fleeing for his life from Cromwell's Roundheads. On his restoration in 1660 the King granted to Colonel Newman the addition of an inescutcheon to be set in the middle of the shield: gules a portcullis imperially crowned or. This was in allusion to Charles's escape through the Worcester city gate as a result of Colonel Newman's efforts. Later on in his escape, the King posed as a servant to Mistress Jane Lane, riding a strawberry roan. The Lanes were given two augmentations. To their shield was added a canton showing the arms of England, and they were also given the crest of a strawberry roan horse couped at the flanks and holding between its feet a royal crown. There were other instances of Charles II's recognition of those who saved him. To Colonel Carlos, who was with him when he hid in the oak tree at Boscobel, he gave a complete grant of arms.

Another augmentation of great interest is that borne by the Howards, Dukes of Norfolk. This consists of the royal arms of Scotland (the lion pierced through the mouth by an arrow), all on a bend. It was granted by Henry VIII to the 2nd Duke who had utterly defeated the Scots at Flodden Field in 1513. The earliest example in England is that of the buckles granted to the Pelhams for Sir John de Pelham's share in capturing King John of France at Poitiers in 1356. There have been many other families which claimed some similar honour, and in the crest of the Wallers (baronets of Braywicke Lodge) there is hanging from a walnut tree a shield which bears a fleur-de-lis. This is supposed to refer to the exploit of a fourteenth-century Waller in helping to capture the French king.

Civic Arms

Heraldry is not a matter only for families, and there are many thousands of arms of cities, schools, universities, churches, monasteries, city companies, and of great financial institutions such as banks and insurance companies. It is easy to see how the conception of civic arms developed as the idea of a corporate personality grew up. The subject is a special one, requiring separate treatment, but is known all over the world wherever European colonisation has taken place. A useful recent work, especially because of its source, is a well-illustrated book called

European Civic Coats of Arms, by Jiri Louda, a Czechoslovakian student of heraldry who lives in Czechoslovakia and whose book was published in England in 1966.

Ecclesiastical Heraldry

One of the Cinderellas of the subject, this has little importance in English or Scottish heraldry. As with other countries which accepted the Continental reformation, the arms of abbots and monasteries disappeared with the uprooting of the Catholic Church. In England, we have still the arms of the sees of the Church of England. They are often of great historical interest and, with the extension of the Anglican Church throughout the world, there are over 500 bishops in communion with the Archbishop of Canterbury. These include the bishops of the Protestant Episcopal Church of America. All, or nearly all, sees in the Anglican Communion have coats of arms, and an interesting book could be written on this aspect of heraldry alone. On the European continent, too, there is a rich field for heraldic study, coupled with the enormous expansion of the Church of Rome into every continent. Popes, bishops, abbots, monasteries, colleges, universities, all have coats of arms. The best book in English on this vast subject is by Woodward who, in addition to his treatise on Heraldry already referred to, produced a one-volume work, *Ecclesiastical Heraldry.* This was written in the last century and clearly requires to be brought up to date and greatly extended. An admirable work published in 1949, *Coutumes et Droit Héraldique de L'Église* by Mgr Bruno Bernard Heim, deals very carefully with the subject of church heraldry.

American Heraldry

Most people anxious to make a study of heraldry are usually interested in the possibility of gaining a coat of arms for themselves. There are several ways in which an American citizen can obtain this honour. (i) The best is undoubtedly to prove descent from someone to whom arms were granted. In English heraldry, such a grant is carried on to all the descendants of the original grantee, so that if a pedigree can be proved from a grantee, then the modern inquirer who has done this has both an English derived pedigree and a coat of arms. In Scotland, as we have seen, the position as to arms is different. (ii) Application can be made to the English, Scots, or Irish authority for a grant of arms, a course which invariably meets with success. The reason for mentioning the three authorities is because a person of English or Welsh descent applies to the English College of Arms; those of Scots descent to the Lord Lyon; Irish-descended folk should apply to the Chief Herald of Ireland; those from the six counties of Northern Ireland, Ulster, to the Norroy and Ulster King of Arms at the College of Arms. But the inquirer must realize that he is petitioning a sovereign foreign state for the grant of an hereditary honour. Consequently, course (iii) may commend itself to him. As a citizen of an independent state which does not officially grant arms he can assume arms of his own devising, and it is much better to work out a coat of arms for yourself than to assume one belonging to someone else, merely because you have the same name.

There is also a fourth method. Many Americans think that American arms should be recorded, and to this end have set up organizations of their own. My book, *The Story of Heraldry*, which is still in print, contains a chapter headed, 'An American College of Arms', referring to the work of the New England Historic Genealogical Society which set up a Committee on Heraldry. This committee has published a number of Rolls of Arms, exactly on the lines of those historic documents produced in England before the sixteenth century. It is understood that the committee will record self-assumed arms, and it should be said that its work is produced by men of great heraldic scholarship. Since the last edition of *The Story of Heraldry* was published, an American College of Arms has been established in Maryland to register, confirm or grant arms, and these it is later intended to include in a register of American armory— a most commendable enterprise. The address, for those who may wish to contact the college, is: The American College of Arms, Heralds Mews on Longdock, Harbourmaster's Building, Baltimore, Maryland, 21202, USA.

Royal Arms

These have in some cases become identified with a country, the most familiar example being that of England. The first royal arms were the lions borne by Richard Coeur de Lion at the end of the twelfth century, and these were adopted by all subsequent sovereigns, the Plantaganets first, then all the other dynasties, Tudor, Stuart, Hanoverian, and now Windsor. True, all succeeding dynasties are connected by blood, and also with the Norman kings and the old English line behind the latter, but the descent is naturally through many female lines, and in several cases the family arms of the particular dynasty have been given up in favour of the historic coat.

Very interesting, too, is the instance of Sweden. The kingdom of Sweden has two coats, the Great and the Small coat of arms. The Small coat shows three crowns of gold in a blue field, and these arms were first used by Albrecht of Mecklenburg in 1364 when he became King of Sweden. The new king relinquished his family coat of arms and adopted the three crowns which have been used by every dynasty since, as in England. Just as the lions of England are quartered with the arms of Scotland and Ireland, so in the Great coat of Sweden we have the three crowns in the first and fourth quarters; in the second and third the field is blue with three silver bends sinister wavy, and over all a crowned golden lion. These arms are those of the Folkung dynasty (1250-1363). The Great coat has been used since 1448, and the usage in Sweden is for the arms of the reigning dynasty to be shown in an inescutcheon in the centre of the quartered coat. Since 1818 the inescutcheon has been that of the Bernadottes.

The above account of Swedish royal arms is taken from a paper by C. G. U. Scheffer, State Herald of Sweden. ('The Coats of Arms of Sweden,' in *The American-Scandinavian Review*, autumn 1963). Mr Scheffer remarks: 'If the dynasty which first adopted a coat of arms governed a country for any length of time, the dynasty's coat of arms gradually came to be recognized as that of the country. Thus the lion with the axe, from having been the arms of the Sverre dynasty, became the national coat of arms of Norway. It was not influenced by subsequent reigning families. The three lions in the shield strewn with hearts which appeared in the arms of the royal family of the Valdemars became Denmark's coat of arms and have remained as the Small coat of arms and as the most important part of the Great coat of arms. Originally the same conditions prevailed in Sweden.'

CHAPTER 13

Titles

No one can study genealogy without coming upon almost as many reference to titles as there are to heraldry. In British genealogy, it is certainly true that both in England and Wales, Scotland and Ireland, immense numbers of people are connected with peerage families, and also with royalty. It should be clearly understood that the great majority of these descents are legitimate, though there are also a number of known illegitimate descents from royalty, such as the families which descend from Charles II. Silly jokes are often heard in this connection when mention is made of the British peerage, so that it is as well to get the facts right. There are four dukes in the British roll of lords who come from Charles II—Buccleuch, Grafton, St Albans, and Gordon & Richmond (the last is one title)—and there is the Earl of Munster from William IV. There is the dukedom of Beaufort from a bastardy of John of Gaunt, Edward III's son. The arms of Lord Hankey have the bordure which here denotes a bastard descent. This gives us seven, and if we make it up to a round dozen to cover the hidden bastardies, it is not much of a percentage against the number of over 1,000 peers on the Roll of the Lords Spiritual and Temporal (this is a printed pamphlet list, published by the British state publishing house, Her Majesty's Stationery Office, [HMSO], every October).

Contrariwise, it is a fair estimate that at least half of the families of British descent have a peer somewhere in their ancestry a few generations back, perhaps nearer. In the writer's own case, for example, a forbear eight generations ago was an earl, through whom the family has also a royal descent. There is nothing uncommon about such lines of ancestry. In the first decade of this century, the Marquis de Ruvigny produced several large volumes on the subject of the Blood Royal of the Plantaganets, in which he traced the descent of some 100,000 men and women of his time from Edward III. That the number traced represented all who had royal Plantaganet blood was far from correct. In fact, so numerous are the known descendants of the Plantaganet kings, that Edward III has been described as the ancestor of the middle-class Englishman !

The reason for this prolific abundance does not indicate for Edward III an activity at home comparable to the energy of his French conquests. It simply means that many of his family lived to maturity and begat children of their own. It also reaffirms that there has never been in England a closed caste system, except for the period of the Hanoverian sovereigns, and that applied only to royalty. The royal house in England and in Scotland married with the families of the nobles, and the latter with the smaller gentry and yeomanry, burghers, tradesmen and so on. Consequently the interconnections between the various classes is very close, added to which noble status in England is limited to the reigning peer and his wife. The younger children, in particular, have always expected to go out and earn a place by their own exertions, knowing that their eldest brother would succeed to the family title and estate. This identification with, and merging into, the people on the part of the aristocratic families is one of the main reasons why there has never been an anti-noble movement in Britain. During the time of the French Revolution, the 1848 Communist uprising in Europe, and the Communist revolutions from 1918 onwards, Britain has never known a move to get rid of the aristocracy. The powers of the House of Lords have been drastically reduced, but even the most determined opponents of privilege have frequently ended as lords themselves. This is true of David Lloyd George (an earl), Herbert Asquith (earl), Philip Snowden (baron), Clement Attlee (earl), David Kirkwood (a baron in 1945, but a deportee from Glasgow in 1915). The nobles have been able to absorb each new rising class in turn. Had the noblesse in Russia, France, Italy, and Germany done the same they would not now be outcast or impotent.

Two main subjects will be dealt with in this chapter: (i) A brief exposition of the British titled system and (ii) a survey of titles as still existing elsewhere in the world. This procedure is not prompted by any obsolete national prejudice, but simply by the fact that Britain is almost alone in retaining a system of titles which are still being granted. The only other state of which I know where titles are still being created is the Vatican, but this is perhaps in a different category since the head of the Vatican state is also the head of the world's largest religion and so a spiritual chief.

The origin of a title in the United Kingdom must come from the Queen, as the Fountain of Honour, or from one of her predecessors on the throne. If the titles or arms are not granted by the sovereign but are of foreign origin, then they should not be used by British subjects without the Queen's approval. (See Note 13, The Queen's own title).

The peerage in the United Kingdom consists of five ranks. The word peer is from the French *pair*, which means equal, and in France this was applied to the great feudal lords, such as the Duke of Brittany or of Burgundy, who were the equals of the Crown although technically vassals to the French king, who was their suzerain or liege lord under the feudal system. On several occasions these French nobles produced a state of near anarchy in France, especially during the Hundred Years' War with the English, but eventually, in the seventeenth century, the Crown succeeded in reducing them to impotence. Louis XIV kept them hanging about at Versailles, the monarchy having then become absolute, and their removal from contact with their estates, combined with the noblesse system, had much to do with the anti-aristocratic movement at the end of the eighteenth century.

Clearly the peers of England were never on the same footing as the French *pairs*. They did succeed in weakening the monarchy at times during the middle ages, but when they reached the zenith of greatness in the internecine strife of the Wars of the Roses (1455-85), they also perished. Richard Nevill, Earl of Warwick, known as the King Maker, was the 'Last of the Barons' (see Lord Lytton's novel of that name for a good account of the age). He died in battle and no other nobleman was ever again allowed to possess an army of retainers. From the Tudor period onward, the nobles have had to be content to be simply peers.

The five ranks of the peerage are (i) dukes, (ii) marquesses, (iii) earls, (iv) viscounts and (v) barons. Only one of these titles is of English origin, that of earl; the rest come from either the military and other high ranks of the later Roman Empire, or from early medieval usages. The title of duke is simply the Latin *dux*, a leader, used of the great military chiefs in the fifth and sixth centuries. The viscount is the *vice comes* or under-count, while the count, or *comes*, was a companion of the emperor. The title of count never caught on in England, though the earl's wife (earl being the equivalent of count) is known as countess. Marquess is from a *marchio* or march (a frontier) because the original holders of this title were keepers of frontiers. The correct English or Scots form is marquess; on the Continent the proper spelling is marquis.

The title of baron is from Norman French and means the king's man. It was originally applied to all the nobles, which explains why the Earl of Warwick was styled the last of the barons. It has now come to denote the lowest rank of the peerage. The title of earl is from the Old English eorl, and was used as a translation of the Norse jarl; the former English title of nobility was that of alderman, or older man (senior senator), which is still used in England to denote senior local councillors.

These five grades in the peerage are subdivided within themselves, so that there are five subgrades within each one. The reason for this is that, as England has grown into the United Kingdom, a new category of the peerage has come into being. In each class of the peers they are sub-divided as follows: (taking the dukes as examples): (i) Dukes of the peerage of England. (ii) Dukes of the peerage of Scotland. The Crowns of England and Scotland were united in 1603, when James VI of Scotland became James I of England, but the two countries continued to be separate entities with separate parliaments under the one Crown until 1707 when, by a treaty of union, the countries were united as one

Coronets.

realm of Great Britain. They retained their separate legal systems, and separate established churches (in England the Church of England, and in Scotland, the Presbyterian Church, the Kirk), but the Scots Parliament was united with that of England. From 1707 no fresh creations have taken place in the English or Scots peerage though there have been revivals of peerages which have become dormant.

The peerage, which dates from 1707, is (iii) the peerage of Great Britain, but at the same time as there were dukes etc of Great Britain, there were also (iv) dukes etc of Ireland, because after 1707 Ireland still continued to be a separate kingdom with its own parliament and its own House of Lords. The present United Kingdom of Great Britain and Northern Ireland is the only country left in the world in which the nobility, or house of peers, forms part of the legislature. The legal implications of this will be explained in Chapter 14. This legislative separation of Britain and Ireland continued until 1801, when the Irish

Parliament was merged in that of Great Britain and the whole realm of three kingdoms was formed into the United Kingdom of Great Britain and Ireland. From this time dates the fifth division in the peerage grades, (v) dukes etc of the United Kingdom. Since then there has been an occasional creation of an Irish peerage, where it was desired to elevate someone like an heir to a peerage, before he could inherit the other title.

When the union of Scotland and England took place, the Scots peers did not all sit in the House of Lords but were allowed to elect sixteen of their number to sit during the life of the parliament. At the union of Ireland with Britain, the Irish peers were allowed to elect twenty-eight of their number to sit in the Lords for life. Thus a peer cannot be simply defined as one who has the right to a seat in the House of Lords. The Scots peers have recently been allowed to sit in the Lords, like the peers of Great Britain or of the United Kingdom. Irish peers have ceased to be elected since 1921, because the twenty-six southern counties of Ireland then became independent of Britain as the Irish Free State, now the Republic of Ireland. The last of the Irish representative peers having died, no Irish peers as such now sit in the Lords, and there are about seventy Irish peers who are thus not entitled to a seat in the Upper House.

There are Scottish and Irish peers who have never been elected to the Lords but who have sat therein, not as Scots or Irish peers but by virtue of their having possessed a peerage of Great Britain or of the United Kingdom in addition to their Scots or Irish title. Just to make the matter even more complicated, when such a peer speaks in the House of Lords, he is, out of courtesy, addressed by the highest title he holds, eg, an Irish earl who sits in the Lords by reason of possessing a United Kingdom barony is addressed as 'the noble earl'. To this little difficulty in understanding may be added another. Under the Act of Union of 1801, an Irish peer who was not elected to the House of Lords could offer himself for, and be elected to, the House of Commons (this privilege never applied to Scots peers). A few years ago, the Father of the House of Commons—the MP with the longest unbroken service—was Earl Winterton, who had been an MP for forty-seven years. He was a real Irish earl but, never having been elected to sit in the Lords, he had been a candidate for the (lower) House of Commons and a member of it for all that time. To add yet another Gilbert and Sullivan opera touch to the whole proceeding, when Earl Winterton retired from the Commons he was given a United Kingdom peerage as Baron Turnour, so that he could sit in the Lords, since as an Irish earl he was not a member of the Lords. This was rather like 'promoting' a colonel to be a

P

captain—one is almost tempted to describe it as an Irish way of doing things, except that Irish folk had no hand in the arrangements.

Another matter which often puzzles newcomers to the peerage is the presence in the Commons of an MP who is styled Lord X, Y, or Z. For instance, for some fifteen years Lord Dunglass represented the Lanark division of Lanarkshire in the House of Commons. *Who's Who*, in his biography, describes the title of Dunglass as 'being a courtesy title while his father held the peerages.' In other words, although Mr Alexander Frederick Douglas Home, MP for Lanark division, was styled, out of courtesy, Lord Dunglass, he was not at that time a peer but only the heir to his father's earldom. When his father, the 13th Earl of Home (pronounced Hume, this being the old spelling of the name) died in 1951, Lord Dunglass succeeded as 14th Earl and, of course, had to give up his seat in the Commons.

Any foreigner who finds all this somewhat difficult to understand, can be assured that even the natives of Britain are by no means clear as to their own system of title, while journalists who venture into the sphere of title seem often quite unable to grasp the meaning of a courtesy title. It is really quite simple. All the higher ranks of the peerage (dukes, marquesses, earls), possess more than one title. The reason is that either their forbears gradually rose in the scale, going up from baron to viscount, then to earl etc in different generations; or, when a commoner is created an earl or higher, he is always granted at the same time another peerage, or perhaps peerages. Prince Philip, Duke of Edinburgh, is also Earl of Merioneth and Baron Greenwich. These three peerages were created together and represent the three countries of Scotland, Wales and England. When the late Clement Attlee resigned as Prime Minister of the United Kingdom, he was created an earl, but he was at the same time made Viscount Prestwood of Walthamstow. His only son, who has succeeded him as Earl Attlee, bore the courtesy title of Viscount Prestwood during his father's lifetime. Such usage is only a courtesy and anyone who wished would have been quite in order in referring to Viscount Prestwood as Mr Martin Attlee.

There are some ceremonial styles set out in the older reference books, so that a duke is His Grace or Your Grace, a marquess the Most Honourable the Marquess of X, an earl, a viscount or a baron, the Right Honourable the Earl of X, the Right Honourable the Viscount Y and the Right Honourable Lord Z. In English usage, one never writes or speaks of 'Baron X' when referring to a British peer. 'Baron' is used in English only of a Continental baron, eg, Baron de Reuter who, though a British subject, was given permission to use the foreign title. In colloquial usage, the style of Lord is used for all peers below the rank of duke, or in general writing; more formally, it is the Marquess of Willingdon, the Earl of Birkenhead and Viscount Hall. Lord and Lady are old English terms, meaning the supplier and giver of bread, and just as in ordinary discourse and writing one uses the word 'Lord', though his peerage rank may be any of the four degrees below duke, so the wives of these four ranks are all styled 'Lady', but more formally, the Marchioness of Reading, the Countess Attlee, and Viscountess Hall. This style of 'Lady X' is also used for the wives of baronets and knights (see below).

The paraphernalia of My Lord, Your Lordship etc and the formal ending of a letter, 'I have the honour to be, my Lord, your Lordship's humble servant (or creeping, bowing and obsequious slave!) is now abandoned and left only to persons trying to get an aristocratic reference or touting for an order. 'Dear Lord X', or a formal 'Sir' is now normal in letters; in conversation it would be 'Lord X'.

Women, with two exceptions, take their style from their husbands. The two exceptions are: a queen regnant, like Her Majesty Elizabeth II, as distinct from a queen consort who is the king's wife and takes her style from him; and a peeress in her own right, when she has inherited the title from her father. She is then the Countess of Seafield (Mrs Studley Herbert). Otherwise a woman derives her style and rank from her husband, so that most married women are Mrs from their husband's Mr. Similarly with duchess (duke), marchioness (marquess), countess (earl), viscountess (viscount) and baroness (baron). What of the courtesy titles? The eldest son of a duke, marquess or earl usually bears the title of one of his father's subsidiary peerages, and his wife takes the same style. Younger sons of dukes are known as 'Lord', followed by the Christian name and surname. Thus the father of Sir Winston Churchill was Lord Randolph Churchill, a younger son of a Duke of Marlborough. He and his wife were Lord and Lady Randolph Churchill. The same rule applies to the younger sons of a marquess and their wives. The eldest daughters of a duke and a marquess are styled Lady Mary X. If she is married to a peer, this courtesy style is lost in the husband's higher substantive rank. Otherwise, when she marries, Lady Mary retains her style, altering merely her surname, and so we have, for instance, Mr Smith and Lady Mary Smith, for husband and wife.

The younger sons of earls, viscounts and barons are called the Honourable (Hon). Their wives are the Hon Mrs —. It is incorrect to address these sons as Mr or Esquire, though it is often done, and in discourse they must be Mr. In writing, they should be addressed as the

Hon John Smith (Dear Sir etc). The daughters of earls are styled Lady —, eg, Lady Mary Smith, and take this style into marriage, as do the daughters of dukes and marquesses.

The sons and daughters of viscounts and barons are styled the Honourable, and the same rules apply as mentioned for the younger sons of earls. The only other case in which a married woman has a style different from that of her husband is when a film star, or a professional woman such as a doctor, keeps her maiden name in ordinary usage after her marriage.

In modern England there are a growing number of life peers, ie, their peerages will die with them, but their styles, and those of their wives and children, are the same as for the hereditary peers. These life peers are, up to the present, all of the rank of baron.

After the peers, there are still two other classes of titles in Britain, the baronets and the knights. The former are peculiar to Britain, and their name is supposed to be derived from the term 'banneret', applied in the middle ages to a knight of exceptional bravery whose fork-ended pennon had been cut square, as a small banner or banneret. However that may be, as an order baronets date from the year 1611, and owe their origin to the chronic lack of money of the first Stuart king of England, James I. He badly needed funds to pay soldiers to conquer the province of Ulster in Ireland, and it was suggested to him by an antiquary, Sir Robert Cotton, that he should revive the so-called order of baronets. The creation was made in no uncertain manner. A lump sum had to be paid by anyone who wanted the honour, and they had to be gentlemen born (three generations of armigers behind them) as well as possessing a good estate. Baronets have the title of Sir—thus Sir Nicholas Bacon—their wives are styled Lady, and the title is hereditary. The word is officially abbreviated to Bt, but Bart is more common and more serviceable. The five classes of the order, with the dates of their institution, are (i) Baronets of England, 1611; (ii) of Ireland, 1611; (iii) of Scotland, 1625; instituted by Charles I, in order to pay for the settlement of Nova Scotia; (iv) of Great Britain, 1707; and (v) of the United Kingdom, 1801. The baronets of Scotland are allowed to wear a badge with a saltire (the St Andrew's Cross) and on the saltire, the royal arms of Scotland. Other baronets have a badge showing the arms of Ulster, a red hand sur-mounted by an imperial crown. The red hand commemorates the settle-ment of Ulster in 1611, and is derived from old legends of the district. These badges are worn suspended round the neck by a ribbon of tawny orange colour.

The order of baronets has known many vicissitudes and at one time seemed likely to lose its proper precedence among British notables. Members of the order then took the sensible step of forming themselves into a trade-union, guild or association in order to defend their rights. In 1902 the Standing Council of the Baronetage was set up and secured one very great advantage, the establishment in 1910 of a Roll of Baronets, to be prepared and maintained by the Home Office, the department under the British Home Secretary. This roll is the equivalent of the roll of the Lords Spiritual and Temporal, but whereas the latter will show the name of a peer even when he has not taken his seat in the Lords, the Home Office Roll bars anyone whose name is not on it from being officially received anywhere as a baronet or addressed as such in formal or official documents. To get his name on the roll, the heir to a baronetcy must register his succession to the title by proving it to the satisfaction of the Home Office. In most cases this means that a claimant proves that he is the eldest legitimate son of the deceased baronet. In some cases where a baronetcy has devolved upon a cousin some degrees removed, more difficulty is experienced. In one remarkable instance, a man who was a grocer in Melbourne, Australia, found to his own surprise that he was heir to a baronetcy. Two of his uncles in Australia had also succeeded to the title though they never knew it. This claimant became in due course Sir Frederick Hay, Bt.

The title of baronet being hereditary, it might be thought to rank its holders with the titled nobility, but this is not so. The order of baronets ranks a good way behind the lowest class in the peerage, that of baron. Baronets come behind knights of the Garter, of the Thistle, and of St Patrick, after the younger sons of barons, and sons of Lords of Appeal in Ordinary (see Chapter 14 for explanation of this last expression). A baronet does not sit in the House of Lords unless he also happens to be a peer; out of some 1,500 baronets, some 250 are also peers. A baronet can sit in the Commons, if he can persuade the voters to put him there. In truth, a baronet has the best of all worlds: a title which is hereditary, and one which does not entail his sitting in the Lords, yet does not bar him from the Commons. He can even alter his surname if he wishes and still retain his title. (A peer cannot do this, because his exact title must be in his letters patent from the sovereign—when a mistake is made, as it sometimes is, the error has to go on for ever!) Perhaps the best definition of a baronet, and the simplest explanation, is that he is an hereditary knight, an explanation which may not suit the pundits but which is accurate. One final thought on baronets: they are anathema to Socialists, who have never allowed any to be created since they came to power in 1964.

The knights cover a wide range of orders, nine in all, plus the Knights Bachelor. The latter is now regarded as the lowest of the orders, and is sometimes rather disparagingly spoken about as the reward of mayors and retired tradesmen—an attitude typical of the misunderstanding which has grown up about the order of knighthood. It developed from the feudal organization of the middle ages, in which the mounted warrior was supreme on the battlefield. Thus the soldiers who won victory for William the Conqueror at Hastings were mainly mounted men, and twenty years later the land had been divided into knights' fees, land holdings sufficient to maintain a knight and his following. At this time any idea of chivalry must have been absent. From the twelfth century onwards, ideals of knightly conduct began to circulate, together with stories about King Arthur and his Round Table, and about Charlemagne and his Paladins. The Crusades added the ingredient of religious enthusiasm to the conception of chivalric ideals. The military origins of the whole movement can be seen from the terms employed in various languages to denote the knights—cavalier, chevalier, caballero, ritter etc. The English knight is derived from a different source—cnicht, the Old English for a boy, a youth or an attendant. The idea grew into an ideal, and the Church, as with most things medieval, began to attach a special meaning to it. Ceremonies in church marked the entry into knighthood. The aspirant watched his arms in the church, then on the morrow he was knighted by the king, or more likely some great lord, and the new knight participated in the Mass. He swore to be faithful to God, the King, and to protect the weak. Like all human institutions, knighthood gradually declined from its high ideals but it did introduce a much-needed civilizing influence during the harsh period between the eleventh and thirteenth centuries. The very perfect gentle knight of Chaucer was the fine flower of chivalry.

From the thirteenth century, western Europe was more settled than at any time since the disintegration of the Roman Empire, and so more elaborate modes of living became possible. In several countries of western Europe, notably in Spain, religious orders of military monks arose. There were the three military orders of Calatrava, Santiago, and Alcantara. Somewhat earlier were the orders of the Knights Templar, of St John of Jerusalem, and of the Teutonic knights. These were orders of men bound together to fight against the Moslems who had seized the Holy Land and invaded Europe. While some of these crusading orders were engaged in Palestine and Syria, the Spanish orders fought the Moslems in Spain, and the Teutonic knights carved out east Prussia battling with primitive pagans in the Baltic forests. Later there were created orders of knighthood, like that of the Garter in England, which dates from 1348.

The crusading orders derive from the monastic ideal, but the English and Scottish orders come from the original conception of the Knights Bachelor. The meaning of this last expression cannot be properly explained, but is probably derived from a corruption of *battelier* or fighter on the battlefield, and confused with the low Latin *baccalaurius*. However that may be, the Knight Bachelor represents the original medieval order of knighthood from which the different orders have been hived off. A present-day knight who does not belong to one of the orders mentioned below is termed a Knight Bachelor, and can put Kt, or Kt Bach after his name. Both he and the members of the nine orders are all called 'Sir', and the holders of these decorations are able to put various letters after their names as shown below, where the dates of institution of the orders are also given:

(1) The Most Noble Order of the Garter, KG, 1348.

(2) The Most Ancient and Most Noble Order of the Thistle, KT. This order is supposed to have been instituted in 809 in Scotland but, on more solid historical ground certainly existed in the fifteenth century. New statutes for the order were promulgated in 1687.

(3) The Most Illustrious Order of St Patrick, KP, 1783. This order is now obsolescent, as only two knights remain, the Duke of Gloucester and the Duke of Windsor. As the bulk of Ireland is independent of the British Crown, the British government has felt unable to recommend to the sovereign the creation of knighthoods of St Patrick.

(4) The Most Honourable Order of the Bath, GCB, KCB. The conventional date for the creation is often given as 1399, but no date can be assigned for the beginning of the order as it arose from the custom of a ceremonial washing before the conferment of knighthood. The order was revived and given statutes and rules in 1725. This order has more than one class. Thus GCB is a Knight Grand Cross; KCB a Knight Commander of the Bath; and CB a Companion of the Bath. The Companions are not knights. They remain plain Misters but are able to put CB after their names. Other orders have the same class of Companions.

(5) The Most Distinguished Order of St Michael and St George, GCMG, KCMG, CMG, 1814. The Knights Grand Cross are GCMG, the Knights Commander are KCMG and the Companions, CMG.

(6) The Royal Victorian Order, 1896. GCVO = Knight Grand Cross; KCVO = Knight Commander; CVO = Companion, and MVO = Member.

(7) The Most Excellent Order of the British Empire, 1917. GBE = Knight Grand Cross; KBE = Knight; CBE = Companion; OBE = Officer; MBE = Member. In addition, a woman in the higher class has the DBE = Dame of the Order.

(8) The Most Exalted Order of the Star of India, 1861. GCSI = Knight Grand Commander; KCSI = Knight Commander, and CSI = Companion. No appointments have been made since 1947.

(9) The Most Eminent Order of the Indian Empire, 1886. GCIE = Knight Grand Commander; KCIE = Knight Commander; CIE = Companion. No appointments since 1947.

More is said in Chapter 15 on the subject of these orders, and those of other countries, but anyone who wishes to read a very detailed study of the British orders should consult *The Queen's Orders of Chivalry*, by Brigadier Sir Ivan de la Bere, 1961.

The knights of St John of Jerusalem are not styled 'Sir', but are entitled to put after their names letters denoting their rank in the order. Thus a Bailiff or Dame Grand Cross is able to put GCStJ after his or her name; a Knight of Justice, KJStJ etc. A man who has been made a knight of one of the orders can be advanced to a higher order or created a Knight Grand Cross without being knighted again. So also anyone who has been made a companion of an order can be made a knight of that or of another order. Wives of Knights Grand Cross are styled Lady Smith, or Brown etc.

After the names of many British folk will be found the abbreviation, Esq, meaning Esquire. This is a rank and comes at the end of the Table of Precedence. The Table is based on an Act of Parliament of 1547, in the reign of Henry VIII, which regulates the relative positions of all persons on all official occasions in England. Originally, an esquire was an attendant on a knight, and most people have heard or read of the squires in medieval warfare whose task it was to attend to the needs of the knights whom they served. Most squires looked forward to attaining knighthood and were themselves of gentle birth. Gradually the term came to apply to the first rank of gentry. Gentry and nobility are really the same thing, the only difference between them being of degree within the same class. Just as the five classes of peers differ in their respective degrees of rank, but are all peers, so all those who bear arms (coats of arms), are of the same class, the nobility, though differing in that class according to their ranks. There are various definitions of the term 'esquire', but these scarcely need elaborating as today publicity agencies and mail-order firms are busily engaged in addressing all British males over the age of twenty-one by the term. Still, for anyone who is seriously studying the subject of ancestry, some useful divisions of the classes of esquire can be given: (i) All those males who are members of the families of peers, baronets and knights and who have themselves no other title (Esquire is never used with any other title, including those of Professor or Doctor). (ii) Holders of certain offices in connection with law and administration, or members of the legal profession.

Mister (Mr) is a colloquial rendering of Master, and is a title of respect; the female equivalent is Mrs (Mistress).

In former times in England, esquires were expressly created as such, and as late as the second half of Queen Victoria's reign, one of her favourite servants, John Brown, was created an esquire by the Queen. Even now there is a continuous creation of esquires, for whenever a grant of arms is conferred upon an untitled person he is termed an esquire in the letters patent which are issued by the Earl Marshal, acting for the sovereign. Letters patent provide the grant of arms, and arms are the distinguishing mark of the lowest rank of nobility, commonly called gentry. The grant of arms is the formal recognition of nobiliary status and this should be understood by anyone who is or becomes armigerous. Letters patent are used to confer the higher rank of nobility, peerages and so on, but it is only a degree in the same nobiliary status of the person who possesses a coat of arms. This truth has been somewhat obscured in England, but not in Scotland, where it has recently been made clear by a Scots herald, Col Gayre of Gayre and Nigg, in several of his writings.

Britain's roll of titles is but the survival and most systematic of the numerous titled systems which have existed in the world. While it is true that many countries have abolished titles—the United States has refused to recognise them from its very inception—there is a natural instinct among human beings which craves for the distinction conferred by a title. Most married women object to being called Miss; some single women resent being described as Mrs. The titles of Reverend, Professor and Doctor are widespread in modern society, and show no signs of disappearing; the curious form, Emeritus, has grown from being a proper description of a retired professor to apply to almost every position, including even organist emeritus. Very few men will tolerate being called Smith, Brown etc, without the addition of Mr. In the political world, presidents, premiers, members of parliament, senators, mayors and councillors, all seem for the most part averse to the omission of their titles. It would therefore seem rather unfair that someone who is a duke, a lord or a knight, should be deemed undemocratic for his use of a title while all around him object to being merely Tom, Dick or Harry. This may help to explain an historical fact: the existence of titles from the earliest records of civilisation. Some of the forms taken by these, especially in the ancient East and among modern Oriental potentates, may sound ridiculous and sometimes even blasphemous. The Old Testament contains numerous instances of monarchs whose pride and greatness were humbled, even in the moment of their apparent superiority to all earthly power, implying the moral that their grandiloquent titles were an affront to the Supreme Power.

In the family history of titles those in use in western Europe derive partly from the usages of the Roman Empire, and partly from the practice in the barbarian states which arose on its ruins. Our emperors, princes, patricians, nobles, senators, consuls, censors, tribunes and pontiffs, all come from Rome. In addition, many Greek titles have reached us through a Roman or Latin medium, eg, episcopate, and the previously mentioned origins of duke, *dux* and count, *comes*. Emperor comes from *imperator*, the title of a successful general and given to the Roman head of state as commander-in-chief of the forces. Prince is from *princeps* or chief, a title adopted by the first Roman, emperor, Augustus Caesar; the surname of the great conqueror, Julius, became the title of the succeeding emperors and was adopted in various forms, such as Tzar of Russia, Kaiser of Germany, and Kaiser-i-Hind (Emperor of India) by the British monarchs. A patrician was a member of the Roman noble families as distinguished from the plebians or lower classes. The nobles (*nobilis, nobiles*) were those who were known or distinguished, as distinct from the *ignobiles* or unknown. Hence the word has passed into the languages of Europe. The senators were the seniors, the older and wiser men, those who had served the state and become members of the Senate. The consuls were the two magistrates elected annually to the administration of the state in peace and in war. Censors had the task of pruning the lists of Roman citizens, and tribunes were officers appointed to defend the rights of the poorer citizens against the nobles. The Pontifex Maximus was the chief priest of the state religion, and the position was held by the emperor. When he withdrew to Constantinople from Rome, the title gradually passed to the Pope who now has it. The episcopus, or overseer, was the Christian bishop.

In several languages, the Latin *rex* has been naturalised; in French, as *roi*, in Spanish as *rey*. 'King' is a Saxon word from a root meaning 'kin' or 'kith', but his attributes are royal or regal, an instance of Latin influence.

Most of the titles like emperor, prince, duke or count began as terms of office and then, as the offices became hereditary, so did the titles. An example occurs in the history of Holland, with the title of Stadtholder becoming hereditary in the family of the Prince of Orange.

Many titles have come into the English language from the east and from the influence of the Moslem or Islamic religion. The first of these is that of Caliph, the successor to the Prophet Mohammed, who was the founder of the Mohammedan or Moslem faith. As the centuries passed, the office of the Caliphate became associated with some Moslem monarchies, including that of the Sultan of Turkey. Sultan means 'power' and has been the title of numerous eastern sovereigns. The female is Sultana. Other Oriental terms are Mahdi (the leader of a great movement in the Sudan in the last century) meaning 'one who is guided aright'. Amir and Emir are terms for Moslem kings or other rulers. The Khedive of Egypt—'Khedive' meaning master or prince—succeeded the Pasha of Egypt, the pasha being a person who held a high administrative position. The commonest title in Egypt is that of effendi, applied to anyone of consequence. The Bey was a governor, as with the Bey of Tunis. The Dey (a word meaning 'maternal uncle!') of Algiers, like his counterpart in Tunis, held an office which became hereditary and so did the title.

In western Europe, numerous titles appeared during the middle ages. The Roman Empire had broken down in the west but the emperor who ruled in Constantinople over the eastern half of the empire never gave up his claim to be the universal Roman emperor. In the year 800 Charlemagne, the only effective western emperor, was crowned by the Pope as head of a revived Roman Empire in the west. This was the start of the Holy Roman Empire which was to last until it was ended by Napoleon in 1806. In theory, the empire was elective and anyone could be elected to its headship. In fact, at various times the position of emperor was offered to a Spanish candidate, and to English candidates. Eventually it came to be hereditary in the Habsburgs of Austria. An electoral college was formed, comprising the German magnates, and in the seventeenth century the Elector of Hanover was a member of the college—hence the references to the first Hanoverian sovereigns of England as German Electors.

The word 'palace' is derived from the Latin *palatium*, or Palatine Hill, where the Roman Caesars had their palace, and a Count Palatine was one who had a very special relationship to the Crown. The most famous Count Palatine (or Palsgrave) was ruler of the Rhineland, where his territory was called the Palatinate. In England, there were two places in which such special jurisdiction existed, namely Durham, near the Scots border, and Chester, facing north Wales, The Bishop of Durham had the position of a prince as well as his episcopal title. The Palatinate of Durham has long ceased to exist, but the arms of the see of Durham show a mitre above the shield, encircled with a ducal coronet, a reminder of the time when the bishop was a great temporal lord. The prince bishop was a fairly common figure on the Continent, as at Liège in Belgium. The other English palatinate, Chester, was annexed to the Crown, and when the sovereign's eldest son is created Prince of Wales, he also becomes Earl of Chester.

The Continental margrave, found in Germany, is the same as a marquis. The title of Serene and Most Serene was used in medieval times for princes who, while sovereign, were not the equal of the rulers of great states like France. The Doge of Venice was thus styled, and so today's Prince of Monaco is His Serene Highness Prince Rainier. Similar explanations help to define the titles of duke and archduke. The former was always a great distinction for a person of vast possessions and influence, like the mighty dukes who were *pairs* of the French Crown. Such in origin was the Tzardom of Russia. The Grand Duke of Muscovy was at first the ruler of a small territory and for some time acted as a tax collector for the Tartar rulers of Russia. In the fourteenth century the Grand Duke became the Grand Prince of Muscovy or Moscow, and in the fifteenth century, in the reign of Ivan III, the Tartar yoke was thrown off. After the fall of the eastern Roman empire, with the capture of Constantinople by the Turks in 1453, the Grand Prince assumed the title of Tzar, the arms of Byzantium or Constantinople, and regarded himself as the successor to the empire. His nobles were termed the boyars, but after the time of Peter the Great (1672-1725), an imitation of western usages set in as regards both titles and armorial bearings. Archdukes are found in Austria, and their titles could more accurately be rendered as Grand Dukes (a style used in Tzarist Russia). The 'grand' does not imply any superiority in jurisdiction over other dukes; it simply meant, in most cases, greater possessions and nearness to the throne.

The German equivalent of count is graf, with the female grafin. The landgrave was one of the great territorial lords of whom there were four; Thuringen, Hesse, Elsatz and Leuchtenburg. The barons were herren, or lords.

Two English titles (one is derived from France) are important. The sheriff was the shire reeve, the ruler of a shire or, as it came later to be called, a county. The office continues to the present day, in England, where it is purely an honorary function, and in the USA where it carries with it practical administrative duties. Constable has become in England the name for a policeman, but in former days it denoted the commander-in-chief of the armed forces. This was also the case in medieval France. The High Constable of England, *pro hac vice*, has already been mentioned earlier.

Indian titles are, of course, quite distinct from those of the west, although in the period of British rule many European titles were imported and bestowed upon Indians. There are three divisions of Indian titles, Hindu, Moslem and the western styles. Raja(h) means 'king'. The term 'Rajput', applied to one of the most warlike of the Indian races, means 'son of a king', and there are many Rajput princes. Maharajah means 'great king'. There are Hindu titles. Nawab, commonly rendered into English as nabob, is a Moslem term denoting a governor or nobleman. The Peshwar, the hereditary sovereign of the Mahratta state, took his title from the Persian word for a chief. Sahib, which came from Arabic into Hindustani, meant 'friend' and was much applied to Europeans by Indians. Bahadur was a title used in connection with officers and means 'brave'.

The Moslems invaded India in the eleventh century and again in 1398, when the Mongols under their leader, Timur the Lame, (Tamburlaine as the name was corrupted in the title of Christopher Marlow's play) entered the country. Just a century later one of Timur's descendants, Babur, established the Mogul empire in India. Mogul is the Persian form of Mongol, and the emperor whose court was at Delhi was known as the Great Moghul.

Under British rule, most of the princes of India received the style of His Highness (HH) followed by the title Maharajah etc. One of the greatest of the princes, the Nizam of Hyderabad, was given by the British government the style of His Exalted Highness, and of 'Faithful Ally of the British Government'.

Since the emergence of India and Pakistan as separate states independent of Britain, the position of the princes has undergone great changes and although their personal wealth was at first unimpaired, they rapidly lost authority over their former territories. Reports in the press in 1968 indicated that the government of India, following upon Congress decisions, now wishes to abolish the privy purses, amounting to £3m per year, as well as the special privileges of the Indian princes.

In the sphere of ecclesiastical titles, the Church has borrowed generously from the State. The principal bishop in the entire church, the Pope or Bishop of Rome, is commonly called the Pope, which means Father. He is wont to sign documents as *Pastor Pastorum*, Shepherd of Shepherds, and is also styled *Servus servorum Dei*, Servant of the servants of God, a title adopted by Pope St Gregory the Great (590-604); *Pontifex*, Pontiff; *Pontifex Maximus*, Chief Pontiff, a title derived from pagan Rome; *Summus Pontifex*; *Romanus Pontifex*, Highest or Roman Pontiff; *Sanctissimus Pater*, Most Holy Father, and *Sanctissimus dominus noster*, Our most holy lord.

The cardinals derive their names from the Latin *cardo*, a hinge on which something turns. The term has come to denote the College of Cardinals, whose members in various ways act as advisers to the Pope. They are the electors of the college, and each is styled His Eminence Cardinal X, followed usually by the name of his see.

Very often found among the titles of the Catholic clergy is that of Monsignor (Mgr). These are addressed as prelates with the title of Right Reverend John Smith. The word 'prelate' itself is derived from a secular usage, meaning merely one set over. A primate, the term applied to some bishops who head a province, is also borrowed from secular Latin usage. The monsignors are members of the papal court.

Archbishops, bishops, deans, archdeacons, canons, priests and deacons are common to both the Catholic and Anglican churches. The styles of archbishops are the Most Reverend, and His Grace the Archbishop of X. The Anglican Archbishops of Canterbury and York are also styled Right Honourable and so addressed as Most Reverend and Right Honourable, the latter title deriving from their membership of the Privy Council. All bishops are Right Reverend, but only the forty-three diocesan bishops of the Anglican Church in England are styled Lord Bishop. This last usage does not apply to Anglican bishops who are suffragans, missionaries, or colonial. Deans are styled the Very Reverend Dean of Y, and the title derives from *decanus*, one set over ten, and is another secular term brought within the ecclesiastical sphere. A provost, who is set over some cathedrals in England, takes his title from the *praepositus*, one placed over, ie, in charge. An archdeacon is styled the Venerable, and canon is a title taken from the Greek word for a rule. Clergymen of all denominations are termed the Reverend, and this applies to rabbis (ie, masters) in the Jewish religion. The Chief Rabbi is styled the Very Reverend.

The eastern Orthodox Church has a considerable extension throughout the world, not least in America. The Chief Patriarch of the Eastern Churches is the Patriarch of Constantinople, who is termed His All Holiness Athenagoras I, Archbishop of Constantinople, the New Rome, and Ecumenical Patriarch. Under him are ecclesiastics bearing the title of Exarchs, a borrowing from the later Roman eastern empire.

The Patriarch of Alexandria is His Holiness, or His Divine Beatitude

Pope and Patriarch of Alexandria and all Africa, 13th Apostle and Judge of the Universe.

The Patriarch of Antioch is His Holiness the Lord X, Patriarch of Antioch, the Great City of God, of Cilicia, of Iberia, of Syria, of Arabia, and of all the East, Father of Fathers, Pastor of Pastors, 13th Apostle.

The Patriarch of Jerusalem is His Holiness, or His Beatitude. These four Patriarchs are the four principal prelates of the Eastern Church.

Monastic institutions abound in the churches, Catholic, Eastern and Anglican. The head of a monastery is the abbot, who is called the Lord Abbot of X. The head of a province in an order of monks is the provincial, referred to as the Very Reverend Father. Dom (short for *dominus*, lord) is often used before the names of monks. The head of a priory is the prior, and the monks are known as brothers. There are many orders of the religious life for women. The head of a nunnery is the mother superior, known as the Reverend Mother. The nuns are sisters and are addressed as Sister Mary etc, according to the Christian name taken when they professed their final vows.

CHAPTER 14

Peerage Law

Almost the only work on Peerage Law in England in the present century was a book by F. B. Palmer, a Bencher of the Inner Temple, published in 1907 under the title, *Peerage Law in England, a Practical Treatise for Lawyers and Laymen.* On the other hand, more Acts of Parliament dealing with the peerage have, unquestionably, been produced in this century than ever before. More especially is this true within the last twenty years, during which many changes have taken place in the legal position of the peers. Palmer, in the work mentioned above, refers to the interest which the subject possesses. Peerage law, he says, 'appeals alike to the lawyer and the statesman, to the student of history and to the antiquarian. *It appeals on personal grounds, to those who are descended, and their number is legion, from ennobled ancestors*; and last, not least, it appeals to those who possess or hope to inherit or recover an existing peerage'. (*op cit*, preface, italics by L. G. P.).

As always happens with English law and the legal systems derived from it, peerage law is composed of statutes and cases dealing with peerages which have arisen from decided usage. Between the reign of Richard II (1377-99), and that of Queen Victoria (1837-1901), only eighteen statutes are cited by Palmer. In our time, and since he wrote, in the past sixty years there has been important legislation as to the powers of the House of Lords (1911 and 1949), on the abolition of the right of peers to be tried by their peers (Criminal Justice Act, 1948), on the creation of life peers (1958), on the right to disclaim or give up a peerage (1963), and, in the same Peerage Act, permission for Scots peers as such to sit in the Lords, and the right of women who possess hereditary peerages to sit in the Lords. Under the Life Peerage Act of 1958, women may be created life peers and sit in the House of Lords. In addition, payment of expenses to peers during their attendance in the House has been introduced, and measures have also been taken to excuse peers who do not wish to attend sittings of the House of Lords. It will thus be seen that much attention has been given to the Lords in our time. They have frequently been threatened with abolition but they still continue to be part of the United Kingdom legislature. We deal then with (1) peers as forming the House of Lords, considering the latter as (a) part of the British Parliament or legislature, and (b) the highest court of law in the United Kingdom; and (2) with the peers as forming a noble class.

Peerage has been defined in law as an incorporeal hereditament, an inheritance, and as being a species of real property, because titles and dignities were formerly, under the feudal system, annexed to lands. This definition will hardly cover the present state of the peerage in which, for the great majority of peers, a title is quite unconnected with land, and when a growing number of peers are life creations. Since this is so, the best definition of a peerage is that it is the rank or dignity of a peer.

Peerage, like everything else in the United Kingdom, has evolved. Ever since the publication of Darwin's *Origin of Species* in 1859, thought has been dominated by the conception of life and institutions evolving or developing from the simple to the more complex. Nowhere is this conception better exemplified than in Britain, though the legal notions in connection with peerage are much more static than dynamic, probably because of the nature of legal thinking.

Nobility is as old as monarchy in England, and is to be found from the earliest times of the English settlement in the fifth century AD. By the time of the Norman Conquest, the great landowners, both lay and ecclesiastical, had been accustomed to meet the King in the Witan (in full, Witenagemot, or meeting of the wise) to decide national policy. This body was the forerunner of the Great Council, as it came to be called in Norman times, and from it has developed the Privy Council which still exists in Britain and which is a body completely distinct from, as it is much older than Parliament. The latter, as we now know it, began at the end of the thirteenth century, from 1265 to 1295. Some of the oldest statutes in English law, such as the well-known *Quia Emptores* (lying at the base of the land law) were passed by parliaments which did not contain more than the Crown and the peerage element. Even now the proper definition of a parliament is the Crown with the Lords and Commons.

The monarchs from William the Conqueror onward were wont to call together from time to time their tenants-in-chief, of whom there were about 200. The ecclesiastics—archbishops, bishops and the greater abbots—were summoned to these assemblies because they were great landowners who held from the Crown what were called the temporalities of their episcopal sees. Two interesting survivals of this ancient

Q

practice still have their place in England. One is the presence in the House of Lords of twenty-six prelates of the Established Church of England. These are the Archbishops of Canterbury and of York, with twenty-four of the other bishops, known as the Lords Spiritual. An Act of Parliament begins with the following preamble: 'Be it enacted by the Queen's most Excellent Majesty, by and with the advice and consent of the Lords Spiritual and Temporal, and Commons in this present Parliament assembled, and by the authority of the same, as follows etc. etc.' The other survival is found in the necessity for a bishop to do homage to the Queen for his temporalities (ie, the lands attached to the see) on his appointment as bishop.

At first, both Houses of Parliament sat together, and it was only towards the end of the fourteenth century that the two houses separated and that we hear of a House of Lords and a House of Commons. There is even an instance of a man who sat in the Lords in one Parliament and in the Commons in the next, thus expressing a preference shared now by the very few peers who have availed themselves of the provisions of the Peerage Act, 1963 (see later). Then, in the fifteenth century, we have the first instance of a creation of a peer, a Baron Beaumont, without the old territorial appendages, as a plain creation by letters patent from the King. For the past 500 years that is how peerages have been created, with a few exceptions such as when the eldest son of a peer has been needed in the Lords and has been summoned by a writ in one of his father's peerages. The method of creation of peerages now is always by letters patent. The other method was by writ of summons, which meant that a man was called to the Great Council of the King, the English legal theory being that the man so summoned was thereby created a peer with the right of inheritance passing to his heir. This theory, like many other legal theories, has no historical basis, but even though it can be shown to be at variance with historical fact, it is settled law in England. In consequence, if anyone can show that he is heir to a barony by writ of summons, then he can claim that barony and the right to a seat in the House of Lords. Nor is this claim dependent upon a male-line descent. Sometimes in cases within the last 100 years, the line of descent has gone through as many as a dozen families spread over several centuries. Women, too, can inherit baronies by writ, the reason being that these are really feudal dignities, and in their case, when a baron had an only child, a daughter, she passed the inherited dignity to her husband.

There are, therefore, two modes of creation of peerages in England, that of the great majority, which is by letters patent, and that of the minority, who hold baronies by writ of summons. There was a third method: the holding of a title because of a property. This was peculiarly feudal and there is no peerage today held or capable of being held on such terms. There is a popular myth to the effect that the earldom of Arundel is held by the tenure of Arundel Castle, so that if the Duke of Norfolk (who is also Earl of Arundel) were to sell the castle, the buyer would become Earl of Arundel. After a very careful examination of a claim to the barony of Berkeley in right of the tenure of Berkeley Castle, in 1858, the House of Lords decided that no such claim could be sustained, and on this Palmer (*op cit*, p 186) remarks, 'it may now be taken as settled that, if there ever were, there are now no longer any peerages by tenure in England; nor is there the smallest likelihood that the title to a peerage by tenure will at any time hereafter be established'.

Considering, then, the way in which Parliament has developed over the course of many hundreds of years, it is not so surprising that it should still form part of the United Kingdom legislature. The British Constitution is unwritten. In theory, this should render it easy for alterations and innovations to be made, but in reality the weight of tradition is often a more powerful barrier to change than anything in the nature of a written constitution. There has been plenty of constitution making and writing in the last twenty years for the numerous states set up on the ruins of the British Empire, but it is very doubtful if they will work. However perfect on paper, the constitution has still to operate among human beings, and under the British Constitution the various institutions can be modified by the requirements of real life. Revolutions of a drastic kind are not popular in England, and only once has a serious effort been made to alter the native constitution. In the period of Parliamentary or Cromwellian rule, from 1645 to 1660, the King, Charles I, was executed, the monarchy and the House of Lords were abolished, the episcopal Church of England was overthrown and a presbyterian church substituted; the Archbishop of Canterbury was beheaded, the office of bishop removed from the Church, and the Book of Common Prayer prohibited. Finally, as though to round off the revolution, a dictatorship evolved and the dictator, in the person of Oliver Cromwell, closed the House of Commons and drove out its members. This experience was apparently enough for the English people, and no such forceful modernization has since occurred. Very great changes have been made, but have been achieved by Act of Parliament.

The House of Lords has long ceased to be a gathering of great feudal lords; they went out with the coming of the Tudors and strong laws were passed, and enforced, to prevent their keeping retainers. The members of the Upper House had, therefore, to be content to be rich men, great landowners, and later, heads of industry and commerce, lawyers and politicians. They recovered from their abolition in 1649, although after a time Cromwell had found it necessary to institute what he called the Other House, just as he sought to restore the monarchy in his own person. When the Stuarts were restored in 1660, all the old institutions came back with the King, but in every case with considerable modification. The monarchy had suffered what, in our jargon, is termed a traumatic experience, and although several of the post-Restoration sovereigns did exercise great powers, it was understood that matters would not be pushed to an extreme by the Crown. As regards the House of Lords, it was tacitly assumed that it would not interfere with a money Bill or financial measure, which came up to it from the Commons. During the seventeenth, eighteenth and nineteenth centuries, members of the same families would be sitting as contemporaries in both Houses. The practice of an heir to a peerage sitting as an MP has been mentioned in Chapter 13 and is still quite common. Thus, in the period between the seventeenth and nineteenth centuries, conflict between the two Houses was unlikely to arise. There was a quarrel over the passage of the Reform Bill of 1832 but this was settled without much trouble. Moreover, the Tory party had no built-in majority in the Lords, and a Whig majority was quite common.

With the twentieth century, conflict between Lords and Commons did occur. The vast changes engendered by the industrial revolution in Britain had produced a class of new poor, dispossessed of all save a wage, and that scanty and hardly earned. These people began to combine in order to secure for themselves a measure of social justice. At first, the incipient Labour or Socialist party was allied with the Liberals (the latter had developed out of the old Whig party as the opponents of the Tories who were now known as Conservatives, later as Unionists). In 1906 a Liberal government came to power, holding 513 out of a total of 640 seats in the Commons. Of the 513, 377 were Liberal held, 53 Labour, and 83 Irish members, giving the Liberals an overall majority of 114 and the assured support of the Labour and Irish members for many of their measures. In the Lords, however, the Conservatives had a majority of 391 out of a total of 602 peers. As the Conservatives found themselves so weak in the Commons, they tried to stem the tide of Liberalism by the aid of their majority in the Lords, which began to use its power to veto Bills sent up from the Commons. So successful was the co-operation between Mr Balfour and Lord Lansdowne, the Conservative leaders respectively in the Commons and in the Lords, that during the first three years of the Liberal government it was impossible to get any measure other than a money Bill passed into law in any form corresponding to the Liberals' intentions.

For two and a half centuries the Lords had left money Bills alone, but at last, in 1909, the Liberals led by the Prime Minister, Mr (later Earl) Asquith, and his Chancellor, Mr (later Earl) Lloyd George, brought forward financial proposals which emboldened the Lords to break their rule and to oppose a money Bill. The reason was that the foundations of the Welfare State were about to be laid. Lloyd George proposed to increase the taxation by some £13 millions in order to provide for old-age pensions and increased expenditure on education and other social services. These charges were to be met by increases in estate or death duties, and in land taxation. Estates of over £1 million were to pay a total duty of one-quarter of their value. Income tax was to be higher and there was to be a tax of 20 per cent on the unearned increment in land values, payable either on the sale of the land or at the death of the owner; there was to be a further tax of one halfpenny in the pound on the value of undeveloped land and minerals; and a 10 per cent duty on any increase in value which accrued to the landlord at the end of a lease.

All these measures were most repugnant to the great noblemen who owned large landed estates, and when the 1909 Budget, which contained the proposals, came before the House of Lords, the Finance Bill (ie, the Budget) was rejected by the peers for the first time in more than 250 years. On the second reading of the Bill, after a long preliminary discussion, the Bill was rejected by 350 to 75 votes, and as the business of the House was normally conducted by 80-100 peers, it was evident that many who only attended very occasionally, and were colloquially termed 'backwoodsmen', had turned up simply and solely to vote against the Bill.

Thus it happened, in the words of Lloyd George, that 500 ordinary men chosen by accident from among the unemployed had been able to override the wishes of the working population of Britain. He made much popular play with comparisons, showing that while a few thousand people owned the soil of Britain, 'the rest of us are trespassers in the land of our birth', and that one man while he was asleep could get more money than his neighbour could obtain in a whole year of honest toil. Lloyd George refused to believe that this dispensation had come about by justice, and rather welcomed the rejection of his Budget by the Lords. Now the Government could appeal to the country with a safe conscience on a constitutional matter; the Lords had rejected a Finance Bill, and by so doing had dared to challenge the supremacy of the all powerful Commons. He was right, and on appeal to the country the Liberal government won a general election, but with a much decreased majority, at the beginning of 1910.

Then followed consultations between Government and Opposition in order to reach that favourite English expedient, a compromise. This proved impossible and a Bill was prepared to reduce the time of the Lords' veto to two years and, of course, to exclude from their veto anything which the Speaker of the Commons should decide was a money Bill. Even so the Lords might not have yielded, had Asquith not had in his possession a final, irresistible weapon. Once, at the time of the Treaty of Utrecht, Queen Anne had been persuaded to create twelve peers in order to ensure a majority in the Lords for the acceptance of the treaty. In 1832, William IV had agreed to create enough lords to give the government a majority in the Upper House, so that the Reform Bill should be passed. This operation, commonly known as 'peer packing', was to have been repeated on a vast scale in 1910, the King, Edward VII, followed by his son George V, who succeeded him in that year, having agreed if necessary to create 500 peers of Asquith's choosing to enter the Lords and, of course, swamp the Conservative opposition. This threat of an avalanche of nobility proved too much for all but the most diehard of the Conservative peers. The Parliament Act of 1911 was passed (in 1910) by a majority of seventeen (131 for and 114 against). Asquith, incidentally, had prepared a list—later found among his effects—of 249 people who were ready to enter the Lords on his terms.

The result of the Parliament Act of 1911 was to shackle the power of the Lords to keep back Commons' legislation. Thereafter, trouble with a left-wing government could not be prolonged for more than two years, and any measure rejected would, if re-presented after two years, automatically become law. When a Labour government was in office in 1929-31, and was dependent on Liberal votes, there were occasional conflicts with the Lords. There were many more in the next Labour government from 1945 to 1950, particularly over a Bill to nationalise the steel industry. Realising that if the measure were held up by the Lords there might not be time for it to become law automatically after the two-year period had expired, the Labour government decided to reduce the period of the veto from two years to one year. Accordingly a second Parliament Bill, that of 1949, was passed to amend the Act of 1911 and so ensure that a Bill turned down by the Lords should become law not more than one year after its rejection. This Act, which at the time of writing governs the powers of the Lords, was preceded by an all-party conference designed to produce a reform of the Lords which would be acceptable to all parties. An agreed statement was issued at the conclusion of the conference to the effect that the conference had failed, because agreement could not be reached on the subjects of the powers and the composition of the House. Two previous conferences in 1908 and 1918 had failed for the same reasons. The Conservative party would have liked a reformed House, possessing powers substantial enough to hold up a Commons' measure and give time for 'second thoughts'. In other words, to set up a Senate, as in the democratic systems of the United States, Canada and Australia. This is exactly what the Labour party does not want, its real object being one-chamber government, either by outright abolition of the House of Lords or by reducing it to such a state of emasculation that it acts merely as a rubber stamp for measures passed by the Commons. By comparison, the written constitution of the USA was produced in the eighteenth century with the then British constitution in mind, and it was designed to provide a system of very valuable checks and balances, between President (replacing the sovereign), Senate (standing for Lords without hereditary element) and House of Representatives (the Commons). That constitution remains, but the British constitution has taken a dangerous slant towards a one-chamber system of rule. When the British Prime Minister, Ramsay Macdonald, visited Washington in the 1930s, he remarked in his gushingly ecstatic manner, 'How alike we are in our political institutions'. There is an outward resemblance.

In 1967, the Labour government again included in its programme a promise of further reform of the Lords. As things are at present, however, the Lords remain part of the legislature of the United Kingdom, the only country in the world to have hereditary legislators, even though their powers have been severely curbed. In Sweden in the last century the House of Nobles ceased to be part of the legislature and was replaced by an elected Upper House.

Such then is the present position of the House of Lords.* Now for its powers as the supreme law court of the United Kingdom. Let us begin with a quotation from Francis Cowper, Barrister-at-Law of Gray's Inn, and of Lincoln's Inn, London. 'The English are rightly proud of the integrity of their judiciary; yet of the administrative details of their legal system they know virtually nothing. Thus while they are vaguely

* See note at end of chapter on White Paper (Nov. 1968) on House of Lords reform.

aware that a case may in the last resort be carried before the House of Lords, they never look at the matter with the fresh clear eyes of a stranger, or ask, like Hilaire Belloc's bewildered American, Mr Petre, when faced with that very contingency, "What in hell has any durned Lord to do with it?" ' (The Judicial Jurisdiction of the House of Lords —*Burke's Peerage*, 1953.) If we recall that the Lords had been in existence, and above all, had passed laws, before the Commons originated, the key to the situation is readily found. Thus, the Great Council (*Magnum Concilium* = the modern British Privy Council) was the Norman equivalent of the Saxon Witan. From it, in course of centuries, hived off Parliament as we now know it, and the law courts, but clearly in matters of the law and its interpretation recourse was had in early times on the greatest matters at least to the King in his Council, comprising the magnates of the realm. The modern equivalent of the orders and directions made in early centuries in England still exists in the form of Orders in Council. These are made in times of emergency when Parliament is not in session, and there is need of some urgent action. A royal proclamation usually accompanies the most urgent of such orders. In this work we are not concerned with the latter, except to say that Orders in Council and royal proclamations come under the heading of delegated legislation; they operate for a limited time and must be reviewed by Parliament. Another form of delegated legislation is that by which ministers are empowered under various Acts of Parliament to make orders having the power of law, and to act as judges in cases of appeal from the decisions of their own ministries, a development which has at the same time produced thousands of orders and very seriously eroded the freedom painfully won by Englishmen from Magna Carta onwards.

Following the development of Parliament and its division into two Houses, the Lords and Commons both took strong objection to legislation by the Council or by proclamation. Much of the seventeenth-century struggle between King and Parliament was on the subject of legislation apart from Parliament. Yet a curious modification occurred. Instead of Parliament as a collective whole being the court of appeal in legal issues, the Lords alone retained that right. 'In Parliament the Commons were newcomers appended as it were to the ancient great council of the realm, the assembly of magnates, barons and prelates, but not a part of it, and it was this ancient part alone, which apparently without challenge, performed the function of final court of appeal belonging originally to the King and his Council in Parliament. When in 1485 the judges stated that this power resided in the Lords alone, they were only making explicit something which had already been recognised for a century.' (Cowper, *op cit.*). This was confirmed again at the passing of the Criminal Appeal Act, 1907, when it was enacted that the final appeal in criminal cases should be to the House of Lords. By usage, confirmed by judicial opinion and Parliamentary enactment, the House of Lords is the supreme law court in the United Kingdom.

Does this then mean that every peer, every 'durn lord' in short, has the right to hear appeals on what must by the time they reach the supreme court be extremely complex legal matters? Most emphatically not, though, as so often in England, restriction of the hearing to peers who are qualified as judges is a matter of practice, not of legislation. Right up to the end of the eighteenth century, peers who were not legally qualified did attend and give their votes on law cases brought before the House, though this was only so in cases which had an interest for them and did not apply to the majority of hearings.

From the beginning of the nineteenth century, a marked change becomes apparent. The business life of the nation was growing ever more complex and the cases coming before the Lords were most unlikely to appeal to laymen. Another important factor was the slowness of the Lords in despatching business. In the Chancellorship of Lord Eldon, it really seemed as if some decisions would never be reached, and these long-drawn-out suits were satirised by Charles Dickens in his novel *Bleak House*, in which the case of Jarndyce against Jarndyce drags on until the estate is exhausted and the suitors likewise. A working rule emerged in the first half of the nineteenth century to the effect that only judicially qualified members of the peerage should hear appeals. In 1844 Daniel O'Connell, the great Irish leader, had been found guilty in the Irish courts of conspiracy, sedition and unlawful assembly, and had appealed to the House of Lords. Some lay peers tried to record their votes, but agreed to withdraw after remonstrance by the judicially qualified lords. In the period 1873-76 the corrective was applied to many abuses in the English legal system. Among other important changes, the Appellate Jurisdiction Act of 1876 laid down that there should be certain persons as Lords of Appeal. These were the Lord Chancellor (always a peer), peers who had held or did hold high judicial office, plus the Lords of Appeal in Ordinary. The last named are life peers created under the provision of the Act, and subsequent Acts have strengthened the position of the Lords of Appeal in Ordinary who in 1968 were nine in number. In practice, from 1876 at least one of these very distinguished judges has been a learned Scots lawyer, in order to deal with appeals from Scotland. Even these reforming Acts never contained a provision excluding unqualified peers from hearing appeals, but common sense has been enough to keep them out, reinforced by a near century of usage to the contrary.

There were three and still are two other judicial functions of the Lords. The first was that of the right to try peers who were charged with treason or criminal offences. This right was abolished by Section 30 of the Criminal Justice Act, 1948. It had become an isolated relic from the provisions of Magna Carta (1215), where it was laid down that a man was to be tried by his peers or equals, ie, a knight by knights, a freeman by freemen, a lord by lords. When such a trial of a peer by peers occurred it was an occasion of great splendour. The last time this procedure was adopted was in 1935, when Lord de Clifford was tried on a charge of manslaughter, arising out of a motor-car accident, and acquitted. At his trial there were present eighty-three Lords Temporal wearing their scarlet and ermine robes, and wearing or carrying their cocked hats. One of the Lords Spiritual, the Bishop of Sheffield, was also present, with four judges of the High Court in their full ceremonial robes and full bottomed wigs. The Lord Chancellor presided as Lord High Steward (appointed as such for the occasion only) dressed in his robes of black and gold. The accused was conducted to the bar of the House by the Gentleman Usher of the Black Rod in court dress. When the trial ended, each lord, beginning with the most junior baron, rose in his place, put his right hand on his breast and delivered his verdict. 'Not Guilty, upon mine honour'. The Lord High Steward then received from Black Rod the wand which was the symbol of the office of High Steward and broke it in two to denote that he had discharged his commission. It was all very picturesque and old-worldy and, not surprisingly, Hollywood reacted by making a film about a peer being tried for murder and, of course, being found guilty and condemned to death. The film featured Robert Montgomery, as the Earl of Chicago, with Edward Arnold as the victim. Those who would like to pursue the subject of trial by peers may care to read *Tried by Their Peers*, by Rupert Furneaux, 1959, which, apart from describing procedure, recounts eight such trials on charges of murder, treason, bigamy and of being accessory to murder, covering the period 1603 to 1901.

The House of Lords still has the jurisdiction in cases of impeachment, though this procedure has not been used since 1805. Impeachment was the initiation by the House of Commons of criminal proceedings against any person, peer or commoner. The other remaining jurisdiction of the Lords is in the matter of privileges, the principal subject of which is that of claims to peerages or to a seat in the Lords. In the case of a claim to revive an old peerage, the House acts only when the matter has been referred to it by the Crown and it then operates through the Committee of Privileges.

In the above account and earlier, reference has been made to life peers, a subject of present importance, which requires special notice.

Life Peerages

In 1856, at a time when legal business was being held up through having too few judges in the Lords, it was decided to confer a life peerage on a distinguished judge, Sir James Parke, who was accordingly created a life peer as Lord Wensleydale. This meant, as it does today for life peers, that the peerage died with him, and could not be inherited. In the same year, however, the Committee of Privileges decided that a life peerage carried with it no right to sit and vote in the Lords: 'evidence was produced that for the last 400 years there was not a single instance of a commoner with a peerage for life taking his seat in the Lords.' (Palmer, *op cit*, p 88). It would be hard to think up a statement more removed from historical fact. In Palmer's own treatise, just quoted, ten instances are given of peerages created for life and with the approval of Parliament. Even stronger testimony is given in *The Complete Peerage*, vol 8, pp 751-53, in which no less than twenty-nine instances are cited of life peerages conferred from 1377 to 1758. Yet a ruling of the Committee of Privileges is regarded as law, and as having been always the law. This is not the only case, as we shall see, in which law and historical fact have become divorced from each other.

The particular problem created by the Committee of Privileges in 1856 was solved by creating Lord Wensleydale an hereditary as well as a life peer. He then sat in the Lords and assisted as a judge. Twenty years later the Lords of Appeal in Ordinary were appointed and admitted as life peers. There the matter rested until 1958 when, under the Conservative government of Mr Harold MacMillan, an Act—Life Peerages Act, 1958—was passed, under which it was ordered that powers should be conferred upon the sovereign to enable her to create life peers and peeresses. In consequence of this Act, women for the first time took their places in the Lords, though those who were hereditary peeresses in their own right as holding baronies by fee were still excluded. The strange thing about this Act is that it should confer on the sovereign powers which, in the judgment of England's greatest legal authorities, she already possessed. Both Sir Edward Coke in the seventeenth century and Sir William Blackstone in the eighteenth century had declared that the Crown can create a man or woman noble for life, and as we have noted, had done so over a period of 400 years. Yet a Conservative government, traditionally 'loyal to Church and Crown', behaved in this manner.

The idea behind the Life Peerage Act was to democratise the House of Lords painlessly and to bring in fresh talent. The life peers are all appointed, not elected, and at the very youngest are usually middle aged. A youthful lord in the Lords will be an hereditary lord. Still, the result has been a considerable alteration in the composition of the House. It has brought women into the House, and the majority of the new life peers are persons who would not have accepted an hereditary peerage. Since the Labour government took office in 1964, only life peerages have been created, so that an appreciable minority on the Roll of the Lords is now composed of life peers. In attendances at the House, the life peers may at times be in a majority.

Women Peers or Peeresses

The entry of women into the House of Lords as life peeresses was a great innovation, although in line with the opening of the Commons to them some forty years earlier. With typical British practicality, the peeresses who had inherited peerages from their male relatives were not admitted to the Lords until 1963 (see below). These ladies are of two categories: (i) holders of ancient baronies by writ, in which the descent of the title can go through the female line. A well-known case is that of the Countess of Erroll, head of the family of Hay, who holds the position of Hereditary High Constable in Scotland; and (ii) those who inherit a peerage by what is called special remainder. This means that when the letters patent are made, by which the peerage is created, it is allowed that, in the lack of male heirs, the peerage can be inherited through the female line. A few such peerages have been made in modern times for several reasons, two examples being the British war leaders, Viscount Portal and Earl Mountbatten, who, having no son to succeed them, have been given the special remainder by which their peerages will pass to their daughters or their daughters' issues. A special remainder can also allow the succession of a brother of a peer, as it did with the First World War leader, Earl Kitchener, a bachelor, whose peerage by special remainder passed to his brother and the latter's issue.

Surrender of Peerages

Another matter in which the legal doctrine of peerages is at variance with historical fact is in connection with the surrender of a peerage. Here the situation must be made absolutely clear. Correspondents have often told me that a peerage or baronetcy at one time existed in their family and that their ancestor gave it up, or more usually passed it to a brother etc. Such stories are entirely without foundation. In Scotland, a peerage could be given up but it was always a formal act of surrender to the Crown, which could then give it to someone else, possibly another member of the same family. No Scots peerages having been created since 1707, for the reasons set out in Chapter 13, any such surrender would have been before than date, and in any event would be well known. (A holder of a Scots peerage antedating the Union of 1707, could perhaps surrender his peerage). In England, it is a fact that the surrender of peerages took place up to the reign of Charles I. Both in Palmer, *op cit* p 154-55, in my book, *The Story of the Peerage*, appendix 9, p 285-86, and in *The Complete Peerage*, vol 3, Appendix A, cases of renunciation of peerages are given. The last-named authority lists eighteen instances, and it is there stated that, in Scotland, surrenders of peerages were frequent, but that after the Union of England and Scotland the power of the Crown to alter the descent of dignities was lost. A case is cited *ibidem* of an Irish barony, Cahir, which was surrendered and regranted in 1585.

The renunciation of peerages is a subject which has been given a great deal of publicity in recent years because of the efforts of Mr Anthony Wedgwood Benn to avoid inheriting the viscounty of Stansgate. He tried to do this in 1955 by getting his father, the first Viscount Stansgate, to bring forward the Wedgwood Benn (Renunciation) Bill. This failed to pass the Lords because, in 1640, that House had resolved that 'no person that hath any honour in him, and a peer of this realm, may alien or transfer the honour to any other person', and again, *nemine contradicente*, 'that no peer of this realm can grant or extinguish his honour, but that it descends unto his descendants neither by surrender, grant, fine, nor any other conveyance to the King.' These declarations had been prompted by alarm at the acceptance by Charles I in 1639 of the surrender of the barony of Stafford from Roger Stafford (see page 65). Again in 1660, and despite the earlier resolutions, Viscount Purbeck gave up his peerage to Charles II. In 1678 Purbeck's son tried to get it back. In 1907, too, it was stated by one of the Law

Lords in another case: 'There is no doubt that a man cannot alien a title of honours either by surrender to the Crown or by grant to a subject.' The law was held to have been the same from the beginning, and the instances already cited of peerages which had been surrendered were simply ignored or, if noticed, held to have been made in ignorance of the law! Consequently it happened that when Viscount Stansgate died in 1960, his son Anthony was his successor in the title.

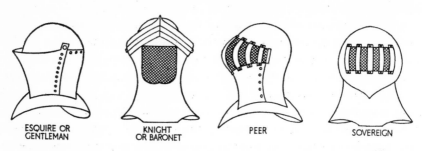

ESQUIRE OR GENTLEMAN   KNIGHT OR BARONET   PEER   SOVEREIGN

Helms.

No one can be compelled to use a title, and there are several peers and baronets who have inherited their titles but who do not, for various reasons, use them. In the case of Mr Wedgwood Benn, the matter was complicated because he was a Member of Parliament. Once he had succeeded to the title he was a peer and could no longer remain in the Commons. He then fought and won the election which resulted from his unwanted elevation to the peerage, but, on seeking to take his seat, was turned back at the door of the House of Commons. His defeated opponent, who had lost by 10,000 votes, was then declared by an Election Court to be the winner and MP for the constituency. To add piquancy to the situation, the new MP was himself the heir to a peerage which would bar him from sitting in the Commons when he succeeded to the title.

The problem was finally solved by the Peerage Act, 1963, often referred to as the Wedgwood Benn Renunciation Act, though it had much wider implications than the surrender of peerages. Sub-section (1) of the first clause of the Act is relevant in the present connection: 'Subject to the provisions of this section, any person, who after the commencement of this Act, succeeds to a peerage in the peerage of England, Scotland, Great Britain, or the United Kingdom may, by an instrument of disclaimer delivered to the Lord Chancellor within the period prescribed by this Act, disclaim that peerage for his life.' Disclaimer means surrender or renunciation, or the giving-up of a peerage.

There is a time limit to the period in which a peer may renounce his peerage. He must make his disclaimer within twelve months beginning with the day on which he succeeds to the peerage or, if he is under twenty-one on succeeding, then the period of twelve months begins with the day on which he attains his majority. Anyone who is an MP and who succeeds to a peerage must, if he wishes to disclaim, do so within a period of one month beginning with the date of his succession, and not later.

A disclaimer does not affect succession to a peerage. The peerage still exists but is in suspension, and the son and heir (or other heir) of the disclaimer can succeed to the title on the disclaimer's death. It is expressly mentioned in the Act that the disclaimer cannot accelerate the succession to the peerage. It could happen that two or three generations might pass before the descendant of a disclaimer might wish to revive the peerage. It would be open to him to do so.

Naturally, Mr Wedgwood Benn availed himself of the provisions of the Act and disclaimed the Stansgate viscounty for life. As soon as it was possible for him to be elected again to the House of Commons for his old seat—in 1963—he was returned with an impressive majority and in 1964 became a minister in the Labour government. He has been married since 1949 to Caroline Middleton, MA, eldest daughter of the late James Milton de Camp of Cincinnati, Ohio.

The total number of renunciations since the Act of 1963 has been small. Those concerned are: the Barony of Altrincham (disclaimed by 2nd Lord, John Grigg); the Barony of Beaverbrook (2nd Baron, Sir John William Maxwell Aitken—he is also a baronet, which cannot be disclaimed); the viscounty of Hailsham, (2nd Viscount, Quintin Hogg); Barony of Fraser of Allander; the Earldom of Home, and the Barony of Douglas, with several other peerages, all disclaimed in 1963 by Sir Alec Douglas-Home on becoming Prime Minister; the Barony of Monkswell (4th Baron, W. A. L. Collier); the Earldom of Sandwich (9th Earl, George Charles Montagu); Barony of Southampton (5th Baron, Charles Fitzroy); —altogether representing less than 1 per cent of the total number of hereditary peerages.

Other changes have resulted from the 1963 Act. Scottish peers are all now eligible to sit in the Lords, so that it is no longer necessary for the Scots peers to elect sixteen of their number to sit there. Peeresses in their own right may also now sit in the Lords. As regards holders of peerages of Ireland who are not also holders of peerages of the United Kingdom, they remain unrepresented in the Upper House and are not entitled to sit there. There are about seventy of these noble outcasts.

The 1963 Act is the most considerable measure for reconstructing the House of Lords to have appeared in the present century. It contains the same curious feature as the Life Peerages Act; viz, it confers on the Crown a power which it already possesses, that of resuming a peerage when the holder wishes to surrender it. It is abundantly clear that this was the practice over several centuries and if the Crown could take the surrender of peerages between 1379 and 1679, it is hard to see how that power could have been lost, or how any declaration of law could alter the facts of history.

Other measures have been taken in recent years which materially alter the position of the peers. In previous centuries they have usually been wealthy persons, and have been able to give of their time to Parliament without remuneration, whereas today many peers are poor men. In Britain, members of the Commons—the MPs—receive very substantial salaries and expenses. Members of the Upper House were not similarly rewarded but now a small sum is paid to each peer for each day of his attendance to meet some of his expenses. Steps have also been taken to meet the criticism that the House can be a receptacle for the backwoodsman or patrician barnacle. Peers who do not propose to apply for a writ of summons, or who are not really interested in the work of the House, can now be excused from attendance by signifying that they do not wish to attend. This removes many who are not politically-minded, as well as the danger of their arriving merely because some favourite subject is on the agenda. An asterisk in the Roll of the Lords now marks the names of peers who are not in receipt of a writ of summons. Most of the twenty-odd pages of the Roll are sprinkled with asterisks, evidence of the House's successful exclusion of many who could have made little useful contribution to the debates. Before this measure was introduced, every peer had the right to a writ of summons —a document couched in old formal language—but though it carried with it a corresponding duty to attend, this was ignored in many instances.

The Privileges of Peerage

These have never been numerous, and some were amusing rather than harsh, as for undergraduates at Oxford and Cambridge who, being noblemen, were allowed to wear tassels on their caps, a practice which gave rise to the English description of a snob as a tuft hunter. The wealthy and powerful, as peers formerly were, have sufficient privileges in their wealth and power to be able to dispense with special rights.

One privilege, however, does remain and could be of importance —that of freedom from arrest in civil actions, eg, in a case of wife maintenance.

The Committee of Privileges

This Committee has already been mentioned and is of interest in connection with claims to revive a peerage in abeyance. The House of Commons also has a Committee of Privileges, since the Commons must have the right to decide who shall and who shall not be members of it. Thus a lengthy report was issued from the Commons' Committee of Privileges over the petition concerning Mr Wedgwood Benn in the Session 1960-61. Similarly, the Lords Committee of Privileges issues reports on claims to revive peerages, as with the Scrymgeour Wedderburn case mentioned in Part I, (Proceedings before the Committee for Privileges and Judgment, Dudhope Peerage, 1952 and Earldom of Dundee, 1953). The constitution of the committee requires that all the lords who come to any Committee for Privileges shall be of that committee, but that in any claim of peerage the committee shall not sit unless three or more Lords of Appeal (the life peers who are judicially qualified) are present.

The law on abeyance is complicated. Abeyance occurs only when the descent of a peerage is being held up by the existence of several co-heirs, no one of whom can make an exclusive claim to the peerage. They cannot share the inheritance as they could with land or other property, because a peerage is an impartible (unsplittable) inheritance. In such an event the peerage passes into abeyance. It still exists but no one possesses it. The Crown has the power to terminate the abeyance in favour of one of the co-heirs, and the peerage then descends to that person. Sir Edward Coke declared: 'Where there be more daughters than one, the eldest shall not have the dignity and power of the earl, that is, to be countess. What then shall become of that dignity? The answer is that in that case the King, who is the sovereign of honour and dignity, may, for the uncertainty, confer the dignity upon which of the daughters he pleases. And this hath been the usage since the Conquest, as it is said.' He who would differ from Coke on the subject of Common Law needs to possess something virtually unknown in the seventeenth century, the gift of historical criticism. As we shall see, Coke's idea of historical continuity partook of the assumptions of that age.

When an abeyance is thus terminated, a writ of summons is issued to the person concerned, unless he is a peer already, when letters patent

R

are made in his favour. Letters patent would also be used if the person selected was a woman. The new holder of the peerage then possesses an old peerage which carries with it the old precedence. Where an abeyance is ended in favour of one of the co-heirs, and subsequently the issue of that co-heir fails, the peerage goes to the next heir of the original grantee. And if this next heir is represented by several co-heirs, it again falls into abeyance.

Also, and these are probably the cases of most interest to persons whose descent is traceable from the holders of ancient peerages, the abeyance will terminate without any intervention by the Crown if the title of the co-heirs becomes united in one person. Thus, if the peerage falls into abeyance between several daughters, and the issue of all the daughters fails except one, then that one or her heir will be entitled to the peerage. A considerable time could elapse before such an event, and the evidence to support a claim would need very careful sifting by the committee.

The propositions about abeyance and the nature of peerages, especially of the baronies by writ, have been reached gradually during the last 300 years. There would be little objection to this but for the fact that a legal theory once accepted as law is—at least in peerage law—held to have been the law, as far back as the limit of legal memory—the reign of Richard I (1189-99). The doctrine of abeyance depends upon the theory, or rather settled law, that baronies were created by writ of summons to Parliament and that the sons of such persons as were summoned became peers after them. In other words, that the writ of summons created an inheritable dignity. Yet it can be shown by examples too numerous to mention that this doctrine is only a theory which subsequently evolved and which is at variance with the facts.

The theory on which abeyance rests owes a great deal to the authority of Sir Edward Coke (sixteenth to seventeenth century), who appears to have been mistaken in his interpretation of the earldom of Chester and its inheritance. From this developed the seventeenth-century doctrine on the subject. For a long time, when a peerage was called out of abeyance it was in favour of co-heirs petitioning for baronies which had been held by near ancestors and which had not long been in suspense. From 1764 a change began; the Botetourt barony was then claimed, and this had been in abeyance for 358 years. After that, until 1916, there were sixteen baronies called out of abeyance in which the period of abeyance in each case was not less than 100 years. In ten cases the period of abeyance exceeded by a large margin 200 years. It was pointed out that in most instances the so-called barony had never existed unless the supposition that a writ of summons to Parliament did create a peerage was to be accepted.

In *The Complete Peerage*, vol 4, there is an appendix running to 50,000 words on, 'Earldoms and Baronies in History and in Law, and the Doctrine of Abeyance'. A quotation from p 723 is a good summary of the position. 'It is time that a strong protest be entered against the continuance of the practice of calling out of abeyance so-called baronies in fee, (*This term "in fee" or "in fee simple", is still applied in English law to land, which, in theory, is held in fee from the Crown, though sold as a freehold; hence its applicability to a peerage dignity. L. G. P.*), most of which never had any existence. The co-heirship possessed by the petitioner usually represents only a small fraction of the alleged barony, and in nearly every case the lands have been alienated for centuries. This right to an estate of honour, which is the most endurable that can be bestowed, has no basis in fact; yet most of these parvenus are given precedence in the House of Lords over the heads of all peers of like degree whose right to their dignities is unquestioned.'

Strong stuff and written in 1916, the year in which four baronies—Burgh, Strabolgi, Dudley and Wharton—were called out of abeyance in one day. According to the severe criticism in *The Complete Peerage*, vol 13, pt 1, page 321, in medieval times the rolls of attendance at the Great Council and those of attendance in Parliament were sometimes mixed, so that when the barony of Strabolgi was revived in favour of the Rev Mathias Kenworthy, an entirely new barony was, in fact, created because the earlier Lords Strabolgi attended the Council but did not sit in Parliament. If this were indeed so, a peerage was created by mistake in 1916. It was probably in view of these criticisms, and also because King George V became seriously concerned over the multiplication of peerages by this and other means, that a select committee on peerages in abeyance was eventually set up in 1926, and reported in the following year.

This select committee took evidence from various authorities on the subject, including Mr Doubleday, the editor of *The Complete Peerage*, who was responsible for the appearance in print of the protest given above. The committee rehearsed the steps by which the doctrine of abeyance had been evolved and then stated, with regard to the fourteenth and fifteenth centuries, that 'there is grave reason to doubt, to say the least of it, whether during these two centuries either sovereign or subject had ever any idea that by a summons to a Parliament a hereditary right either was being or had been created.' It pointed out that 'the law, however, if settled, cannot be unsettled in this way', ie, by the criticisms of scholars. With regard to recent cases, 'we accept them, and recognise that the claims established by them now stand beyond challenge'.

After summarising the findings they had deduced from the evidence of the experts, the committee went on to add some general recommendations which were submitted to the King. These, which follow, are of great importance to anyone who is thinking of putting forward a peerage claim.

'In the absence of special circumstances or special reasons to the contrary:

'1. No abeyance should be terminated the first commencement of which occurred more than one hundred years before the presentation of the petition.

'2. No petition should be allowed to proceed where the petitioner represents less than one-third of the entire dignity.

'3. Except in the case of petitions which have already been presented, it should be an instruction to the Attorney General that his report to the Crown should advise that no further proceeding be taken in the case of any petition which does not comply with these two requirements.

'4. When the Committee for Privileges is satisfied that any arrangement entered into between the petitioner and any co-heir is tainted with any impropriety, no report should be made by it upon the petition except that such arrangement is not shown to have been a proper one.

'5. In considering whether or not the sovereign should be advised to extend his grace to the petitioner for a termination of an abeyance, the like regard should be had to character, position, services, and fitness as would be had in the case of a subject on whom it is in contemplation to recommend that a peerage should be conferred.' (Report referred to above, p 11.)

These recommendations meet most of the criticisms which have been voiced, but they also serve to demonstrate the rigidity of the law; once settled, there cannot be any unsettling of its results or even of the principles which it formulates. The proviso that no barony should be called out of abeyance if the period of abeyance has lasted for more than 100 years has prevented what might be called foolhardy claims. It has not prevented a just claim, as in the Scrymgeour Wedderburn case.

The Formal Opening of Parliament

The ceremony which marks the sovereign's opening of a new session of Parliament is perhaps the best visual illustration of how all the forms of the British Constitution have been retained even though their underlying reality has completely changed. When the Queen opens Parliament, she does so with all the pomp and ceremony of centuries past, and anyone who has seen a print of Elizabeth I opening Parliament, or reading the Gracious Speech from the Throne, will know that, in all the essentials, the scene has not altered under Elizabeth II. The sovereign, gorgeously robed and wearing her crown, has proceeded into the Houses of Parliament and taken her seat on the throne in the House of Lords. Round her are her family (in the case of Elizabeth I, she sat alone beneath the canopy of state) and her great officers of state like the Lord Great Chamberlain and the Earl Marshal. Nearest to the Lord Chancellor's seat (known as the Woolsack because it is made of wool, the source of the country's early wealth) are the Lords Spiritual—the archbishops and bishops; behind and around them are the Temporal Lords, though only a selection of these since, the peerage now being ten times as large as it was under Elizabeth I, not all the 1,000 peers could get in if they wanted to. Facing the sovereign are the clerks or officials of Parliament. At the bottom of the Chamber, standing at the Bar, are the Prime Minister with the Cabinet and as many MPs as can squeeze themselves into the limited standing space. In the far distance at the other end of the Parliament House is the seat of the Speaker of the House of Commons. When the Queen is seated on the throne, the Commons are summoned by Black Rod, an official so named because he carries a black rod as a sign of authority. As he nears the door of the House of Commons, it is slammed to in his face. Then he knocks and has to state his business through the grill of the Commons' door. On admittance to the Bar of the Commons, Black Rod states his purpose. This archaic procedure is derived from an event of 300 years ago when King Charles I entered the Commons and tried to seize five MPs. Since then the Commons have been on the watch against any such attempt, hence the slamming of their door.

Having received the royal summons, the Commons go through to the Lords. They walk in crocodile with the Prime Minister and leader of the Opposition (a salaried post in England) side by side, followed by the rest of the MPs, paired on the same principle. Arriving in the Lords, the Prime Minister and the MPs stand listening humbly (in appearance) to the Queen's Speech, which the Prime Minister has written for her to deliver. Afterwards this same Gracious Speech will be pulled to pieces in the Commons by the Opposition, because it expresses not the Queen's views but those of the Government. Centuries ago, the positions adopted by the chief actors corresponded to reality. The sovereign really ruled; the Commons were the humblest part of Parliament; the Prime Minister might be a peer—and indeed frequently was, until the opening of the twentieth century—and his duty was to act as minister to his sovereign and carry out the monarch's wishes. In fact, it was only very gradually that the office of Prime Minister evolved; until 1905 no such creature was officially known, and to give him a place recognised in the Table of Precedence, he held, in addition, the post of First Lord of the Treasury.

There have been times when I have called the state or formal opening of Parliament a charade, or dubbed it the Westminster Miracle Play, but for those who know the facts it serves as a useful reminder of British history, a colourful eruption of the past into the dull round of the present. The extent to which it also serves to mislead those who are not well versed in history is another matter; a Gallup poll in England not long ago revealed that a majority of those questioned thought that the Queen still ruled. The attraction of the state opening is undoubtedly great, especially if one can get a place in the Parliament House. The procession from Buckingham Palace, with the Life Guards on horseback in full-dress uniform and the Yeomen of the Guard walking beside the state coach, is a memorable sight.

The Houses of Parliament are really the Palace of Westminster, and the sovereign allows Lords and Commons to meet there. The official responsible for the Palace is the Lord Great Chamberlain, who is a member of the Queen's Household. His office is hereditary between families who hold the office in turns. The Lord Chamberlain holds another office, which is not hereditary. He orders matters of social importance for the Queen, such as admission to the royal enclosure at Ascot racecourse and for a long time was responsible for licensing plays.

Letters Patent

These have been mentioned in connection with the creation of peers and are so called because they are open for all to see. Their opposite is letters sealed, which contain matter of a secret or confidential nature. The form of the letters patent is of interest as it employs much old-time language. Here, for example, is the document for creating the most numerous class of peers—the barons, though the style would not vary very much for other ranks:

'Elizabeth the Second by the Grace of God, of the United Kingdom of Great Britain and Northern Ireland and of Our other Realms and Territories Queen, Head of the Commonwealth, Defender of the Faith, To all Lords Spiritual and Temporal and all other Our Subjects whatsoever to whom these Presents shall come, Greeting. Know Ye that We of Our especial grace, certain knowledge and mere motion do by these Presents advance, create and prefer Our trusty and well beloved A . . . B . . . Esquire, to the state degree style dignity title and honour of Baron X . . . of Y . . . in the county of Z . . . And for Us Our heirs and successors do appoint give and grant unto him the said name state degree style dignity title and honour of Baron X . . . to have and to hold unto him and the heirs male of his body lawfully begotten and to be begotten Willing and by these Presents granting for Us our heirs and successors that he and his heirs male aforesaid and every of them successively may have hold and possess a seat place and voice in the Parliaments and Public Assemblies and Councils of Us Our Heirs and successors within Our United Kingdom amongst other Barons And also that he and his heirs male aforesaid successively may enjoy and use all the rights privileges pre-eminences immunities and advantages to the degree of a Baron duly and of right belonging which other Barons of Our United Kingdom have heretofore used and enjoyed or as they do at present use and enjoy in Witness whereof We have caused these Our Letters to be made Patent Witness Ourself at Westminster the . . . day of . . . in the . . . year of Our Reign.—By Warrant under the Queen's Sign Manual'.

Couched in very archaic language with its use of the royal first person plural, this document belongs to an older time and, as with old-fashioned legal documents, has no punctuation marks. The passage about the descent of the peerage deals only with male descent, but in those few peerages in which the descent is allowed through daughters (or other relatives) a special remainder is inserted to the effect that, failing legitimate male issue, the peerage can pass to female heirs lawfully begotten. In still fewer cases the remainder clause states that the peerage can devolve upon a brother of the grantee, or that brother's sons. In another sense, too, the above document may well become an anachronism, as, since 1964, only life and not hereditary peerages have been created. The same situation existed as regards baronetcies from 1945 to 1951, when only about one a year of these hereditary titles was created, but when Churchill returned to power in 1951 he allowed the creation of baronets again. A period of six years with a creation only once a year was not sufficient to put into permanent cold storage an institution which had lasted some 350 years and had over 1,500 members. Since 1964, the Labour government has not created any baronetcies, and it is unlikely that a future Conservative government would care to stir up party political strife by reviving the creation of baronets.

The same could well be true of hereditary peerages. Should the Labour party remain in power as long as their Conservative predecessors—thirteen years from 1951 to 1964, it is very much to be doubted whether any further creation of hereditary peerages would occur. The normal style of letters patent may then be that for a life peer, which is as follows, omitting the preamble listing the Queen's titles etc :

'. . . We of Our especial grace, certain knowledge and mere motion in pursuance of the Life Peerages Act 1958 and of all other powers in that behalf Us enabling do by these Presents advance create and prefer Our . . . to the state degree style dignity title and honour of Baron . . . And for Us Our Heirs and Successor do appoint give and grant unto him the said name state degree style dignity title and honour of Baron . . . to have and to hold unto him for his life Willing and by these Presents granting for Us Our Heirs and Successors that he may have hold and possess a seat place and voice in the Parliaments and Public Assemblies and Councils of Us Our Heirs and Successors etc. etc.'—London Gazette, No 41462, 4 August 1958.

Here, surely, is as curious an amalgamation as could be found of ancient royal power with modern democratic procedure; an amalgamation symptomatic of the erosion of the old substance of nobility while retaining the form. 'All other powers in that behalf Us enabling'—what an expression for a former sovereign monarchy ! The styles of the wives and children of life peers—which are the same as for those of hereditary peers—were set out in a royal warrant (London Gazette No 41454, 22 July 1958). In the above Gazette, No 41462, the style of a life peeress's patent was given : her children can be styled Honourable, but her husband does not become a peer.

The Sale of Honours

This is a subject which has occasioned a great deal of comment but the facts about it can be briefly stated. The sale of titles began in England in the reign of James I, who sold peerages right and left, besides instituting the baronets' order. Large sums, as much as £10,000 a time, were paid for peerages and the practice lasted throughout the Stuart period. Under the Hanoverian kings, however, the Prime Minister exercised patronage and became responsible for the creation of peers. This meant that corruption took other forms, as all sorts of persons were made peers merely because they supported the government, and not because they had paid large sums of money for their honours. With the rise of the great modern political parties, a money element again appeared in the distribution of honours, and large contributions to party funds were rewarded with various titles.

There are many instances of peerages being bought in this manner during the present century. Under the regime of David Lloyd George, Prime Minister 1916-22, and much later an earl, there was considerable sale of honours. In 1925 the Honours (Prevention of Abuses) Act was passed, following the recommendations of a Royal Commission set up in 1922 to examine alleged abuses in connection with the honours system. Lloyd George fell from power in 1922, never to return to office, but trafficking in honours did continue, and ten years after 1922 a man named Maundy Gregory, who was reputed to have had an income of £30,000 per year from no visible source, and certainly lived at that rate, was summoned under the 1925 Act. His case was heard at Bow Street in London on 16 and 21 February 1933, and on being found guilty of the offence, he was sent to prison for two months, and fined £50 and 50 guineas costs. An engrossing account of this incident and of all that led up to it is to be found in *Honours for Sale—The Strange Story of Maundy Gregory*, by Gerald MacMillan, 1954. This is the only case to have been brought under the 1925 Act, but it has sufficed. The sale of honours no longer takes place.

The Table, or Order of Precedence

The Table of Precedence, which has previously been referred to, is based on an Act of Parliament, 1539, of Henry VIII for Placing the Lords; it has proved on the whole a useful framework for arranging the order in which official personages are to appear or to sit. By means of emendations, recognition is given to the changes wrought by developing institutions. Thus in 1905 the office of Prime Minister was accorded formal recognition by royal warrant. Similarly, the High Commissioners for member countries of the Commonwealth were given the same precedence as foreign ambassadors. The Precedence Table does, of course, represent many offices as they were centuries ago, eg, the Lord Chancellor comes before the Prime Minister who appoints him, but whose official position is some 700 years younger than that of the Chancellor. The Chancellor of the Exchequer, the second most important member of the government, comes behind all the peers and behind the knights of the great orders. This is because he was only a clerk in days when peers and knights were the magnates of the realm.

Forfeitures of Honours

In days gone by anyone found guilty of treason or other felony was held to be corrupted in blood, and therefore unable to transmit any estate, title or honour which he possessed. This situation was gradually ameliorated by different statutes, and by an Act of 1870, 'to abolish Forfeitures for Treason and Felony, and to otherwise amend the Law relating thereto.' Attainder, corruption of blood, forfeiture, and escheat for treason or felony were wholly abolished, escheat having been the forfeiture of land to the Crown following upon treason or felony. Consequently, a peer now found guilty of treason or other felonies would not forfeit his peerage or estates and these would pass to his son.

NOTE: At the beginning of November 1968, the Government brought out a White Paper in which were set forth its intentions for the reform of the House of Lords, a reform twice announced in a Queen's Speech, in 1967 and in 1968. They were as follows:

(i) The reformed House is to be two-tiered, having about 250 peers who have the right to speak and to vote; secondly, in the second tier, non-voting peers (mainly hereditary), with the right to speak but not to vote.

(ii) After reform, succession to a peerage would not carry a right to a seat, but existing peers, by succession, would have the right to sit but not to vote for their lifetimes.

(iii) Voting members would be exclusively life peers or created peers. Some of the hereditary peers would be granted life peerages, which would thus give them voting rights.

(iv) Hereditary peers at the time of reform could withdraw from the House.

(v) Future and existing peers by succession who chose to renounce membership of the Lords would be able to sit in the Commons if elected.

(vi) All peers would be qualified to vote in Parliamentary elections.

(vii) Voting peers will be expected to attend not less than one-third of the sittings. There will ultimately be a retiring age of seventy-two.

(viii) Voting peers are to be paid. The amount is not yet settled, but the White Paper refers to a sum of £2,000 having been mentioned by some parties.

(ix) The voting House is initially to consist of about 230 peers, so distributed as to give the government of the day a small majority over opposition parties.

(x) Non-voting peers will be able to ask questions in the House, to move motions and to serve on committees.

(xi) The delaying power of the Lords is to be reduced to six months.

(xii) The number of bishops who attend the House is to be reduced from twenty-six to sixteen.

(xiii) The Law Lords are to continue their existing judicial functions.

(xiv) Patronage, as regards 'topping up' (the words of the Paper) is to be exercised by the Prime Minister, and the leaders of the Opposition parties in recommendations to him.

The above proposals were considered in great detail, especially in the House of Commons, and as a result the Government decided not to proceed with the Bill.

CHAPTER 15

Orders of Chivalry and Decorations of Honour

THE distinction between these two and medals is as follows: an order is really one of chivalry and would in the great majority of cases imply knighthood at least in older times. There are in the United Kingdom two orders—of Merit, and of the Companions of Honour—which do not confer the title of 'Sir'. In countries outside the UK, such as Russia, an order carries no title. Decorations are those distinctions which are not orders of chivalry and yet are not medals. Among decorations are awards made for valour, such as the British Victoria Cross or the US Congressional Medal of Honour. Medals are given for a great variety of reasons, such as long service or to commemorate particular campaigns or wars, and the number of awards throughout the world is so large that it would be impossible to deal here with even a small fraction of them. Attention has, therefore, been confined to orders of chivalry and decorations of honour, though here again space restricts us to the minimum of detail.

From very ancient times, valorous conduct in war has been noted and recognised by special marks of approval. The ancient Romans signalised the feat of saving the life of a citizen by bestowing upon the rescuer an oak leaf crown, and Julius Caesar in his youth won this award. At other times and places gifts of gold chains or badges, or of arms and armour, marked valorous distinction; substantial grants of land or money were also made, especially under the feudal system. One of the most interesting scenes in the Bayeux Tapestry shows William the Conqueror bestowing arms (ie, weapons), upon Harold in recognition of his bravery in the Norman conquest of Maine.

The modern system of knighthood grew up, as mentioned in Chapter 13, from the original institution of mounted and mailed warriors of feudal times. In each country there developed from this practical fighting force the orders of chivalry, the earliest being those crusading companies of knights in Spain, the Holy Land and Prussia. Among these religious military orders, that of the Knights Templars, founded in 1118, came to a disastrous end in 1312 when it was suppressed by the King of France and the Pope. The Teutonic knights were secularized in 1525 as a result of the Reformation, when the Grand Master became a Lutheran and a duke of Prussia, and the order has lingered on in an attenuated form up to the present day. The order of Knights Hospitallers of St John of Jerusalem or, as they are best known, Knights of Malta, has also continued. It is mainly a Catholic order, controlled ultimately by the Pope, but two non-Catholic organisations are derived from it, the bailiwick of Brandenburg, and the order of St John of Jerusalem in England. The latter was authorised by royal charter in 1888 and though the British monarch is sovereign of the order, recipients of knighthoods in that order may not use the title of 'Sir'. The St John's Ambulance Brigade and Association is under the control of this order.

Spanish and Portuguese religious military orders also still exist, though in an attenuated or suspended form. Spain is indeed almost a museum of these institutions for, in addition to the three military orders, Alcantara (founded 1160), Calatrava (1158) and Santiago (*circa* 1160), there are five maestranzas or royal corporations of chivalry. They are of Seville, Granada, Ronda, Valencia and Zaragoza; all organisations or very old associations of knights and gentlemen whose object is to exercise themselves in horsemanship. These maestranzas, which originated as schools for the management of arms on horseback, were reorganised in the eighteenth century. Spain today being, as it were, a monarchical state in suspense, with a Council of Regency to act when General Franco dies, the Spanish orders just mentioned are preserved, but there are several others. Among them are the Red Arrows (1937) an allusion by title and badge to the Falange organisation; Charles III (1771); St Ferdinand (1811); St Hermengilde (1814); Isabella the Catholic (1815); Alfonso X (1939); Raymond of Penafort (1944) and others.

The most famous order associated with Spain is that of the Golden Fleece, founded in 1430 by Philip the Good, Duke of Burgundy. The title derives from the story of the ancient Argonauts who went to Colchis in search of the Golden Fleece, and alludes to the wealth of Flanders which was largely based on the wool trade. The Spanish branch of the Habsburg family came to control the Netherlands, but in 1700, when the Spanish line died out, the rule over the order should have passed to the Austrian Habsburgs, but the Spanish kings considered themselves as sovereigns of the order, so that both Spain and Austria continued to bestow it. If a king is restored to Spain, he may revive this splendid order.

Spain has been dealt with first in this section because much of the old constitutional position was restored with the Franco victory, and many orders exist there in suspense. In many other European countries, by contrast, old orders have disappeared with the change from monarchy to republic or in coming under Communist control. Again, many orders now existing and bestowed, have tended to become not orders of chivalry but of merit, and carrying no title.

Now to deal briefly with the British orders and their principal decorations before turning to those of other lands. The nine great British orders previously mentioned in Chapter 13 have always entailed the wearing of special robes, hats, cloaks and of course the insignia, which usually include a chain with a badge, a ribbon and a star, together with some distinction peculiar to the particular order.

(1) Thus the insignia of The Garter (England, 1348) are the collar with the appendant showing St George trampling on the dragon, the riband with the lesser George, which is worn on the right hip from a broad dark blue ribbon which passes over the left shoulder; the Garter—the special mark of this order—to be tied round the left leg; and an eight-pointed star to be worn on the left breast. These insignia are worn in entirety only on the most ceremonial occasions, as when the annual service is held in St George's chapel at Windsor. At this time there is a procession of the Queen and the knights with their attendants from the castle to the chapel which, incidentally, has more heraldic devices to the square yard than any other building in the world. On other high occasions, a knight may wear the ribbon and the star, usually with evening dress. The ribbon of the order is not worn with ordinary clothes and this applies equally to the other great British orders. The Garter motto is: *Honi soit qui mal y pense* (Evil be to him who evil thinks), and St George's Day—23 April (which is also Shakespeare's birthday) is the anniversary day of the order.

(2) The Thistle is composed of the sovereign and sixteen knights, plus royal knights and Queen Elizabeth, the Queen Mother, as a lady of the order. There are no foreign knights, nor have there been for more than two centuries. The colour of the order is deep green, the insignia consist of a mantle of green velvet ornamented with a figure of St Andrew bearing his cross—the familiar X or Greek Cross; a gold collar with the motif of thistles and rue, and, hanging from the collar, the badge showing St Andrew with cross; a silver star in the form of St Andrew's Cross. The motto is: *Nemo me impune lacessit* (No one harms me with

impunity), and the anniversary day is St Andrew's festival, 30 November. The chapel of the order is in St Giles' Cathedral, Edinburgh. When the Earl of Home renounced his peerages and became Sir Alec Douglas Home, his sole remaining title of knighthood was that of the Thistle.

(3) St Patrick. Insignia: a sky blue mantle; a gold collar composed of roses and harps, and attached to the collar a gold badge surrounded by a wreath of shamrock within which is the motto, *Quis separabit* (Who shall divide); a light blue ribbon hanging from the right shoulder, with a smaller badge. The order consisted of twenty-two knights, and the anniversary day was no doubt St Patrick's Day, 17 March, but when the Protestant Episcopal Church of Ireland was disestablished in 1871, the religious ceremonies which had been held in St Patrick's Cathedral, Dublin, were abolished and subsequent investitures took place in Dublin Castle or at Windsor.

(4) The Bath, as previously mentioned, has three classes. The Knights Grand Cross (GCB) have mantles of crimson satin lined with white taffeta, with a star of the order on the left. The military GCBs have for insignia: a gold collar pendant therefrom a gold Maltese Cross, a silver star with centred a gold Maltese Cross. The civil GCBs have a similar mantle but a slightly different badge and star. Knights Commander have similar but smaller insignia. So, too, with the Companions. The motto is *Tria juncta in uno* (three joined in one), and services of the order are held in Westminster Abbey every four years.

(5) St Michael and St George. There are a maximum of 100 GCMGs, 355 KCMGs, and 1,435 CMGs, together with several officials of the order and extra royal knights. The insignia are, for GCMGs, a Saxon-blue satin mantle, with a representation of the star of the order on the left; a gold collar composed of the lions of England, Maltese Crosses and the cyphers SM and SG; hanging from this is the badge, which has St George's Cross on one side, St Michael trampling on the devil in the centre, and on the other side, St George slaying the dragon; the ribbon is Saxon-blue with a scarlet central stripe. For KCMGs the insignia are similar but they have no collars and the badge is smaller, as it is smaller for a CMG. The chapel of the order is St Paul's Cathedral and services are held annually. Occasionally, distinguished foreigners are made honorary knights. Motto: *Auspicium melioris aevi* (Auspice of a better age).

(6) The Royal Victorian order is given only to those who have rendered some personal service to the sovereign. The anniversary day is 20 June, the day when Queen Victoria, founder of the order, succeeded to the throne. The chapel is the Queen's Chapel of the Savoy, in London,

a relic of the ancient Savoy Palace which stood on the site now occupied by the Savoy Hotel before it was burned down in the Peasants' War in 1381. The chapel was saved and is the private possession of the sovereign as Duke of Lancaster. (Note that the title of Duchess is never used for the Queen, she, like a king, is styled Duke of Lancaster when in Lancashire). The insignia of GCVOs are a mantle of dark blue silk, edged with red satin and lined with white silk; on the left the representation of the star; a gold collar having the inscription, 'Victoria Britt. Reg. Def. Fid. Ind. Imp.' in frames between the oval pieces; the badge is a white Maltese Cross, which has in the centre the image and monogram of Queen Victoria. On certain occasions the badge is worn suspended from the ribbon, which is dark blue with three stripes, red, white and red, on either side. The KCVOs wear a ribbon round their necks, and the badge is the same as that of the GCVOs but smaller. CVOs have a ribbon and badge; MVOs of the 4th and 5th classes also have ribbons and badges but either smaller or of lesser quality. The motto is *Victoria*. In connection with this order may be mentioned (i) the Royal Victorian Medal, awarded for very long service and (ii) the Royal Victorian Chain which is not part of the order but was instituted in 1902 by Edward VII. The Chain, which is of gold and composed of lotuses, trefoils, thistles and roses, is a mark of high distinction from the sovereign.

(7) The British Empire. The chapel is in the crypt of St Paul's Cathedral, London, and the motto is *For God and the Empire*. The insignia are: for GBEs a collar of six medallions of the royal arms and six of the cypher of King George V, set out alternatively and linked by work showing the imperial crown between two sea lions; from this collar hangs the badge of a cross surmounted by the imperial crown; when the collar is not worn the badge is worn suspended from a ribbon of rose-pink edged with pearl grey; the military GBEs have in the centre of the ribbon a pearl grey stripe, a quarter of an inch in width; the star is of silver with a gold medallion depicting the crowned effigies of King George V and Queen Mary; the mantle is of rose-pink satin and has a representation of the star on the left. KBEs have a badge and star of similar pattern but smaller, and CBEs have a similar badge. Officers and members—OBEs and MBEs—have similar but smaller badges. The total permissible number of members in all five classes is 1,705 in any one year. There is also a medal of the order, the British Empire Medal.

(8) The Star of India, now obsolete. The ribbon of the order was pale blue edged with white. There was a mantle, collar, badge and star, and

the insignia were ornamented with diamonds. Motto: *Heaven's Light our Guide.*

(9) The Indian Empire, also obsolete. Insignia were mantle, collar, badge and ribbon of dark blue. Motto: *Imperatricis auspiciis.* (Under the auspices of the Empress).

(10) Imperial Order of the Crown of India, founded 1877 and now obsolete. The ribbon was of light blue edged with white.

(11) The Order of Merit is of the type mentioned above, where the order does not confer a title. It was founded by Edward VII in 1902, there are twenty-four members, and very rarely honorary membership is given to a foreigner. The badge is a gold cross of red and blue enamel, with the motto, *For Merit,* in the centre. The ribbon is half blue, half crimson. For military members, two silver swords are added to the badge. Holders are allowed to put the letters 'OM' after their names.

(12) Companions of Honour, abbreviated to 'CH' after the holder's name, is an order founded in 1917 by King George V. The ribbon is red or crimson, and the motto: *In action faithful and in honour clear.* The badge is of gold, an oval-shaped medallion with a representation of an oak tree; from the latter is a shield bearing the royal arms and on the right the design is of a mounted knight in armour.

In addition to the above, there are many decorations of honour in the United Kingdom, the most notable and the one which precedes all others, even the Garter, being the Victoria Cross. This was instituted in 1856 by Queen Victoria, and is the supreme award for any member of the armed forces. The Cross has often been bestowed posthumously, and a bar to the Cross may be awarded if warranted. Fewer than 1,400 VCs have been awarded from 1856 to the present. The ribbon is of a claret colour, and the Cross is of bronze (a cross patée). On the obverse is a lion passant guardant standing on the Royal Crown, below which are the words, *For Valour,* in a scroll.

The George Cross, instituted by George VI in 1940, ranks next to the Victoria Cross. It is awarded for acts of heroism on the part of civilians, or to personnel of the three services, in actions in which military honours would not usually be granted, eg, when soldiers are engaged in assisting the civil power in connection with fires, floods, etc. The Cross is of plain silver with a circular medallion in the centre having a representation of St George trampling the dragon and surrounded by the words *For Gallantry.* On the reverse is the recipient's name. The ribbon is blue with a silver cross.

The George Medal is awarded in similar circumstances to the George Cross but when the conditions are not as exacting. The ribbon is in

s

alternate stripes of red and blue. The medal is of silver, the obverse carrying the effigy of George VI, and the reverse showing St George slaying the dragon on the coasts of England.

The Distinguished Service Order was founded in 1886 for rewarding acts of meritorious service in war. It is awarded only to officers, and the ribbon is red edged with blue.

The Imperial Service Order and Medal were instituted by King Edward VII (1902) to reward members of the civil service. The letters 'ISO' can be used after the recipient's name.

The Royal Order of Victoria and Albert, founded by Queen Victoria in 1862 after the death of her husband, Albert the Prince Consort, consists of the sovereign and forty-five ladies. The ribbon is of white moiré.

The Royal Guelphic Order is now obsolete but was a Hanoverian order founded in 1815 by the Prince Regent, later George IV. In nineteenth-century biographies accounts are found of knights of this order, which was discontinued after 1837, when Victoria became Queen, as she was unable to accede to the throne of Hanover because the Salic law of that country did not allow women to reign.

Other British Decorations

The Royal Red Cross (RRC) instituted by Queen Victoria in 1883 for ladies in the nursing services. Ribbon: blue edged with red.

Distinguished Service Cross (DSC), founded by Edward VII in 1901 for bravery, and exclusively a naval decoration. Ribbon: dark blue with white middle stripe. The original title was Conspicuous Service Cross.

Military Cross (MC) instituted 31 December 1914, for Army officers. Ribbon: white with purple middle stripe.

Distinguished Flying Cross (DFC) instituted in 1918 for acts of gallantry by Air Force officers and warrant officers when flying in active operations against the enemy. Ribbon: diagonal strips of purple and white.

Air Force Cross (AFC) instituted in 1918 for acts of valour when not engaged in active operations against the enemy. Awarded to officers and warrant officers. Ribbon: diagonal red and white stripes.

The Albert Medals are awarded for gallantry in saving life at sea or on land. They were established in 1866 by Queen Victoria and are so named because they are said to have been designed by the Prince Consort, Albert. There are four medals, one in gold for saving life at sea, ribbon: thin blue and white stripes; a bronze medal, ribbon: white, blue and white, edged with blue; a gold medal for saving life on land, ribbon:

thin red and white stripes, and a bronze medal, ribbon: white, red, white fringed in red. These medals are now superseded by the George Cross and George Medal, except in cases of posthumous award.

Distinguished Conduct Medal (DCM) instituted in 1854 and awarded to non-commissioned officers and enlisted men for bravery in the field; ribbon: red, dark blue and red.

Conspicuous Gallantry Medal (CGM) for other than commissioned officers in the Royal Navy and Royal Marines, and to men of the Merchant Navy. Ribbon: white edged with dark blue. Originally instituted in 1855 and reinstituted 1874.

Conspicuous Gallantry Medal (CGM) Royal Air Force, instituted in 1943 and awarded to non-commissioned RAF personnel and also Army personnel, glider pilots etc.

The Distinguished Service Medal (DSM), instituted in 1914 and awarded for bravery in action by petty officers and men of the Royal Navy, non-commissioned officers and men of the Royal Marines and all other persons holding equivalent position in Her Majesty's service afloat. Also, since 1942, to Merchant Marine personnel. Ribbon: dark blue, white and dark blue stripe on central white.

The Military Medal (MM), instituted in 1916 and awarded for gallantry to warrant and non-commissioned officers, enlisted men and women of the Army. Later extended to include RAF personnel for gallantry on the ground. Ribbon: blue with five narrow alternate white and red stripes in the centre.

The Distinguished Flying Medal (DFM), instituted in 1918 and awarded to warrant and non-commissioned officers and men of the Air Forces for gallantry in action, as with the DFC for officers. Ribbon: thin diagonal stripes of purple and white.

The Air Force Medal (AFM), instituted in 1918, is awarded for equivalent services as for the Air Force Cross to warrant and non-commissioned officers and men of the Air Forces. Ribbon: thin diagonal red and white stripes.

Dominion Countries

The names of nationals of Australia and New Zealand still figure in the Honours Lists of the United Kingdom, and some Canadians still have British, non-hereditary honours.

United States of America

The most valued decoration is the Congressional Medal of Honour, instituted by Congress in 1861 for the Navy and in 1862 for the Army. It is the American equivalent of the Victoria Cross and is open to all ranks for bravery in action over and beyond the call of duty. The design of the Army medal is that of a bronze five-pointed star, on a laurel wreath, and having in the centre a representation of the head of Minerva within a circle bearing the words, 'United States of America'. The ribbon is light blue with thirteen stars, and the medal hangs from it, by a bar having on it the word 'Valor' and above it, a spread eagle. The Navy medal has a five-pointed bronze star and in the centre, Minerva (as representing the USA) repulsing enemies, within a circle of thirty-four stars, the number of states in the Union in 1862.

The Distinguished Service Cross is peculiar to the Army and dates from 1918; it is awarded for gallantry in action. The Cross is of bronze with the American eagle superimposed and in a scroll beneath the eagle, the words 'For Valor'. The ribbon is blue-edged with white and red stripes.

The Distinguished Service Medal, instituted in 1918, is awarded to Army and Navy personnel who have rendered meritorious service, whether in combat or in some other sphere. The medal for the Army is of bronze, having on the front the coat of arms of the USA, surrounded by a circle of blue enamel, with the words 'For Distinguished Service', and 1918 in Roman numerals 'MCMXVIII'. The ribbon is white-edged with red and thin blue stripes. The medal for the Navy is of gilded bronze with the American eagle in the centre, having a blue enamelled circle around it, and thereon the words 'United States of America, Navy'. On the reverse is Neptune's trident within a laurel wreath and having on the surrounding circle the words 'For Distinguished Service'. Ribbon: dark blue with a central yellow stripe.

The Navy Cross, instituted in 1919, is for award in cases of gallantry where the Medal of Honour, or the DSM would not be appropriate. It is of bronze with laurel points where the limbs of the cross join, and in the centre is the representation of a caravel or ancient ship. Ribbon: dark blue with white central stripe.

The Silver Star, as it is now, was instituted in 1932 for award in cases of bravery in action which did not justify the Medal of Honour or the DSM. Previously, the Star had been worn on the medal ribbon (rather as the British oak leaf symbol is used on a campaign medal to denote a mention in despatches). The Silver Star is of bronze, having in the centre a laurel wreath surrounding a silver star. Ribbon: white with a red stripe, and fringed with blue having a thin white stripe.

The Legion of Merit was established in 1942, and is awarded for meritorious service; all ranks are eligible. The design is of a five-rayed cross, with double points, and having in the centre a circular plaque of blue, thereon thirteen white stars. The cross is on a wreath of green with crossed arrows in gold between the arms of the cross. The ribbon is crimson, fringed with white. This decoration can also be awarded to personnel of the armed forces of foreign nations.

The Distinguished Flying Cross was instituted in 1926 for award to members of the Air Corps in recognition of heroism or extraordinary achievement in a flight. The decoration is of bronze, the design that of a four-bladed propeller on a cross, behind this a square of rays. Ribbon: blue with three stripes, white, red (edged with white) and white.

The Soldier's Medal, instituted in 1926, is awarded to Army personnel in recognition of acts of heroism in peacetime or when not in actual combat with an enemy. The medal is of bronze and octagonal, with the American eagle standing on the fasces (bundle of rods), with thirteen stars, six on one side, seven on the other. Ribbon: blue with a central part in alternate thin white and red stripes.

The Navy and Marine Corps Medal, instituted in 1942, is for Naval and Marine personnel, and is awarded on same terms as for the Soldier's Medal. The medal is octagonal and the design shows an eagle standing on an anchor resting on a globe. The ribbon, in equal portions, is purple, orange and red.

The Bronze Star was instituted in 1944 for acts of heroism in combat or in support of combat operations. It is a five-pointed star, in the middle a small star within a circle. Ribbon: red edged with white and having a blue stripe also edged with white in the middle. The Bronze Star may be awarded to personnel of all services.

The Commendation Ribbon (Navy), for services in action, is green with two broad white stripes. The Commendation Pendant (Army) is a metal pendant, worn from the ribbon, which is green edged with white and having five thin white stripes in the middle.

The Air Medal is awarded to aircrew for notable service, but not up to DFC level. It is a bronze star, sixteen-pointed, with an eagle in flight in the centre. Ribbon: dark blue with two orange stripes.

The Purple Heart is a very interesting decoration, originally created by George Washington towards the end of the War of Independence in 1782, when it is thought that only three awards were made. The decoration was then forgotten but was rediscovered and reinstituted on the 200th anniversary of Washington's birth, 22 February 1932. By subsequent decision in 1942, the Purple Heart is awarded to all military personnel who are wounded in action. The design is heart-shaped, the centre being of purple enamel bordered in light bronze. On the front a bust of George Washington as a general is shown in relief. The reverse is of bronze and has the inscription 'For Military Merit'. The ribbon is purple bordered with white, and the ring attaching the Heart thereto incorporates the Washington coat of arms, from which the Stars and Stripes are derived.

The Medal for Merit was established in 1942 for award to civilians of foreign nations who had assisted in the war effort in the Second World War. The design shows the American eagle standing on a plinth and surrounded by a circle on which are thirteen stars. Ribbon: claret colour with two central stripes in white.

The Medal of Freedom is an award junior to the Medal for Merit. It is of bronze and the ribbon is in red moiré with four narrow central white stripes.

The Oak Leaf Cluster, as with the British bar to a decoration, denotes the second award of the particular medal and is worn on the ribbon of the medal.

There are numerous American campaign medals.

Orders and Decorations of Other Nations

The immensity of this field can be judged by the fact that while several large volumes have been produced on the orders of many countries, no work exists which claims to list all the orders and decorations of honour of every country in the world. In fact, no single work could ever contain an account of all the medals which have been struck in response to the well nigh universal demand for signs of recognition.

Very few countries are without decorations of any sort, though Uruguay has none, and Switzerland hardly any, except, it is believed, two or three awards for life saving. The position with Red China is uncertain but if the practice in the USSR is any guide, then there may well be such decorations in present-day China. To deal adequately with all the orders and decorations still being conferred today would require a work as long as the present book and it will be possible here to give only the briefest details of some countries' decorations.

To begin with a few principles:

(i) An article in the most recent edition of *Chambers' Encyclopedia* lists in six pages the entries for all countries from Abyssinia to Zanzibar. To take one country alone, Mexico, this source lists only the order of the Aztec Eagle, instituted in 1933 for award to foreigners. Yet it requires very little reading to know that in former eras in Mexico there have been other orders. In 1821, for instance, an adventurer named Iturbide had himself crowned as monarch of Mexico and determined to provide his new empire with all the trappings of European monarchy. 'In August the order of Guadalupe was instituted with fifty grand crosses, one hundred knights and an indefinite number of companions.' (A *History of Mexico*, by H. Bamford Parkes, p 185, 1950, Houghton Miflin Co.). The Iturbide government lasted a very short time, and the rest of its history can be read engagingly enough in Mr Parkes' book, but it remains true that anyone making inquiries into the genealogies of Mexican families is quite likely to find references to membership in the order of Our Lady of Guadalupe, Iturbide having been a devout Catholic. The Imperial Order of Guadalupe was extinguished with the fall of Iturbide, but General Santa Anna restored it in 1853. On his fall in 1855, it was again extinguished, restored by the Regency in 1863, and confirmed by the Emperor Maximilian in 1864. It was finally extinguished in 1867 after the emperor's execution. Maximilian also founded in 1865 an Imperial Order of the Mexican Eagle and the Imperial Order of San Carlos, both of which ended with his death. The above details are taken from Lucas de Palacio, *De Genealogiá y Heráldica* (Mexico, D F 1946), pp 131-132.

(ii) As this example from Mexico well illustrates, there are in most countries as many decorations as there have been regimes. The succeeding regime repudiates the honours granted by its predecessor, and this process may be repeated many times. Consequently, the historian, or compiler of honours, finds that he can very rarely give a straightforward account but must continually, as it were, retrace his steps. One of the best compilations on the subject is still Sir Bernard Burke's *Book of Orders and Decorations* published in 1858, but then, of course, the number of independent states was much less than it is now. No volume of the same size could be produced today and purport to cover the whole field. Later compilers have often produced fine works, but anyone who studies them will see that, while they include much that was unknown to Sir Bernard Burke, a great deal which he included is no longer relevant. The student of honours must then be prepared to consult half-a-dozen general works and to supplement these with the special brochures which may be obtained from various governments.

(iii) This is the century of revolution. Only thirty years ago there were some sixty independent governments in the world. Today there are probably not less than double that number. In a world in which the small island of Jersey, one of the English Channel Islands, can contemplate following Southern Rhodesia's example of UDI (Unilateral Declaration of Independence), and in which growing nationalist movements in Scotland and in Wales demand independence, fissiparous tendencies are very obviously on the increase.

(iv) Not only do governments proliferate, but regimes have been changed in our century with considerable frequency. The only countries which can claim stability in form while undergoing great changes in substance are what may be termed the Anglo-Saxon countries and Japan. With Scandinavia and the Netherlands, the United States, the United Kingdom, Australia, Canada, New Zealand and South Africa have all known great changes but have preserved their outward form, although South Africa has passed out of the British Commonwealth and become a republic instead of a nominal monarchy.

Even before it left the Commonwealth, the South African government had prepared in 1952 a series of decorations which were intended to replace the British decorations formerly bestowed upon South African citizens. The ruling caste in the republic is the Afrikaans Dutch-descended majority of white people. Next, come the white minority of British descent, after them the Cape Coloureds of mixed Indian ancestry, and, at the base of the social pyramid, the mass of the blacks. The South African decorations are largely reminiscent of the Dutch heroes and pioneers who contributed to the provinces and republics—Cape Colony, Natal, Orange Free State and Transvaal—which now comprise the republic. Queen Elizabeth II would only have approved these decorations on condition that her royal cypher or crown appeared on the reverse of the designs, and no doubt there have been changes since 1962 when South Africa left the Commonwealth.

The chief South African decorations are the Castle of Good Hope (Casteel de Goede Hoop) for valour in battle; the Van Riebeeck, awarded to officers for distinguished service against the enemy; a Van Riebeeck medal, for award to non-commissioned officers and enlisted men; the *Honoris Crux* (Cross of Honour, Erekruis), also awarded for gallantry in action; the Louw Wepener (named after a man who lost his life in 1865), and awarded for heroism, not in war; the Star of South Africa (Ster van Suid Afrika) for award to officers for meritorious service in peace or war; and finally—omitting the usual medals, such as the Korean Medal for participation by SA troops in the United Nations' Korean campaign —a decoration which recalls the very large British contribution to the development of South Africa. This is the John Chard Decoration and John Chard Medal, awarded as long-service decorations. They commemorate the epic defence at Rorke's Drift, on the Tugela river, by Lieutenants Chard and Bromhead with a small number of British soldiers against several thousands of Zulus. The best account of this heroic fight has been written by an American historian who bids fair to become as laurel-wreathed as Prescott and Motley—Donald R. Morris, author of *The Washing of the Spears, the Rise and Fall of the Zulu Nation*, published in 1966.

A full account of the changes in heraldic design resulting from South Africa's transition from republic to monarchy and to republic again is to be read in *Lions and Virgins* (1965) (Heraldic state symbols, coats of arms, flags, seals and other symbols of authority in South Africa 1487-1962) by Dr C. Pama, an author of Dutch birth now settled in South Africa.

Turning now to Japan as another country which can claim stability in form, she still keeps her ancient monarchy, although by the revolution of 1866 she changed from the Shogunate to a more modern state constitution. Her orders of chivalry are of comparatively late date, being based on the deliberate imitation of things western in the later nineteenth century, but taking their symbols either from the *mon* or from references to Japanese history. These orders are: The Chrysanthemum (1876) derived from the *mon* of the emperor's family and bestowed only on royalty or heads of state. There is a badge consisting of a star of thirty points with chrysanthemums between the longer rays, a ribbon of scarlet moiré with violet borders which is worn across the body with the badge resting on the hip, and another star to be worn on the breast. The Rising Sun, founded in 1876, has eight classes and what is really a highest class, that of the Paulownia Sun (1888). The Sacred Treasure (1888), refers to the original treasures of the monarchy—a mirror, swords etc—lost in a battle centuries ago. The Golden Kite (1890) is awarded for bravery in action to members of the armed forces. Cultural Merit (1937) is clearly derived both in title and objects from western models. Finally, there is the Crown (1888), for ladies.

The Scandinavian states and the Netherlands can be considered comparable to the Anglo-Saxon countries as being, on the whole, stable and slow to change. Taking Denmark first, we have a very distinguished order indeed, that of the Elephant, which was brought to the notice of the British public in 1950 when it was conferred on Sir Winston Churchill. Founded in the later fifteenth century (1458 and 1462 are given as dates by various authorities), it fell into disuse in the sixteenth century but was revived by King Christian V in 1693. There is only one class, which makes bestowal of the order a salute to greatness. The insignia consist of badges, ribbon and star. The badge is of great beauty, being an elephant in gold, enamelled in white, having its harness and a carpet on its back in blue and surmounted by a tower, before which sits an Indian dressed in purple with a gold spear in his hand. On one side of the animal is a cross of five diamonds, with brilliants for the eyes. The star is eight-pointed with rays between the points and a cross surrounded by a laurel wreath in the centre on a red ground. The ribbon is light watered blue, and is worn over the shoulder with the badge on the right hip. The origin of the title is unknown, though the ubiquitous Crusaders have, as usual, been involved by historical detectives in search of clues.

The Dannebrog is said to have originated in the thirteenth century; it was revived in 1671 and the statutes have been laid down and changed several times since. The insignia are a badge, star and ribbon (white moiré edged with scarlet); there are seven classes, the last being a badge of honour. There is also the order of the Icelandic Falcon founded by the King of Denmark in 1921 and which has continued under the Republic of Iceland.

Norway has only one order, that of St Olaf, founded by King Oscar I in 1847, and having four classes: Grand Cross, Commander, and Knight First and Second Class. The insignia vary for the classes. There is also the St Olaf Medal, instituted in 1939 for contributions to the well-being of Norway, and a War Cross of 1941 for bravery in the Second World War. Norway and Sweden were united for nearly a century until 1905. In 1904 the order of the Lion was founded but it is no longer conferred, evidence that even in Scandinavian countries political changes can affect orders.

Sweden has five orders. The Seraphim was reconstituted under its present name by Frederick I in 1748, from a predecessor going back to the thirteenth century and known at one time as the order of the Saviour. There is only one class and the order is conferred on a select number, among whom Swedes must already be members of the order of the Sword, or of the Polar Star. The insignia are very elaborate, consisting of collar, badge and star, in which the heads of the seraphim are a motif. The ribbon is light blue. The Sword, supposedly founded in 1522 but reconstituted in 1748, has five classes and is awarded to military personnel. The ribbon is yellow with blue stripes towards either edge. The Polar Star or North Star (1748) is in three classes and rewards civil merit. The ribbon is black. The Vasa (1772) has a green ribbon and is awarded for services to nationalised industries etc. There are three classes. The Charles XII (1811) has only one class and is awarded to masons of high rank. The ribbon is red.

The last of the five Scandinavian countries, Finland, has three orders, the Cross of Liberty (1918); the White Rose (1919), connected with the Orthodox Church; and the Lion (1942).

The Netherlands has the military order of William, founded in 1815 by King William I and awarded to military personnel for gallantry, and to civilians for bravery in presence of the enemy. Corresponding to the British Victoria Cross, it has four classes, a badge of a Maltese Cross, and a yellow ribbon with blue stripes towards the edges. The Lion of the Netherlands, founded by King William I in 1815, is awarded for various services and can be bestowed on military and civilians alike. It has three classes, and the ribbon is blue with broad central stripes of orange. The Orange Nassau, 1892, for services to the state, has five classes and the ribbon is orange with edges of blue, the colours being separated by a thin white stripe. The House of Orange (1905), like the British Royal Victorian order, is awarded for services to the royal house. It has six classes, and an orange ribbon. There are also in the Netherlands, the Resistance Cross (1946), the Bronze Cross (1940), the Cross for Merit (1941), and the Flying Cross (1941).

(v) Passing now to countries which have experienced revolutions and complete changes of regime, perhaps the most interesting is the USSR, in which some of the old Tzarist orders have been revived. Even after the collapse of the Tzardom in 1917 and the execution of the last Tzar, Nicholas II in 1918, the next head of the House of Romanoff, the Grand Duke Cyril, continued to bestow some of the great Russian orders. The Russian system also incorporated the orders of conquered peoples, such as that of St Stanislas and the White Eagle of Poland. The order of St Alexander Nevsky, founded in 1725, has been used afresh by the Soviets, having been re-established in 1942 without the title of 'St'. It is a very high decoration for commanders, has only one class, and the ribbon is pale blue with a red central stripe. The old Tzarist order of St George (1769) was very highly valued and could even be worn with the Soviet uniform. In 1943 the order of Glory was instituted for NCOs and men of the Army, and junior lieutenants of the Air Force. The ribbon, orange with three black stripes, is the same as that of the order of St George. Again, the order of Suvorov (1942) recalls a pre-Soviet decoration.

Most of the Soviet orders date from the time of the war against Germany; thus, the order of Victory (1943) for successful higher commanding personnel; of Kutuzov (1942) again for commanders and named after a Tzarist general; of the Patriotic War (1942) for those who showed heroism against the Fascist invader; of Bogdan Khmelnitsky (1943); Ushakov (Navy, 1944); and Nakimov (Navy, 1944). Most of these decorations have classes, as with western orders. In addition to the above, there are other orders created before the war of 1941-45. The Gold Star Medal (1939) is that of the Heroes of the Soviet Union, and is the highest of all awards. The Hammer and Sickle gold medal is awarded to Heroes of Socialist Labour, and both these and Heroes of the Soviet Union are automatically awarded the order of Lenin. The latter was established in 1930 and is given to individuals and organisations for work of national importance. Lenin's effigy appears in the badge, as with the effigies of saints and kings in western orders. The order of the Red Banner (1932) is a military award, and the Red Banner of Labour (1928) is for services in production and scientific research. The order of the Red Star (1930) is for personnel of the armed forces, the badge showing a soldier of the Red Army surrounded by the Russian inscription, 'Workers of all countries, Unite'. There are also a very large number of service medals. In the case of some orders, the names of recipients are inscribed on a roll of honour, and holders of the order of Victory have their names in the Grand Kremlin Palace.

Germany is another of the greater countries which has passed through revolutionary experiences. Not only that, but before 1870, Germany was a number of kingdoms each with its own orders, and despite union in one empire under the rule of Prussia, these kingdoms and principalities continued right up to 1918, when a republic briefly replaced the empire. Consequently there were these principal orders in the following states: Anhalt: order of Albert the Bear (1836). Baden: Fidelity (1715). Bavaria: St Hubert (1709), St Michael (1693), St George (1729), St Elizabeth (1766), and St Theresa (1827), the last two being for ladies and requiring rigorous proof of genealogy and arms bearing, as with so many of the old German orders. Brunswick: Henry the Lion (1834). Hanover had the Guelphic order already mentioned under British orders, also St George (1839) and Ernest Augustus (1865). Hesse: the Golden Lion (1770). Hohenlohe: the Phoenix (1759). Lippe: the Cross of Honour (1890), and the Rose (1898). Mecklenburg: the Crown of the Wendes (1864), and the Griffin (1884). Oldenburg: Peter Frederich Louis (1838). Prussia had many orders; the Black Eagle (1701), and the Royal House of Hohenzollern (1851), still being conferred by the head of that same royal house. Saxony: the Crown of Rue (1807) was one of a number of orders and the only one to be awarded by the former princely house. Waldeck: the order of Merit (1857). Württemberg: the Golden Eagle (1702) and the Crown (1818). As noted, many of these orders are still conferred by the heads of the royal houses, although they no longer rule.

For Germany in general, there were the decorations of Prussia which the Kaiser conferred. The most famous were the Pour le Mérite, founded in 1667 and renamed as the order of Merit (1740), having both military and civil sections; and the Iron Cross (1813) as an award for gallantry. This was refounded with several classes in 1939 by Hitler, who also instituted a great many orders and distinctions, the memory of which may remain. Under the Federal Republic, an order of Merit (1951) in eight classes exists, the ribbon being scarlet with fringes of gold, black, gold. The badge is a cross with the German eagle in centre.

France had many distinctions under the old monarchy previous to the revolution in 1789. A very great order was that of the Saint Esprit, or Holy Ghost (1578); others included those of St Michael (1469) and St Louis (1693). These have all passed into the limbo of lost honours. In 1802 Napoleon instituted the Legion of Honour to which he made 48,000 appointments, nor have numbers fallen away in more recent times. There are five grades in the Legion, the ribbon is red, and the badge is a five-pointed star with the centrepiece showing the female head symbolic of the Republic with the wording around it 'Republique Française'. The Médaille Militaire (1852), awarded to officers for distinguished conduct in war, and the Croix de Guerre (1915) to commemorate mention in despatches, are the most important French distinctions. In their former colonial empire in Indo-China, Africa and elsewhere, the French recognised a large number of orders of the native regimes.

Italy had some orders of chivalry of which one at least ranked among the highest European distinctions. This was the Annunziata (or Annunciation), founded in 1362 by the Counts of Savoy, ancestors of the royal line of Italy. There were only fifteen knights of the order and the costume was of great magnificence. The Collar, the name formerly given to this order, was of gold with a badge representing the Annunciation. The order of St Maurice (1434) and St Lazarus represented the union of two orders, and there were five classes. This order has been preserved in a sense by the Italian republic in a charitable context. So, too, has the Military Order, now of Italy, formerly of Savoy, founded in 1815 for rewarding distinguished service in war and peace. The Civil Order of Savoy (1831) was of one class and limited to seventy knights. The Crown of Italy (1868) had five classes and commemorated the union of Italy in 1870.

Austria had, as already noted, the Golden Fleece, and there was also the Military Order of Maria Theresa (1755), which conferred hereditary nobility. The Crown of Leopold (1808), the Iron Crown (1805), and Francis Joseph (1849), with two orders for ladies, Elizabeth (1898) and the Starry Cross (1668), were Austrian distinctions, as the old empire included the kingdom of Hungary. There were also the Hungarian orders of the Golden Spur and of St Stephen (1764). The modern Hungarian republic has an order of Merit and medals of Merit (1950).

The Vatican, or Holy See, possesses a number of knighthoods, the best known of which are those of St Gregory the Great (1831), Pius (1849) and St Silvester (1905).

Belgium has the order of Leopold (1832) awarded to officers for bravery in action and for long service, and to NCOs for good service. There are five classes. The Crown (1897), originally for the Congo State; Leopold II (1900); the African Star (1888), and the royal order of the Lion (1891) were all Congolese orders. Belgium has a Military Cross, a Croix de Guerre, and a Croix de Feu.

Brazil was an empire under a branch of the Portuguese royal family of Braganza before the present republic. Under the emperors, there were the Southern Cross (1822), revived by the republic in 1933; Peter I (1826); the Rose (1829), and also some orders of the home country of Portugal. The republic has instituted an order of Military, Naval and Aeronautical Merit.

Imperial China had the interestingly named order of the Double Dragon (1881) and the Striped Tiger. The republic, precursor of the Communist regime, had the orders of Jade, the Precious Tripod, and the Pavilion in the Sky.

Greece has the orders of the Saviour (1833), George I (1915), the Phoenix (1926) and St Olga and St Sophia (1938).

Liechtenstein has an order of Merit (1937), and Luxembourg possesses the Golden Lion and Adolphus of Nassau (both 1858).

Poland, in 1921, revived the White Eagle, which had been founded in 1705 by the former king of Poland. Also revived in 1918 was the Virtuti Militari (1792) awarded for bravery, and there was instituted an order of Polonia Restituta (1921).

Portugal has, with Spain, the distinction of possessing some of the oldest orders in the world. Several of these have been retained by the present regime, although they are no longer orders of chivalry but rather of merit. Among these are St Benedict of Aviz (1162), St James of the Sword (1177), and the military order of Christ (1317). The badges are almost the same under the new arrangements. There is also the

Tower and Sword (1459), reconstituted in 1832 as an order of merit, together with various other modern orders.

Outside Europe, there are some orders which are well known, often because they have been conferred on Europeans. Ethiopia has the order of the Seal of Solomon (1874), and several later orders; Turkey had the Medjidie (1852) and Osmanie (1861); Egypt's orders of Mohammed Ali (1915) are distinguished. Numerous decorations, often very ephemeral, have been produced in the central and south American states. Cuba has more orders than a couple of medium-sized European states, and Haiti has had enough decorations to justify the production of a beautiful and elaborate work on the subject.

In the Republic of Ireland there are several decorations or medals to commemorate the successful 1916-21 struggle against the British. Most modern states have added creations of some kind of honorary distinction to their assumption of independence. That it has been found necessary to do this even in Communist states is a proof of the saying, 'Man does not live by bread alone'. Economic forces are not sufficient by themselves to inspire human beings.

PART 3

The Clan System

T

CHAPTER 16

The Clan System

C LAN history is of great importance to any student of Scottish genealogy, since without it he cannot understand the study and will certainly not make headway until he does. The word 'clan' is used extensively throughout the English-speaking world, as applied to all sorts of nations, and in this context the word is probably equivalent to 'tribe'. In numerous books there are references to tribes in Afghanistan, in Arabia, in central and southern Africa and, in historical narrative, to tribes among the ancient Germans. The term is also constantly applied in the Bible to the descendants of Abraham; the Israelites descended from his grandson, Jacob, or Israel, who later became split into two political entities, Israel with ten tribes and Judah with two. Again, in Japanese heraldry we find many references to clans among the great families of Japan.

In all these cases the basic idea is the same, of individuals, and of families, united as a common blood stock. Usually there is the claim of descent from an ancestor; sometimes, as with Israel, as the physical ancestor of the whole people; sometimes as the eponym or name figure, as with Romulus for the Romans, or the ancestor of the royal lines of the Germans, Woden. In all these instances, while there was most probably an original core having a common descent, there must also have been a gathering under the tribal umbrella of persons not related to the main stock but who came to be known by its name. We see this very clearly in the Old Testament. When Abraham was commanded to circumcise all the males in his household, it is expressly declared: 'And all the men of his house born in the house, and bought with money of the stranger, were circumcised with him.' (Genesis ch 17, v 27). Further we read (Exodus ch 12, v 38) that when Abraham's descendants left Egypt, 'a mixed multitude went up also with them'. It is very unlikely that these alien elements left no progeny to be included under the heading of Israelites. (See Chapter 10 on Jewry.)

Similar was the position of the Highland clans of Scotland. The latest writer on the clans, Sir Iain Moncreiffe, Albany Herald, says: 'Many (ie, the chief of the clan's tenants) were true clansmen whose genealogies went back at least nominally to the forefather of the whole clan. . . . The rest of the fighting force were made up of newcomers who had sought the chief's protection.' (*The Highland Clans*, p 27, 1967). Again he remarks: 'Younger sons were settled within the appanage that formed the clan territory. Their children in turn settled there and thus the clan took roots. For the word *clan* simply means "children" and originally each clan was made up only of the immediate descendants of the man after whom it was named.' (p 30). From consideration of these quotations and the use of common sense, we can deduce that the Highland clans would, in each case, have had an original nucleus grouped around or derived from a progenitor who gave his name to the clan. This is the reason for the 'Mac' used in so many surnames, and which means simply 'son of'.

The next matter of importance is the distinction to be made between Highland and Lowland clans. In the majority of modern works on the subject it is quite clear that the Highlands are meant when clans are mentioned. The largest work on the subject is *The Clans, Septs, and Regiments of the Scottish Highlands*, by Frank Adam, revised by the greatest Scottish authority, Sir Thomas Innes of Learney, Lord Lyon King of Arms (sixth edition, 1960). The late Robert Bain's *The Clans and Tartans of Scotland* (fourth edition, 1960, enlarged and re-edited by Margaret O. MacDougall) covers Lowland clans as well as Highland. In Johnston's *Clan Map of the Scottish Highlands*, that portion of the country below the Forth and Clyde estuaries is shown with clan names, eg, Johnstones, Maxwells, Kennedys etc, but all in one uniform colour, whereas the Highland clans are shown with a separate colour for each tribal area. In former times the Scottish Parliament regarded the Border families as being clans, and an Act of 1587, for the quieting and keeping in obedience of the people of the Borders, Highlands and Isles, refers to the clans on the Borders as well as in the Highlands. It has also been observed by some Scots historians that the King's title was that of King of Scots, not of Scotland, since the King was the Chief of Chiefs.

Nonetheless, the popular conception of a clan as Highland, and the Highlanders as wearing the kilt, equipped with target and claymore, and with bagpipes playing, is a correct view within certain wide limits. Not all the clans of the Highlands are of Celtic or Gaelic origin, nor is the wearing of tartan, as distinct from the kilt, confined to Highlanders.

It remains true that the Highlanders were for the most part distinct in race from the Lowlanders. There was also a cleavage between the two areas, especially after the sixteenth-seventeenth century, in manners and religion—many Highland clans adhered to the Church of Rome—as well as in language.

The famous historian, Lord Macaulay, himself derived from an ancient but somewhat depressed clan, has a vivid description of the Scottish Highlands in Chapter 13 of his *History of England*. The whole chapter should be read by the student of clan history, but the following passage is particularly relevant. 'Soon the vulgar imagination was so completely occupied by plaids, targets and claymores, that by most Englishmen, Scotchman and Highlander were regarded as synonymous words. Few people seemed to be aware that, at no remote period, a MacDonald or a MacGregor in his tartan was to a citizen of Edinburgh or Glasgow what an Indian hunter in his war paint is to an inhabitant of Philadelphia or Boston. Artists and actors represented Bruce and Douglas in striped petticoats. They might as well have represented Washington brandishing a tomahawk and girt with a string of scalps.' A few years ago, in a representation of Shakespeare's first part of *Henry IV*, the noble and knightly Douglas was brought on in a kilt, with target and claymore, and depicted fighting thus among the mail clad-warriors at the battle of Shrewsbury, and all this on the English stage in London.

During the later eighteenth century, when the American privateer, Paul Jones, threatened Leith, the Scots authorities declined an offer from some Highlanders to defend the coast because they feared what these terrible men might do once they had arms in their hands.

In this connection nothing can be more instructive than the attitude taken by Scotland's greatest man of letters. Sir Walter Scott was descended from the Scotts of Harden, one of the Border families. He certainly was not a Highlander and himself admitted that, through ignorance, much bad Gaelic appeared in his novels. The views about the Highlands which he puts into the mouths of characters in his novels reflect the attitude taken by Lowland Scots in the eighteenth century (Scott was born in 1770) towards the Highlanders. In *The Fair Maid of Perth*, much of the story turns on the troubles in the Highlands between Clan Chattan and Clan Quhele, two confederacies of clans, each of which claimed supremacy in the Highlands. Throughout the story, and particularly in Chapter 13, the view taken by Lowlanders of all classes is that the Highlanders are caterans, thieves, savages, and well-nigh pagans. The climax of the story turns upon a combat on the North Inch (Island) at Perth before the Scots king, between the two groups of clans.

This is no fiction but took place in 1396, and the Clan Quhele—now thought by some to be the Cummins—was thoroughly vanquished with great loss of life on both sides. In others of Scott's novels, *A Legend of Montrose*, and *Rob Roy*, to say nothing of *Waverley*, the Lowlanders' views of their Highland neighbours are, to put it mildly, pejorative. This is not to suggest that these views are historically accurate for the whole period of Scottish history, but they were certainly those of Scotsmen in the Lowlands some 200 years ago.

The truth about the racial make-up of Scotland cannot be put more succinctly than it was by Sir Iain Moncrieffe: 'Scotland is in the main made up of five formerly separate realms, three of which spoke Celtic languages in historic times, while the other two were founded by more recent Teutonic conquerors who did not exterminate the subjugated Celtic peoples in their territories. Generalising broadly: in the west lay the kingdom of the Gaelic-speaking Scots, and to the east and north-east that of the Picts, while the Western Isles (and for a long time the far north) were under Norse rule. In the south-west was a kingdom of the Welsh-speaking Britons, and the south-east was ruled by English-speaking Angles.' ('Landed Gentry of Scotland', one of a number of introductory articles in *Burke's Landed Gentry*, 1952).

The Scots came from Ireland where, as already mentioned under Irish genealogy, a similar system of clans has existed from a remote period. For some centuries there was hostility between Picts and Scots, but in 843 Kenneth MacAlpine, King of Dalriada, succeeded to the kingship of the Picts in right of his mother. He was crowned King of Scots at Scone, where once was kept the Stone of Destiny, now under the Coronation chair in Westminster Abbey. The older line of Scots kings descended from Kenneth, who thus became the High King (Ard Righ as in Ireland) over the whole of the old Alban realm in Scotland. With Malcolm Cenmore ('Big Head'), who was killed in 1093, great changes took place, and from his time can be dated the consolidation of the clan or tribal system in Scotland which was to last until after Culloden (1746). In 1070 Malcolm married Margaret, the sister of Edgar Atheling, the heir to the English throne, and with the advent of these English exiles many more refugees from England settled in Scotland. Later, under Malcolm's son David I, Norman as well as English settlers came north and the feudalism of the Anglo-Normans entered Scotland. Briefly, under feudalism the king owned the land and let it out to his great tenants. Under the clan system, though the king was the Chief of Chiefs, it was the great chiefs who ruled over the domains of the clans, each clan being like a family which owned a territory administered by its chief. Queen Margaret was instrumental in bringing Saxon nobles to Scotland, changing the court language from Gaelic to English, and bringing the Celtic Church into conformity with Rome.

Succession to the chiefship of a clan was hereditary, but did not necessarily pass to the eldest son. The selection had to be made from among the kin of the chief, and a successor could be chosen from the derbhfine, a group of nine kinsmen nearest to the chief, or under the law of tanistry the chief could nominate his successor, the tanist who must be a kinsman. As head of the clan, the chief is entitled to wear three eagle's feathers; chieftains are the heads of junior branches—the cadet lines of the clan—and are entitled to wear one eagle's feather. The word 'chief' was brought to Scotland by Norman settlers and adopted into the Gaelic usage. Another word also used to denote a chief was 'captain', derived from the Latin *caput*, head. It is used of the greatest chiefs, as Captain of Clan Chattan.

The branches of the clan are called the septs, and these may, and usually do, bear surnames quite different from that of the main line. The usage as to surnames was very fluid in the Highlands and similar to that which prevailed among the Welsh. Thus the celebrated clan Mackintosh has for its septs the following: McKeggie, MacCombie, MacOmie, Mac-Thomas, Shaw, MacAy, MacHay, Tosh, Tosbach, Hossach, Adamson, Ayson, Esson, Hardy, MacHardie, MacCardney, Crerar, Noble, Mc-Conchy, MacAndrew, McKillican, MacGlashan, Glen, Glennie, Ritchie, Macritchie, Macniven, Niven, Seath and Seth. Because of this affiliation the Anglo-Irish dramatist, Bernard Shaw, joined a clan Mackintosh association, since his ancestry was certainly not Irish, but Scottish-English.

The history of the clan system is full of turbulence, warfare, cruelty, romance, and loyalty. As with many fierce and semi-savage peoples, the Highlanders could be capable of splendid qualities combined with the most revolting cruelties. Anyone who reads casually in the 'Mac' entries in *Burke's Peerages*, or *Burke's Landed Gentry*, will be horrified by the sober recital of murder and rapine in the annals of the most notable chiefs. Even more peculiar is the pride felt by the most cultured gentlemen of the present day at descent from some who can only be fairly described as thieves and murderers.

The rule of the King of Scots was acknowledged by Highlanders in a spasmodic manner, much like the rule of the High King in Ireland. The Lords of the Isles, the MacDonalds, were in fact serious rivals to the Scottish king. At Bannockburn, the MacDonalds stood on the right wing, a position which they claimed as theirs of right, fighting for

Robert Bruce. The Scottish throne was never a secure seat and it was not until the end of the fifteenth century that the Norse rule was finally ended in what is geographically Scotland. After this the Orkneys, Shetlands and outer Hebrides were securely united to the realm of Scotland, though to this day in the Orkneys and Shetlands, the Scotsman is as much a foreigner as the Englishman.

When James VI of Scotland became James I of England, and could control both sides of the Border, the turbulence of this area began to subside and it soon became as peaceful as the rest of the Lowlands. The Highlands, however, remained a territory apart, and their way of life changed little. North of the Highland line, all was unsettled and in the eighteenth century a French map-maker could write across the area of the Grampian mountains, 'terre inculte, habitée par les sauvages'. The last battle between clans occurred in the later seventeenth century, but this did not mean that the turbulence of the clans had ceased. There were constant forays against the Lowlands, to avoid which the landed gentlemen of the districts near the Highlands would often pay money to the Highland freebooters in what was called blackmail (ie, rent) to ensure that their cattle were not lifted.

The problem of the Highlands was accentuated by the exile of the Stuart dynasty. In the days of Cromwell, the King's general in Scotland, the Marquess of Montrose, found his best support in the Highlanders. When William of Orange replaced James II, Viscount Claverhouse (Bonnie Dundee) led the Highlanders to victory at Killiecrankie against the Government troops, and only his death prevented his army from winning further successes. In 1715 the Highlanders rose again and won the battle of Sheriffmuir on behalf of the Old Pretender (James VIII to the Scots). After this, attempts were made to pacify the Highlands. General Wade constructed roads through them, and forts were built in strategic places—Fort George, Fort Augustus and Fort William—from Inverness to the south-west down the Great Glen, the present Caledonian canal. In 1745 came the final outburst. Bonnie Prince Charlie, the Young Pretender and son of James VIII, landed in Scotland and gathered an army from the clans. He won the battle of Prestonpans, near Edinburgh, capturing all except the castle, and marched on into England as far as Derby. He was then forced to retreat, gained a victory at Falkirk, but was finally defeated with heavy slaughter at Culloden (Drumossie Moor) near Inverness in 1746. The Prince escaped, despite a price of £30,000 on his head.

This rebellion meant the end of the clan system. The British Parliament passed three measures, one of which forbade the wearing of weapons by Highlanders, and another the wearing of Highland garb in any form. (This Act was repealed in 1782.) 'But the great and effective measure—expected after 1715 but delayed—was the abolition of hereditary claims of feudal superiors to military service, and the substitution of "sheriff deputies" advocates for the old hereditary jurisdictions. . . .' (Andrew Lang, *History of Scotland*, vol 4, p 521, 1907). This was the Hereditable Jurisdictions Act, 1747. Under it, 'compensation was paid to the holders of hereditable jurisdictions. The Duke of Argyll received £21,000; the Duchess of Gordon, £25. The Duke of Buccleuch had but £3,400 to Morton's £7,240 and Eglinton's £7,800 . . . the whole sum was £152,237 15s 4d, while claims had been put in for £583,090 16s 8d.' (*op cit*, pp 521-2.) Compensation was not, of course, paid to anyone who had been in rebellion, and large areas of the Highlands thus became forfeited to the Crown.

It is very difficult to assess the number of people living in the Highlands at the time of the rising for the Stuarts. In 1314, at Bannockburn, there are supposed to have been 10,000 clansmen representing twenty-one clans on Bruce's side, with four or five clans fighting for England. The first time we are able to obtain a definite figure is in 1724, when General Wade reported that there were 22,000 fighting men in the Highlands, of whom about 10,000 were vassals of loyal chiefs; the rest were either disaffected to the Government or had been in arms against it. This argues a population, all told, of about 130,000-200,000. Prince Charlie's army was not above 6,000 men, and at Culloden there were more Scotsmen against him than there were Englishmen. There was a great increase in the Highland population in the nineteenth century and, by 1851, it had risen to 334,475. Then came the necessity for emigration, along with the famous, or rather infamous 'clearances', when the land was cleared of the poor clansmen to make room for sheep, cattle and deer forests. The constant pressure of economic forces has compelled many chiefs to sell their ancestral property; those who remain are often in dire straits.

Before dealing with the clans individually, the subject of dress falls to be considered. Tartans are probably the cause of more misunderstanding than even coats of arms, and there is a clear distinction between them and Highland dress in general. From early times, the belted plaid was worn, measuring some 18 feet in length and 6 feet in width. Plaited in the middle, it was so arranged that its great size did not impede the wearer, and served both as a cloak by day and a blanket by night. When, some 250-300 years ago, the modern-style kilt was evolved, this was done by cutting off the lower part of the belted plaid and, as it had no pockets, putting the purse, or sporran, in front. The result was a garment admirably adapted to use in the mountains.

Now as regards tartan, meaning a coloured or striped cloth, this had been called 'tweed' up to the eighteenth and nineteenth centuries. It had been known for many centuries in Scotland but there is no evidence of definite clan pattern or significance before the year 1800. Proof of this is found in old prints and illustrations of tartans, which rarely, if ever, can be related to those now in use, although in many cases the person shown in the print is known to have been a member of a particular clan. This is not surprising, for two good reasons. First, the tartans of past days, being made from a few dye-producing plants, were simple in design and limited to a small range of colour and pattern. Secondly, the prohibition for nearly forty years against the wearing of Highland dress meant that the secrets of weaving had mostly disappeared. 'Tartan was almost a thing of the past; many of the old weavers had died and with their passing details of old patterns were lost; the wooden pattern sticks had rotted away and such fragments of old tartan cloth as remained were so worn and perished that they were of little value in adding to the little knowledge that remained of pre-1745 tartans.' (Bain, *op cit*, p 27).

With George IV's arrival in Edinburgh in 1822, a great revival set in. The royal visit was stage-managed by Sir Walter Scott. George held court at Holyrood House, and wore the royal Stuart tartan. He was the first king to visit Scotland for 171 years. The last of the Jacobite princes Henry Stuart, Cardinal York, died in 1807. George III had settled on him an annuity of £4,000 per annum and in due course the Cardinal (to the Jacobites, Henry IX) settled on George III the remaining Crown jewels left in his possession. By this transaction the cardinal, so the Jacobites hold, appointed George III as his tanist; hence the enthusiasm for George IV, and the loyalty now shown to the British sovereign by descendants of the Jacobites.

Although the clan structure in the old semi-feudal style ended 200 years ago, the clan idea has never ended, and to this day, all over the world, there are clan associations with chiefs and chieftains. Some of the clan stories can be glanced at. Recognition of a clan chief is a matter for the Lord Lyon, and in 1959 he granted recognition as head of the clan McBain to Mr Hughson Maynard McBain, an American business man, then chairman of Marshall Field & Co, and a director of the First National Bank of Chicago. He was reported as hoping to buy land in Inverness-shire where his ancestors had lived. The only woman chief, Dame Flora Macleod of Macleod of Dunvegan Castle, Isle of Skye, invited members of the clan from all over the world in 1955 to contribute to the renovation of the castle.

There have been some interesting exchanges between Old World and New in this matter of clans and chiefships. In 1822, the 13th chief MacNab decided to start afresh in Canada and set up a feudal clan regime with a body of clansmen, but the project failed through his own hardness. A far different story is that of Robert MacNeil, the 45th chief of Barra. An American citizen who also has British nationality, he has bought back 9,000 of his ancestral acres on Barra and restored Kisimul Castle.

Not all the clans are of Celtic origin, even though they may have lived as Highlanders for centuries. Gunn, for instance, is of Norse descent, and the Frasers, the Cummings (Comyns), and Chisholms are of Norman origin. In ancient days it was said that only three persons in the world were entitled to put 'The' before their names: The Pope, The King and The Chisholm. Originally, the Chisholms were found on the Borders in Roxburgh and Berwickshire; later in the Highlands. At Culloden, the chief and his clan fought for Prince Charles. Today the head of the family, through the female line, is Chisholm of Chisholm. The prefix 'The' was first used in connection with chiefs in the seventeenth century but is now frequently employed, eg, The Mackintosh, The MacNab.

No clan is more renowned in story and legend than MacGregor, and in olden days they possessed much territory on the borders of Perthshire and Argyllshire. In the latter county they were exposed to the encroachments of the Campbells, the most hated among the clans, mainly because of their skill in winning territory. The MacGregors defended themselves so vigorously that they gained a reputation for turbulence and wrongdoing. At last, in the year 1603, after the Mac-Gregors had inflicted a particularly bloody defeat on their neighbours, the widows and orphans of the slain went in procession to James VI, wearing the bloodstained shirts of the dead and demanding justice against the slayers. The MacGregors were put to the horn, ie, outlawed. They were not allowed to use their surname and every man's hand was against them. Likewise, their hand was against every man's and the famous Rob Roy MacGregor, known as Mr Campbell during much of his career, led a dangerous wandering life, managing however to die in his bed. Eventually, in 1775, the name of MacGregor was restored by Act of Parliament and 856 MacGregors promptly came forward to endorse the claim of John Murray MacGregor as 18th chief. He was created a baronet in 1795, having been recognized as Chief of the

Children of the Mist (the Highland name of the clan). This, then, is not only the most unfortunate of the clans but also the purest blooded, at least since 1603, for between that date and 1775 no one would have claimed to be a MacGregor unless it were true, and no one from another clan would have sought to join the outlawed.

The clan Chattan (pronounced Hattan) is a confederacy of clans which has continued for centuries. It includes the clan Mackintosh, the chief of which is the Chief of clan Chattan, and also the clan Macpherson. The Mackintosh chief's home is Moy, on Loch Moy. It so happens that one of the chiefs emigrated to America in the eighteenth century and intermarried with the Creek Indians, so that Waldo E. MacIntosh is now principal chief of the Creek nation. 'His Redskin name is Tustunuggee Micco and his tribe numbers over 20,000 mostly in Oklahoma, where there is a McIntosh county.' (Moncreiffe, *op cit*, p 128). The Macpherson (the name means 'son of the parson', probably one of the lay vicars of the middle ages), although no longer possessing all their old territory, have a good clan association through which some of the old Cluny chief's lands have been rebought. One of their chieftains, W. Cheyne Macpherson of Dalchully, was the clan historian.

Heraldry developed late among the Highlanders and, as in other Celtic lands, derived from the feudal knights and lords. The clan badges were used from early times and these have often been incorporated in shields of arms, or used as crests. Very famous is the Macpherson badge of a wild cat or cat-a-mountain, with the motto, 'Touch not the cat bot a glove'. The badge is used within the buckle which is worn on caps and on plaids. Incidentally, the greatest care should be taken by any buyer of tartan or clan badges for, without expert advice, it is very easy to be fobbed off with a device or scheme of tartan which never belonged to any clan.

The MacDonalds

They are the largest clan and for grandeur and romance, no clan can be of greater standing than the MacDonalds. The founder of their race, Somerled, son of Gillebride, did not deign to lower his crest even to the King of Scots. The proud title, Lord of the Isles, was annexed to the Scottish Crown in 1540, and is now borne by the Prince of Wales, but in earlier centuries, when the kingdom of Scotland was not yet fully constituted, the title denoted an independent sovereign who waged war on the King of Scotland, or of Norway, and concluded a treaty with the King of England as an equal.

The largest of the clans of the Scottish Highlands, the clan Donald had nine main branches, among them the MacDonalds of Sleat, of Islay, of Keppoch, of Clanranald, of Glencoe (sometimes referred to as Mac-Ians), and the MacAlisters of Loup. In addition, in descent from Somer-led, there are the MacDougalls, who form a separate clan, and the Mac-Donnells of Glengarry. Beside these great branches of the clan there are the septs, numbering, according to some authorities, no less than 182. A sept may be defined as 'the branch of a line which is itself a main clan stem, also an unaffiliated in-taken tribe'. (Sir Thomas Innes of Learney).

When Somerled, whose Norse name means Samuel, appears in history, he comes as a great chief or king, but of his predecessors we know nothing beyond the fact that his father was Gillebride, a Gaelic name. Somerled lived in the early part of the twelfth century and is first heard of as an exile at the hands of the Norwegians, apparently driven from extensive possessions and living in Morvern, in northern Argyllshire, opposite Mull. At this time the Norwegians controlled all the islands of Scotland, right down to the Isle of Man. Not until 1468-9, on the marriage of James III of Scotland to Margaret, Princess of Norway, did the sovereignty of the Shetlands and Orkneys pass to the Scottish Crown. In the twelfth century the western islands were exposed to an aftermath of the Viking age, which had earlier so afflicted England, France, and Ireland. About the year 1130, Somerled led the men of Morvern against the Norwegian pirates and land ravagers, and drove them out, thus becoming ruler of Morvern, Lochaber, and most of northern and southern Argyllshire.

About 1135, King David I, the Scots king, conquered Man, Arran and Bute from the Norwegians. These territories, according to some accounts, were then held by Somerled as a feudal grant from the Crown, but whatever the origin of his possessions, Somerled became sufficiently strong to disturb the balance of power in the western isles. He aided an invasion of Scotland by Wimond, an English monk who had gone to the Isle of Man and put forward pretensions to the earldom of Moray, and made an alliance with Olaf, the Norwegian King of the Isles by marrying his daughter, Ragnhildis. On Olaf's murder, Somerled invaded Man on behalf of his son Dougall (of Lorn, ancestor of the clan Mac-Dougall), and after several fierce battles, including one at sea in 1156, in which Somerled had a force of eighty galleys, he succeeded in gaining control of Man and of the south islands. The latter included all islands south of Ardnarmurchan Point in Argyllshire down to Bute; the peninsula of Kintyre was reckoned as an island among the south islands.

The north islands, which were the outer Hebrides and the Inner Hebrides north of Ardnamurchan Point, remained under Norwegian control.

Somerled was now very powerful and could afford to try conclusions with the Scots king, Malcolm IV. For a time, their differences were composed by a treaty made in 1159, but in 1164 Somerled brought a fleet of 160 galleys up the Clyde to Renfrew and landed with a large army. He was met by the High Steward of Scotland and in the ensuing battle both Somerled and his son (by his first marriage), Gilliecolum, were killed. Thus ended the career of a man who had come near to establishing a monarchy on the west of Scotland, independent of the sovereign who reigned in Edinburgh. After Somerled's death the custom of gavelkind (equal division of the father's estate among his sons) prevented, as in Celtic Wales, the rise of a strong power. Dougall, the eldest son, received Mull, Coll, Tiree and Jura, with the district of Lorn on the mainland of Argyllshire. Islay and Kintyre went to Reginald, and Bute to Angus, Arran being shared between Angus and Reginald. The territories of Argyllshire which had been held by Somerled passed to his namesake and grandson, Somerled, son of Gilliecolum.

In the centuries which followed this distribution of Somerled's kingdom, right up to the annexation of the title of Lord of the Isles to the Scots crown in 1540, the chiefs of the clan continued to be semi-independent rulers, their fortunes being chequered according to the strength or weakness of the Scottish king. Despite vicissitudes, this mighty clan spread from the Outer Hebrides (north and south Uist), the Inner Hebrides (Skye, Rum, Eig, Islay, Jura) to Kintyre, Argyllshire, and Ross, though in the last-named territory they did not secure a permanent footing.

Of the three sons of Somerled mentioned above, the youngest, Angus, and his male issue were killed in battle by the men of Skye. A granddaughter of Angus, Jean, married Alexander, the 4th High Steward of Scotland and ancestor of the royal house of Stuart. In right of his wife, Alexander claimed and seized the territories of Bute and Arran. The surviving sons of Somerled, Dougall and Reginald, were both styled Kings of the Isles. Dougall was the founder of the great clan MacDougall of Argyll and Lorn. Reginald was the founder of two families; his son Donald begat the clan Donald or MacDonalds of Islay; the younger son Roderick, or Ruari, was ancestor of the clan Rorie or MacRories of Bute. When the Scots under the High Steward began to press hard upon their territories, the Kings of the Isles sought the assistance of the Norwegian king who, being now weaker in the western isles than the King of Scots, was a much less dangerous foe. In consequence Haco, King of Norway, invaded Scotland in 1263, but was defeated by King Alexander III at Largs, and compelled to cede the Hebrides to the Scottish Crown. Thus the appeal to Norway had turned out very unfortunately for the Mac-Donalds, for although Alexander III pardoned their share in the Norwegian invasion, it was as vassals of the Scottish Crown that they were confirmed in their lands. Skye, Lewis, Man, Arran and Bute were lost to them, though the MacRories secured fresh land in the northern isles. The male line of the chiefs of the MacRories expired in 1346, when Ranald was murdered at Perth, but his only sister, Amy, was married to John, chief of the clan Donald.

In the terrible time of the War of Independence, when Scotland was devastated by the struggles of Wallace, and later Bruce, with the English, the MacDonalds were equally unfortunate. The chiefs of the clan Dougall and of the clan Donald both sided with the Baliols and Comyns against King Robert Bruce. One of the most prized possessions of the chiefs of MacDougall down the ages has been the famous Brooch of Lorn, which came into the family in 1306 when Sir John MacDougall, the 5th laird of Dunollie, defeated Bruce. Covering the retreat of his fleeing men, Bruce was assaulted by several of the MacDougall clan, and such was his valour that even his enemies likened him to the heroes of antiquity. But although he slew the clansmen who had seized him, he was forced to unclasp his brooch and leave it and his cloak in the tenacious grasp of one of the dying men. Hence that treasured heirloom, the Brooch of Lorn.

On Bruce's triumph at Bannockburn in 1314, when Scotland's independence was for ever assured, the chiefs of clan Dougall and of clan Donald had to forfeit much of their land. It would have fared ill with the race of MacDonald had not Angus Og, the brother of Alexander, chief of clan Donald, sided with Bruce and led a large body of the clan to fight at Bannockburn. It was this Angus Og whose name was altered for reasons of poetic euphony by Sir Walter Scott in his poem 'The Lord of the Isles', and it is to him that Bruce is represented in the poem as saying:

> 'One effort more and Scotland's free;
> Lord of the Isles, my trust in thee
> Is firm as Ailsa Rock;
> Rush on with Highland sword and targe,
> I, with my Carrick spearmen charge,
> Now, forward to the shock!'

From their position and their services at Bannockburn, the Mac-Donalds claimed the hereditary right to be placed on the right wing in battle, and neglect of this custom some 400 years later was to have serious consequences.

Angus' two sons were John, chief of clan Donald, and John Og, ancestor of the MacIans or MacDonalds of Glencoe. The name of this branch of the clan will ever be memorable for the dreadful tragedy of Glencoe in 1692, when an attempt was made by the British government to extirpate in cold blood 'that set of thieves', as the MacDonalds of Glencoe were called owing to their predatory habits. About forty were thus murdered, but the bulk of the clan escaped and in 1745 could marshal 130 able-bodied men in the field.

Reverting to John, chief of clan Donald, he, with the peculiar genius of his family for siding with the losers, supported the later English nominee to the Scottish throne, Edward Baliol, and when Baliol was ignominiously chased out of Scotland, John lost much of his land. However, he was pardoned by King David II, not so much out of clemency as for fear of discontenting his powerful clan, both MacDonald and MacRorie being in possession of vast areas. About this time, 1344, originated the branch MacIan, or MacDonald, of Ardna-murchan, which is thought to have become extinct 300 years ago although a family named MacRain now claims the representation.

John, chief of the clan Donald, styled himself Lord of the Isles after 1346, when he succeeded to the representation of the MacRorie branch. He married twice, having put away his first wife, Amy, to make a royal marriage with Margaret, daughter of Robert, the 7th High Steward of Scotland. The Steward eventually became King Robert II, first of the House of Stuart, and by arrangement between him and John Mac-Donald, the chiefship of the clan and the Lordship of the Isles were made to descend to the sons of John's second marriage. John, Lord of the Isles, died in 1380 and was succeeded by his son, Donald, who was in conflict with the infamous Regent of Scotland, the Duke of Albany, who had murdered the heir to the throne. In consequence, Donald over-ran the northern Highlands and there occurred the great battle of the 'Red' Harlaw in 1411, fought between Donald and his Highlanders and a small body of armoured chivalry fifteen miles from Aberdeen. The battle was drawn, but as the Highlanders retreated it is regarded as a Lowland victory. It was the last great trial of strength between the Gaelic and the Saxon elements in Scotland.

It was this battle of Harlaw which Sir Walter Scott mentioned in his novel *The Antiquary*. He describes how 200 knights set out and,

'They hadna ridden a mile, a mile,
A mile but barely ten,
When Donald came branking down the brae,
Wi twenty thousand men.
Their tartans they were waving wide,
Their glaives were glancing clear,
The pibrochs rung frae side to side
Would deafen ye to hear.'

Donald had been in alliance with Scotland's mortal enemy, the English king, Henry IV. This pointed to a dangerous tendency which culminated in 1462 when Donald's grandson, John, made a treaty with Edward IV of England whereby all Scotland was to be partitioned between the Lord of the Isles, the Earl of Douglas, and others and to be held in vassalage of the English Crown. In prosecution of this treaty various rebellions were raised and Inverness was captured, but the government suppressed the rebels. John, Lord of the Isles, was for a time restored to his earldom of Ross, but after repeated troubles caused by his nephew, Alexander, and his bastard son, Angus, the titles and possessions of the Lord of the Isles were declared in 1493 to be forfeited to the Crown.

Troubled and disturbed times followed, and Donald Dubb, the son of Angus mentioned above and grandson of John, the last Lord of the Isles, made several attempts to restore the independence of his house. Donald Dubb had been kidnapped as an infant and held captive during most of his life by Argyll, head of the Campbells, the sworn foes of the MacDonalds, but in the intervals when he was able to escape, Dubb led several fierce risings against the King of Scots. In the last and most serious of these, he had 4,000 picked fighting men with 160 galleys and was in alliance with King Henry VIII of England. This was in 1545, but Donald Dubb died in the rebellion and from then on the cause of the MacDonalds declined. The last Lord of the Isles had died in 1498, and after that the main branches became, in effect, separate clans. They acknowledged the Scots king, and indeed gave an allegiance to the royal line of Stuart at least as whole-hearted as ever they had bestowed upon their chiefs. The great poverty prevailing in the Highlands led such branches of MacDonald as those of Keppoch and Glencoe to raid their Lowland neighbours' cattle, but so long as a Stuart king reigned there were no more rebellions.

The fall of the ancient Lordship of the Isles meant the end of a Gaelic culture, for at their courts the old poems had been recited, the old airs played, and the tribal culture of the Gaels had flourished without the assistance of later civilizations. Before leaving this part of the subject,

U

it is well to recall the solemn ceremony whereby the kings, or Lords of the Isles, were installed. The Bishop of the Isles was present at the ceremony, with the chieftains of all the principal families. The king to be installed took his stand upon a large square stone, in which was graven a footprint to show that he would follow in the steps of his predecessors. In token of his integrity of heart, he wore white raiment and received at first a white wand in token that he ruled, not as a tyrant, but as father of his people; he then received his father's sword as a symbol of his duty to defend them. Mass was celebrated, and afterwards the new Lord of the Isles gave his people a feast, which lasted for a week. The Lord had his council of sixteen in Islay, and when he delivered lands to his vassals it was done with all due ceremony, the recipients kneeling before their chief and swearing to 'maintain, defend and support thee, as I wish the Lord in my need to help me.'

After the last male Stuart—James VII of Scotland and James II of England—had left the throne in 1688, the Scottish Highlands continued in a state of semi-independence. The Highland chiefs gave a loose allegiance to the British government and submitted to some measure of control, but they were still able under their old feudal jurisdiction to call out in rebellion hundreds of armed followers, and still liable to indulge their ancient practice of raiding the Lowlanders' cattle. In the three periods of trouble in 1689, 1715 and 1745, the MacDonalds were always to the fore. In 1689 they took part in the wild charge at the pass of Killiecrankie which destroyed the army of William III led by General Mackay. Afterwards, as already described, one branch of the clan, MacDonald of Glencoe, was marked out for brutal and cold-blooded destruction. In 1715 the MacDonalds were in the Jacobite army at Sheriffmuir, but the rising collapsed.

In 1745 the last attempt of the exiled Stuarts saw Bonnie Prince Charlie land in Moidart with seven men. He was soon provided with a bodyguard of the brave MacDonalds of Clanranald, and with this as a nucleus, began his effort to reconquer three kingdoms. That design was ruined on 16 April 1746 on Culloden Moor. The three MacDonald regiments of Glengarry, Keppoch, and Clanranald were stationed on the left wing of the Jacobite army, despite their plea that since the battle of Bannockburn in 1314 they had always stood on the right wing. They therefore refused to charge, and when one of their chiefs, the venerable Keppoch, advanced almost alone and was shot down, he exclaimed as he fell, 'My God, have my children forsaken me?' After exchanging a few rounds of musketry with the British troops, the MacDonalds marched off the field with colours flying and pipes playing.

Whatever the truth of this story, it is a fact that the Prince owed his safety after the battle to a lady of the clan, Flora MacDonald, the daughter of MacDonald of Milton in South Uist, and the stepdaughter of MacDonald of Armdale in Skye. With the aid of this lady and of Lady Clanranald, the Prince was smuggled across to Skye disguised as Flora's maid, much as his collateral ancestor, Charles II, had travelled after Worcester as Jane Lane's servant. The 'Skye Boat Song' commemorates this incident in the well-known lines:

> 'Speed bonny boat like a bird on the wing!
> Onward! the sailors cry,
> Carry the lad that is born to the King,
> Over the sea to Skye.'

The Prince was taken to the house of Sir Alexander MacDonald of Sleat, by whose wife he was further helped to safety. And all this while a reward of £30,000 was being offered by the government for the Prince's capture; a sum which would have been wealth untold to the poor Highlanders but which, in their loyalty, presented no temptation to them. Flora MacDonald married Allan MacDonald of Kingsburgh and they, like many others of the clan, emigrated to the American colonies where they fought for Britain in the American War of Independence. Since then, MacDonalds have fought in every war in which the British Empire has been engaged and have built an enduring monument to their valour.

The present chief of the names and arms of MacDonald is Lord Mac-Donald, who is a baron of the Irish peerage, his title having been created in 1776. By a decree of the Lyon Court on 1 May 1947, he was granted the undifferenced ancient arms of MacDonald of MacDonald, as inheritor of the feudal barony of MacDonald. Lord MacDonald is a member of the order of the British Empire, has been Lord Lieutenant of Inverness-shire and served in the Second World War. He descends from Somerled's son, Reginald, through the MacDonalds of Sleat. The present and 25th chief of Sleat is Sir Ian Godfrey Bosville MacDonald, who is the 17th baronet in a Scottish baronetcy creation of 1625. Lord Mac-Donald and Sir Ian are cousins, for both descend from the marriage of the 3rd Lord MacDonald. Sir Ian's progenitor was illegitimate according to the technicalities of English and Irish peerage law, but legitimate under Scottish law. He therefore succeeded to the estates of Bosville of Thorpe, his maternal grandfather, while the Irish barony of MacDonald passed to his younger brother, Godfrey, 4th Lord MacDonald. The present baronet's great-grandfather secured a decree of legitimacy in the Court of Session in 1910, and so inherited the Scottish baronetcy.

Other existing branches of the clan with their chiefs may be noted here. James Alexander Ranald MacDonald of Balranald, DL and JP, and Honorary Sheriff for Inverness-shire, descends from the MacDonalds of Sleat through Donald Herraich MacDonald of Griminish, who possessed Balranald in North Uist. Of this Donald a curious story is told. He was engaged by his natural brother Gillespie Dubb in a jumping competition in his hall and an accomplice concealed above contrived to drop a noose over his head as he jumped. Donald was rendered helpless and Gillespie was able to murder him by running a red-hot spit through his body.

William Malcolm Bell of Rammerscales, Dumfrieshire, JP, BSc, FRSA, who served in the First World War with the Canadian Engineers, descends from Allan MacDonald, 9th chief of Clanranald, through Donald MacDonald. The latter was a MacDonald Highlander at the battle of Killiecrankie and his claymore is still preserved by the family.

John Lachlan MacDonald of Tote in the Isle of Skye, formerly a major in Lovat's Scouts, descends from Charles MacDonald who, in the 1745 rising, led 150 men to Bonnie Prince Charlie's standard and fought through all the campaign.

John Maxwell MacDonald of Largie in Argyllshire, who served in the 1939-45 war with the Argyll and Sutherland Highlanders, descends from John, Lord of the Isles, son of Angus Og, of Bannockburn. Under his genealogy in *Burke's Landed Gentry* comes the history of the Mac-Donalds of Clanranald and of Keppoch. The MacDonnells of Glengarry also descend from the same John, Lord of the Isles, and the present and 22nd chief of the MacDonalds is Wing Commander Aeneas Ranald Donald MacDonald, DFC.

The Earls of Antrim descend from the Lords of the Isles, their ancestor being John, second son of John, Lord of the Isles, who married as his second wife the Princess Margaret Stuart.

Notes

1, page 16. On the subject of Hitler's ancestry, there is a deeply interesting account in the book: *Der Fuehrer: Hitler's Rise to Power*, by Konrad Heider (English edition, 1967). Heider writes: 'There are Jewish Hitlers, though the name is rather rare. This has led to a search for a Jewish strain in Adolph Hitler. There is no proof, however; all the facts and internal evidence at our disposal argue against the idea.' (p 36). Hitler's father, Alois, was the illegitimate son of a poor peasant girl, one Maria Anne Schicklgruber. It is argued that the father was Johann Georg Heidler, but another view is that it was his brother, Johann von Nepomuk Hitler. On this Konrad Heiden remarks: 'But there is one curious fact which cannot be argued away: the later National Socialist racial legislation requires everyone aspiring to pass as an Aryan to provide four Aryan grandparents; if brought before strict judges, Adolf Hitler might have difficulty proving the identity of his paternal grandfather.' A genealogical chart in the book shows what Heiden calls 'family relations so restricted as to border on incest'.

Thus once more genealogy comes in to explain matters of profound importance; the physical and psychological composition of the man whom Winston Churchill described as a 'maniac of genius'. Genealogy also illumines the character of many of the most ferocious and dangerous nationalist leaders. They come, as their ancestry shows, from the periphery of a great nation. Hitler was an Austrian; Stalin a Georgian; De Valera is not by any means purely Irish, nor were many of the leaders in the Irish revolt against England in 1916-21. Further back in history, Napoleon was a Corsican who spoke French with an Italian accent; Cromwell was in the male line of Welsh origin, and Disraeli of Italian Jewish stock.

2, page 17. When the Norman Conquest had been concluded and the land of England divided among William's followers, there were recorded in the Domesday Book (1086) about 180-200 great tenants who held their lands direct from the Crown. As a general rule, their property was split up and divided; although considerable in the aggregate, it did not allow for an easy mobilisation of vassals in rebellion against the throne. With the passage of 400 years the process of amalgamation had, by the time of the warring Roses, produced a far smaller baronage. The great nobles had followed the principles of business tycoons in the present day and had formed mergers, so that their possessions were increased by marriage of heirs and by the fact that a husband could hold an earldom or barony in right of his wife. Thus Richard Neville, the famous Kingmaker, and 'Last of the Barons', held two earldoms by right of his marriage. The Bohuns, who were hereditary High Constables of England, were Earls of Hereford, of Essex and of Northampton. In this way the number of the barons decreased while their revenues and powers increased. In the close nexus of relationships, many of them were cousins of the sovereign, and the majority related to each other. As the powers of the nobles grew, their smaller numbers rendered them much more vulnerable if they fell out with the sovereign and were worsted in battle. This was proved when the Tudor dynasty supplanted the Plantaganet. Many of the older nobility perished in battle or on the scaffold, but not a majority of them. A new race of nobles dates from the Tudor period, but of the older peerage, many survived the Wars of the Roses only to be destroyed in intrigues and manufactured cases of alleged high treason under the first Tudor sovereigns. A full account of this process is given in my book, *The Story of the Peerage*, Appendix 2.

3, page 21. Hebrew Genealogies. The Bible abounds in genealogies. A little more than 100 years ago a world history could be written by a distinguished scholar, Philip Smith, brother of Sir William Smith, in which the subtitle of the first volume was: 'Ancient History: From the creation of the world to the accession of Philip of Macedon.' In this, the starting date of the narrative is the same as that still given in many of our Bibles, namely 4004 BC. The literal acceptance of the Old Testament is assumed, and the genealogies are taken as completely correct. There are some ten genealogies in the Book of Genesis and few of the other historical books are without them; they occupy a good deal of space in Numbers and 1st Chronicles. In the New Testament, genealogies are used only to describe the descent of Christ. In St Matthew's Gospel, forty-two generations are given as covering the period from Abraham to Christ. This gives a period of some 1,300 years allowing, as modern genealogists do, thirty years to a generation, or 1,700 years if, like the old Greek historians, we reckon forty years to a generation. We must also allow for the greater than average age of the patriarchs, Abraham, Isaac and Jacob, with whom this genealogy begins.

Making these reservations it can be seen that forty-two generations would bridge the period from the birth of Christ to the age of Abraham, circa 1850 BC (by the Usherite chronology). This would also imply that there were only ten generations between Judah and David, covering a period of some 700 years. In St Luke's Gospel, a total of seventy-five generations cover the whole period of 4,000 years between Adam 'which was the son of God' and Christ. No doubt in the mind of Biblical writers, the period of some 2,200 years from Adam to Abraham was adequately covered by some thirty generations owing to the much greater longevity of persons in the earlier generations.

These Biblical genealogies have fared badly at the hands of the German Higher Critics. After a very long period in which the Bible was accepted as the veritable Word of God, the only book in the human library written by God not man, we have during the last 100 years arrived at a reaction which often shows very little evidence of common sense. Few books of the Bible, according to these pontificating countrymen of Luther, were written by the men whose names they bear but, as Hilaire Belloc remarked, by other men of the same names. Not unnaturally, these critics have found in the names in many of the genealogies, not individuals but tribes. The names of the twelve sons of Jacob are looked upon as tribal names and not as those of individuals, forgetting that even the largest tribe must begin at some time with an individual or a few individuals. Another way of regarding the names in the Biblical genealogies is to see individual names as eponymous, that is as being of persons who gave their names to a people, place or institution. This is only a more involved way of saying the same thing as in the Scriptural narratives.

A good analogy is found in the clans (really tribes) of the Scottish Highlands. The chief has his line of descent from the founder or eponym of the clan, and this pedigree can be substantiated; but not all those who bear the name are necessarily descended from the eponym. This was true in the case of Israel, but there is no need to exercise undue scepticism as to the possibility of the sons of Jacob being progenitors of the two million Israelites who, 400 years later, left Egypt to settle in Palestine. A modern parallel to the growth of a people from a very small nucleus is provided in the history of the thirteen American colonies which became the USA. Many family genealogies in great detail have been kept showing how numerous are the descendants in 300 years of a single pair. For example, William Learned came from Bermondsey, Surrey, England, to Massachusetts Bay Colony in 1630. From him have come more than 4,000 direct and traced descendants (*The Learned Family in America, 1630-1967*, by Mrs Eugenia Learned James.)

4, page 28. *A propos* of the Japanese belief in the divine origin of their nation, the story goes that one of the Japanese learned in conversation with an American scholar conceded that the Darwinian theory might be accurate enough for the Americans and other inferior races, but added with exquisite politeness that it could not apply to the Japanese who knew their biological origin. The best rider to this little story is the fact that the Chinese name of Japan was for long, 'The Kingdom of the Monkey Men'.

5, page 53. To this day the prelates of the Established Church of England are required to do homage to the Sovereign for the temporalities attached to their sees. When Queen Elizabeth II was crowned, she received the homage of the peers. First of these was the Archbishop of Canterbury who, on his knees, swore that he would be true and faithful to the Sovereign, ending: 'And I will do, and truly acknowledge, the service of the lands which I claim to hold of you, as in right of the Church. So help me God.' Nowhere else in the world does this feudal rite survive. After the archbishop came the royal dukes to render homage, headed by the Duke of Edinburgh. He said, 'I, Philip, Duke of Edinburgh, do become your liege man of life and limb, and of earthly worship; and faith and truth I will bear unto you, to live and die, against all manner of folks. So help me God.' The directions are that the Duke takes off his coronet, the other royal dukes (in this case the Duke of Gloucester only) taking off their coronets likewise, kneeling and repeating the words of homage after Prince Philip. Then, each duke touches the crown on the Queen's head. The non-royal dukes, the marquesses, the earls, viscounts and barons then perform the same ritual, the first in each degree kneeling before the Queen while the rest follow him in his oath of fealty.

6, page 61. The greatest authority on the subject of the Common Law, the celebrated Sir Edward Coke, Chief Justice in the reign of James I and ancestor of the Earls of Leicester, says of Grand Serjeanty, that 'tenure by Grand Serjeanty is, where a man holds his lands or tenements of our Sovereign Lord the King by such services as he ought to do in his proper person to the King as to carry the banner of the King or his lance, or to lead his army, or to be his Marshall, or to carry his sword before him at his Coronation, or to be his Sewer at his Coronation, or his Carver, or his Butler, or to be one of his Chamberlains of the receipt of his Exchequer, or to do other like services' (*Coke upon Littleton*, book 2, ch 8, s 153).

When the long reign of Queen Victoria ended, there was no one who could remember what manner of claims had been put forward at her coronation. The customary procedure is for a Court of Claims to be appointed by the new sovereign. This will have the Lord Chancellor as president, and will naturally include the Lord Chamberlain, the hereditary Earl Marshal (the Duke of Norfolk), and several eminent judges. When the court sat in 1901 in preparation for the coronation of Victoria's son and successor, Edward VII, 'it was stated that no written precedents were known to exist, and that if any minutes of the proceedings of previous Courts had ever been taken, beyond the "Coronation Rolls", they were retained by the person who took them, and had never found their way into any of the public offices. It was probable therefore that the procedure would be largely regulated by the Court itself, at its first sitting.' (*Coronation*

Claims, 1910, p 25, by Sir Gerald Woods Wollaston, followed by a small supplement in 1936).

The most interesting point about this truly medieval survival is that it persisted right up to 1952-53, for the coronation of Elizabeth II. The court sat in a sombre government chamber in Downing Street and its proceedings were enlivened by the oddity of some of the petitions. One petitioner, who did not appear, claimed to be ruler of an independent principality bordering upon the river Shannon in Ireland. In the case of the manor of Worksop, the holder claimed the right to provide a glove for the sovereign's right hand. In 1902 and 1911 (coronations of Edward VII and of George V) the Duke of Newcastle had been allowed this privilege, but vast political and social changes had occurred since then. The coal mines had been nationalised and the National Coal Board now owned the manor of Worksop. Would the Board claim the right to send a representative with the glove for Her Majesty to Westminster Abbey? How this would have been settled, we do not know, as the National Coal Board decided to remain content with its own flag and the coat of arms for which it had petitioned the Earl Marshal on its establishment, and did not venture further into medievalism.

One of the most interesting of the claims to be found in the Coronation Rolls is that of the Dymokes of Scrivelsby in Lincolnshire, a still existing family which descends through female lines from Roger Marmion, a Norman lord of Scrivelsby, 850 years ago. For over 600 years, the Dymokes (as successors to the Marmions, to whom the privilege was granted), have been the Champions of England. They held, and hold, their lands on Grand Serjeanty, of appearing, armed head to foot in full armour and mounted on a steed, in Westminster Hall at the coronation banquet. There it is their duty to throw down a gauntlet to all and sundry who should presume to challenge the sovereign's right to the throne, and to do battle with any such. The last occasion when this colourful ceremony was carried out was on 29 July 1821, at the coronation banquet of George IV, when Sir Henry Dymoke rode a horse, borrowed from Astley's Circus, into Westminster Hall. At the next coronation, of William IV in 1832, there was no banquet, as one of the British government's periodical economy drives was in progress—the King himself even suggested doing without a coronation! Again in 1838, when Victoria was crowned, there was no banquet, for the somewhat more creditable reason that the function was hardly suitable for a girl of eighteen. The custom, once broken, has never been resumed and, instead, the Dymoke of the day carries the standard of England at the coronation. He has no knighthood or other title save the proud distinction of being 'The Honourable the Queen's Champion and Standard Bearer of England'. His motto is, *Pro rege Dimico*. 'I fight for the Sovereign', and the Dymoke badge is, appropriately, a sword.

To turn from this glittering display of chivalry to the dry records of the Rolls series may seem an anti-climax, but it is from such apparently dry-as-dust materials that family histories are traced and the spark of family romance and glamour is kindled. In proof of this let us look at a case history parallel in one respect to the Dymokes'—that of the family of Scrymgeour-Wedderburn. The head of this line is the Earl of Dundee who, besides three other peerages, has also the style of Hereditary Royal Standard Bearer of Scotland and Constable for Dundee. As such, the earl and his predecessors have borne the Scottish royal standard at the coronation of many monarchs. Behind all the glamour and magnificence of the ancient title there is a story of deprivation and star-crossed fortunes which would have been dismissed as too impossible even in fiction had a novelist written the tale. In 1298, the great Scottish patriot, Sir William Wallace, granted the lands of Dudhope (pronounced 'Durrop') and the Constableship of Dundee to Sir Alexander Scrymgeour in return for his services as standard bearer. The legend in the family makes the Scrymgeours to have become hereditary standard bearers in the time of Alexander III (died 1285), because the previous standard bearer, Bannerman, had refused to accompany the king in an expedition across the river Spey. In passing, the Bannermans have not even now forgotten their ancient honour and still recall it in their pedigrees. The head of the Bannermans is a baronet and the main charge in the coat of arms is a banner displayed with, in the top right-hand corner, the badge of Scotland. Such is the tenacity of Scottish tradition and family pride.

Sir Alexander Scrymgeour's son carried the royal standard at the battle of Bannockburn in 1314, and from then on the heads of the family in each succeeding generation had the same privilege. Peerages were conferred— the Viscounty of Dudhope in 1641, and the Earldom of Dundee in 1660. So far, it is the common success story of a British family going up through the different social and titled grades. Then, with the death of the first earl in 1668, the family misfortunes began. The earl had had the ill luck to incur the hatred of the most powerful man in Scotland, the Duke of Lauderdale, who possessed all the ingredients of the villain in popular novels, and infinitely more skill and success. He was a great favourite of Charles II, and used his influence to deprive the Scrymgeour-Wedderburn (the latter an additional surname acquired on a marriage) heir of both titles and land. He even went to the extent of destroying their patent of nobility so that the mode of descent of the peerages should not be known. Thus the unfortunate family was left for nearly 300 years until, in 1952, the Committee of Privileges of the House of Lords accepted Henry James Scrymgeour-Wedderburn as having made out his claim to the titles, honours and dignities of Viscount Dudhope and Lord Scrymgeour in the peerage of Scotland.

The following year, on 18 May 1953, just two weeks before the coronation of Elizabeth II, the committee allowed the claims to the earldom of

Dundee, and the barony of Inverkeithing. The claimant was told that he could prepare himself for the coronation as an earl. The injustice of 300 years was put right but, in the peerage books, the Earls of Dundee from the 2nd to the 10th appear as *de jure*, not *de facto*, having been kept out of their peerage titles by the machinations of the old Duke of Lauderdale. The family estates were lost, and even the privilege of hereditary standard bearer was in danger for, as late as 1902, the Earl of Lauderdale (the dukedom had become extinct) was still claiming even that right. Only patient research in documents and records regained for the family its rightful honours.

7, page 62. Serfdom. In the course of three centuries from the Norman Conquest the bonds of serfdom began to be loosened. The Black Death in 1348 rendered labour scarce and it became much more difficult to enforce permanency on a manor. The Peasants' Revolts in 1381 and 1450, although they were put down, gave warning of the dangers of trying to maintain serfdom. It had died out by the end of the fifteenth century and the copyholder long before that time could no longer be equated with a villein. Peasantry from the thirteenth century onward were not the downtrodden creatures known in France. Copyholders were often in quite good financial positions, corresponding to our leaseholders.

These facts have considerable bearing on the tracing of pedigrees. Someone has to be descended from the serfs, and perhaps most people do so descend, though blood of peer and peasant is greatly mixed in England. One of the first principles in genealogical research is never to be ashamed, or for that matter unduly proud, of anything one finds in one's pedigree. The right attitude is that shown in the family history of the Elmhirsts of Elmhirst, whose seat is near Barnsley in Yorkshire. This family starts its pedigree with Robert of Elmhirst, who was born about 1300 and who lived as a serf on the lands which his descendants still own. He died about 1350 and, going down the pedigree after him, we can see how his descendants became first copyholders and then freeholders, purchasing the lands where their ancestors had toiled. There was not always such a poetically appropriate and happy ending, but there was a greater security of tenure than many people imagine.

In Bedfordshire, for instance, careful research has shown short pedigrees for villeins of 100-150 years, as much as many peers' families can show in modern England. The following example is instructive: 'Against this general background of tenures and obligations the history of some of the families can be followed. Among the bond tenants, William Algor constantly appeared as a surety for his neighbours. In 1290 both he and Douce, his mother, were presented (ie, brought before the manorial court) for subletting land in Tebworth. . . . He had a son, Reginald, and probably two others, John and Simon, for he was pledge for the last named when Simon acknowledged in court that he was a bondman. . . . Eleven years later Simon paid 6d for many defaults of his services. In 1303 he had given 20s fine to marry Lucy, widow of William Yuggeleis, and to take over the third of a virgate (an old English measure of surface, from Latin *virga*, a rod), which she held as dower. This family did not rid itself of its servile status during the century and is represented in the 1376 rental by John and Agnes Algor, both bond tenants.' (Publications of the Bedfordshire Historical Record Society, vol 28, Court Roll of Chalgrave Manor, 1278-1313. Ed by Marian K. Dale, p 27, 1950). In the same source, the pedigree of the Poleyn family is traceable from 1213 to 1376.

Quite a number of villein pedigrees have been carried back through the manorial records to the fifteenth century and even 200 years earlier, as with the Elmhirsts. The importance of this class of record having been stressed, it is important to the searcher to know where to find the manorial rolls. Unfortunately they were never gathered into a central depository and are much dispersed. Some have found their way to the British Museum, and other libraries. Sometimes county libraries have collections of valuable documents of this nature; often they can be found in the County Record Office, in the county capital. The best course for the inquirer is to consult the county public library of the area in which he is interested and obtain guidance there.

8, page 72. The quality of pedigrees certified by heralds. 'The certifications of the kings of arms for the most part are liable to error. In this respect the priest, Don Manteo Escagedo Salmon, says, "The ancient kings of arms (there are some hundreds of volumes in the manuscript section of the National Library) tended more to the stupid flattery of those with whose drafts they were commissioned (for whom they solicited magnificent parchments as empty of documentation as they were inflated with legends) rather than to the conscientious and documented investigation of their work." ' This opinion, which is quoted in *De Genealogia y Heraldica* by Lucas de Palacio, p 16, 1946, as applicable to the Spanish genealogies, is an instructive parallel to the even more vitriolic views expressed by the great English genealogical scholar, John Horace Round. In the very valuable but long-defunct quarterly, *The Ancestor*, vol 3, p 34, 1902, Round wrote of a pedigree of the Lambert family which had been sealed and certified by the Kings of Arms in the seventeenth century, 'But what their witness really proves is the worthlessness of such authority. When the three Kings and Somerset Herald attested the Lambert pedigree, it was in the days when the British Solomon (ie, King James I) rejoiced in his descent from "Brute the most noble founder of the Britains" even as his predecessor had exulted in her heraldic pedigree from Adam. What have heralds to do with history? What with facts? Among their dead legends they linger still.' It is not suggested that a forged pedigree would now be accepted, attested and sealed by three Kings of Arms and a Herald, but the curious anomaly remains that in an English court of law, a pedigree certified by the College of Arms could be accepted as a legally admissible document whereas the learned paper which destructively criticises the pedigree could not be put in as evidence because it would not be an official document.

9, page 140. Although Luxembourg is a small country this does not mean that settlers have not emigrated from it. I may mention M. Emile Erpelding of 23 rue de Rochefort, Beggen, Luxembourg, who has traced his own genealogy to 1650 and is experienced in the problems of overseas enquirers.

10, page 141. On one occasion an enquirer came to me asking about the possibility of discovering the coat of arms of his Russian grandfather, who had occupied an official position which, in Tzarist days, entitled the holder to armorial bearings. It was quite impossible to get from the Soviet authorities anything beyond a reply at the Embassy in London that the enquiry had been forwarded to Moscow. This is, in my experience, by no means an isolated case.

11, page 183. A ludicrous instance of the lack of heraldic knowledge in the very place where one would expect to find it, occurred a few years back—in Buckingham Palace. The arms of the Duke of Edinburgh were being processed by the College of Arms. One of the supporters of the shield was described as a Hercules. I had to arrange the drawing of the arms for inclusion in *Burke's Peerage* and, being pushed for time, I was forced to get my own artists to make the drawing, instead of having a sketch from the college. When I was preparing the next edition of the work I was told by the Palace authorities that the illustration as shown in the text was incorrect. On asking for specific details, I was informed that they did not understand heraldry and that the matter rested with the college. It turned out that my drawing was heraldically correct, but had not been made by the proper trade union (I may mention that there can be as many fashions in heraldic drawings as there are heraldic centuries, but all can be correct). The Queen is the Fountain of Honour, which means that she grants all titles, honours, and coats of arms, yet the gentlemen of her household did not know the elementary facts of heraldry—the very science of gentility! The result of this objection was that the excellent Hercules devised by my artist—a real broad-shouldered, beetle-browed figure suitable indeed to uphold the stars—was dropped in favour of a pansy-looking creature more fitted for the shapes of Carnaby Street.

12, page 193. A very useful study of the *mon* has been made by Dr H. Carroll Parish, who has set out his conclusions in a paper, entitled, 'The Japanese Family Badge or House Mark' in *The Augustan* (vol 11, no 1, Jan-

Feb 1968), the journal of the Augustan Society Inc, of 18002 Faysmith Avenue, Torrance, California, 90504, USA. Dr Parish shows that the *mon* is seen as approximating to different heraldic terms according to the viewpoint of various western nations. Thus some of the books prepared on the subject by Japanese scholars and rendered into English refer to Japanese crests which English heralds generally reject as a translation of the word *mon*. In Germany the latter has been translated as *wappen*, the German word for a coat of arms. This the *mon* most certainly is not. The better translation is 'family badge', or 'heraldic badge' or, 'house mark'. Several similarities exist between Japanese and European heraldry. Both developed in the twelfth century, but as body armour of the very elaborate western kind was not used in Japan, the initial use of the *mon* was on the ornate clothes of the Japanese noblemen, and later in a simple form on the standards and tents of warriors in the Kamakura period (1185-1338). Its latter use was for the same reason as in Europe, to differentiate between one clan and another. Then, also as in the west, with the passing of 400 years the *mon* became much more stylised, with the necessity of differencing patterns, and the use of the devices spread to many other classes apart from nobles and warriors, such as merchants, priests and scholars.

No central body such as the English College of Arms existed in Japan, but in 1642 the Shogun Iyemitsu ordered all the warrior families to register their *mon*, and not to vary them thereafter. It also appears as a considerable difference from the western system that a family could and did possess more than one *mon*, there being a fixed *mon* (*jomon*) worn on important official functions, and a device known as the *kayemon* which was used on ordinary occasions. The retainers wore the *jomon* on their armour, much as in medieval Europe. From the seventeenth century onward, the *mon* became used by all manner of persons, although the devices of the great lords were of course restricted to them. In the heavily feudal society which existed for 200 years of the period of exclusion, when Japan was a forbidden country to Europeans, it would probably have been a matter of punishment by death for one of the lower classes to have used the *mon* borne by a samurai.

Of the characters of the *mon*, Dr Parish remarks: 'Of some 500 prominent and aristocratic Japanese families mentioned in an 1880 publication listing 3,040 *mon*, one-half are from the vegetable kingdom, one-fourth are artificial objects and one-fourth are geometrical forms. No fish are listed and only a few animals, birds, reptiles or insects are included. In contrast, western charges are mostly from the animal kingdom and include only ten vegetables. The Japanese concentration on the vegetable kingdom is probably the result of the influence of Buddhism which placed a taboo on the hunting and raising of animals for food and the popularity of flowers as objects of admiration and study as far back as the Nara period.'

There is also a similarity between Japanese and Scottish heraldry in so far as the law of primogeniture in Japan gave the eldest son jurisdiction over the whole family. Hence what we should call the cadet branches were bound to adopt *mon* of their own, distinct from that of the head of the clan. Finally, in the modern period when Japan changed from a feudal to an up to date country in fifty years, all Japanese were required to take family names, and a *mon* usually went with a surname. This would correspond to the completely erroneous view, widely held among people of British descent—that every surname has a crest or coat of arms.

13, page 223. The Queen's own title. The title of the Queen is: Elizabeth II, by the Grace of God, of the United Kingdom of Great Britain and Northern Ireland, and of her other realms and territories, Queen, Head of the Commonwealth, Defender of the Faith. This title is at once the product of historical evolution and the result of political developments in the twentieth century. From 1340 until as late as 1800 the British sovereign styled himself King of France, though the claim was only likely to have become realistic in the fifteenth century. English kings were called Lords of Ireland until Henry VIII took, by Act of Parliament, the title of King of Ireland. Henry VIII was given by the Pope the title of *Fidei Defensor*, (Defender of the Faith), because of the book he wrote against the Protestant, Martin Luther. Later, when Henry broke with Rome over the subject of his divorce from his first wife, the Pope revoked the title, but Henry had it regranted by his parliament. The present Queen's father bore the title of Emperor of India until 1947, his predecessors having also borne it from 1877 when the Prime Minister, Benjamin Disraeli later Earl of Beaconsfield, had it granted to Queen Victoria by Act of Parliament. The term 'Head of the Commonwealth' is as easy to define as the Commonwealth itself. The subject of the royal titles over the ages needs to be studied in greater detail than space here permits. The reader is referred to the royal lineage as it appears in the several editions of *Burke's Peerage*, also to my own work, now out of print but available at second-hand, *Ramshackledom, A Critical Appraisal of the Establishment*, (1962), particularly Appendix I, The Growth of the Imperial Idea.

The title of Prince of Wales is not that of a peerage nor of an office, but simply the style borne by the eldest son of the sovereign, when and only when the sovereign chooses to bestow it upon him. On the accession of the sovereign, his or her eldest son becomes Duke of Cornwall, under a charter of Edward III, 1337. Then, when the sovereign wishes, the title of Prince of Wales is granted to the Duke of Cornwall. The present Prince of Wales was so created in July 1958. The full list of the titles of the Prince is: His Royal Highness, Prince Charles Philip Arthur George, Prince of Wales and Earl of Chester, (this always goes with the princedom of Wales), Duke of Cornwall, Duke of Rothesay, Earl of Carrick, and Baron of Renfrew, Lord of the Isles and Great Steward of Scotland. The last five titles are of Scottish derivation, as the Crowns of England and Scotland were united in 1603. The title of Prince of Wales originated after King Edward I of England had conquered Wales in 1284. The first Prince of Wales was his son, created 1301, who became Edward II. There have been twenty-one Princes of Wales.

The surname of the British royal house is Windsor, and was adopted by royal proclamation in 1917. The royal family did not have a surname before that date as they were older than the custom of adoption of surnames. They were usually mentioned in history books as the House of Guelph (Welf), or more often as of Hanover; sometimes of Saxe Coburg Gotha, after the marriage of Queen Victoria with Prince Albert of Saxe Coburg. The marriage of Elizabeth II with Prince Philip Mountbatten did not result in the creation of a House of Mountbatten. By a proclamation of 9 April 1952, the Queen declared that she and her descendants would bear the surname of Windsor. A slight modification of this ruling was made by the Queen in 1960 when she decided that some of her remoter descendants should bear the name Mountbatten-Windsor, the first time that a hyphenated surname has appeared in the royal family. The styles of the other members of the royal family are governed by letters patent of 30 October 1917 from George V. Under these, the children of the sovereign and the children of his/her sons, and the eldest living son of the eldest son of the Prince of Wales, are HRH and Prince. The other great-grand-children of the sovereign in the male line are not princes but bear the styles of the children of dukes, while their children have no titles. Thus there can be Mr and Miss Windsor. It is well known that George VI refused the title of Her Royal Highness to the Duchess of Windsor.

Glossary of
Heraldic Terms in common use

Abased: When an ordinary is placed below its usual position.

Accosted: Placed side by side.

Accrued: Come to maturity.

Achievement: A full coat of arms.

Acorned: Bearing acorns (applied to an oak tree).

Addorsed: Placed back to back.

Affrontée: Full-faced.

Agnus Dei: (Lamb of God), the Paschal Lamb (Christ) carrying a cross, and with a halo round the head.

Ailé or aislé: Winged.

Alant: A mastiff with short ears.

Allerion: An eagle without beak or feet.

Ambulant: Walking, (as in passant).

Annulet: A ring, a mark of cadency.

Antique Crown: See Eastern Crown.

Appaumé: The hand open, presenting the palm.

Argent: Silver or white.

Armed: A term applied to the horns, hoofs, beaks and talons of an animal when they differ from the colour of the rest of the body.

Arrondie: Circular or rounded.

Aspersed: Sprinkled or strewed.

Attired: Of the horns of deer, when they differ from the colour of the rest of the body.

Attires: The horns of a stag or buck.

Azure: Blue.

Baillonné: When an animal holds a staff in its mouth.

Banded: Encircled with a band.

Bar: A diminutive of the fesse, and taking up one-fifth of the shield.

Barbed: A term used to describe the natural colouring of the five leaves which appear in the outside of a full blown rose.

Barnacles: An instrument used to compress the nostrils of a horse.

Baron and femme: Husband and wife.

Barrulet: Diminutive of the bar.

Barruly: Covered with ten or more barrulets.

Barry: When the field, or charge, is divided by horizontal lines.

Bars gemel: When two bars or barrulets are parallel to each other (Gemel = twin).

Base: Lower part of the shield.

Basilisk: An heraldic monster, like a wyvern with the head of a dragon at the end of its tail.

Basnet or Basinet: A helmet.

Baton: A staff or cudgel which is cut at the ends instead of reaching from one side of the shield to the other.

Battlements: See *Embattled.*

Beacon: An iron grate or basket set on a pole, and containing fire.

Beaked: As with armed, when the beak of the bird is of a different colour from the body.

Bearing: Applied to any single charge.

Belled: Said of any creature to which bells are attached.

Bend: Two lines drawn diagonally from dexter chief to sinister base.

Bendlet: A diminutive of the bend.

Bend sinister: When the bend is drawn from the sinister chief.

Bendy: The shield covered with bends.

Bezant: The ancient gold coin of the Byzantine Empire, a round flat gold piece.

Bezantée: Semée or strewn of bezants.

Billets: Oblong squares.

Billeté: Semée of billets.

Bird bolt: A small arrow with a blunted head.

Bordered: With an edge of a different tincture.

Bordure: A border on the inside of a shield and occupying one-fifth of the shield.

Botonny (or Botonnée): Applied to a cross whose arms resemble a trefoil.

Bouget: See *Water bouget.*

Bourdon: A pilgrim's staff.

Braced: Interlaced, linked together.

Brassarts: Armour for elbows and arms.

Bretessé: With battlements on both sides, one against the other.

Breys: Barnacles (qv).

Brigantine: A coat of mail.

Brimsey: A gadfly.

Brisure: A mark of cadency.

Burgonet: A steel cap.

Cabossed or *Caboshed:* When the head of an animal is shown full-faced or looking right forward, no part of the neck being seen.

Cabrée: A horse salient or on its hind feet.

Cadency: Charges in a shield or arrangements therein to denote younger members or lines of a family from the senior stock.

Cadet: A younger son or other junior member of a family.

Caduceus: A wand with two snakes entwined round it, often used to denote a man of learning or of medical attainments.

Caltrap: A ball of iron with projecting spikes meant to catch the feet of cavalry, as used by the Scots at Bannockburn.

Calvary, or *Passion Cross:* A plain cross mounted on three steps.

Canting arms, (*Armes parlantes*): In which there is a pun on the owner's name.

Canton: A division of one-third of the chief in the right-hand corner.

Cap of Maintenance: Head gear of crimson velvet turned up with ermine, used originally by the barons in Parliament.

Caparison: Trappings of a war horse.

Carbuncle: See *Escarbuncle.*

Cartouche: An oval shield.

Casque: A helmet.

Castle: Usually shown with two towers, having a wall and gateway between them; sometimes with a third tower behind the gateway, then said to be triple-towered.

Cat-a-Mountain: A wild cat shown always guardant.

Catharine wheel: An instrument of torture with iron teeth, the means of martyrdom of St Catharine.

Celestial Crown: An eastern or antique crown with a star on each point.

Centaur: A mythological creature, the upper part man, the lower part horse.

Cercellée: See *Recercellée.*

Chamber: A short piece of ordnance.

Champagne: A narrow piece cut off the base of a shield.

Chapeau: See *Cap of Maintenance.*

Chaplet: A garland of leaves and flowers.

Charge: Any figure borne on the field.

Charged: Applied to a field or bearing upon which a charge is placed.

Chaussé: Shod.

Chequy or *Checky:* A field covered with small squares of alternate tinctures like a chessboard.

Cherub: Shown as an infant's head between wings.

Chess rook: The castle used in the game of chess.

Chevron: A division occupying one-third or one-fifth of the shield, like an inverted stripe in a sergeant's badge of rank.

Chevronel: A diminutive of the chevron.

Chief: The upper part of a shield.

Chimera: A mythical figure, having a maiden's face, a lion's mane and legs, a goat's body and a dragon's tail.

Chough: See *Cornish chough*.

Cinquefoil: A herb with five leaves.

Civic Crown: A wreath of oak leaves and acorns.

Clarion or *Claricord:* By some, called the rest for a lance, but in all probability a species of musical instrument like a mouth organ.

Close: When the wings of a bird are not expanded.

Closet: A diminutive of the bar.

Cockatrice: A mythological creature with wings and legs of a fowl, and the tail of a snake.

Collared: Having a collar around the neck; also applied to a shield when ornamented with the collar or ribbon of a knightly order.

Combatant: Fighting or rampant face to face.

Compartment: The base on which a shield rests, particularly with supporters.

Componé, Compony: When a single row of rectangular pieces is made up of alternate tinctures.

Confronté: Facing each other.

Conjoined: United.

Conjoined in lure: Applied to two wings joined together with their tips downwards.

Contourné: When an animal faces the sinister side of the shield.

Corbie: A raven (cf. the well-known surname Corbett, which means raven).

Corded: A charge bound with cords.

Cornish Chough: A crow with red or yellowish beak and legs.

Coronets: Used for princes or peers.

Cotise: A diminutive of the bend, usually borne in pairs, with a charge between them.

Cotised: Placed between two cotises. On either side of a fesse or bend are described as a fesse etc cotised.

Couchant: Lying down with head uplifted.

Couché: A shield suspended by one corner from a belt.

Counter changed: Where a field is divided per bend etc, and the charges in each section are of the tincture of the field in the other section.

Counter embattled: (See *Embattled*) when the charge is marked with battlements on each side.

Counter embowed: Bent in the reverse direction.

Counter flory: A treasure flory, in which the alternate fleurs-de-lis are reversed.

Counter vair: See *Vair*, from which it differs in that the bells of the same colour are arranged base to base and point to point.

Couped: Cut off by a straight line (contrast erased), applied to the head or limbs of an animal.

Couple close: Diminutive of a chevronel, always borne in pairs.

Courant: Running.

Coward: An animal shown with its tail between its legs.

Cramp: A piece of iron, usually borne in couples and turned up at each end.

Crampons: Hooks used in building.

Crenellée: See *Embattled*.

Crest: Object shown on top of the helmet.

Crest coronet: The small crown from which a crest rises.

Crested: When the crest or comb of a cock or cockatrice is of a different tincture to the rest of the body.

Crined: When the beard or hair of an object differs in tincture from the body.

Cronel: The blunted head of a tilting spear.

Cross: Probably the most extensively used of all heraldic devices. The types generally encountered in coats of arms are shown in the illustration.

Crozier: A prelate's staff, used by archbishops, bishops, abbots etc.

Crusily: When the field is charged with crosses.

Cubit-arm: The hand and arm cut off at the elbow.

Cuisses: Armour covering thighs and knees.

Dancetté: When lines of which the teeth or indents are larger or wider than those of the line indented.

Debruised: When an ordinary such as a bend, is placed across another charge.

Dechaussé: See *Dismembered* or *Demembered*.

Decked: When the feathers of a bird are trimmed at the edges with a tincture different from the rest of the body.

Decrescent: When the moon is in its last quarter, with the horns turned towards the sinister side of the shield.

Defamed: When an animal is shown minus its tail.

Degrees: Having steps at the base, as of a cross calvary, hence degraded.

Dejected: Anything thrown down.

Demi: Half, applied to head or top unless otherwise stated.

Despectant: An animal looking down.

Dexter: Right hand, it must always be understood that a shield is supposed to be held by someone, hence the right of the shield corresponds to the viewer's left hand.

Diapered: A covering of floral-type enrichment, where the colour differs from that of the rest of the charge.

Differenced: Implies brisures or marks of cadency.

Dimidiated: Divided into two equal parts.

Disclosed: Wings expanded, of tame birds.

Dismembered, or *Demembered:* When an animal or other charge has portions severed from it, and set at a little distance from each other, yet still keeping the outline of the figure.

Displayed: Wings extended, of birds of prey.

Disponed: Arranged.

Distilling: Letting fall drops of blood.

Dormant: Sleeping (of an animal) but with the head resting on the forepaws; contrast *Couchant.*

Double queued: Having two tails.

Double tressure: One tressure within another.

Doubled: When a lambrequin is lined of a different tincture.

Dovetailed: In form of wedges.

Dragon: A mythical monster, shown as a quadruped in English heraldry.

Drawing iron: An instrument used by wiredrawers.

Ducal coronet: Really the same as *Crest coronet,* composed of four leaves all of the same height above the rim.

Eastern Crown: A band of gold from which rise pointed rays.

Eclipsed: Said of the sun when shown in red or black tincture.

Eft: A newt.

Eight foil: An eight-leaved grass.

Elevated: Of wings raised above the head.

Embattled: Battlements as of a fortress; see also *Counter embattled.*

Embowed: Bowed or bent.

Embrued: Stained with drops of blood.

Endorse: A diminutive of the pale.

Endorsed: See *Addorsed.*

Enfield: A mythological animal, with the head of a fox, legs of an eagle, body and hind legs of a greyhound, and the tail of a lion. Very rare, but the crest of the O'Kelly family.

Enfiled: When a charge is pierced by the blade of a sword or other weapon.

Engoulant: Devouring.

Engoulé: When a charge has its end in the mouth of an animal.

Engrailed: A partition line scalloped.

Enhanced: When an ordinary is placed above its usual position.

Enmanche: See *Manch,* a sleeve.

Ensigned: When a charge has another placed above, or is 'adorned' with it.

Enté: Grafted.

Enté en Pointe: A division of the shield which rises from base towards fesse point. Used in Continental heraldry.

Environed: Surrounded.

Epaulier: Armour used on the shoulder.

Equipped: A horse fully armed and provided with trappings.

Eradicated: When trees are shown torn up by the roots.

Erased: In contrast to *Couped,* means forcibly torn off the body, leaving the severed part jagged.

Erect: Upright.

Ermine: White fur with black spots.

Ermines: Black fur with white spots.

Erminois: Gold fur with black spots.

Escallop shell: The well-known badge of the pilgrims to the Holy Land or other shrines.

Escarbuncle: A charge derived from the iron bands which radiated from the boss of a shield and helped to strengthen it.

Escutcheon: Shield.

Escutcheon of pretence: A small shield placed in the middle of a man's shield and bearing upon it the arms of his wife, when the latter is an heraldic heiress.

Esquire: A term applied to a form of the gyron.

Estoile: A star with six points, whereas a mullet has five.

Evett, or Lizard: A small creature like a miniature crocodile.

Expanded: Opened or displayed.

Falchion: A broadsword.

False: Voided (qv).

Fan: A winnowing instrument for blowing away chaff.

Feathered: Arrows which have wings different in tincture from the shaft. See also *Flighted.*

Fer-de-Fourchette: When crosses end in a forked iron.

Fer-de-moline: A millrind, ie, the iron fixed in the middle of a millstone.

Fermail: The buckle of a belt.

Fesse: An ordinary formed by two horizontal lines across the shield, taking up one-third of the area.

Fessepoint: Centre of the shield.

Fessewise: Placed in the direction of a fesse.

Fettered: See *Spancelled.*

Fetter lock: A shackle with a lock.

Field: Surface of the shield on which charges may be borne.

Figured: When the sun or other objects have a human face.

File: Label (qv).

Fillet: A diminutive of the chief.

Fimbriated: A narrow bordure with a different tincture.

Fireball: A grenade or bomb with flames coming from the top.

Firme: Applied to a cross patée when it extends to the edge of the escutcheon.

Finned: When the teeth, tail and fins (eg, of a whale) are tinctured gules.

Fitchée: Pointed at end, to fix in ground.

Flanches or *Flaunches:* When the shield has on both sides a segment of a circle drawn from chief to base.

Flanks: Sides of the shield.

Fleece: The badge of the order of the Golden Fleece.

Fleuretty: A surface semé of fleur-de-lis.

Fleur-de-lis: Flower of the lily, the heraldic variety of which has three leaves only.

Fleury: Ornamented with fleur-de-lis.

Flexed: Bent or bowed.

Flighted: See *Feathered.*

Flory, Floretty: Fleuretty.

Flotant: Floating.

Flowered: Used of plants when they show their flowers.

Foliated: Leaved.

Formée: Patée.

Fountain: A roundel wavy argent and azure.

Fourchée: Forked.

Fracted: Broken.

Fraise: A strawberry-leaf, in Scotland a cinquefoil.

Fresnée: Rearing or standing on the hind legs.

Fret: An ordinary (see illustration, p 110).

Fretty: When a field is covered with frets.

Fructed: Fruited, bearing fruit.

Fumant: Emitting smoke.

Furnished: Equipped as of a horse with saddle, bridle etc.

Fusil: A narrow lozenge.

Fusilly: Covered with fusils.

Gads: Plates of steel and iron.

Galley: Ship driven by sails and oars; see also *Lymphad*.

Gamb: The whole foreleg of a beast, as apart from a paw, which is shown as couped or erased from the middle joint.

Garb: A wheatsheaf, or if of other grain, the kind must be specified.

Gardant: Guardant, full-faced.

Gardebras: Armour covering the elbows.

Garde-visure: The visor of a helmet.

Garland: A wreath of leaves or flowers.

Garnished: Ornamented.

Gauntlet: A steel glove.

Gaze, At: An animal of the chase, when looking full front *Guardant* = At gaze.

Gemell: See *Bars gemel*.

Genet: A small animal like a weasel or a fox.

Gerated: Differenced by small charges.

Geratting: The process of such differencing.

Gillyflower: A blood-red carnation.

Giron: See *Gyron*.

Girt, Girded: Bound round with a band.

Gliding: Applied to snakes moving fesseways.

Glory: Rays surrounding a charge.

Gobony: See *Compony*.

Gonfanon or *Gonfalon*: A standard.

Gorge, or Gurge: A water bouget.

Gorged: Wearing a collar.

Gorges: A whirlpool (the punning coat of a famous family of that name, Gorges).

Gorget: Breast armour.

Y

Goutte: A drop.

Gouttée, Guttée: Semée of drops.

Gradient: As of a tortoise walking.

Greaves: Armour for the legs.

Grice: A young wild boar.

Grieces: Steps.

Griffin, or *Gryphon:* A mythical animal, the upper half an eagle, the lower a lion. The male version has no wings.

Gringolée: Crosses whose ends are the heads of serpents.

Guardant: Full-faced.

Guidon: A pennon or flag.

Guivre: Guingolée.

Gules: Red.

Guttée: Semée of drops, as of water (d'eau), of blood (de sang) etc.

Gyron: Lower half of a quarter formed by a diagonal line.

Gyronny: The division of the shield by cross and saltire, in parts from 6-12. The well-known coat of the Campbells, the Dukes of Argyll, is gyronny of eight, or and sable.

Habergeon: A coat of mail without sleeves.

Habited: Clothed.

Haie: A hedge.

Handled: Applicable to spears.

Harpy: A fabulous creature, a bird with a virgin's face, neck and breasts, and the body and legs of a vulture.

Hart: A stag in its sixth year.

Harvest fly: A butterfly.

Hatchment: The representation of a person's arms formerly placed on his house after his death. Often found in old churches in England.

Hauberk: A coat of chain mail armour.

Hauriant: When a fish is shown in the perpendicular position, as if sucking in air.

Haussé: Enchanted.

Hawk's bells and jesses: The latter being the thongs which fastened the bells to the hawk's legs.

Hawk's lure: Made up of two wings conjoined with the tips downwards, with a line attached ending in a ring. Wings thus shown are said to be in lure or conjoined in lure.

Hay fork: See *Shakefork.*

Heads: Shown in profile unless otherwise stated.

Hempbreak: Hackle.

Hillock: In heraldry, denotes more than one hill.

Hilted: The hilt of a sword when its tincture differs from that of the blade.

Hind: The female deer, usually shown as trippant (tripping).

Hirondelle: A swallow.

Hood: Coif or hood of a monk.

Hooded: Said of the human face when the head-dress is of a different tincture; also of a hawk when the latter wears a hood or mask, as in falconry.

Hoofed: When the hoofs are of a different tincture.

Horned: When the horns are of a different tincture.

Humetté: When an ordinary is couped so that it does not touch the sides of the shield.

Hurst: A clump of trees.

Hurt: An azure roundel.

Hurtée: Charged, or semée with hurts.

Hydra: A fabulous many-headed dragon.

Ibex: An animal with straight horns (in British armory).

Imbrued: Embrued.

Impaled: Two coats in the same shield in pale.

Imperial Crown: Much the same as a regal crown. Imperially Crowned, when the charge etc is thus crowned.

In lure: Hawk's lure.

In pride: Said of a peacock having its tail expanded.

In splendour: When the sun is surrounded by rays.

Incensed: When animals have flames issuing from mouth and ears.

Indented: A line having small indentations (contrast dancettée).

Inescutcheon: Escutcheon of pretence.

Ink moline: A mill rind.

Invected: Similar to engrailed but with spikes pointing inwards instead of outwards.

Issuant: Rising out of. When said of an animal, only the upper half of the animal is shown.

Jellop: The comb of a cock; hence 'jelloped'.

Jessant: Shooting forth; only half of the charge is shown when blazoned thus.

Jessant de lis: A leopard's face with fleur-de-lis passing through the mouth.

Joinant: Conjoined.

Jupon: A surcoat.

Knotted: Said of trees.

Knowed: See *Nowed*.

Label: A cadency mark, a rectangular piece having three pendants.

Ladder, Scaling: A ladder with hooks, used in sieges.

Lamb, Paschal: See *Agnus Dei*.

Lambrequin: Mantling.

Langued: When the tongue of an animal is of a different tincture.

Larmes: Tears.

Lattice: Trellis.

Laver: A cutter, or ploughshare.

Legged: When the legs of a bird are of a different tincture.

Leopards: In French heraldry the same as a lion, passant guardant, hence the former blazoning of the royal lions of England as leopards.

Leopard's face: When the head is represented affrontée or guardant, and no part of the neck is visible.

Leopard's head: When the head is in profile or affrontée, if part of the neck is visible.

Lever: A cormorant.

Lined: When the inside lining of a mantle etc is of a different tincture.

Lioncel: A young lion.

Lion poisson (sea lion): A mythical creature, a lion in the upper half, fish in the lower.

Liston: Scroll of the motto.

Lodged: When the stag etc is lying on the ground or at rest.

Lozenge: A charge shaped like a diamond and four-sided.

Lozengy: Covered with lozenges.

Lucy, or *Luce:* A pike fish.

Lure: See *Hawk's lure*.

Lymphad: A galley.

Maiden's head: The head and neck of a woman couped below the breast, the head wreathed with roses, and crowned with an antique crown.

Manch or *Maunch:* A sleeve.

Manchet: A cake of bread.

Maned: When the mane is of a different tincture.

Martlet: A bird without legs, otherwise a martin or swallow, with tufts of feathers where the legs join the body.

Mascle: A voided lozenge.

Masculy: Covered with mascles.

Masoned, or *Massonné:* A division by lines to depict the mortar between the stones of buildings.

Membered: When the beak and legs of a bird are of a different tincture.

Merlion: A martlet.

Merlé: Mingled.

Metals: Or and argent.

Millrind: Fer de Moline.

Mort: A death's head or skull.

Moor's Head: Head of a negro in profile, couped at the neck, wreathed about the temples.

Morion: A steel cap.

Morné, or *Mortné:* A lion without tongue, teeth or claws.

Morse: A sea lion.

Mound: An orb or globe (of the world) denoting sovereignty.

Mount: When a hill is shown in the base of the shield.

Mounted: When a horse bearing a rider is shown.

Mounting: Animals of the chase shown in the same position as an animal of prey—which is rampant.

Mourné: Mourned, blunted.

Mullet: A star of five points.

Mullet pierced: A mullet which is pierced in the centre, like the rowel of a spur.

Muraillé: Walled.

Mural crown: A coronet of gold.

Murrey: The colour sanguine.

Muzzled: When a bear or other animal has its mouth tied with bands.

Naiant: Swimming, as of fish shown horizontally.

Naissant: Rising or coming out of the middle of an ordinary.

Narcissus: A flower of six petals.

Naval crown: A gold coronet composed of sterns and sails of ships on the upper edge.

Nebulée or *Nebuly:* A line of partition.

Newed: When the fibres of leaves and plants are of a different tincture.

Newt: An effet or eft.

Nislée, or *Nillé:* Formed of slender or narrow lines.

Nombril: A point in a shield last but one from the base.

Nowed: Knotted, said of the tails of serpents.

Ombré: Shaded.

Ondé, Undy or *Undée:* Wavy.

Opinicus: Mythical creature, with a lion's legs, eagle's head and neck, with wings and a short tail.

Oppressed: See *Debruised.*

Or: The metal gold.

Orb: See *Mound.*

Ordinary: Some heraldic charges very frequently used. Called honourable ordinaries.

Ordinaries, sub—: Charges also frequently used but of lesser importance than the ordinaries.

Oreiller: A cushion.

Organ rest: A clarion (qv).

Orle: A narrow bordure, but detached from the edge of the shield; charges said to be in orle are arranged in this manner.

Orlé: Bordered.

Ounce: A lynx, the upper part of the animal is tawny white, the lower of an ash colour, over all there is a sprinkling of black dots.

Overall: When a charge is placed over all other bearings.

Overt: Open, as with birds having wings open for taking flight.

Owl: Always shown full-faced.

Pale: An ordinary, a band placed vertically in the centre of a shield.

Palisado Crown: A gold coronet ornamented with golden palisades on the upper rim.

Palisse: A division of the field by piles, meant to give the appearance of palisades.

Pall, or *Pallium:* An archiepiscopal vestment made of white lamb's wool, in the shape of the letter Y, bearing five crosses patées fitchées.

Pallet: A diminutive of the pale.

Paly: Divided into perpendicular divisions like pales with alternate tinctures and the number of such divisions must be given as paly of six etc.

Paly bendy: Divided into lozenge shapes by lines paleways and bendways.

Palmer's staff: A pilgrim's staff.

Panther: A wild animal shown with fire issuing from mouth and ears.

Papilonné: A form of the fur vair, but covered with scales like a butterfly's wings.

Party per bend etc: Said when the field or charge is divided by a line drawn in the direction of the particular ordinary.

Paschal lamb: See *Agnus Dei.*

Passant: When an animal is walking and looking straight before it.

Passant guardant: Said of a beast walking but full-faced (affrontée).

Passant reguardant: Walking but looking backwards.

Passion Cross: Differs from the Calvary Cross (qv) in not having steps.

Passion nail: A long spike with a rectangular head.

Pattes: Paws of a beast.

Patonce: A floriated form of the cross.

Patty, Patée: A cross with each arm expanding from the centre and ending in a straight line.

Pavilion: A tent; also the canopy under which the arms of a sovereign are shown.

Pean: A fur, like ermine but with sable ground and golden spots.

Peel: An instrument used by bakers for drawing bread out of an oven.

Pegasus: A mythical winged horse.

Pelican: Represented usually wtih wings, expanded and vulning her breast from which drops of blood are falling. When she feeds her young in this way, she is said to be 'in her piety'.

Pellet: A sable roundel.

Pelletty: Semée of pellets.

Pennon: An oblong flag.

Pennoncel: A small flag.

Penny-yard-penny: A silver coin.

Per: See *Party.*

Perforated: Voided or pierced.

Petionel: A pistol.

Pheon: The head of an arrow or dart.

Phoenix: A mythical bird, rising from flames.

Pierced: When a charge is perforated so as to show the field.

Piety: See *Pelican.*

Pile: One of the ordinaries.

Pilgrim's scrip: A wallet, or bag.

Plate: A flat silver roundel.

Playing tables: Backgammon boards.

Plenitude: Applied to the moon when full.

Ployé: Bent or curved.

Poing: The hand closed (appaumé = open).

Point, In: When piles, swords etc are arranged as approaching each other in the base of the shield.

Pomegranate: A foreign fruit. The blazon must always state that it is slipped, leaved or seeded.

Pomme: A green roundel, pl. pomies.

Pommelly or *Pommetty:* Of a cross whose arms end in balls.

Popinjay: A parrot.

Portcullis: The grating closing a fortress gate, usually shown with spikes in the base and chains attached to its upper beam.

Posed: Statant.

Potent: (i) a crutch, (ii) a fur made of crutch or T-shaped divisions.

Pouldron: Armour for the shoulder.

Pounce: Talons of a bird of prey.

Powdered: Semée.

Prester John: Erroneous description of the figure of Christ.

Pretence, Escutcheon of: The small shield borne in the middle of a shield to denote the arms of an heiress.

Pride, In its: Applied to peacock etc with tail expanded.

Proper: Borne in its natural colour.

Purfled: Bordered.

Purpure: Purple.

Pyot: A magpie.

Quarter: A sub ordinary.

Quartered: Divided into quarters.

Quarterings: Different coats combined into one shield, more than four in most cases.

Quarterly: When the shield is divided into four equal sections by lines.

Quatrefoil: A herb with four leaves.

Queue: The tail of an animal.

Queue fourchée: Double queued (qv).

Quise, A la: At the thigh.

Radiant: Shining with rays.

Raguly: Used of a line or partition, the projections being oblique. It can be described also as like the stem of a tree from which the branches have been cut. (See illustration on p 206.)

Ramé: Branched or attired.

Rampant: When an animal is shown standing erect on its hind legs, as with the lion rampant of Scotland.

Rampant guardant: Standing on the hind legs but with face affrontée.

Rampant reguardant: Standing on the hind legs with the head looking backwards.

Rampant sejant: Sitting in profile with the forelegs raised.

Rangé: Arranged in order.

Ravissant: When a beast of prey is carrying its victim in its jaws.

Rayonnant: Adorned with beams of light.

Rays of the sun: Sixteen in number, nine round an estoile.

Razed: See *Erased.*

Rebated: When a portion of the end is removed.

Rebus: Similar to a canting coat, when the charges allude to the bearer's name.

Recercellée: Applied to a cross similar to a cross moline but with the ends turned round more.

Reclinant: Bending backwards.

Recontre: See *Cabossed.*

Reflexed, or *Reflected:* Bent back.

Reguardant: Looking backward.

Reindeer: A stag with double attires.

Remora: A serpent.

Removed: When an ordinary has fallen or been taken from its proper position.

Renverse: When anything is shown contrary to its natural position.

Rere-mouse: A bat.

Respectant, or *Respecting:* When animals are shown face to face.

Reserved: Contrary to usual positions.

Retorted: Bent or twisted back, as serpents are shown wreathed one in another.

Retranché: Again divided in a bend, cf, recoupé when in a field divided per fesse, a piece is again divided per fesse.

Reversed: Turned upside down.

Riband: A diminutive of the bendlet.

Rising: When birds are shown as if preparing for flight.

Rompu, Rompé: Broken.

Rose: Always shown as full blown, the petals expanded, seeded in the middle with five green barbs or leaves behind them. An heraldic red rose is blazoned gules, not proper. The terms 'barbed' and 'seeded proper' mean that the barbs are green and the seeds yellow.

Roundels: Sub-ordinaries.

Rousant: Rising, said of a bird preparing to fly.

Rustre: A lozenge with a circular piercing.

Sable: Black.

Sagittarius, or *Sagittary:* A centaur (qv) with bow and arrows.

Salamander: A mythical animal, supposed to be born in fire; shown as green surrounded by flames.

Saliant: Leaping.

Salmon spear: A harpoon.

Saltant: When an animal is shown as springing forward.

Saltire: The ordinary formed like an 'X'.

Saltirewise or *Saltireways:* In the form of a saltire.

Saltorels: Small saltires.

Sanglant: Bloody, torn off.

Sanglier: A wild boar.

Sanguine: Blood colour (or murrey).

Saracen's head: Same as a Moor's head (qv).

Sarcellée: Cut through in the middle.

Satyr: A mythical creature, half antelope, half man.

Scallop: A shell.

Scarpe: A diminutive of the bend sinister.

Scintillant: Sparkling.

Scorpion: Resembles a crayfish and is shown erect.

Scrip: A pilgrim's purse.

Scruttle: A winnowing fin.

Seadog: Drawn like a seal but with a beaver's tail, a finned crest along the whole back, the legs scaled and the feet webbed.

Sea horse: A mythical creature, the forepart and head resembling a horse with webbed feet, and the hind part having a fish's tail.

Sea lion: Like the preceding, but with the head and mane of a lion.

Sea mew: A kind of seagull.

Seapie: A dark-brown water fowl, with red head and white neck and wings.

Seax: A scimitar with a semi-circular notch hollowed out of the back of the blade. A weapon associated with the Saxons who invaded Britain, and whose name is preserved in Essex, Sussex, Middlesex etc. The coats of arms of Essex and Middlesex have seaxes.

Seeded: When roses, lilies etc are of different tincture.

Segreant: Said of a griffin rampant, wings addorsed.

Sejant, or *Segeant:* Sitting.

Sejant addorsed: When two animals are sitting back to back.

Semée: Strewed or powdered with small charges.

Sengreen: A house leek.

Seraph's head: That of a child between three pairs of wings, one pair in chief, one in fesse and one in base.

Serrated: With indentations like those of a saw.

Sexfoil: Like a cinquefoil but with six leaves.

Shackle: A link of a fetter.

Shackbolt: A fetter.

Shafted: Handle of a spear.

Shakefork: Much the same as a pall, but does not touch the edges of the shield.

Shambrough: A kind of slipper.

Shapewined: In a curved line.

Sheaf: See *Garb.*

Sheldrake: A variety of duck.

Shivered: Broken or splintered irregularly.

Single: The tail of a deer.

Sinister: Left-hand side (contrast *Dexter*).

Sinople: The French term for vert (green).

Siren or *Syren:* A mermaid.

Shean or *Shene:* A dagger.

Slashed: When the sleeves of a garment are cut open lengthwise, and the apertures show a different colour.

Slay or *Slea:* An instrument used by weavers.

Slipped: Said of leaves and flowers when a slip or stalk is torn from the stem.

Spancelled: When a horse has its fore and hind legs fettered together.

Speed, At: When a stag is shown running.

Sperver: A tent.

Sphinx: A mythical creature with head and breasts of a woman, body of a lion and wings of an eagle.

Spindle: See *Fusil.*

Spit: A spade.

Splendour: Said of the sun shown with a human face and irradiated (qv).

Staple: An iron fastening.

Star: See *Estoile.*

Starved: Stripped of leaves.

Statant: Standing.

Stellion: A lizard or snake.

Stringed: When an instrument, eg, a bugle or horn, has strings of a different tincture.

Sub-ordinaries: See p 334.

Subverted: Reversed, or turned upside down.

Sufflue: Rest or clarion.

Sun: Shown with a human face, irradiated, and is then called a sun in splendour.

Supporters: Figures placed on either side of a shield.

Surcoat: The coat worn over the armour.

Surgeant: Rising.

Surmounted: When one charge is placed upon another.

Surtout: (lit. over all). Said of an escutcheon of pretence.

Swepe: A balista, or machine used for throwing stones.

Swivel: Two iron links which turn on a bolt.

Sykes: A fountain (qv).

Tabard: A surcoat, sleeveless, embroidered with arms and now worn by the heralds in England and Scotland.

Tabernacle: A tent.

Tailed: Said of comets and animals.

Talbot: An old English hunting dog.

Targant, or Torgant: Bending or twisting like an S. (See also *Torqued.*)

Target: A round shield.

Tasces: The armour which covered the thighs.

Tau: A cross in the shape of the Greek letter 'T'.

Tawny, or Tenné: Orange.

Teazel: The head of a kind of thistle.

Tenné: Tawny (see above).

Terrace, or Terras: A narrow mount at the bottom of the base.

Thoye: A lynx.

Threstle, or Trestle: A three-legged stool.

Thunderbolt: A twisted bar in pale, inflamed at each end, winged and with four forked and barbed darts in saltire issuing from the centre.

Tiara: The Papal mitre.

Tiercé: When the field is divided into three equal areas of different colours.

Timbre: The helmet with wreath, lambrequin and crest, placed over the arms.

Tincture: A heraldic colour; metal, colour or fur.

Tirret, or Turret: Manacles.

Toison d'or: The Golden Fleece, the badge of the order of that name.

Torn: A spinning wheel.

Torqued: Wreathed or twisted. (See *Targant*).

Torse: The wreath on which the crest is placed.

Torteau: A red roundel.

Torteaux: Discs of colour on a field.

Tortillé: Semée of torteaux.

Tourne: See *Reguardant.*

Tower: Triple-towered.

Towered: Having turrets.

Transfixed: Pierced through.

Transfluent: When a stream passes through the arches of a bridge.

Transmuted: Counterchanged.

Transpierced: Pierced through.

Transposed: Turned from the ordinary position.

Traversed: Turned to the sinister side.

Trefoiled: As of a cross when its arms end in trefoils, of another ordinary that is edged with trefoils.

Trefoil: A three-leaved grass.

Treillé: Latticed.

Tressure: A diminutive of the orle (half the size).

Tressure flory: A tressure having fleurs-de-lis at intervals around it.

Tressure flory counter flory: The royal tressure in the arms of Scotland, in which alternate fleur-de-lis point to the centre of the field.

Trevet: A tripod of iron.

Triyle: Formed of three arches.

Tricorporate: When three animals are united in one head in the centre of the shield.

Trident: A long-handled fish spear with three prongs.

Trien: Three.

Triparted: Divided into three.

Trippant: When animals of the chase are walking; counter tripping, when two beasts are passing in opposite directions.

Triton: A merman.

Triumphal crown: A crown of laurel leaves.

Trononée: Dismembered (qv).

Truncated: When trees are cut smoothly off at top and bottom.

Trunked: When the trunk is of a different colour.

Trundles: Quills of gold thread.

Trunk of a tree: When the root of the tree has been torn up and the top cut off.

Trussed: Close (qv).

Trussing: When a bird of prey has seized another animal.

Tuberated: Swollen out.

Tun: A barrel.

Turned up: When the lining of a cap is of a different colour and is turned up over one edge.

Turreted: Having small towers.

Tusked: When an animal's tusks are of a different tincture.

Tynes: The branches of the antlers of stags and bucks.

Umbraced, or *Umbrated:* Shadowed.

Undée, Undy: Wavy.

Unguled: When the hooves of an animal are of a different tincture.

Unicorn: A mythical animal with the body of a horse, one long twisted horn rising out of its forehead, and with cloven feet.

Unifoil: A single-leaved grass.

Upright: As rampant but applied to reptiles and fish.

Urchin: A hedgehog.

Urinant: Of a fish with head in base.

Urvant, or *Urved:* Turned or bowed upwards.

Vair: One of the heraldic furs.

Vallary Crown: Composed of a circle of gold, surmounted by a number of flat pointed strips.

Vambrace: Armour of the arm.

Vambraced: When the arm is covered with armour.

Vamplate, or *Vamplet:* A steel plate fixed on the tilting lance to protect the hand.

Varvelled: When the hawk's jesses have rings at the end.

Verblée: When a hunting horn is edged with metal of a different colour.

Vert: Green.

Verted: Flexed.

Vervels: Small rings.

Vested: Clothed.

View: The track, or footing, of all fallow deer and of a buck.

Vigilance: The stone held by a stork or crane in its uplifted foot.

Vigilant: When a cat is on the lookout for prey.

Visor: The moveable part of a helmet.

Voided: When an ordinary has the interior removed to leave the field visible.

Vol: A pair of wings conjoined.

Volant: Flying.

Vorant (or *Engoulant*) : Devouring.

Vulnant: Wounding.

Vulned: Wounded.

Wallet: See *Pilgrim's scrip.*

Wastel cakes: Round cakes of bread.

Water bougets (or *budgets*) : Vessels to carry water.

Wattled: A term applied to the gills of a cock etc, when the colour has to be mentioned.

Wavy: Formed like waves.

Weare, Weir: Made of stakes and osier twigs interwoven to keep back water.

Wedge: A tool with which to split timber.

Weel: A pot in which to catch fish.

Wellbucket: One with three legs.

Welt (or *Edge*) : A narrow border to a charge.

Wervels: Vervels (qv).

Wharrow spindle: Fusil (qv).

Wheatsheaf: See *Garb.*

Whirlpool: See *Gorges.*

Wings: Having wings.

Wings conjoined: Wings expanded, elevated and united at the base.

Winnowing basket: For winnowing grain.

Wood: Hurst.

Woodman: A savage.

Wreath: That on which the crest is borne, also a garland or chaplet for the head.

Wreathed: Having or wearing a wreath.

Wyvern: A mythical animal with the wings and upper part of a dragon, the lower part with nowed tail as of a snake.

Yale: A mythical creature, coloured argent with spots in gold (or). It is maned, tufted, hoofed, horned and tusked or. The yale is shown by artists as able to swivel its horns at will, so that one horn points forwards and the other backwards.

Glossary of Technical Terms used in the Work

Abeyance: Applied to a peerage, succession to which has failed in the male line; the succession is between daughters and is terminated when one male heir arises from the daughters' descendants; or when by permission of the Crown the abeyance is terminated in favour of one of the heirs.

Allegations: Copies of applications to Church of England bishops asking for the grant of a licence to marry.

Ard Righ: High King in Scotland, previous to Kenneth MacAlpine.

Ard Ri: Similar monarch in Ireland.

Baron: Norman French, the king's man. Lowest rank in the British peerage.

Baronet: An hereditary title of Sir, in the United Kingdom. Abbreviated to Bart or Bt.

Bretwalda: Ruler of the Britons, a title applied to the paramount old English kings, and especially to Egbert of Wessex, ancestor of the present royal family of Britain.

Cadets: The younger sons, or junior members of a family.

Calendared: When records have been arranged chronologically.

Caliph: The name given to the successors of Mohammed (Arabic: *Khalifah*, successor).

Captain: A term used of the greatest Scottish Highland chiefs, eg, The Mackintosh, the Captain of clan Chattan. (Latin: *caput*).

Carucate: Originally, as much land as a team of oxen could plough in one season. Low Latin: *carruca*, a plough. About 120 acres.

Charter Rolls: In England, consist of grants of privileges to various bodies and persons.

C(h) artularies: Books which contain records of all charters relating to lands and properties of a religious house or landed family. From *c(h)artu-(l)arium* = register.

Chief: Of a clan, entitled to wear a single eagle's feather.

Chieftain: Head of a sept, entitled to wear three eagle's feathers.

Clan Chattan: (Pronounced Hattan), an association of Highland clans, of which the chief is Mackintosh.

Close Rolls: Records of transactions which were sent out closed or sealed.

Cognomen: The third of a Roman's names, corresponding to our surname. See also *gens* and *praenomen*.

Commendation: The act by which a man placed himself under the protection of a lord. (Latin : *commendatio*).

Copyholder: One who held his land as a tenant by copy of the court roll, ie, the customary usage entered on the roll of the local baronial court.

Count: Equivalent of English earl. (Latin : *comes*, a companion).

Court Baron: The local court of the lord of the manor.

Curia Regis: The King's Court dealing with pleas touching the Crown.

Derbhfine (Gaelic) : A group of nine kinsmen nearest to the chief in a Scottish Highland clan, from whom a chief's successor could be chosen.

Disclaimer: The surrender, or renunciation of a peerage.

Dormant: A term used to denote a peerage to which there may be an heir but to which an heir has not yet been proved.

Duke: The highest grade in the peerage. (Latin : *dux*, leader).

De Diem clausit extremum: Name of a writ issued by the English king to his escheator to hold an inquiry into a landholder's estate on his death.

Deforceant: Defendant.

De Quo Warranto: The name of a prerogative writ; ie, arising from the powers of the English Crown and inquiring into the authority by which an estate etc was held.

Earl: Third rank in British peerage; the Continental equivalent is Count.

Eponym: One who gives his name to something, especially to a people or place. (Greek : Επὶ upon; ὀυομα a name).

Equity: The name given to a system of law in England arising out of the defects of the Common Law. Equity and Common Law were merged in 1876.

Escheat: The process by which property was forfeited to the Crown, not always by treason.

Eyre, Justices in: The English king's judges, who had roving commissions to hear cases. (Latin *errare*, to wander; French *errer*).

Fee: An estate in land held of a superior lord by a vassal. See *Feudal System*. From Latin *feudum*, or *feodum*; rendered into Old French as fief, and into English as fee.

z

Fee simple: In English law, the nearest approach to absolute ownership, being an estate limited to a man and his heirs. In practical terms, a freehold. See *Fee.*

Feudal system: A term invented by historians of the middle ages to denote the system of land tenure by which a vassal held land from his lord and owed him fealty for it.

Fine, or Oblata Rolls: Records of fines or sums levied by the English Crown for the performance of certain acts.

Fines and Recoveries: These relate to proceedings taken in order to convey estates and free them from charges.

Gavelkind: The equal division of property among sons, a system formerly prevailing in Kent (England), and in Wales.

Genealogy: Study or science of family history. (Greek γενέα birth, λόγος study).

Gens: The second of a Roman's names denoting the clan or race to which he belonged. See also *Praenomen* and *Cognomen.* (Latin : race).

Graf: The German equivalent of Count (female, *grafin*).

Grand Serjeanty: Honorary services by which a man held lands from the Crown, eg, serving the sovereign at a banquet.

Homage: The act by which the vassal gave fealty to the lord for his land. (From Latin *homo*, man).

Hundred Rolls: A hundred was originally an area sufficient to support 100 families.

Ilk, Of that: A term used in Scottish genealogy when the surname of a family is identical with that of its property; eg. Swinton of that ilk = Swinton of Swinton.

Inquisitiones post damnum: Inquiries by the English Crown as to loss of revenues incurred by a tenant's actions.

Inquisitiones post mortem: Inquiries made by the Crown on the death of an estate owner as to sums due before the heir could enter upon his inheritance.

Knight Bachelor: The name of the original order of knights; the bachelor in the title is supposed to be derived from battelier or fighter. Abbreviated to Kt Bach, Kt, or Knt.

Knight of the Shire: A medieval term for an MP of a county constituency.

Knight's fee: The amount of land capable of supporting a mounted knight and his retinue; about two carucates = 240 acres.

Lancaster, Duke of: A title borne by the British sovereign (whether king or queen) when in Lancashire; derived from the fact that in 1399 the Duke of Lancaster became king as Henry IV and the title then merged in the Crown.

Letters Patent: Letters open and for all to read ('to all and singular'), usually now denoting the document by which a peer is created.

Liberate Rolls: (Literally 'set free'). Orders to the English royal treasurers to pay various sums of money.

Lords of Appeal: Life peers created under legislation, the Appellate Jurisdiction Act of 1876, being learned judges acting as Supreme Court of Appeal in the House of Lords.

Manor: The economic unit of rural life in medieval times.

Margrave: The German equivalent of marquis (English marquess). Female, *margravine*.

Marquess: (Continental form, marquis). From the Italian *marchio* or march = frontier; second grade in British peerage.

Mediatised princes: Those whose states had been considered princely under the old Holy Roman Empire (ended 1806) and who were accorded the titles of Serene and Illustrious Highness.

Mon: The Japanese heraldic symbol, similar to the western heraldic badge.

Mortmain: (Literally 'dead hand'). Statutes were passed in England in the middle ages and onward to restrict the rights of corporations to take lands by grant or devise. The law of mortmain was abolished by the Charities Act, 1960.

Muniment chest or room: Containing records of a family, usually relating to land or property; from Latin *munire*, to fortify, ie, to strengthen or make good a claim.

Name and arms clause: In a will, clause which requires the beneficiary to take the surname and arms of the testator as a condition of inheriting the estate.

Patent Rolls: Open, or patent for all to read.

Peculiar: A term applied to certain ecclesiastical jurisdictions in England which came directly under the Crown.

Pedigree: The setting-out of a family history in chart or other written form. Latin, *pes*— a foot, *grus*, a crane; a sign resembling a crane's foot was used in medieval times in Europe to indicate line of descent, thus ↓ .

Petty serjeanty: Land tenure on rendering some object, eg, a rose to the Crown on specific occasion.

Pipe Rolls (or Great Roll of the Pipe): So called as being written on a roll and wound round a stick. They are English Exchequer records.

Placita: Pleas, records of English medieval law cases. Pleas of the Crown.

Praenomen: The first of a Roman's names, corresponding to our Christian or forename. See also *Gens* and *Cognomen.*

PCC: Prerogative Court of Canterbury where, before 1858, wills were proved if the testator had property in more than one ecclesiastical jurisdiction.

PC(I): Prerogative Court of Ireland.

Quipu: A knot, a Peruvian arrangement for making arithmetical calculations and for assisting the memory.

Red Book, Liber Rubeus: Records of feudal dues from time of Henry II to Henry III, 1154-1272.

Rico Hombre: The term used in Spain and Portugal to denote the feudal baron, one of whose symbols was a cauldron, symbolising his duty to feed his followers.

Sasines: Seisin (qv).

Scutage: Commutation of military obligation; payment of money in place of military service; Latin *scutum*, a shield.

Seisin: The taking possession of land.

Sennachie (y): Tribal genealogist among the Scottish clans.

Sept: A branch of a Scottish Highland clan.

Serf: A person unable to leave an estate without permission of the lord, a villein (qv). Not a slave (*servus*) = a person who is the property of another.

Serjeanty: See *Grand* and *Petty Serjeanty.*

Special Remainder: A clause in the letters patent by which a peerage is created and by which, in default of direct male heirs, the peerage can go to either the male heirs of a brother or to daughters and their children.

Suzerain: The superior lord to whom a vassal did homage.

Tanist: The person nominated by the chief of a clan as his successor.

Tanistry: The system in the Celtic races by which succession to land and clan chiefship lay with the clan elders and not with the individual.

Temporalities of a see: The lands attached to an English bishopric and for which the holder must do homage to the sovereign.

Tenants-in-capite: Tenants-in-chief; the greatest landowners in England after 1086, holding their estates from the Crown.

Testa de Nevill: Written in reign of Henry III, 1216-72. It contains records of feudal dues.

Vassal: Low Latin, *vassus,* from Celtic *gwas,* a boy.

Villein: A person working on an estate and unable to move from it without permission of the lord of the estate; a serf. (From Latin, *villa,* or country estate; hence *villanus*).

Virgate: Old English term for quarter of an acre (supposed to be a peasant tenement) and sometimes as equivalent to 30 acres (a quarter of a carucate).

Viscount: Deputy to a Count. (Latin, *vice comes*).

Visitations: Conducted by the English heralds between 1530 and 1688 to examine coats of arms.

Voivodship, (Wojewodzhie): A Polish term denoting the administration of an area similar to an English county.

WS: Writer to the Signet. The lower branch of the legal profession in Scotland, practically equivalent to the English solicitor.

NOTE: The meaning of the terms: virgate, bovate, carucate and hide is still much debated by medievalists. The terms apparently had different meanings in different parts of England and in various contexts.

Modern Pedigree Sketch

The word 'modern' used above is perhaps a little arbitrary, but to a genealogist an English pedigree of some 250 years, back to 1700 or so, is viewed as comparatively modern, in contrast to those which can be traced before 1600. For the overwhelming majority of English people whose forbears have been living in England for any length of time, the tracing of a pedigree for 250-300 years does not normally present any insuperable difficulties. Before that time, ie, before the reign of Charles II (1660-85) the tracing of a pedigree depends largely upon records of ownership of land, and it is in the period previous to 1660 that the Visitation-type pedigree comes into existence.

William Orme married at St Michael's Church, Stone, Staffordshire on 31 December 1734. William Orme was of the parish of Stone, where record of his baptism is not available in the period 1700-1720. There are, however, to be found two small areas in the registers which have been damp for some time, and which are now quite illegible. It could be that William Orme's baptism was recorded on the unreadable pages. This is mentioned only as an example of some of the difficulties encountered in searching the parish records.

William Orme's bride, Mary Emery, was of the parish of Stoke-upon-Trent. There is no indication of the parentage or ages of the parties—information which should have been, but is not, given. According to some old family papers, Mary was the daughter of John Emery, and she and William Orme had seven children, of whom six are recorded in the baptismal registers of Stone.

They were:　1.　A dau., baptized 19 Feb. 1735.
　　　　　　2.　Mary, bapt. 7 May 1738.
　　　　　　3.　Cecilia, bapt. 9 Nov. 1740.
　　　　　　4.　Thomas, bapt. 18 Aug. 1745.
　　　　　　5.　Francis, bapt. 10 April 1748.
　　　　　　6.　Robert, bapt. 10 June 1750.

The fifth of these children,

Francis Orme, bapt. 10 April 1748, m. 15 July 1771, Anne Timmis, at Bucknall Church, Staffs and had issue, (his will is dated 24 Feb. 1821),

　　　　　　　　1.　Josiah, b. 19 April, bapt. 10 May 1772.
　　　　　　　　2.　Anne, b. 7 Feb., bapt. 6 Mar. 1774.
　　　　　　　　3.　Hannah, b. 14 April, bapt. 10 May 1778.
　　　　　　　　4.　Elizabeth, b. 20 July, bapt. 17 Sept. 1780, m. Geo. Silcock.
　　　　　　　　5.　Anne, (Nanny), b. 10 July, bapt. 3 Aug. 1783, m. Job Bagnall and had issue.
　　　　　　　　6.　Mary, b. 19 June, bapt. 10 July 1785, m. William Griffin.
　　　　　　　　7.　John, b. 4 Oct. bapt. 2 Dec. 1787, (?) had a son, John.
　　　　　　　　8.　Michael, b. 10 July, bapt. 1 Aug. 1790.

The youngest of the above eight children,

Michael Orme, is mentioned in the 1841 Census as of Burslem, Dale Hall, (New Church Lane). His age is there given as 49 (discrepancies in exact age are of frequent occurence in the records), and he is described as a botanist. In the same census, the other members of his family are given as Francis, age 14, a botanist; Michael, age 20, a botanist, and Jane, age 20. In the 1851 census his wife's name is given as Mary, age 70, b. May Bank, Staffs, and he is there described as having a son Elijah, aged 5, b. Burslem and a granddau., Ellen, aged 8. He must then clearly have been married before, but it would seem that some mistake occurred, and Ellen his granddau., (see below) was aged 5, not 8. It appears that he died in 1870, being buried at Dale Hall Church, Burslem. From the 1871 census further details are available about members of Michael Orme's family, as follows:

1. Michael, age 20 in 1841, a joiner, (according to 1871 census, this occupation being apparently concurrent with the earlier mentioned botanist) residing in 1871 at 63 Howard Street, Burslem, Stoke-upon-Trent, b. at Tittensor, 1819, (age 52 in 1871). His wife, Jane, age 50, born at Leek; his six daus., all b. at Burslem, were:

    (1) Elizabeth, 17, warehouse woman, pottery.
    (2) Marian, 15, painter (pottery).
    (3) Mary, 15, painter (pottery).
    (4) Martha, 11, pottery at home.
    (5) Agnes, 9, scholar.
    (6) Sarah J., 7, scholar.

   Also residing with him was a granddau., Agnes J. Beech. Michael d. 6 Jan. 1872, and was bur. in Dale Hall Church.

2. Francis, a botanist (in 1841 census) and a joiner, on his marriage certificate, b. 1827, m. 29 Dec. 1845, Tamar, dau. of John Oakes, of George Street, Newcastle-under-Lyme, a collier, and d. 30 July 1849, being bur. at sea on his way to America, having had issue,

Ellen, b. 11 Mar. 1846, m. William Cooke, and grandmother of present living descendant, to whom I am obliged for permission to include the above account.

Thus a pedigree of seven generations can be constructed by the combined use of parochial records, Somerset House registers, census returns, and family papers. It is quite possible that earlier generations of this family will be found in the same area in Staffordshire. A former vicar of Tittensor made notes that, in 1597, Sir Gilbert Gerrard rebuilt a manor house at Tittensor, and that William Orme occupied the manor (the Ormes, it is added, were a yeoman family from Hanch (?) Hall, Longsden). In 1643 the manor house was destroyed and after 1660 it was rebuilt by William Orme and Sir Charles Gerrard. It appears reasonable to conclude that further research will indicate a connection between William Orme of 1660 and William Orme of 1734, (born probably 1700-14). Moreover, there was a Visitation family of Orme in Staffordshire.

Visitation Pedigree Sketch

In selecting the family of Hooke of Crookes for illustration of a good Visitation pedigree, I have been guided by three considerations. The family (1) was recorded in every one of the Heralds' Visitations of Gloucestershire, in 1583, 1623 and 1683; (2) is still existing, and still possesses the ancient property of Crookes; and (3) like other truly old landed gentry families, the Hookes are lineally traced long before the Visitations. The connected descent begins with Thomas Hooke, of *circa* 1415, whose sword is in possession of the family, and who fought at Agincourt. An ancient tradition assigns to him the grant of Crookes from Henry V. The family's muniment chest contains a marriage settlement dated 7 July 1435, in which Thomas Hooke's son, another Thomas Hooke, was contracted to Margaret, only daughter of Sir Guy Whityngton, who with his son, Robert, witnessed the marriage settlement. Sir Guy, who was Lord of the Manor of Pauntley in Gloucestershire and High Sheriff of that county in 1428, commanded a company at Agincourt. He was nephew of Sir Richard Whittington, Lord Mayor of London.

The issue of this marriage was Guy Hooke of Crookes, who was living *circa* 1470 (Visitations of Gloucestershire, 1583, and 1623; Harleian MSS. 1041 and 1543, British Museum) and had issue,

Richard Hooke, of Crookes, living *circa* 1510, who married Alice, dau. of William Wirrall, and d. (will dated 18 April, proved 7 July 1547) having had issue etc, etc.

The documentation of this family as preserved in their muniment chest is very extensive and of a nature which cannot be found apart from continuous possession of land. Owing to their ownership of estates in the same area extending over a period of 550 years, the Hookes possess a very large number of documents including wills, marriage settlements, leases, purchases and sales of property, which are invaluable in tracing their family history. Clearly the sources used in tracing a more modern style genealogy—birth, marriage, and death certificates, census returns and the like—assume at most a very subordinate importance in this case.

It is of interest to note that before the connected pedigree begins in the early fifteenth century, there are for upwards of two centuries mentions of Hookes in Gloucestershire. These show how deep are the roots of the family in the county. It is in the highest degree likely that the persons mentioned below were of the same stock; in fact, in more than one case there is documentary proof that they were.

(1) Walter Hoke (spelling is always varied at this date), was a juror in Gloucestershire, 1247-8.

(2) Richard de la Hoke, was party to an oath in an Inquisition taken at Tetbury, 1327.

(3) By a charter dated 5 Nov. 1433, a certain Thomas Philpot granted to Thomas Hoke and others, all lands in the vill of Morton Folet.

(4) By another charter bearing same date Thomas Philpot granted other lands to the same parties.

(5) There was a presentation in 1411 of William Hoke, parson of the church of Brommester in the diocese of Hereford, to the church of Redmarley Abitot in the diocese of Worcester being in the King's gift (Calendar of Patent Rolls, G. 112).

(6) In 1412, in the same record as above, Philip Hoke and Agnes his wife, are commissioners appointed to receive the oath of the following: Guy Whityngton and Thomas Hoke, mentioned in the marriage settlement of Thomas and Margaret Hooke, 1435 (see above).

(7) The chantry of St James and St Anne was founded by one John Hooke and another by licence of King Henry VI.

(8) Parish of Little Dean, Trinity Chantry founded by Philip Hooke.

(9) In the guide to the church of St Mary the Virgin, Newent (written by Mr Irvine E. Gray, MBE, MA, FSA, County Records Officer for Gloucestershire) in the list of incumbents are the names of Robert Hoke, 1393, and John Hoke, 1434. The former is mentioned in the marriage settlement of 1435, as also the William Hoke, (5) above.

The pedigree of Hooke of Crookes Park is given in full in *Burke's Landed Gentry*, (17th edition, 1952) and in the 18th edition, vol 2 down to and including the present head of the family, Sqdn. Ldr. Douglas Hooke, of Crookes Park, his son, Lt-Cmdr. Michael Hooke, and the latter's children. The details from (1) to (9) above do not appear in the *Landed Gentry* account, which gives the pedigree generation by generation from 1415, and I am much obliged to Sqdn. Ldr. Hooke for supplying them and for permission to include this account.

It is perfectly clear that there were Hookes in Gloucestershire from the early thirteenth century, but the pedigree of this family is honourably distinguished from first to last by a refusal to include anything in the nature of undocumented material. Perhaps the unbroken possession of land, pedigree and coat armour for five and a half centuries—far antedating the records of more than half our peerage —precludes any desire to strain after earlier items, whose connection can, however, be assumed with a high degree of probability.

Note: Mr. Enoch Powell's History of The House of Lords

While I was writing this book Mr J. Enoch Powell's book (in conjunction with Mr Keith Wallis) was published—*The House of Lords in the Middle Ages*. A very learned study of the development of the House of Lords up to the year 1540, it needs considerable analysis in detail but I do not consider from a first reading that it conflicts with any views expressed in my work. Mr Powell's study heavily underlines the fact that the Peerage, and consequently the House of Lords, has developed and, in fact, evolved without any attempt by anyone to set up a model House of Lords or Constitution of the same. I should be inclined to say that his study is quite fatal to the normal English legal theory of a Peerage. In passing, I should also say that I think the bearings of his studies upon the origins of the House of Commons should find their way into popular histories at an early date. I would advise all students of the Peerage to read this book.

Index